BETWEEN LANGUAGES AND CULTURES

Between Languages and Cultures

Colonial and Postcolonial Readings of Gabrielle Roy

ROSEMARY CHAPMAN

McGill-Queen's University Press
Montreal & Kingston • London • Ithaca

© McGill-Queen's University Press 2009

ISBN 978-0-7735-3496-4

Legal deposit second quarter 2009
Bibliothèque nationale du Québec

Printed in Canada on acid-free paper that is 100% ancient forest free
(100% post-consumer recycled), processed chlorine free

This book has been published with the help of a grant from the
Canadian Federation for the Humanities and Social Sciences,
through the Aid to Scholarly Publications Programme, using funds
provided by the Social Sciences and Humanities Research Council of
Canada. Funding has also been received from the International
Council for Canadian Studies through its Publishing Fund.

McGill-Queen's University Press acknowledges the support of the
Canada Council for the Arts for our publishing program. We also
acknowledge the financial support of the Government of Canada
through the Book Publishing Industry Development Program (BPIDP)
for our publishing activities.

Library and Archives Canada Cataloguing in Publication

Chapman, Rosemary, 1951–
    Between languages and cultures : colonial and postcolonial
readings of Gabrielle Roy / Rosemary Chapman.

Includes bibliographical references and index.
ISBN 978-0-7735-3496-4

1. Roy, Gabrielle, 1909–1983 – Criticism and interpretation.
2. Bilingualism and literature. 3. Biculturalism in literature.
4. Culture conflict in literature. 5. Canada – In literature. I. Title.

PS8535.095Z59 2009   C843'.54   C2008–906533–6

Typeset by Jay Tee Graphics Ltd. in 10.5/13 Sabon

I wish to dedicate this book
to the memory of my parents,
Peter and Jean Drew.

Contents

Tables

Acknowledgments

The completion and publication of this book were made possible by the generous support of a number of individuals and funding bodies. Initial archival work was undertaken during an inspiring research trip to Manitoba in 2002, partly funded by an award under the Canadian Government Faculty Research scheme. Staff at the Centre du patrimoine franco-manitobain, Saint-Boniface, Manitoba, the Department of Education Library (IRU), Winnipeg, and the Provincial Archives of Manitoba, Winnipeg offered valuable advice. In 2005–06 I was granted a matching Study Leave by the AHRB, during which the manuscript was completed. I wish to record my thanks to those who helped me during my research trip to Montreal and Ottawa in the summer of 2005: Professor Jane Everett for generously allowing me to consult unpublished materials on Joyce Marshall; Professor François Ricard for granting me permission to work on the archival holdings of the Fonds Gabrielle Roy at Library and Archives Canada, Ottawa; Monique Ostiguy at Library and Archives Canada for preparing the material for me to access from the Roy archival holdings. The University of Nottingham has generously given additional support for my research trips to Canada. I am also grateful to Roger Martin at MQUP for his encouragement of the project, to Joan McGilvray for guiding me through the various production processes, and to Jane McWhinney, my editor, whose sensitive reading of the manuscript has improved the final product. Finally, I thank Graham and Joe for their love and support.

Earlier versions of material discussed in sections of chapters 3, 4, and 5 were first published in the following articles:

1. An earlier version of the first section of chapter 3 has appeared in "French and English in Gabrielle Roy's Autobiographical Work," *The French Review*, special issue, "Le Québec et le Canada francophone," 78, 6 (May 2005): 1127–37.

2. An earlier version of part of the second section of chapter 5 has appeared in "Writing of/from the Fourth World: Gabrielle Roy and Ungava," *Québec Studies* 35 (spring/summer 2003): 45–62.

3. Sections of the first part of chapter 4 have appeared in a different version in "Translating difference: Gabrielle Roy's Inuit stories in French and English," *International Journal of Francophone Studies* 9, 3, (2006): 329–46. These sections have been reprinted by permission of the editors.

I am indebted to François Ricard for granting me permission to quote from the archival holdings of the Fonds Gabrielle Roy and to reproduce one of the photographs from the archive on the cover.

BETWEEN LANGUAGES AND CULTURES

Introduction: Power Relations in
Roy's Manitoba

In her autobiography *La Détresse et l'enchantement*, Gabrielle Roy captures a moment from her schooldays in Saint-Boniface that reveals the complex cultural situation of the Franco-Manitoban minority in the 1920s. Recalling a visit from the (anglophone) inspector from the Department of Education, she describes the kind of bicultural role-play expected of French-speaking Manitoban pupils: "Il me demanda si je connaissais quelque passage de la pièce. Je ne perdis pas une minute, imprimai sur mon visage le masque de la tragédie et me lançai à fond de train: *Is this a dagger* ... [He asked me if I knew some passage of the play by heart. I lost no time in drawing the mask of tragedy over my face and launching full tilt into 'Is this a dagger ... ']."[1] Roy then comments on the pleasure this ritual seems to produce: "C'était la première fois que je découvrais à quel point nos adversaires anglophones peuvent nous chérir, quand nous jouons le jeu et nous montrons de bons enfants dociles [That was when I first discovered how dearly our English-speaking adversaries can love us, providing we play the game and show what good, obedient children we are]" (DE 75; 56). As Roy implies, the scene confirms power relations between anglophone and francophone in Manitoba (Franco-Manitobans as children and anglophone power symbolically justified by the Shakespearean text). It is essentially a colonial scene, in which recitation becomes "a ritual act of obedience, often performed by a child before an audience of admiring adults."[2] Roy analyses the ambivalent positioning of her young self vis-à-vis English and French culture. In a tone half admiring and half self-mocking she declares: "Mais j'avais, je pense bien, un petit côté cabotin, peut-être en partie entretenu par notre sentiment collectif d'infériorité, et qui me faisait rechercher l'approbation de tous côtés [But I was a bit of a show-off, I think, perhaps owing partly to our collective inferiority complex, which led me to seek approval at every opportunity]" (DE 73; 55). Indeed, Roy's education, her family situation, and her personal aspirations required her to become bilingual and bicultural.

Roy's relationship with the English and French languages is complex. Her parents, both born in Quebec, had met in the Prairie province of Manitoba and moved to Saint-Boniface, a small town with a sizable francophone community, across the Red River from Winnipeg, provincial capital of Manitoba. Born in 1909, Roy was educated and then employed as a teacher within the Manitoban Department of Education. During this period, the dominance of the English language relegated both the French language and other minority languages to a marginal and inferior status. In her late twenties Roy decided to leave Manitoba. She travelled to Europe (both France and Britain) to complete her linguistic and cultural education and on her return to Canada in 1939 chose to settle in Quebec and pursue a career as a writer, having decided in the late 1930s that French would be her language of literary expression. This series of choices can be interpreted as a response to the linguistic and cultural inferiority and uncertainty that Roy had internalized as a Franco-Manitoban. Her sense of identification with Canada, with Manitoba and Quebec, and with France and Britain are all complicated by her origins within a linguistic and cultural minority. Yet, as I shall propose in the course of this book, a decentred relationship to various forms of dominant culture can also be understood as a form of cultural hybridity that opens up possibilities of thinking outside the binaries of Empire, colonization, majority and minority, and essentializing notions of identity.

The causes and effects of such a relationship to language and culture are the focus of this book. What did it mean to be born into the marginalized Franco-Manitoban community in 1909 and become first a school pupil, then a trainee teacher, and finally an elementary school teacher in that context? How did the feeling of cultural inferiority play out in subsequent relationships to the different linguistic communities of Canada (parts of the English-speaking majority, the various French-speaking minorities, immigrants, and indigenous peoples), and to the centres of cultural authority that were Britain and France? As a result of her decision in the late 1930s to use French as her language of literary expression, it would seem that Roy joined the ranks of francophone writers. But the linguistic situation of many non-metropolitan francophone writers is complex and marked by the processes of colonialism that their countries of origin have experienced. Roy's relationship with Quebec (and that of Quebec with Roy) is a subject for another book, but two brief examples indicate that it was not straightforward on either side. In an interview with David Cobb in 1976, Roy recalled that when *Bonheur d'occasion* was published, she was attacked from the pulpit by Catholic priests "wanting to know what '*this stranger in our midst*' was up to, bringing all this poverty and hard times to such harsh and public light."[3] In the same interview Roy stated that her loyalties were divided between Quebec and the Canadian West: "I'm inclined to agree with the ultimate separatist aim of more autonomy – but I have a great fondness for the rest of Canada, too. To some Quebeckers that makes me a bizarre creature, my western heritage is a curse as well as, to me, a blessing."[4] In Roy's case, the enduring fact of her bilingualism and biculturalism, and the colonial and neo-colonial implications of this dual identification are of deep significance to a full appreciation of her work.

After returning to Canada, Roy went on to become the first Franco-Canadian writer to achieve wide international recognition, with the dazzling success of her first novel, *Bonheur d'occasion*, in 1945 and its English translation, *The Tin Flute*, in 1947. She is regularly claimed as a founding figure of Quebec literature. Lori Saint-Martin, for example, refers to her as "one of the leading figures of Quebec literature" in her introductory essay to *Lectures contemporaines de Gabrielle Roy*.[5] She is a frequent figure of intertextual reference in work by other Québécois writers such as Michel Tremblay or Jovette Marchessault. After a passing acknowledgment of Roy's birth in Saint-Boniface, many critics and literary historians have assimilated her unproblematically into the canon of Quebec literature. There are, of course, notable exceptions to this relative neglect of Roy's Prairie origins. François Ricard's outstanding biography discusses in detail Roy's relationship with Manitoba and was one of the inspirations behind this present study. Carol J. Harvey, among a number of Manitoba-based academics, has published extensively on the Western settings and themes of Roy's writing, and Roy's work dominates the bookshops of Saint-Boniface. But this study is not about regionalism or the construction of minor literary canons; it is about the very specific experiences of culture that are produced in different geographical, social, and historical contexts by the complex processes of colonialism, and about the distinctive local responses to the practices of assimilation and acculturation that colonial situations impose. These experiences and responses can be traced in various forms throughout the work of Gabrielle Roy.

This book was inspired by the desire to read Roy's work through the lens of her bilingual and bicultural consciousness. It brings together three distinct strands of enquiry. I have drawn on a range of theoretical and empirical studies of colonialism and post-colonialism, to provide a conceptual framework for key areas of investigation: the education process, language, the status and practice of translation, migration, hybridity, and the place of the indigenous population in Canada. But since I am interested in the very specific case of the francophone minority in Manitoba, I have applied this conceptual framework to a particular body of archival material – textbooks, examination papers, correspondence, and annual reports relating to education in both English and French in Manitoba in the period from 1916 to 1937. This archival research was invaluable for the insight it gave into what Franco-Manitobans like Roy would have studied at school, both in English and in French. And it also revealed much about what she, as a First Grade teacher, would have taught her own pupils, for many of whom English and French were both foreign languages. The third strand of this study is, of course, the work of Gabrielle Roy itself, which I have read through these perspectives and shall discuss within the context of the broad organizing themes of the book.

After a general consideration of the relationship between education and colonialism, and the role of English language and literature studies in the context of colonialism and imperialism, I present the background to the particular case of education in Manitoba. Roy's schooling in Saint-Boniface began at a critical turning point in the history of the young province, when pressures toward acculturation to an Anglo-Canadian norm were at their most intense.

EDUCATION: A COLONIAL PROJECT?

It is commonly accepted that education is a key tool of colonial and imperial governance. Colonial and subsequent imperial powers influence not only the structure and the content of schooling but, more important, are the source of an ideology that justifies and continues the work of domination. An educated colonial subject will have learned to see the world through the categories of the coloniser, as John Willinsky suggests: "Imperialism afforded lessons in how to divide the world. It taught people to read the exotic, primitive, and timeless identity of the other, whether in skin colour, hair texture, or in the inflections of taste and tongue. Its themes of conquering, civilizing, converting, collecting, and classifying inspired educational metaphors equally concerned with taking possession of the world."[6] Within the colonial project, education served the creation of a cultural elite whose function was to mediate the values of empire, which had themselves been ideologically influenced by the values and claims to universality of the colonial culture. The most famously cited evidence of this "civilizing mission" is the "Minute on Indian Education" of Thomas Macaulay, which in 1835 defined the aim of education in India: "to form a class of persons, Indians in blood and colour, but English in taste, in opinions, in morals and in intellect."[7] Clearly the specific nature of this mission differed according to the requirements of the Empire in different areas of the world colonized by Britain, taking on distinctive dynamics in different contexts. In a "colony of occupation" in Asia or Africa, for example, the educational project focused more narrowly on the creation of an elite than it did in a colony of settlement such as Australia or Canada.[8]

In colonies of settlement, referred to as "settler-invader colonies" – or, in Diana Brydon's chronological revision of the term, "invader-settler colonies" – the relationship of the settler to the culture of the colonial power is also mediated through education.[9] For the settler both is and is not the representative of that power, as Alan Lawson argues. The "Second World," that of the settler, is "a place caught between two First Worlds, two origins of authority and authenticity: the originating world of Europe, the imperium, as source of the Second World's principal cultural authority; and that other First World, that of the First Nations, whose authority the settlers not only effaced and replaced but also desired."[10] As a result of this ambivalent placement between the source of power and its object, the colonized people, the settler can be said to embody the process of colonization: "The settler subject is, in a sense, the very type of the non-unified subject and the very distillation of colonial power, the place where the operations of colonial power as negotiation are most intensely visible."[11] In Canada, one is faced with the unusual complication of two established groups of settler subjects, the one conquered by the other and so existing in a relationship of unequal power. Given the colonial and post-colonial history of the anglophone and francophone presence in Canada, the implications of Lawson's point become all the more complex. Power relations between the settler populations produced changing patterns of negotiation, different degrees of visibility, and a range of possible subject positions for subjects caught between not just two, but three worlds. The education system provides an ideal stage for us to witness these processes of negotiation being played out. And the very existence of such processes of negotiation justifies – and indeed requires – that Canada, like other invader-settler colonies, be included in the broad field of postcolonial studies.

The place of Canada within this field is, of course, a matter of some controversy.[12] But the complexity and ambivalence produced by the education system in Manitoba in the period of Roy's education and teaching career can only be fully appreciated by taking the realities of both British imperial power and the French colonial legacy into account. As Bill Ashcroft has pointed out, "education is perhaps the most insidious and in some ways the most cryptic of colonialist survivals, older systems now passing, sometimes imperceptibly, into neo-colonialist configurations."[13] Roy's case exposes a whole network of tensions between competing notions of identity and culture (between British and French; between Anglo-Canadian and Franco-Canadian; between majority and First Nations, Métis, or immigrant minorities), notions relating both to the history and to the future of the Franco-Manitoban population.

So far I have referred to education in its broadest terms, as an institutionalized system or as a body of required learning divided into disciplines and delivered via a syllabus.

Before turning to look at the ways in which English (and French) were taught in Manitoban schools during Roy's time there, it is worth reflecting on the wider significance of the study of English within the British Empire. The study of English is deeply implicated in the process of Empire building, just as the study of French language and literature has been crucial to the French "civilizing mission." In studying the example of nineteenth-century Ontario, Robert Morgan analyses the discourse of educational tracts and finds a widespread image at work, that of the Empire as "a giant classroom for the teaching of English."[14] He cites a speech by the Reverend J. George in which George speaks of England as a schoolmistress "commissioned to teach a universal language to the world."[15] Claims to universalism help obscure the actual process of linguistic imperialism taking place, a process that R. Phillipson describes as seeking to "legitimate, effectuate, and reproduce an unequal division of power and resources ... between groups which are defined on the basis of language."[16] The teaching of literature also performs this work of legitimization. As Gauri Viswanathan reminds us, the study of English literature as an integral part of "English" began in India long before it became the norm in Britain: "The British educational system had no firm place for it until the last quarter of the nineteenth century, when the challenge posed by the middle classes to the existing structure resulted in the creation of alternative institutions devoted to 'modern' studies."[17] Until then, "literature" in Britain was represented either by classical texts, in the case of the upper classes, or by religious studies among the lower classes. Given the strict controls in British India on the teaching of Christianity, literature took on an important function as a surrogate source of moral teaching. At the same time Indian pupils' exposure to English literary texts created a myth of idealized Englishness, apparently untainted by the real business of colonialist expansion. As Charles Trevelyan, a civil servant in India from 1826–1838 with a particular interest in the field of education, admitted: "[The Indians] daily converse with the best and wisest Englishmen through the medium of their works, and form ideas, perhaps higher ideas of our nation than if their intercourse with it were of a more personal kind."[18] The colonial subject acquired a British-tinted view of the world and Britain's special place in that world. Individual subjects also learned how to speak, to name themselves as "I" and "we," in the language learned at school. As Morgan sees it: "From this perspective, English is a training in how to say 'I,' and the establishing of the social horizons within which this utterance takes place."[19]

However, as Heather Murray observes in her study of the development of English Studies in Canada, the process is not one of simple imposition, whereby English Studies act "as a conduit through which English literature and its accompanying values are transported from the centre to the margins."[20] She argues that the local conditions of educational establishments on the "margins" led to

strategic adaptations and innovations at the level of curriculum or
the development of a discipline that were in advance of the colonial
centre. In addition to the case of India she cites those of Scotland
and Canada where vernacular literary studies developed before
they did in England. Education acts as an arm of imperial governance, and the specific model of education that develops in a colony
or a dominion will serve both imperial and local interests. Murray
concludes that the relationship between English Studies and the
British Empire cannot be fully understood by a simple centre-
periphery model: "What is needed is more detailed attention to the
operations and oppositions of the colonial classroom ... The picture
will be very different when we try to see what colonized people did
to and with English, rather than what English 'did' to them."[21] One
of the key aims of this book is precisely to achieve an insight into
the "operations and oppositions of the colonial classroom" in Manitoba in the period 1916–1937, in respect to the teaching of both
French and English.

THE HISTORICAL BACKGROUND TO THE
MANITOBA SCHOOLS QUESTION

In September 1915 Gabrielle Roy began school at the Académie
Saint-Joseph in Saint-Boniface, a school run by the Sœurs des Saints
Noms de Jésus et de Marie, founded in 1898 and operated as a
French, Catholic school under the bilingual system. By the time she
entered Grade 11, the bilingual system had been abolished in Manitoba, making English the sole language of instruction. Consequently Roy's schooling, her teacher training at the Central Normal
School in Winnipeg, and her years as an elementary school teacher
in rural Manitoba and Saint-Boniface coincide with the period
when the linguistic rights of the francophone minority were the
most severely challenged. But the twin issues of language of instruction and denominational schooling dated from the arrival in the
West of White settlers.[22]

From the beginning of European settlement of the Red River Col-
ony in the area of modern-day Winnipeg in the early nineteenth
century, the population had been anglophone and francophone,
Protestant and Catholic. The first school was established in 1818 by
Bishop Norbert Provencher and later became le Collège de Saint-
Boniface. On the opposite bank in the parish of Saint John's, Angli-

can missionaries opened the Red River Academy in 1820. As C.J. Jaenen points out, this dualism was the natural consequence of the pattern of settlement: "It was not due to any structure imposed by Ottawa or London."[23] Until the entry of a small part of modern-day Manitoba into the Canadian Confederation in 1870, this territory was part of Rupert's Land, Canada's hinterland, but separate from Canada. When Manitoba joined Confederation, Article 23 of the 1870 *Manitoba Act*, based on the 1867 *British North America Act*, confirmed the existing situation of education in the Red River Colony, thereby guaranteeing the language rights of francophones and anglophones in Manitoba. Article 22 formalized the existence of a denominational education system, with a Catholic and a Protestant section.

In *L'Enseignement français au Canada*, the French-Canadian nationalist and historian Lionel Groulx describes the operation of the bilingual system during the first twenty years of Manitoba's existence as a perfect example of the co-existence of anglophone and francophone: "All the legal rights and privileges that form the basis of educational freedom are at the heart of the Manitoban legislation and remain an integral part of it until 1889."[24] When Manitoba entered Confederation, its population was split fairly equally between anglophones and francophones. Groulx gives the figures as follows: of about 14,000 inhabitants, there were 1,565 Whites, 556 Indians, and 11,963 Métis, of whom just over half were francophone.[25] The fact that the population was predominantly Métis recalls the history of initial contact between the male guides and traders working for the Hudson's Bay Company and its rival the North West Company (prior to their amalgamation in 1821) and the First Nations population through the fur trade and related trades (supplies and exchange, for example). These men found partners and had families with women from the indigenous population, and many of the families settled in the Red River Valley. From the outset, education for the Métis population in the Red River Colony and subsequently for First Nations children, was automatically delivered in the language of the settler, either English or French, in keeping with the principles of assimilation – linguistic, cultural, and religious. This practice illustrates the point made by Johnston and Lawson that in the context of the Second World the (predominantly) white settler acted as "an agent of colonial rule over the proportionally, and usually numerically shrinking indigenous population."[26]

Table 1
Population figures for Manitoba, 1881–1981

Year	Total population of Manitoba	Percentage of French origin	Percentage of English origin
1881	62,260	15.6	59.7
1901	255,211	6.3	64.4
1911	461,394	6.8	59.9
1931	700,139	6.7	52.6
1981	1,013,705	7.1	36.9

SOURCE: Figures from *Statistique Canada*

In the post-Confederation years, the Catholic bishop of Saint-Boniface, Monseigneur Taché, and renowned recruiting priests such as Father Albert Lacombe campaigned vigorously to recruit new settlers from Quebec and other parts of North America in order to maintain a strong francophone presence in the West. In fact the family of Roy's mother decided to migrate to Manitoba as the result of just such a recruitment drive in 1881.[27] But despite the efforts of the Catholic Church, demographic changes over the first two decades of Manitoba's existence meant that the francophone population was soon outnumbered. The table above shows the relative size of the populations of "English" origin and "French" origin.[28]

It is interesting that figures for the Métis population, available for 1870, then disappear from official Canadian statistics until 1941. In the intervening years the Métis were likely counted according to their French or British descent. Yet Manitobans were clearly aware of Métis identity throughout this period. When Roy goes to teach in Marchand in the summer of 1929, the village is described as "a Métis village."[29] The archives of the Association d'Education des Canadiens-Français du Manitoba (AECFM) also identify Métis pupils separately in figures given for the school population of the Ecole Sainte-Anne in AECFM reports for 1922: 119 of the 125 pupils in the school were described as French-Canadian, Métis, or Belgian in origin.[30] All were Catholic. As the table shows, while the population of English origin was growing rapidly from inward migration, the total population was also diversifying; as a result, the proportion of English origin dropped from nearly two-thirds in 1901 to just over a half in 1931. The size of other groups fluctuated according to patterns of migration as well as birth rates. In 1881 immigrants from German-speaking countries represented 13.6% of the population, almost equalling the proportion of French origin. By 1911 their proportion had dropped to 4.9% but new waves of migration saw Ukrainians forming 5.6%, Scandinavians 2.3%, and Poles 1.5% of the population.[31] All these groups could exercise their right to schooling under the bilingual system, where numbers allowed. Against this background of a diversifying and rapidly growing population, the status of French as an official language and the existence of the bilingual, denominational education system were discontinued in Manitoba in 1890.

For the following six years all schools had to teach according to the English system, but in 1896 a compromise was negotiated. The Laurier-Greenway compromise, enacted in 1897 as an amendment to the *School Act*, allowed teaching to be conducted in a minority language (not only in French) according to the bilingual system, and permitted religious education between 3:30 and 4:00 in the afternoon, where numbers warranted. By 1915, however, concerns had developed about the effects of the bilingual system on the standards of English in a province where a quarter of all schools were bilingual. The new Liberal government in Manitoba was committed to reforming the education system, making school attendance obligatory, and reducing the proportion of time allotted under the bilingual system to the teaching of minority languages. A report published on 14 January 1916 gave detailed evidence about schools' performances. A further factor was that the outbreak of the Great War had heightened tensions among groups of different national and racial origins in Canada, because of their varying degrees of allegiance to the British Empire. An increased emphasis on learning English, it was felt, would hasten the emergence of a common (Anglo-) Canadian identity. Indeed, in Legislative debates the view was expressed that the bilingual clause must be removed from the *School Act* "if a common citizenship were to be built up in Canada."[32] On 10 March 1916 the *Act to Further Amend the Public Schools Act* (known as the *Thornton Act*) was passed despite vigorous opposition from French members and the Ukrainian member (but with the support of the representatives of the Icelandic and Scandinavian communities, who favoured assimilation in the public sphere, happy to maintain their language and culture in the private sphere of home and family). The French members' response was that the legislation was "an attempt on our national life."[33] The francophone Liberal, Talbot, declared: "The French are a distinctive race, and we will not be assimilated, whether you like it or not."[34] This stance was, of course, more than a simple refusal to accept the domination of the language, culture, and ideology of the anglophone majority in Manitoba, or even in Canada. English was still the language of Empire, and the teaching of English was still entangled with the practices of that Empire. Franco-Manitobans' determination to resist the legislation was clearly a function of their colonial past.

The 1916 legislation made teaching *in* French illegal. Under the bilingual system some teaching had been allowed in a minority language from Grade 1 onward, but most subjects still had to be taught and examined in English. After 1916 the French language could only be taught at the secondary level as a second language, and religious education, as between 1897 and 1916 was permitted only in the half-hour after the official end of the school day (where numbers justified). Francophones from Saint-Boniface, such as Gabrielle Roy, now had to attend the Central Normal School in Winnipeg and receive their training in English (whereas three of Roy's older sisters, Anna, Adèle, and Bernadette, had trained as bilingual teachers in neighbouring Saint-Boniface). It was only in 1967 that the bilingual principle was once again recognized in Manitoba, after fifty years of organized resistance from the Franco-Manitoban community.[35]

With the bilingual system abolished, and the introduction of compulsory, non-denominational, English-language schooling throughout the province, one might well have expected that Manitoba would fall all the more easily into the vision of the British Empire as "a giant classroom for the teaching of English." Certainly the British Empire was a very real presence in schools in Manitoba throughout the period under discussion. Then, as now, education was a provincial not a federal responsibility; the Department of Education reported not to Ottawa but to the lieutenant-governor of Manitoba, the king's representative. All teachers seeking a teacher's licence were required to swear an oath of allegiance to the Crown, and non-British citizens were only allowed a temporary licence. In the half-yearly records of attendance returned to the Department of Education, each teacher had to sign two declarations: first, that no religious education had been taught in school apart from in the half-hour period after 3:30, in accordance with the law; second, that "the regulations respecting the flying of the 'Union Jack' at the school have been complied with during the present term and that the said 'Union Jack' in use in the said School District is now in good condition and repair."[36] The classroom was supplied with maps and a globe to remind pupils of the shape of the Empire and their place within it. Elementary school readers featured photographs of the reigning monarch and other images of Empire.

This was only one side of the picture, however. Roy's accounts of her education in La Détresse et l'enchantement and several of her other autobiographical and fictional works demonstrate that a bilingual system was continued, even though this continuation defied the provincial law and had to be concealed from Department of Education officials. It was in 1928 that Groulx visited Manitoba to research the state of francophone education in the province, the year in which Roy completed her Grade XII examinations at the Académie Saint-Joseph. As he records in L'Enseignement français au Canada, he was highly impressed by Franco-Manitobans' "constructive resistance" to linguistic and cultural assimilation.[37] What Groulx found in Saint-Boniface was evidence of a clandestine parallel system of education administered by the AECFM. The association came into being as a response to the debates paving the way for the 1916 legislation. A preliminary meeting had been held on 25 February 1916 at the Collège Saint-Boniface. The first document with a typed letterhead in the AECFM archives referring to the foundation of the organization is dated 15 March 1916, that is, just five days after the passage of the Thornton Act. The organization was only disbanded in 1968 after the principle of bilingual education had been fully reinstated in provincial legislation (Bill 59, 1967).

While the Liberal members of the Manitoba legislature had been at pains to reassure Catholics that the banning of the bilingual system in 1916 was not an attack on their religion, and that the arrangements for religious education would continue as before, language and faith went hand in hand for Franco-Manitobans. The AECFM relied on this link, using it as "the vehicle for a resistance movement whose goal was the protection of the French language, guardian of the faith."[38] The lay founders of the association had a close relationship with the Catholic Church, and the authority and patronage of the Church strengthened the control of the association over parents, teachers, and pupils. Now that education was obligatory in Manitoba, all pupils had to sit the provincial examinations. But from 1923 to 1967 the association ran a concours, in effect a rigorous examination of the parallel curriculum in French language, literature, history, and religious instruction, from grades IV to XII.[39] Association correspondence reveals the amount of work that the organization of the *concours* required, notably in the matter of sponsorship for the numerous prizes.[40] Among the organizations supporting the event by the donation of medals, and prizes of books and cash were the Société Saint-Jean-Baptiste in Montreal, the Association catholique de la jeunesse canadienne française, and the Chevaliers du Colomb in Quebec. The French-language newspaper *La Liberté* published the annual results of the *concours* and other news about the association's activities (helping to ensure the high profile of the association's work in the Franco-Manitoban population and encouraging their continued support).[41] At the 1926 awards ceremony on 31 July, Gabrielle Roy won the top award in Grade X, the Prix provincial, la Médaille de la France with 93% for her performance.[42] The prize for the best performance at Grade XII, the last year of high school, was a cheque for a year's fees at the Normal School in Winnipeg. In 1928 Roy duly won this prize as well, and she began her teacher training in the following autumn.

While the AECFM ensured that education continued to be delivered at least partly in French in Manitoba after 1916 and that Catholicism did not disappear from the curriculum, this was only part of the story. What developed was a curious form of cultural resistance. All those involved in delivering an alternative French education had to play a double game. In correspondence the AECFM reminded teachers of the need for secrecy and subterfuge. A recommendation concerning the provision of supplementary reading for pupils is accompanied with the caveat, "Make sure that the inspectors do not see those books."[43] As far as the Department of Education was concerned, the parallel system did not exist, at least not in any official way. Department of Education Archives in Winnipeg make no reference to the clandestine resistance. For example, in 1929–30 (the year before Gabrielle Roy joined the staff as Reception Class teacher) the Institut Provencher opened a brand new wing with eight additional classrooms. The annual report recorded this proudly with a photograph, but made no reference to the fact that much of the teaching there was to be carried out in French. It would seem the teaching in francophone school districts was a taboo subject in official reports (as policy concerning the First Nations' residential schools also seems to have been). The AECFM archives reveal that there was in fact a certain amount of contact – lobbying (on matters like school libraries) and even consultation (on curriculum reviews) – with the Department of Education. But the AECFM's real influence was within the classrooms in French-speaking areas.

Roy's schooling in Saint-Boniface began at a critical turning point in Manitoba, when the province was still less than fifty years old and pressures toward acculturation to an Anglo-Canadian norm were at their strongest. My first two chapters, "Learning to be Canadian" and "Becoming a Teacher," will examine the curriculum and the pedagogical climate of the times. In chapters 3 and 4, I explore the relationships to language that emerge in Roy's works in the light of her bilingual and bicultural background. Chapter 3, "Bilingualism, Diglossia, and the Other's Language," discusses ways in which *La Détresse et l'enchantement* is marked by traces of English (the language of the dominant culture?) and how encounters between languages are represented within a number of her texts. Can the presence of other languages in Roy's texts be related to processes of linguistic and cultural assimilation or to various forms of hybridity? In chapter 4, I address Roy's status as a *Canadian* writer through an examination of her work in translation. To what extent does the translation from the language of the minority to the language of the majority constitute an act of assimilation? What happens to the linguistic specificity of her works and how is linguistic difference treated in specific translations – does it disappear or is it given a new meaning? Some of the different translation strategies of Roy's translators are also examined in detail.

Chapter 5 develops some of the implications of the preceding chapters on education and language to consider Roy's writing as an attempt to "write Canada" in a way that is influenced by her very particular positioning and non-belonging. The dislocating effects of what has been described as a split consciousness, a sense of being between languages and cultures, and consequently open to others' linguistic and cultural differences, can be found through an analysis of selected works in which Roy represents Canada and some of its minorities, in her early journalism for *Le Bulletin des Agriculteurs*, as well as in a much later text, *La Rivière sans repos*.

My overall aim is to offer a reappraisal of Roy's work as a Canadian writer *in French*. Bilingualism and biculturalism are terms that can be conceptualized in a variety of ways. They may, for example, suggest a relationship of complementarity between two equal parts. Or, the doubling of language and culture may introduce layers of inequality, as a dominant language or culture seeks to contain or restrict the territory of the minority language. A bilingual or bicultural individual may feel a sense of belonging to both or to neither, or may have a preference for one language or culture. In Roy's case, what emerges is not so much a preference or even a balanced dualism, but a sense of fluidity, a constant attraction toward other identities and experiences, and a rejection of any fixed pattern of identification based solely on language or culture. For this reason, Roy's work seems to me to represent a movement that is produced by colonial power relations but prefigures and explores the possibilities of the post-colonial.

I

The Ambivalences of Learning to Be Canadian

For the Department of Education in Manitoba, the new legislation in 1916, which at last made schooling compulsory between ages 6 and 14 (grades I–VIII), opened up the prospect of educating the new generation of Manitobans as English-speaking Canadians. However, particularly in the context of the early years of the Great War, these young Manitobans were also still being taught to be British citizens. The teaching of English played an essential role in constructing a model of Britishness. As Robert Morgan puts it: "Imperialism was just as much a set of literary pedagogical practices as it was an international economic or military order."[1] In order to resist the assimilatory aims of English-language education, Franco-Manitobans needed to exercise their own control over what young Franco-Manitobans learned.

CURRICULUM MATTERS IN A POST-COLONIAL PROVINCE

The Association d'Education des Canadiens-Français du Manitoba was determined not simply to continue teaching *in* French but to deliver a "French" curriculum to counterbalance the English, non-denominational curriculum.[2] As *Le Bulletin des Institutrices Catholiques de l'Ouest* stated in 1935, looking back on Franco-Manitobans' response to the 1916 legislation: "What are we going to do? It is decided in no time at all: we will resist, we want to finish our children as we have started them off: Catholic and French."[3] This language of resistance is evident throughout the AECFM archives, as in correspondence with the president of the Société

Saint-Jean-Baptiste, Quebec, 6.12.1928: "As long as the former mother province does not forget her motto, the francophone diaspora in the west will feel stronger against the onslaught of assimilation, and their children will continue to sing the sweet-sounding language of France." This chapter examines the double curriculum of Franco-Manitoban schools. Through an analysis of the parallel curricula, the textbooks used to teach French, the examinations set by the Department of Education, and the English-language readers used in all schools in Manitoba, it becomes clear that a range of competing visions and ideologies were at work in the classroom. Not only did pupils of Roy's generation receive a double education but that education comprised multiple points of identification because of the enduring effects of colonial relationships with both France and Britain. It also bore the marks of a longstanding tradition of a separate Franco-Canadian, conservative Catholic identity and the more recent emphasis on a collective Anglo-Canadian identity that was replacing the more relaxed attitudes of the Canadian West under the old bilingual system. In such a highly charged context, bilingualism became for Roy not only a survival tactic but also a source of power and pleasure.

The Curriculum

The AECFM played a variety of roles as unofficial Department of French Education, exercising moral, if not official, authority within the Franco-Manitoban community, aided by its close ally, the Catholic Church. But by far the most significant activities of the association were the coordination, revision, and monitoring of the French curriculum in schools and the organization of the annual *concours*, which served to enforce and monitor the delivery of the curriculum. The AECFM archives do not have copies of the unofficial French curriculum for the period 1916–37, but there are many references to its existence, and some details of set texts are given in minutes and correspondence for this period. The account that follows is therefore based on the information that was available in these sources. The French curriculum was taught in about a hundred schools in fifty Manitoba parishes.[4] One of the earliest records of AECFM activity is a letter from the president of the new association to the *commissaires* of the former bilingual school districts advising them what to tell their teachers ... to continue as before: "That would

Table 2
Elementary School Curriculum, 1922
(French Syllabus)

All Grades	
Lecture	Reading
Orthographe	Spelling
Arithmétique	Arithmetic
Leçons de choses	Nature lessons
Vocabulaire	Vocabulary
Instruction religieuse	Religious instruction
Ecriture	Writing
Grammaire	Grammar
Dictée	Dictation
Analyse	Parsing
Rédaction écrite/orale	Written/oral composition
Grades V and VI	
L'histoire sainte	Scripture
L'histoire du Canada	Canadian history

SOURCE: Jean-Marie Taillefer, "Les Franco-manitobains et l'éducation 1870–1970: une étude quantitative," University of Manitoba, 1988, 284–5.

mean following the curriculum that they had last year and therefore using the same books."[5] In 1922 the association appointed two school visitors to shadow the role of the Department's inspectors but concentrate on the teaching of French and religion in schools.[6] Teachers were expected to teach the French syllabus in addition to the official English syllabus as set out in the Department of Education Program of Study. A report of an inspection of an elementary school, Ecole Sainte-Anne, in 1922 shows what the (French) curriculum comprised (see table 2).[7]

While the AECFM initially recommended that schools continue to use the French textbooks as before, after a period of adjustment to their clandestine status a new syllabus was prepared by two teaching nuns at Gabrielle Roy's school.[8]

It is clear from archival evidence that the association instructed its schools on all matters of curriculum, set texts, school library provision, and classroom displays. In 1925–26, for example, they recommended specific sections of *Le petit catéchisme du Québec* for grades III to V and sections of Lafargues's catechism for grades VI, VII, and VIII. In 1924–25 pupils in grades III and IV studied the Old Testament; in 1925–26 the New Testament. The AECFM also specified the period of history to be taught: in 1924–25 grades IV and v studied French rule in Canada, and in the following year they studied British rule.[9] According to Jean-Marie Taillefer other texts used at elementary school level included a reader edited by the Frères de Sainte-Croix, as well as *L'Histoire sainte* and *L'Histoire du Canada* by the Clercs Saint-Viateur.[10] Pupils were clearly examined on the catechism in the annual *concours* organized by the AECFM, showing that religious instruction was considered an integral part of the curriculum, not an optional extra-curricular item, as the Laurier-Greenway amendment of 1896 had intended.[11] Teachers were encouraged to enter all their pupils, not just the best, for the *concours* and in recognition of the effects of the "foreign environment" in which some pupils were growing up, those with weaker French could be entered for a lower grade than their school year.[12] Composition in French was considered a key element of assessment, counting for 30 percent of the total for lower grades and 40 percent for higher grades.[13]

The parallel curriculum and its monitoring through the *concours* were particularly important for the elementary grades I to VIII, as pupils in grades IX to XII were allowed to continue with French and take the optional papers set for French speakers. But as the curriculum for these higher grades continued more or less unchanged (see Tables 3 and 4 below) the AECFM had to ensure that pupils had by then acquired a high enough standard of written French and had read widely enough to cope with reading Corneille, Lamartine, or Veuillot. As these tables show, there is a striking continuity in terms of set texts and authors from Grade IX onward before and after the ban, despite the official removal of French teaching from the lower grades.

Key texts that show the continuity of the secondary school curriculum before and after the end of the bilingual system include *Leçons de langue française* and *Modèles français: extraits des meilleurs écrivains avec notices*. These texts give an insight into what was considered crucial to the survival of a francophone community in Manitoba and into the kind of education Roy herself doubtless received at the Académie Saint-Joseph. What notions of Frenchness did the texts convey? In what ways did Catholicism permeate the content, and to what extent did these texts encourage a sense of identification with France, as a former colonial power, or with neo-colonial authority? In the 150 years since the Conquest, Franco-Canadian identity had widely diverged from the values and

Table 3
Curriculum for French under the "Bilingual System"

	Department of Education, Manitoba, Set Texts In French, 1914–1916	
	(Last 2 Years of Bilingual System)	
Grade III	*Leçons de langue française,* cours élémentaire	*Second livre de lecture*
Grade IV	*Leçons de langue française,* cours élémentaire	*Livre de lecture,* série bilingue anglais/français
Grade V	*Leçons de langue française,* cours moyen	*Livre de lecture,* série bilingue anglais/français
Grade VI	*Leçons de langue française,* cours moyen	
Grade VII	*Leçons de langue française,* cours moyen *Etude de l'art épistolaire* (ibid.)	*Modèles français,* Père Edmond Procès (Bruxelles) cours inférieur
Grade VIII	*Leçons de langue française,* cours moyen *Etude de l'art épistolaire* (ibid.)	*Modèles français,* P.E. Procès (Bruxelles) *Notices littéraires des auteurs canadiens-français, cours supérieur,* pp. 368–74
	Grade IX – Bilingual Certificate Route for Intending Teachers	
Grade XI		Racine, *Esther* Fénélon, *Télémaque*
Grade XII (Additional French)		*Modèles français,* III, Seconde, P.E. Procès (Bruxelles) (Bossuet, Laprade, St Marc-Girardin). *Causeries,* III, P. van Tricht

SOURCE: Rosemary Chapman from Manitoba Department of Education Archives, Instructional Resources Unit, Winnipeg.

trends of metropolitan France. Interestingly, these set texts were written and published in Quebec and Brussels respectively, natural sources of teaching materials for a denominational education. In France, of course, education had been free and compulsory, but non-denominational since the *Lois Ferry* in the 1880s. In Quebec there had been no such break between education and the Church, and education was delivered by parallel Catholic and Protestant sectors until the eventual educational reform of the *Révolution tranquille* in the 1960s. In Belgium a dual denominational and linguistic system also operated. The use in Manitoba of text books from Quebec and Belgium acted as an important mediation of French culture, as an analysis of their content demonstrates.

Table 4
Sample of Curriculum for French Optional Teachers Course

	1923	1927	1930	1933
Grade IX			*Leçons de langue française,* cours supérieur, FEC, nouvelle édition, pp. 1–146 *Notions de style,* ibid., pp. 271–306	*Leçons de langue française,* cours supérieur, FEC, nouvelle édition, pp. 1–146 *Notions de style,* ibid., pp. 271–306
Grade X	*Leçons de langue française,* cours supérieur, FEC, nouvelle édition, *Manuel de littérature,* II, pp. 45–166, P.J. Verest (Bruxelles), 1920. *Modèles français,* P.E. Procès (Bruxelles) Laure Conan, *L'Oublié*	*Leçons de langue française,* cours supérieur, FEC, nouvelle édition, pp. 1–146 (Analyse littéraire d'extraits de la Fontaine, de Ségur, Bossuet, Lemay). *Notions de style,* ibid., pp. 271–353. *Lectures littéraires* par FIC Jean Rivard Gérin-Lajoie, *Le Défricheur*	*Leçons de langue française,* cours supérieur, FEC, nouvelle édition, pp. 147–270, + analyses littéraires *Notions de style,* ibid., pp. 306–53. *Lectures littéraires* par FIC. Laure Conan, *L'Oublié*	*Leçons de langue française,* cours supérieur, FEC, nouvelle édition, pp. 147–270, + analyses littéraires *Notions de style,* ibid., pp. 306–53. *Lectures littéraires* par FIC. Laure Conan, *L'Oublié*

Table 4 continued

Grade XI	Modèles français, P.E. Procès (Bruxelles) Manuel de littérature, II, pp. 416–527, P. J. Verest (Bruxelles), 1920. Manuel d'histoire de la littérature canadienne-française, C. Roy. Précis d'histoire littéraire, FEC (Montréal). Racine, Esther. Fénelon, Télémaque.	Précis d'histoire littéraire, FEC (Montréal) Cours de littérature par une réunion de professeurs. Racine, Esther. Manuel d'histoire de la littérature canadienne-française, C. Roy, 1925. (Groulx, Bourassa, Buies, Tardivel, Casgrain, Garneau, Fréchette)	Précis d'histoire littéraire, FEC (Montréal) Manuel d'histoire de la littérature canadienne-française, C. Roy, 1925. Racine, Esther	Précis d'histoire littéraire, FEC (Montréal) Manuel d'histoire de la littérature canadienne-française, C. Roy, 1930. Racine, Athalie. Alonié de Lestres, Au cap Blomidon.
Grade XII	Modèles français, P.E. Procès (Bruxelles) Précis d'histoire littéraire, FEC (Montréal). Corneille, Polyeucte.	Modèles français, P.E. Procès (Bruxelles) Précis d'histoire littéraire, FEC (Montréal). Corneille, Polyeucte.	Modèles français, P.E. Procès (Bruxelles) Précis d'histoire littéraire, FEC (Montréal). Corneille, Polyeucte.	Modèles français, P.E. Procès (Bruxelles) Précis d'histoire littéraire, FEC (Montréal). (Lamartine, Veuillot, Vigny, Bossuet, Saint-Simon). Corneille, Le Cid.

SOURCE: Rosemary Chapman from Manitoba Department of Education Archives, Instructional Resources Unit, Winnipeg

FIC: Les Frères de l'Instruction Chrétienne
FEC: Les Frères des Ecoles Catholiques

Textbooks

The advanced course of the Leçons de langue française combined the
teaching of language and literature. It consisted of written and oral
exercises with readings and analyses of short passages. Written by
the Frères des Ecoles Chrétiennes, the text was used in Grade x in
1923 and 1927, but in Grade ix in 1930 and 1933. Under the bilingual system the elementary course of this series had been used as
early as Grade iii, allowing pupils to progress to the intermediate
course by Grade v. Edmond Procès's series, *Modèles français,* continued to be used in grades x to xii in 1923, although by 1927 it was
restricted to Grade xii. Once again this was the advanced level of a
well-established series of textbooks, published in Belgium. The series
was subtitled: "Extraits des meilleurs écrivains avec notices par
Edmond Procès de la compagnie de Jésus [Extracts from the greatest
writers with explanatory notes by Edmond Procès of the Society of
Jesus]." It showed the enduring influence of the Jesuits on Franco-
Canadian education and reflected the principles of the humanist tradition established in Canada, notably in the *collèges classiques.*[14]
Other textbooks recommended both in Manitoba and Quebec were
the work of teaching orders such as the Frères des Ecoles Catholiques
(established in Quebec in 1837), the Clercs de Saint-Viateur (1847),
and the Frères de l'Instruction Chrétienne (1886).[15]

Leçons de langue française, cours supérieur was an all-purpose
textbook. Grammar, subdivided into sections devoted to *phoné-*
tique, morphologie, syntaxe, and *notions de style,* formed the main
body of the book, and a range of texts was interspersed either for
guided *explication de texte* or for other types of exercise, including
dictées, phraséologie, and *composition.* This section closed with
a series of *Notices littéraires* about the authors of the selected
passages. *Leçons de langue française* concluded with a section of
writing tasks such as essays and literary analysis. In the choice of
extracts, essay topics, and vocabulary used in grammar exercises,
Leçons de langue française is strongly marked by Catholic teaching.
A brief passage describing a traveller's impressions of Lourdes, for
example, is used first for a résumé exercise, encouraging children to
absorb and express the scene in their own words. Then detailed
questions give a guided *analyse de texte,* an exercise that was central to the pedagogical practices of classical humanist education. As
Normand Renaud observes in his study of the aims and methods of

the *collège classique*: "The teacher's textual commentary tends to set the text up as a model."[16] While many of the questions concern language and stylistic effect, some require additional knowledge, which the teacher could provide, such as: "Qu'est-ce que *la grotte de l'apparition* dont parle l'auteur? En quelle année eurent lieu les apparitions? Qu'est-ce qu'*un pèlerin*? [What is the *cave of the apparition* that the author refers to? In which year did the apparitions take place? What is *a pilgrim*?]" (338). Further examples of the many religious topics: are "Le courage chrétien," "Le Sanctus à la maison," and "L'Angélus du soir" [Christian courage, The Sanctus in the home, The evening Angelus].

In addition to references to French Catholic traditions, there are also references to Quebec, the second spiritual, and national, pole. French-Canadian topics include: "Québec littéraire en 1760," "De Québec à Montréal en 1643," "La fête nationale," and "Inauguration du monument Laval" [Literary life in Quebec in 1760, From Quebec to Montreal in 1643, The national holiday, Inauguration of the Laval monument (referring to the unveiling of a statue to Monseigneur de Laval in June 1908)]. Written exercises show the same cultural, moral, and religious bias. Exercices in guided composition include such topics as "Le nouveau Salomon," "Une bonne action," and "Repentir et pardon" [The new Solomon, A good deed, Repentance and forgiveness]. Letter-writing tasks include "Un jeune homme au curé de sa paroisse" and "A un jeune frère qui va faire sa première communion" [A young man to his parish priest; To a younger brother about to take his first communion]. The vocabulary in gap-filling language exercises also has a clear moral function:

(Add the missing pronoun to the following) "Si l'__ observait bien la tempérance en toute chose, __ se porterait toujours mieux [If __ observed temperance in all things, __ would always be in better health]";

"Les hommes ont chacun __ vocation providentielle [Every man has __ heaven-sent vocation]";

(Add either *même*, *quelque*, or *tout*) "__ ait été l'astuce, la ruse, la finesse des ariens, des nestoriens, des luthériens, etc., ses dogmes sont demeurés les __
[(Whatever) the clever tricks, ruses, or subtle arguments of the

Arians, the Nestorians, the Lutherans, etc. may have been, their teachings remained unchanged]."

The attitude to the French language being taught is highly normative, encouraging pupils to avoid anglicisms and positing metropolitan French as the norm: "Les fautes les plus opposées à la correction du langage sont: le barbarisme, le solécisme et, pour le Canada, l'anglicisme [The most serious kinds of mistakes in French are: barbarisms, solecisms and, in the case of Canada, anglicisms]" (116).

In contrast to the text's assumption of the centrality of France as linguistic authority, the literary extracts in the textbooks include a significant number by French-Canadian authors. What is striking is the difference in the way French and French-Canadian authors are presented in the *Notices littéraires* (368–74). French authors are listed alphabetically by century. In their case the "Notices" deliver a heavy dose of judgment – positive or negative. The *Philosophes* are the main target, as the following examples illustrate: "Rempli de haine contre le christianisme et profondément corrompu, [Voltaire] a exercé par ses écrits la plus funeste influence [full of hatred for Christianity and profoundly corrupt, [Voltaire] exerted the most harmful influence through his writings]" (365); "les erreurs jansénistes [erroneous Jansenist thinking]" (with reference to Racine, 365); "Le théâtre de Molière respecte peu la religion, et encore moins les lois de la décence et de la morale [Molière's theatre shows little respect for religion and still less for the laws of decency and morality]" (364); André Chénier's poems are written "avec beaucoup de grâce et de pureté, mais [sont] trop souvent licencieuses [with much grace and purity but [are] too often licentious]" (365). Nineteenth-century authors are also criticized on moral grounds: Musset is a "poète d'un très grand talent, mais qui, dans ses ouvrages: Comédies, Elégies, Nouvelles, Contes, Proverbes, etc., se montre aussi licencieux qu'incrédule et impie [a highly talented poet, but one who, in his various works: comedies, elegies, short stories, tales, proverbs, etc., proves to be as licentious as he is agnostic and irreligious]" (366); Michelet is described as an "écrivain de talent, mais immoral et plein d'impiété [a talented writer, but immoral and full of ungodliness]" (367). Authors who are regularly set for study at the advanced level, such as Coppée, Veuillot, or Joseph de Maistre, tend to be positively presented. The note on Coppée, for instance, reads: "La maladie le ramena à la foi, et il écrivit alors, en des pages exquises, 'La Bonne Souffrance' [Ill health restored his faith, and it was then that he composed the exquisite pages of 'Good Suffering' (1898)]" (368). This alleged harmony between the formal qualities of a literary text and the moral quality of the author is totally in keeping with the principles of classical humanism.

In the section on "Auteurs canadiens-français" comments tend to relate more to the author's place in the history of French Canada and the emergence of its literature. Terms such as *canadien, Canada, Québec, patriotisme,* and *nationalisme* appear in the great majority of entries, either in titles of works or in brief comments. Quotations are often included from l'abbé Camille Roy's *Tableau de l'histoire de la littérature canadienne-française* (itself listed as a set text throughout the 1920s and 1930s). Evaluative judgments such as this characterization of de Crémazie are typical: "une âme sincèrement canadienne [a sincerely Canadian soul]." Nationalism, then, emerges as the prime asset of French-Canadian authors, and their religious or moral qualities seem either to be less important or less troublesome. This unequal treatment of French authors and French-Canadian authors underlines the sense that French-Canadian culture is a minor culture, requiring definition in terms of its national (but peripheral) situation in comparison with the dominant (if flawed) culture of France.[17]

Procès's *Modèles français: extraits des meilleurs écrivains avec notices* shows a similar use of commentary. Again this text fits in clearly with the pedagogical premises of classical humanism: "Teaching the rules of the art of writing through the study of an example, rather than referring to theoretical principles in textbooks, is the ideal method of classical education."[18] By studying selections from the "best" authors, the pupil will learn to appreciate their form, sense of order, and harmonious expression, which they will then doubtless imitate in their own use of language. Procès's "Notices" criticize instances of, or supposed leanings toward, socialism, Protestantism, atheism, and immorality (of content). Irony is not appreciated. The "notice" on Anatole France, for example, reads as follows: "Un merveilleux écrivain ... mais profondément sceptique, il a déversé l'ironie sur les choses les plus sacrées, même sur le patriotisme et la religion. Aussi son œuvre est immorale et malfaisante: elle a justement mérité la condamnation de l'Eglise [A marvellous writer ... but profoundly sceptical, he

poured irony on what is most sacred, even on patriotism and religion. Consequently his work is immoral and has an evil influence: it
has quite rightly earned the condemnation of the Church]."[19]

Biographical notes on writers make particular mention of religious or moral conversions; La Fontaine, for example, "mourut
chrétiennement en 1695 [died as a Christian in 1695]."[20] Readers,
or more probably their teachers (as only a select number of extracts
were set for study), are warned against certain writers such as Loti
and Flaubert ("une œuvre dangereuse [a dangerous body of
work]").[21] But as Procès was Belgian and his text was published in
Brussels, his selection does not contain the same French-Canadian
feeling, nor does he provide a list of French-Canadian authors.
However, several Belgian authors are included, and that selection,
together with the censorious attitude to many mainstream French
writers, once again has the effect of slightly decentring the anthology from the French canon.

Roy's memories of her study of French literature in *La Détresse et
l'enchantement* are clearly haunted by this textbook and its contents (representing as they did her final year of literature study). She
describes the curriculum in negative terms and emphasizes the limited range of authors studied: "Quelle idée pouvions-nous avoir de
la poésie française ramenée presque entièrement à François Coppée,
à Sully Prudhomme et au *Lac* de Lamartine, si longtemps rabâché
qu'aujourd'hui par un curieux phénomène – de rejet peut-être – je
n'en saurais retrouver un seul vers [And what idea could we have of
French poetry when it was reduced almost exclusively to François
Coppée, Sully Prudhomme, and Lamartine's 'Le Lac,' which we
parrotted so many times that today, by some curious reaction –
mental block perhaps – I couldn't recite a single line of it]" (DE 71;
54). The authors Roy targets for her strongest criticism, Veuillot
and Montalembert, are both Catholic authors. Veuillot was a mili-
tant journalist, in favour of ultramontanism and, according to
Gérard Tougas, "the French writer the most universally admired in
French Canada during the Second Empire."[22] Montalembert was a
publicist, politician, and liberal catholic. It may well have been,
however, that it was also the ideology of the manuals that so alienated Roy, an ideology that presented a moralistic and censorious
view of French literature.

The omissions from the French syllabus are given as much space
in Roy's account as the inclusions. She cites Zola, Flaubert,

Table 5
High School timetable, 1930–31

Subject	Number of periods per week
English	8
History	5
Maths	5
Science	4
Art/Music	2
PE	3
Optional	
French Option	4
Foreign language*	4

SOURCE: Rosemary Chapman from Manitoba Programme of Study, 1930–31

*In 1930–31, for example, foreign languages that could be taught in Manitoba at this level included Latin, Greek, French, German, and Icelandic.

Maupassant, and Balzac, and later adds Rimbaud, Verlaine, Baudelaire, and Radiguet. By contrast, the account of her early study of English literature is expressed very positively: "La littérature anglaise, portes grandes ouvertes, nous livrait alors accès à ses plus hauts génies [The doors to English literature, however, were open wide and gave us access to its greatest minds]" (DE 71; 54). She lists Hardy, Eliot, the Brontës, Austen, Keats, Shelley, Byron, the Lake poets and, above all, perhaps, Shakespeare (taught right from Grade VII).

Studying French as a second language

The model of French culture and literature that francophone pupils received through the unofficial French curriculum was mediated through a traditional, Catholic ideology that privileged the values of pre-Revolutionary France and edited out unacceptable, progressive elements of French culture. By contrast, anglophone pupils in Manitoba probably gained a very different notion of France and Frenchness. French could be studied as a second language from Grade IX onward, as shown in table 5.

The set text for students of French as a second language was *Mes Premiers Pas en français*, by M.L. Chapuzet and W.M. Daniels, authorized for use in Manitoba from 1920 to 1929 at Grade IX. The authors were both schoolteachers from Britain, one apparently francophone and the other anglophone, who taught at Wakefield Girls High School and Westminster City School. The book was published in Boston for use in the United States and its focus could not have been more different from that of the French textbooks published in Quebec and Brussels. It was a new edition, with grammar rules, and used the direct method. The authors' stated aims are to build up a good vocabulary, not totally avoiding the mother tongue, and to make use of music and dramatic instinct. It offers clear lesson plans, with a high emphasis on oral work, scenes, songs, poetry, pictures, and enjoyment. The textbook is entirely Eurocentric, Frenchness being associated with stereotypical environments such as *le château* and *le marché*. Its only map reveals the British-French origin of the text; it shows a large chunk of Britain with a section of northwest France. Arguably this is to help pupils with a specific exercise: "Un voyage en France par Southampton et le Havre [A journey to France via Southampton and Le Havre]" (110), but it is still rather curious as the only geographical representation of "France" in the book. Considering that the text was recommended in Manitoba, the vocabulary section has surprising omissions (it has, for example, *église* but not *prêtre*). The one reference to North America in a brief dialogue has an exoticizing Eurocentric tone:

"L'oncle Louis a été partout. Il a été en Australie et en Afrique."
"En Afrique chez les nègres?" demande Marie.
"Oui," dit M. Louis. "J'ai été aussi en Amérique chez les Peaux-Rouges."
["Uncle Louis has been everywhere. He has been to Australia and to Africa."
"To Africa where the Negroes live?" asks Marie.
"Yes," says Mr Louis. "I've also been to America where the Redskins live."] (107–8)

Yet while this text is clearly Eurocentric, its method seems to conform to statements that appear in the Manitoba Department of Education's guidelines for second language teaching: "As much emphasis as possible should be put upon the conversational use of language; careful attention to be given to reading aloud, dictation, memorizing."[23] Whether this lively, communicative method really transferred to the anglophone Canadian classroom is put in doubt, though, by the comments of one of the more radical school inspectors of the time, Andrew Moore. Moore himself comes over in the reports as strongly in favour of the study of French, even though his own justification for it is somewhat contradictory, at once liberal and yet tinged with an echo of Empire: "Aside from the cultural value, anyone who can speak both English and French is at home practically anywhere in the civilized world."[24] But he regrets that French is one of the least popular school subjects at present and writes: "The ability to speak French and an ordinary reading knowledge of the language is much more desirable than the present grammatical grind."[25] He encourages the use of radio, gramophone, and conversation from Grade VII onward where possible. Clearly there was a gap between the kind of set text chosen and its use in the classroom, probably by teachers who themselves had a poor grasp of the method. This would seem to confirm that exchanges between francophones and anglophones were uneven, the minority being forced to communicate in the language of the majority, but the majority regarding French as an alien, European language with little to offer them.

Department of Education examination papers

The examination system and the examination papers set by the Manitoba Department of Education to assess the official curriculum give a point of comparison between the teaching of French and English at high school level. By comparing the papers set in 1928, the year in which Roy sat her Grade XII examinations, with those set in 1915, the last year of the bilingual system, one finds a number of contrasts and also some signs of development. The detailed table below lists the examination papers and the set texts for the year when Roy sat her Grade XII examinations.

In addition to the French literature set for Grade XII, Grade X pupils also studied works by some French-Canadian writers, notably *L'Oublié*, one of Laure Conan's many historical and hagiographical works. Plays by Racine (*Esther* and *Athalie*, set texts in the 1920s, both with biblical subjects) were studied in Grade XI. Given the fact that the syllabus for Additional French (for native speakers) continued to use the same set texts as under the bilingual system and led on naturally from the clandestine Catholic education, it is interesting to compare the examination papers set for Additional

Table 6
Examinations and Set Texts for Grade XII in 1927–28

Examination Paper	Set Texts
Composition	800-word essay (some subjects correspond to the prose literature paper)
Rhetoric and Prose Literature	*Pilgrim's Progress* (Bunyan, Pt I)
	Select essays of Addison (ed. Thurber), 1–80
	Rob Roy (Scott)
	Sesame and Lilies (Ruskin)
	Far from the Madding Crowd (Hardy)
	Modern English Prose (Carpenter and Brewster, MacMillan) including Poe, Kipling, London, Dickens, Lincoln, Thoreau, Mill (a mixture of British English and U.S. texts with an occasional Canadian item)
Poetical Literature	*English Poetry: Its Principles and Progress* (Milton, Dryden, Lake poets, Arnold, Kipling, Yeats, De la Mare, Masefield)
History of English Literature	*English Literature* (Long), pp. 186–560
	NB: A student who made more than five spelling mistakes had to take a supplementary paper
Algebra	
Analytical Geometry	
Physics	
(or Chemistry)	
French* (non-native speakers) (or Latin)	a) French Grammar and Composition *The New Fraser and Squair Complete French Grammar*, Pt II
	b) French Authors *Le Petit Chose* (Daudet) *Le Chien du Capitaine Evault*
	c) Short stories, edited by C. Lafontaine *La petite Fadette* (Sand)
History (or Plane trigonometry or Science 2)	*Short History of the English People* (Green), chaps. 3, 6, 7–10
	A Survey of Modern History (Hodges)
Additional English Papers*	a) Bacon, Swift, Burke, Chaucer, Spenser, Milton
	b) Ruskin, Carlyle, Arnold Huxley, Shakespeare: *Midsummer Night's Dream, Twelfth Night, Romeo and Juliet, Macbeth*
Additional French Papers*	a) *Précis d'histoire littéraire* – par une réunion de professeurs III–V
	b) *Polyeucte*
	c) *Modèles français*, P. E. Procès, III, seconde; *Morceaux choisis*: Molière, *Mercure et Sosie*; Bossuet, *Alexandre*; Montalembert, *S. Columba en Calédonie*; Boileau, *L'Art poétique*; Félix, *Le Beau*; La Bruyère,

Table 6 continued

Additional French Papers*	*Du mérite personnel*; de la Prade; Lamartine, *L'Homme*; Veuillot, *A la cime de Moléson*; S-Marc Girardin; de Broglie; Déroulède, *Le Turco*; Coppée, *L'Epave*

SOURCE: Rosemary Chapman from Manitoba Programme of Study, 1927–28

* Women students not taking any foreign languages could omit Maths and take additional papers in French or English.
Anglophone students who took no foreign language studied Chemistry and Physics, Trigonometry, and History.

French with the equivalent language and literature papers set for English. A number of comparisons are possible. In the Optional Literature Papers for French and English, the questions on the French paper seem in some cases to require general knowledge of a text, possibly based on the study of an extract and brief *Notices* rather than the full text, as in the following examples from Optional French – A:

1. Commentez brièvement le [sic] sujets suivants: (1) Les lettres de Mme de Sévigné. (2) Le talent de la Fontaine. (3) Le génie de Victor Hugo. (4) L'académie française.
2. Boileau: son but, son caractère, son œuvre, son influence.
[1. Comment briefly on the following topics: (1) The letters of Mme de Sévigné. (2) The talent of la Fontaine. (3) The genius of Victor Hugo. (4) The Académie française.
2. Boileau: his aims, his character, his work, his influence.]

In Optional French – B, the questions presuppose answers that confirm the qualities of the set text as stated in the question:

"Avec Laprade on ne quitte pas les sommets."
Etablissez la vérité de cette citation à l'égard du style et de la pensée du poème, 'Symphonie du Torrent.'
["With Laprade one never leaves the heights." Demonstrate the truth of this quotation with respect to the style and the thoughts expressed in the poem 'Symphony of the Torrent.']

Optional English literature papers seem to require slightly more analysis and phrase their questions in a more open manner, as in the following example from Optional English – B:

"The sole end for which mankind are warranted, individually or
collectively, in interfering with the liberty of action of any of
their number, is self-protection." How does Mill (a) develop, (b)
limit, this statement?"

Another set of comparisons can be made between the prose composition questions set on English and French examination papers. In
principle, the education system in Manitoba had been secular since
1890. However, as we have seen by looking at the curriculum
before and after 1916, the francophone sector had ignored this law
and continued to teach the Catholic faith not only in separate religious instruction classes but also throughout the curriculum delivered in French. If we compare examination questions for prose
composition in 1915 and 1928, the effects of this practice are clear.
Under the bilingual system in 1915, students of Grade XII English
Composition (not less than five hundred words) had the following
choices:

A Journey from the Aegean to the Black Sea
King Charles the First
Globigerinae
Harry Esmond's College Life
A Duel
Action Essential to the Scholar
The Pretender

These titles offer students a rather Eurocentric set of topics to discuss, and many assume knowledge of British history, literature, or
culture. The equivalent paper in French at Grade XII (Composition
en prose) proposes the following:

(a) Par une bienveillante Providence, Dieu a mis dans la nature
la fécondité, qui satisfait les besoins de notre vie, et la beauté
qui fait le charme de notre âme. Il a droit à notre reconnaissance.
(b) Les qualités de notre belle langue française (clarté, souplesse,
harmonie, richesse)
(c) Les raisons qu'ont les Canadiens de combattre dans la guerre
actuelle; loyauté envers l'Angleterre, sympathie pour la France,
défense de la civilisation menacée

(d) Le bienfait de l'éducation pour la formation de l'esprit, du cœur et de la volouté [sic]

(e) Les avantages de la vie à la compagne [sic]

[(a) By the hand of a benevolent Providence, God has endowed nature with fruitfulness, which satisfies our physical needs, and beauty which enchants our soul. He deserves our gratitude.

(b) The qualities of our beautiful French language (clarity, suppleness, harmony, richness)

(c) The reasons which Canadians have for fighting in the current war; loyalty towards England, sympathy for France, defence of the civilization which is under threat

(d) The benefit of education for the development of the mind, the heart and the will

(e) The advantages of life in the countryside]

(Note: The typographical errors, quite common in papers set for French, suggest that typesetters in Winnipeg were anglophone.)

Here the questions overtly exemplify the moral and religious content of teaching in French. As composition topics, they look very different from the English choices and have the effect of indicating the required response (a feature already found in *Leçons de langue française*). They are also interesting in a number of other respects. The question on the War was clearly topical, but predates the controversy about the conscription of francophones that was to divide Quebec from the rest of Canada in 1917. It is noteworthy, in the context of Manitoba, that loyalty toward "l'Angleterre" is listed before sympathy with France; equally significant is the choice of abstract noun in each case. Question (e) reinforces the recurrent association between French Canadians and rural life, which the Catholic Church, and indeed traditional nationalists such as Lionel Groulx, play on throughout the 1920s and 1930s. Question (b) shows that pupils had been taught a particular view of the superior qualities of the French language which recurs in traditional teaching of French language and literature.

The questions set in the parallel papers for 1928 give a further point of comparison. The composition examination for French is now part of Grade XI and sets the following three questions:

(a) La Reconnaissance aux parents (b) Moyens modernes de communication – par terre, par eau et par air (c) "Je chante, je

pleure." Développer les idées que fait surgir cette inscription sur
la cloche d'une église.
[(a) Gratitude to one's parents (b) Modern means of communication – by land, water and air (c) "I sing, I weep." Develop the
ideas that are inspired by this engraving on a church bell.]

The English Composition paper for Grade XII required an essay of
eight hundred words on one of the following:

A Chance Meeting at a Country Fair
Gabriel Oak
In the Macgregor Country
In Praise of Reading
Thomas Hardy, Last of the Victorians
Radio Television
Mining Development in Manitoba
The Choice of a Profession
The Need for Scientific Research in Canada
My Favorite Canadian Author

The difference in emphasis has not changed, but the scope has
developed in both papers to include topics relating to modern technology. Otherwise, the French paper continued to set moral and
religious topics, while the English paper kept English literature at
its heart, confirming the pattern that developed in the nineteenth
century, when the teaching of English Literature throughout the
British Empire was a way of imposing "British" values and confirming British authority. At the same time, it is interesting to note
the appearance of Canadian and Manitoban references in the
questions, perhaps a sign of the growing confidence of Anglo-
Canadian nationalism.

The role of English-language Readers

So far, we have focused on the ways in which francophone schools
in Manitoba managed the transition from a bilingual system to an
English language system, and in particular how they managed to
retain the confessionality of their teaching in French through the
delivery of a parallel curriculum between grades I and VIII. But
francophone pupils were at the same time following the English
curriculum, learning to read English literature from the same text-

Table 7
English Curriculum, 1924–25

Readers and English Literature Texts, Department of Education, Manitoba, 1924–25	
Grade I	The Canadian Reader, Book 1
Grade II	The Canadian Reader, Book 2
Grade III	The Canadian Reader, Book 3
Grade IV	The Canadian Reader, Book 4
Grade V	The Canadian Reader, Book 5 (first half)
Grade VI	The Manitoba Readers, Book 5 (second half)*
Grades VII & VIII	As You Like It
	Neighbours Unknown (Roberts)
	Selections in Prose and Verse, Pt I
Grades IX & X	Treasure Island
	Richard II
	Lay of the Last Minstrel (Scott)
	Narrative and Lyric Poems
Grade XI	Alexander's Anthology
	Addison, Macaulay,
	Silas Marner
	Hamlet
	Twelfth Night
	(in examination: Milton, Shakespeare, Johnson, Wordsworth, Tennyson)
Grade XII	English Poetry, its Principles and Progress (Poetical Literature Paper)
	Pilgrim's Progress
	Robinson Crusoe
	The de Coverley Papers
	Sesame and Lilies (Ruskin)
	Essays of Elia (Lamb) (Rhetoric and Prose Literature Paper)
	The History of English Literature (Long) 1 Paper

SOURCE: Rosemary Chapman from Manitoba Programme of Study, 1924–25

* This year marked the final stage of the transition from The Manitoba Readers to The Canadian Reader, which was introduced in 1923.

books as all Manitoban schoolchildren, learning to say "I" and "we" in English as well as French. As with Leçons de Langue Française the pupils were introduced to literature through a series of anthologies, or readers. They then progressed toward being able to read full-length texts from Grade VII onwards. Table 7 shows the full English curriculum, using the details of set texts studied in 1924–25 as examples. Table 8 shows the curriculum across all subjects at the elementary level in 1929, the year Roy began her teaching career, in a one-class school where she would have been expected to cover the full range and also to satisfy the AECFM by teaching the parallel curriculum in French.

Table 8
Elementary School Curriculum in 1929–30

Elementary Grades I–VIII	
Grade I	*The Canadian Reader*, Book 1 (Macmillan & Co) (nursery rhymes, simple tales, many traditional)
Grade II	*The Canadian Reader*, Book 2 *Canadian Speller*, Book 1 (W.J. Gage & Co.) Graphic Drawing
Grades III	*The Canadian Reader*, Book 3 *Canadian Speller*, Book 1 Music Drawing
Grade IV	*The Canadian Reader*, Book 4 *Freehand Practice Copy Books III & IV* (Copp Clark) *Manitoba Arithmetic for Elementary Grades* *The Book of Boys and Girls* (Dent) Geography *Canadian Speller*, Book 1 Music Drawing
Grades V	*The Canadian Reader*, Book 5 *Freehand Practice Copy Book V* *Manitoba Public School Book 1* (Gage) Arithmetic *Public School Geography* (Gage) *Pages from Canada's Story*, Part I (Dent) *Canadian Speller*, Book II *Physiology and Hygiene: Canadian Health Book* (Copp Clark)
Grade VI	*The Canadian Reader*, Book 5 *Freehand Practice Copy Book VII* *An English Grammar for Public Schools* *Manitoba Arithmetic for Elementary Grades* *Public School Geography* (Gage) *Pages from Canada's Story*, Part II (Dent) Music, Drawing, Spelling, Hygiene and Nature Study Work Books
Grade VII & VIII (taught combined except for English grammar and Arithmetic)	*The Gold Diggers* *Selections in English Literature for Grades VII and VIII*, Part I (Copp Clark) *Lamb's Tales from Shakespeare* (or *The Taming of the Shrew*) Supplemental Reading: Stories (Marryat, Alcott, Ballantyre, Kipling) Legend/Scripture (Bible Reader, *Odyssey*, Norse legends, *Iliad*, *Story of Roland*, *The Wonder Book*) Adventure (heroic, sagas, the wild, etc.) Biography (Joan of Arc, Captain Cook, Raleigh, "Honorable Men") These to be available in school libraries *The British Empire in Relation to the Rest of the World* (Gage) *The English People: A Junior History*, Robert Jones (Dent & Son)

Table 8 continued

Grade VII & VIII (taught combined except for English grammar and Arithmetic)	(Grade VIII History and Civics) *The Story of Canada*, Ryerson Press *An English Grammar for Public Schools*, Pt IV Elementary Science (list of apparatus and supplies required, 2-year programme) Foreign language study begins in Grade VIII "where possible in larger schools" p. 9 *Latin Grammar*, Hamilton & Carlyle *First French Course*, Nelson

SOURCE: Rosemary Chapman, from Manitoba Elementary School Programme of Study 1929–30

The first readers authorized in Manitoba date back to 1881. Readers were regularly updated, and new series were introduced as follows:

1881-1897	*The Canadian Readers* (later editions were entitled *The New Canadian Readers*)
1897–1911	*The Victorian Readers*
1911–23	*The Manitoba Readers*
1923–34	*The Canadian Readers*
1934–47	*Highways to Reading*

As Diana Brydon states in her reflections on curricular reform: "Anthologies involve choices and they always reveal a bias."[26] Just as in the French language equivalent, these readers introduced pupils not only to reading but also to English literature and to certain notions of Englishness and Canadianness. The Canadian presence in the titles for most of the period is telling, as is the reference to Queen Victoria for the series adopted in 1897, the year of her Diamond Jubilee. The first series, *The Canadian Readers*, was particularly Canadian in focus, appearing only eleven years after the entry of Manitoba into Confederation at a time when the population was growing rapidly from inward migration. Its contents suggest the desire to establish a distinctive sense of Canadian identity and build a notion of Canada being a more liberal place than either the United States or Great Britain. One particularly significant text in this respect is a poem by Miss Janet Carnochan, "Has Canada a History?" (a title that recalls the 1839 Durham Report, which referred to French Canadians as "a people with no history and no

literature").[27] Interestingly for a province in which the majority of
the population had been Métis at the entry into the Confederation,
the poem constructs Canadians ("Us") as a tolerant, but White,
nation and gives an idealized image of relations between settlers
and First Nations:

> We boast of freedom real – to black and red,
> Nor foot of serf our sacred soil may tread,
> That long ere Britain's dusky slaves were free,
> While Wilberforce was battling generously,
> Ere Southern neighbours dreamt the slave a man
> [...]
> Our legislators [...]
> Declared our slaves were free on land or seas.
> Our treaties with the red man in his need
> Have all been straightly kept in word or deed.
> Let each his part build, strong and true and sure;
> Then shall we have a history to endure,
> And Canada – our Canada – shall be
> A noble, Christian nation, great and free.
>   (*The Canadian Readers*, Book III, 238–40)

The volume as a whole makes frequent reference to Canada and to
social and moral preoccupations of the period (as in the extract
"About strong Drink"). Nancy Sheehan, in her study of Albertan
examples, finds a similar concern with moral education in early
readers: "Textbooks, particularly readers, were published with the
content expressly promoting this aim; and departmental examinations questioned a moral or value based knowledge."[28] Titles indicating this focus on Canadian identity include "British Columbia,"
"The Death of Wolfe," "Canada's Progress," "The Beaver," "The
Canadian Song Sparrow," and "How Canada is Governed." There
are also some stories of British exploration and Empire, "Mungo
Park and the Negro Woman," and "The Traveller in Africa" (a
poem of the same story written by the Duchess of Devonshire). The
seeming lack of awareness of the contradiction between strong
appeals to a sense of Canadian identity on the one hand and the
assumption of loyalty on the part of subjects of the British Empire
on the other is typical of textbooks of the time. In 1900 the Ontario

educationalist George Ross – premier of Ontario (1899-1905), former Minister of Education, and anthologizer of *Patriotic Recitations and Arbor Day Exercises* (1893) – declared: "There is no antagonism in my opinion between Canadianism and Imperialism. The one is but the expansion of the other. To be a true Canadian, under existing conditions, is to place yourself in harmony with the spirit of the empire ... with its interest in all that refines and ennobles the human race ... That is imperialism as I understand it. That is Canadianism as I would want it to be."[29]

In later series of *The Canadian Readers* these two components – Canada and Empire – are blended in different ways, Canada being subsumed within Empire, and so within "all that refines and ennobles the human race." Young readers discover themselves first as British citizens, and only later in their education, as Canadian citizens. *The Manitoba Reader*, Grade III, in use from 1911 to 1923 (so during Roy's own elementary school years) is far less clearly targeted at a Canadian readership than the first series. It does, however, open with "My Country," a tribute to Canada, closes with "God Save the King," and also contains a passage about "The Good Queen" (Victoria), so framing the contents in terms of Canada's place within the Empire. The selection of extracts has the familiar mix of animal stories,[30] descriptions of the seasons, Bible stories retold, fables, and heroic tales using British role models including Grace Darling, Lord Nelson, and Sir Philip Sydney. After an account of an act of self-sacrifice by Sydney, the text concludes: "Is it any wonder that, with such men to lead them, British soldiers have done so much in the world?" (74). In the following series (1923–34), although the extract is retained, this patriotic and supremacist comment is suppressed, indicating that a certain amount of editing, revision, and censorship went on between editions and series. Another text that is included in this series but dropped from the subsequent series is a racialist little poem by R.L. Stevenson called "Foreign Children":

Little Indian, Sioux or Crow,
Little Frosty Eskimo,
Little Turk or Japanee,
Oh don't you wish that you were me?
    (*The Manitoba Reader*, vol. III, 58–9)

Apart from these dismissive references to the aboriginal peoples there are a number of items in the *Manitoba Readers* that concern North American Indians, although none relates explicitly to Canada. Two pre-contact tales – "The Star and the Lily" and "How the Indians got the Corn," an adaptation from Longfellow's *Hiawatha* – seem to fit the pattern of representing the indigenous population as primitive and outside history. The *Hiawatha* excerpt is initially presented in the *Handbook* as an "Indian nature-myth." Yet the notes that follow have more than a hint of a distinctly colonial mission: "The Indian is here taught that *transformation can be effected only by labor and perseverance*" (the italics are in the original).[31] The other two extracts have clear colonial content. "The Jack o'Lantern" is a story of a pioneer family in New England using a pumpkin lantern to scare off the local Indians, who saw it and thought it was the Great Fire Spirit (White children outwitting childlike Indians). Finally, to accompany "The Indian Mother's Lullaby" by Chas Myall, there is a picture of an Indian woman, her baby in a papoose, apparently sitting in a White family's living room, the object of the gaze of two White children.

This volume can be compared with *The Canadian Readers*, Book III (1930 edition), from the series that was in use when Roy began teaching. In Book III the text is again framed by the Canada-Empire axis; the Canadian coat of arms is printed on the front with the Canadian motto *A mari usque ad mare* and a photograph of King George V. The extracts open with the text of "O Canada" and close with "God Save Our Gracious King." A further photograph shows the king reviewing troops in France with the Prince of Wales, a clear reference to the Great War. Contents of this 1930 edition for Grade III pupils show considerable overlap with the selection in *The Manitoba Reader* (asterisks show items that appear in both). The selections include Bible stories ("Joseph and his Brethren"* and "The Good Samaritan"*); stories from classical mythology ("Androcles and the Lion," "Midas," and "Pandora's Box"*); traditional tales ("The Pied Piper of Hamelin," "Aladdin," "Robin Hood"); and excerpts from Defoe's *Robinson Crusoe*,* and works of Sir Walter Scott, R.L. Stevenson, Lewis Carroll,* Edward Lear, Robert Browning, and Longfellow; "How the Indians got the Corn,"* and "Jack o'Lantern."* There are tales of British science and invention (James Watt), medical advance and duty (Florence Nightingale), military feats (Lord Nelson, Sir Philip Sydney*), and plucky boys who grew up to be fine Britons (Sir Cloudesley Shovel, who became a great admiral and "helped to capture the great fortress of Gibraltar, in Spain, which has ever since been held by Great Britain") (*The Manitoba Reader*, Book III, 125).

The way such anthologies serve the interests of the Empire is clear. Morgan argues with reference to education in Ontario: "While at first glance, school anthologies appeared to be omniscient samplers of various cultural voices and historical periods ... by systematically manipulating cultural identities, diagramming them in relation to a dominant and invisible axis, they amounted to a form of textual imperialism."[32] The manipulation of cultural identities operates in a number of linked ways: by creating a cultural genealogy for pupils, by reinforcing the values and ideology of Empire, and by constructing racial difference. Young Manitobans in the 1920s and 1930s were offered through the series of *Readers* a metaphorical genealogy that linked them via a network of cultural references to an image of "Man" that appeared to be universal but was in fact very particular.[33] Greek, Roman, German, Russian, Norse, Finnish, and Biblical stories establish a common core. North-American Indian tales are included within this web, so placing the First Nations in the realm of pre-history. Then, as if by direct descent from this common mythical heritage, comes a modern, civilized British identity, which these young "British" citizens (many of Ukrainian, French, or German descent) are enjoined to love and respect, as the poem "Children of the Empire" reminds them:

Uphold your noble heritage – oh, never let it fall –
And love the land that bore you, but the Empire best of all.
(Edward Shirley, *The Canadian Readers*, Book IV, 49)

The second task of the *Readers* was to make the Empire at once familiar and unquestionable as the source of all authority and values, and as the endpoint of historical development. The Union Jack (visible on the flagpole outside the schoolhouse) reappears in the texts of the anthology, as in a passage in Book III, "The Sand Castle," in which the sandcastle (a heavily fortified affair) clearly symbolizes enduring imperial authority. As the notes in the *Handbook* point out: "The castle is so strongly built that it will not fall before any 'common shock,' but if it should fall, there is still a way open

over the causeway, and even then the flag of old England will be flying still."[34] The lasting trauma of the Great War (an uncommon
shock?) is evident in the high number of selections in *The Canadian
Readers* in the 1920s that recall acts of heroism, including the part
played by Canadians (see "Canadians – Canadians – That's All!"
Book v, 284–7). The overriding image is not victory, but patriotic
duty. Most of the named heroes are dead heroes, some eminent,
some from close to home (a passage about Kitchener of Khartoum
is followed by the story of young Alan McLeod, v.c., a Manitoban
casualty of war, Book v, 72–9). Poems such as "Immortality" and
"In Flanders Fields" (Book v, 229 and 416) urge their ten- and
eleven-year old readers to honour the fallen and not to fail them:

> Take up our quarrel with the foe;
> To you from failing hands we throw
> The torch; be yours to hold it high.
>   (*The Canadian Readers*, Book v, 416)

"The Torch of Life," with its central image of an English public
school cricket field, and Kipling's poem "The Recessional" similarly remind Canadians of their place within the Empire. The recital
and memorization of such poems served an ideological function, as
the notes in the *Handbook* make clear. Referring to "The Recessional," the commentator writes: "It was reprinted in all parts of
the British Empire, repeated from a thousand pulpits, and memo-
rized by nearly every person."[35]

In contrast with the recurrent, troubling association between the
Empire and death in passages about the Great War, other more
upbeat "Empire-tinged"[36] extracts seem to belong to a more innocent age. A second poem by Kipling, "The Overland Mail," offers
an image of the vastness and the cohesion of the Empire, the mail
service in British India symbolizing the efficiency of its administra-
tive structure. The colonizers ("We," the recipients of the service)
are loyally served by the educated colonized who, on foot, carry out
the physical duties of the delivery:

> In the name of the Empress of India, make way,
> O Lords of the Jungle, wherever you roam!
> The woods are astir at the close of the day;

We exiles are waiting for letters from Home.
   (*The Canadian Readers*, Book v, 122)

"Home" (Great Britain) is another image that reinforces the myth
of the place that Britain should occupy in the hearts of all British
citizens. Not only is Britain (usually identified as "England") the
centre of power and order but it is also the source of moral values
and virtue. In a tale about British settlers in the harsh landscape of
Australia, a poor English woman's caged lark (brought over on the
ship) moves the rough miners to stop swearing and think of England: "The pure strains dwelt upon their spirits, and refreshed and
purified these sojourners in an evil place."[37]
   The unquestioned location of "Home" as Great Britain is one
link in a semiological chain of Englishness (language, literature,
landscape, moral character, race) that creates a continuum between
Canada, England, and the British Empire. As an assimilative process, this would seem to be an inclusive strategy to wipe out difference by strengthening common values. However, the principle of
*in*clusion is founded on the power of *ex*clusion. As Morgan writes
of Ontario, anthologies such as *The Canadian Readers* mediate
"between a variety of social voices, embodying the 'nation' by holding in relation Irish [an important immigrant group in Ontario],
English, French and Native peoples through the selected themes,
images and, more invisibly, the inclusions and exclusions enacted."[38]
Indeed, racial difference is the underlying explanation for all colonialist ideologies. It is behind the construction of First Nations or
other minority groups as the Other.
   The question is, then, where are francophone minority and
aboriginal populations in these readers? The First Nations are present in the anthologies, as we have seen, but usually either as
ahistorical – a freedom-loving but dying race (see "Tecumseh and
the Eagles," *The Canadian Readers*, Book v, 322–5) – or an exotic
object of the colonial gaze. They do not appear as part of the modern territory of Canada. This is also true of the representations of
the francophone minority. In Books iv and v of *The Canadian
Readers*, francophones are represented in historical terms; that is,
not ahistorically as a primitive people but firmly situated in the
past. They appear as archetypal figures from another age: explorers
such as Jacques Cartier (Book v, 79–81) and La Vérendrye (Book v,

55–8), "The Old Coureur-de-Bois" (Book v, 42), and "The Red River Voyageur" (Book v, 91), which is accompanied by an illustration subtitled "In the Olden Days." There are brave women settlers who survive or thwart attacks from Indians: "A Pioneer Woman" tells of the tenacity of the Métis matriarch Mme Lajimodière (Book IV, 105), and "The Heroine of Verchères" recalls the bravery of a seigneur's daughter (Book IV, 294). For a brief period in the late 1920s, Book v included an excerpt from W.H. Blake's translation of *Maria Chapdelaine*, entitled "A Pioneer's Wife."[39] These representations of French Canadians place them on a timeline that points backward to the "olden days," not forward to (Western) civilization. Figures like the *coureur de bois* ("a child of nature")[40] are ambivalently placed *between* First Nations and white colonizers.

The difference of the francophone (whether linguistic, religious, or cultural) is rarely explicit, but one poem does attempt to give the francophone a voice, albeit with the oddest effect. W.H. Drummond's *"habitant"* poems are written in what the *Handbook* describes as "the dialect of the French-Canadian *habitant*," but which is, of course, English with a phonetically conveyed accent.[41] The example in the *Reader*, "Dominique" (Book v, 273), gives a would-be comic account of a desperate and clueless father discussing suitable punishment for his wild, truant son:

"dat's good advice for sure, very good,
On de cellar, bread an' water – it'll do,
De nice sweet castor ile geeve him ev'ry leetle w'ile,
An' de jail to finish up wit' w'en he's t'roo!"
   (*The Canadian Readers*, Book v, 274)

The voice of the *Handbook* reassures teachers that if children are encouraged to pronounce the words as they are spelled, their effort "will be well repaid."[42] The effect of performing the poem aloud would clearly position the francophone as linguistically inferior, as a bad speaker of English, in an education system where, it must be remembered, "every lesson should be a [English] language lesson."[43] Equally, the positioning of this poem between a scene from the story of William Tell and the account from *Lorna Doone* of a rescue, which includes the line "And the least drop of English blood is worth the best of any other when it comes to lasting out,"[44] leaves any reader (anglophone, francophone, or allophone) in no doubt about where francophones might fit into the hierarchically structured world of the Empire/anthology.

SCHOOL PERFORMANCES: ROY'S REPRESENTATIONS OF HER SCHOOLING

The Introduction opened with a brief discussion of the scene from *La Détresse et l'enchantement* which recounts Roy's recitation from *Macbeth* and its effect on the school inspector. The analysis of the educational context of that scene and the curricula, official and unofficial, that were in use in Manitoban schools at the time, helped place that episode in relation to the wider picture. We have seen how the Department of Education in Manitoba was able to adapt or inflect the education system so that the curriculum served both local and British interests. Equally, the teaching and textbooks of the parallel francophone curriculum presented an amalgam of linguistic, moral, and religious elements that served the ideology of the Franco-Canadian minorities in the interwar years. Curricula, set texts, and evaluation were strategically important within the Manitoban classroom. A further factor in the "operations and oppositions"[45] of this education system was the way in which pupils chose to position themselves in relation to the divergent ideologies of the dual system – total assimilation to the anglophone norm being at one end of the spectrum of possible outcomes, retrenchment into the francophone community being at the other. Differing responses to the ideological processes at work produced a wide range of patterns of assimilation or resistance as individual students underwent their own process of internalization of that institutional framework during their education. Several representations of the educational process and the educational experience of pupil and teacher appear throughout Roy's work – in short journalistic pieces, in extended autobiographical form, and in (auto)-fictional writing. Four autobiographical accounts of Roy's own schooling are particularly significant.

The four accounts were published over a period of more than forty years. The earliest is "Souvenirs du Manitoba" (to be referred to as A), which was written as a lecture for a meeting of Royal Society of Canada at the University of Manitoba, Winnipeg, on 31 May 1954.[46] Roy had been elected to the French section in 1947 as its first woman writer, and in her address at her admission ceremony had expressed strong anti-capitalist views in what François Ricard describes as "a kind of testament," it being arguably the last public exposition of her ideological sympathies.[47] The far less polemical 1954 lecture appeared in different forms in four different publications that reached readers across Canada and in France.[48] While "Souvenirs du Manitoba" places Roy's education at its centre, it begins with a description of the sense of "sécurité profonde [profound security]" (A 13) that she experienced as a child in a community held together by a shared past (identified with Quebec), and the atmosphere of the "vie de la paroisse [parish life]" (A 13) that was maintained in Saint-Boniface and the francophone villages. The speech closes with images of the huge skies, a straight country road between fields of wheat at sunset, and the sense of the infinite that these helped to evoke. The lyrical tone of this childhood memory frames a text that is positive in its account of Manitoba's ethnic diversity, theatrical productions at Winnipeg's Walker Theatre, and education in Saint-Boniface. Schools are described as "la fierté de Saint-Boniface [the pride of Saint-Boniface]" (A 15). The francophone experience of education is conveyed with a humorous account of the skill of Roy's headmistress – "une femme très souple, fine mouche s'il en fut jamais [a very adaptable woman, a clever performer if ever there was]" (A 20) – in presenting her school appropriately both to anglophone visitors from the Board of Education and to francophone church dignitaries.

A second account, "Mes études à Saint-Boniface" (B), was commissioned in English in 1976 for the Toronto-based *Globe and Mail*, and the choice of subject was left to Roy. She wrote the piece in French and Alan Brown, her official translator at the time, translated it. The target audience was therefore anglophone Canada (the newspaper being distributed throughout Canada). The original French text remained unpublished until its inclusion in *Le Pays de Bonheur d'occasion* in 2000.[49] The editors' notes in the posthumous edition suggest that it can be seen as an early version of a passage from the fifth chapter of *La Détresse et l'enchantement*, "with which it will be interesting to compare it in order to gain an insight into Gabrielle Roy's 'method.'"[50] The following, rather wider comparison will bear this out. Compared with "Souvenirs du Manitoba," "Mes études à Saint-Boniface" focuses much more directly on education rather than on childhood and personal memories. A clear pattern of binary oppositions structures this account, giving a stronger sense of the political context, the anglophone domination of the francophone minority, and the power games at play. The structure of the text is close to that of the autobiography and many specific phrases are already there, suggesting that this is a clear pre-text of *La Détresse et l'enchantement*.[51] As will be seen later, though, there is not a complete match between thematic elements; neither is the overall effect of the passage identical in the two texts. The second passage singles itself out from the rest of the corpus by its incorporation of a paragraph that comprises a series of quotations from poets, arranged so as to alternate English with French sources.

The third piece related to Roy's own schooling, "Ma petite rue qui m'a menée autour du monde" (c), unpublished in Roy's lifetime, was written about 1978 and contains a reference to *Ces Enfants de ma vie* (1977) as a recent work.[52] This timing situates it in the period preceding Quebec's 1980 referendum on sovereignty-association, which, as the editors of *Le Pays de* Bonheur d'occasion suggest, may account for its apparent preoccupation with Canadian unity.[53] As the title indicates, this piece explores the link between Roy's Saint-Boniface home and the wider world. References to education, to the learning of English, and to English literature are therefore set within this vision of an opening up to the world beyond, where Roy felt she belonged. The article gives a succinct historical survey of francophone colonization in the West and the "fanatisme [fanaticism]" that led to the end of bilingual education in Manitoba (c 47). The sections on Roy's own education and later teaching career are brief, but some familiar elements emerge, notably her emphasis on English literature and her academic success.

In *La Détresse et l'enchantement* (D), published posthumously in 1984, Roy's schooling, her teacher training, and her teaching career are the central topic of chapters 5 to 10, although other related memories and anecdotes are woven into the chronological framework of those years.[54] The specific section on her schooling (in chapter 5) focuses more strongly on Roy herself – her own performance, her effect on others, her family relationships – and perhaps rather less on the "nous" of the Franco-Manitoban collectivity than is the case with the other texts. It gives greater emphasis to the psychological experience of the individuals involved, and, being in a lengthier form, allows more reflection and digression. As part of a longer work, the chapter also includes pointers to future developments (particularly concerning the fate of her school medals) and

Table 9
Core Elements Found Within Two or More Extracts

Core Element	Text A	Text B	Text C	Text D
Link between religion and education	✓	✓	✓	✓
Manitoban laws	X	✓	✓	✓
Department of Education	✓	✓	X	✓
Visits of school inspectors	✓	✓	✓	✓
Clandestine curriculum	✓	✓	✓	✓
French literature	✓	✓	X	✓
English literature	✓	✓	✓	✓
Shakespeare	✓	✓	X	✓
Production of *Merchant of Venice*	✓	✓	X	✓
Recitation of speech from *Macbeth*	X	✓	X	✓
Quoting of English poetry	X	✓	✓	X
Game-playing, negotiation	✓	✓	✓	✓
Roy's academic success	X	✓	✓	✓

SOURCE: Extracts referred to are from:

A: "Souvenirs de Manitoba"
B: "Mes études à Saint-Boniface"
C: "Ma petite rue qui m'a menée autour du monde"
D: *La Détresse et l'enchantement*

incorporates more general themes that run through *La Détresse et l'enchantement* as a whole (notably the role of the mother and Roy as future writer). However, one can see quite clearly the similarity of structure between "Mes études à Saint-Boniface" and chapter 5 of *La Détresse et l'enchantement*, as both follow largely the same sequence of topics.

Although these four autobiographical texts were produced at different times, for different reading publics, and in different political contexts, they are all structured around a common core of thematic elements. The presentation in tabular form in table 9 indicates the presence or absence of significant references. With one exception, texts B and D cover the same topics, although, as will be shown, to rather different effect.

Closer analysis of three of the general themes that emerge from this corpus give a sense of how differently Roy represents her education in the four contexts. It also shows what underlying similarities can be detected. The first theme is the representation of francophone education in terms of resistance to anglophone domination. As we have seen, this discourse of resistance, which typified the ideological position of the AECFM in the interwar years, is associated with the survival of the French language in the Canadian West. The second recurrent theme is that of Roy's academic success within both the clandestine French curriculum and the official English curriculum. The third related theme is that of the place of English literature within the four accounts.

The discourse of resistance

"Souvenirs du Manitoba" (text A) is not a polemical text and makes little use of the discourse of resistance. Its treatment of education is structured in terms of duality rather than power-based hierarchy. It does refer to the double curriculum, but without explaining the political, historical, or legal context. The curriculum is an oddity, a quirky fact of life: "Nous avions un singulier programme d'études en ce temps-là. Nous devions étudier plusieurs matières en français [We had a peculiar curriculum in those days. We were required to study several subjects in French]" (A 19). "En ce temps-là" suggests a time long gone, whereas the AECFM was still in existence in Manitoba at the time of this lecture and the legislation was not yet amended. Equally, the phrasing of the second sentence ("nous devions étudier") makes teaching in French seem to be an obligation or imposition rather than a resistant response to anglophone domination. The treatment of French literature adds to this negative impression, as elsewhere in this corpus, because of its association with the textbooks in use: "la littérature française telle qu'assez singulièrement résumée par nos manuels de ce temps-là [French literature as summarized in rather an odd way by our textbooks at that time]" (A 19–20). The text does set up an opposition between anglophone and francophone authority in the account of visits by Catholic dignitaries and representatives from the "Board of Education of Manitoba" (A 20). "Le langage de la survivance, de la cause canadienne-française [the language of survivalism, of the French-Canadian cause]" is contrasted with "[l]'allégeance britannique, [la] loyauté à notre souverain et ... un Canada s'étendant d'un océan à l'autre [allegiance to Britain, loyalty to our sovereign and ... a Canada that stretched from one ocean to the other]" (A 20). However, the emphasis here is on the subtlety of the *directrice* in playing to both audiences as appropriate, surviving by means of cleverness, not resisting the one in loyalty to the other. So, while the distinctive nature of education in Manitoba is alluded to, it is not associated in this text with a sense of fervent francophone resistance to a dominant anglophone culture.

The second passage, "Mes études à Saint-Boniface," opens with an equally open-minded comment, the use of "curieuse" echoing that of "singulière" in A: "Mes études à Saint-Boniface, îlot de culture française en pleine mer anglophone, se déroulèrent de la plus curieuse façon. Encore aujourd'hui je serais en peine de décider si elles m'ont apporté plus de bienfaits que d'inconvénients [My studies in Saint-Boniface, a little island of French culture in the midst of an anglophone sea, took place in the most curious way. Even today I would find it difficult to judge whether they gave me more advantages than disadvantages]" (B 35). As the title indicates, in this case the whole piece is concerned with Roy's studies. The combination of the reference to the Franco-Manitoban minority's situation with an ambivalent assessment of her own education sets the tone for what follows. However, as the article continues, the association of religious sentiment, the French language, and education becomes more insistent: "La ferveur des enfants dût faire le reste, car le miracle s'accomplit: on parla français, chez nous, tout aussi bien, dans l'ensemble, qu'au Québec, à la même époque, selon les classes sociales [the commitment of the children must have done the rest, for the miracle happened: we spoke French, at home, just as well, on the whole, as in Quebec at the same period, according to our social class]" (B 35). The curriculum is presented in partisan terms. The subjects taught in French are referred to as:

les matières dont ne se souciait aucunement le Department of Education: le catéchisme, l'histoire sainte, et même, en partie, l'histoire du Canada, d'après un manuel du Québec, qui était en flagrant délit de contradiction avec la version imposée par le School Board. Nous apprenions, d'une part, que les Anglais avaient toujours voulu notre perte, de l'autre, qu'ils étaient loin de nous avoir porté malheur.
[subjects about which the Department of Education was utterly indifferent: catechism, religious history, and even, to some extent, the history of Canada, according to a Quebec textbook which flagrantly contradicted the version imposed by the School Board. On the one hand we learned that the English had always wanted to defeat us, eradicate us, on the other that they were far from doing us harm.] (B 36)

It is worth noting the order of subjects listed above: Roy makes no reference to French language and literature at this point; the cate-chism heads the list, followed by religious history, objects of anglo-phone/Protestant indifference but francophone reverence. Emotive, even sentimental terms are used to identify Franco-Manitobans as victims, Roy among them, "nous, pauvre petit peuple ballotté [we, poor little people pushed this way and that]" (B 39). But the ambi-valence of the opening reflection – "plus de bienfaits que d'in-convénients [more advantages than disadvantages]" – as well as the positive representation of English literature once more work against the effects of partisan terminology, casting them in an ironic light.

In text C, "Ma petite rue qui m'a menée autour du monde," signs of the language of resistance appear, suggesting Roy's positive iden-tification with the Franco-Manitoban population. This interpreta-tion is strengthened by their being positioned just after a summary of the francophone settlement of Manitoba, which cites the iconic figures of the La Vérendrye family, Jean-Baptiste Lagimodière, his wife Rose Gaboury, les Sœurs Grises, and the coureurs de bois (but not Louis Riel). The banning of the bilingual education system is presented as an undated single event (rather than in its different stages – 1890, 1897, and 1916) and termed "la cruelle loi [the cruel law]." It is overtly linked with "les passions du racisme [racist pas-sions]" and "la poussée du fanatisme [the spread/influence of fanat-icism" (C 47). Rather than making a sentimental reference to a "pauvre petit peuple ballotté," Roy is explicit about the injustice: "Ainsi, descendants des premiers colonisateurs du Canada, étions-nous, en notre propre pays, pris au piège, traités en étrangers, ou citoyens de deuxième ordre [In this way, descendants of the first colonizers of Canada, we were, in our own land, trapped, treated as foreigners or second-class citizens]" (C 47). The rhetoric of resis-tance is then continued in the imagery of a battleground, with refer-ences to "cette atmosphère enfiévrée [this feverish atmosphere]" and "des sentiments d'héroïque défiance [feelings of heroic defi-ance]" in support of the nuns' tactics "pour désarmer l'inspecteur [to disarm the inspector]" (C 48), and a characterization of the anglophones as "l'ennemi [the enemy]" (C 49). But this language of Anglo-Franco hostility, which emerged so strongly in the historical summary, becomes more and more attenuated as the account of Roy's education proceeds. The terms are qualified, or undermined, by the presentation of contradictory evidence. We hear about the visit of the anglophone school inspector "qui, d'ailleurs, sans trop le laisser voir, était de notre côté [who, by the way, without letting it show too much, was on our side]" (c 48). And Roy speaks of the change in her own attitude in the course of her contact with the English language and the anglophone population: "J'accomplissais des progrès chez l'ennemi qui, à le fréquenter, se révélait moins un adversaire, bien souvent, que quelqu'un qui nous connaissait mal comme nous le connaissions mal [I was making progress with our enemies who, as I came into contact with them, would often reveal themselves to be less of an adversary and more people who did not know us well, just as we did not know them well]" (c 49). So the use of the AECFM's discourse of resistance and religious fervour is turned in the course of the text from polemical tool to ironic effect, thereby undermining the divide between French and English, francophone and anglophone.

The treatment of Roy's schooling in *La Détresse et l'enchantement* (D), as suggested above, benefits from the fact that the text is a much longer work, an overtly subjective exploration of, and reflection on, memories which at the same time creates a forward-looking trajectory. As Sophie Marcotte has argued, Roy's autobiographical project required such a structure in order to "anchor in childhood the origins of a life project which was ultimately to have occupied her, or rather obsessed her, for forty years."[55] While early drafts of D were probably produced around the same time as B (1976) and c (c. 1978), although thematically related to B and c they are developed in a slightly different perspective, to resonate with the book as a whole. The language of resistance certainly appears in Roy's account of her schooldays, in particular, of relations with the "Department of Education" (referred to in English almost throughout Roy's "Manitoban" works as a sign of the post-1916 assimilationist policy). Relations are framed in terms of "provocation," as "un regain d'hostilité de la part de petits groupes de fanatiques [an upsurge of hostility from small groups of fanatics]" (D 70; 53), or even as guerilla warfare: "Alors reprenait notre sourde guérilla usant peut-être mieux notre adversaire qu'une révolte ouverte [then ... our passive resistance would resume, which perhaps wore down the enemy more effectively than an open revolt]" (D 71; 53). The conflict ebbs and flows, as rumours circulate. But Roy's retrospective reflection acknowledges that this atmosphere might have been promoted for ideological reasons, and that dangers may have been exaggerated so as to encourage that binary divide between Protestant and Catholic, anglophone and francophone: "Toutefois le danger était bien réel et il exaltait nos âmes. Nous le sentions rôder autour de nous; peut-être nos maîtresses en entretenaient-elles quelque peu le sentiment [Yet the danger was quite real and it galvinized us. We used to feel it around us; perhaps our teachers had something to do with maintaining the feeling" (D 70-1; 53). The force of this rhetoric is surely ironic, as the older narrator constructs the mental and ideological resistance with the language of warfare. The opposition between two camps is also undermined in other ways. Roy reverses the power relation briefly as she imagines the anglophone school inspector, now the object of her curious gaze, visiting "en territoire ennemi [in enemy territory]" (D 74; 56). When it comes to the description of the curriculum, with certain subjects taught in English and others in French, the list is less polemically presented than in C. The catechism is not mentioned, and Roy makes a comment stressing the mental gymnastics this required rather than pointing to the anglophone disregard for the Catholic faith: "Cela nous faisait un curieux esprit, constamment occupé à rajuster notre vision [this gave us an odd turn of mind, constantly alert to readjusting our focus]" (D 71; 53). The following paragraph opens with cautious praise of the system: "Parfois c'était tout de même bienfait [Sometimes this was a blessing]" (D 71; 53], before going on to compare the French literature curriculum very unfavorably to the program of English literature.

The final set piece of this section of *La Détresse et l'enchantement* is the account of Roy's recitation of the speech from *Macbeth*, already cited as an example of colonial mimicry. While Roy's performance placates the inspector, reassuring him that the francophones are "de bons enfants dociles [good, obedient children]" (D 75; 56), for her it is a double-edged victory. It may have made her the equal of the *directrice* praised in "Souvenirs du Manitoba" for her ability to play the game, "fine mouche s'il en fut jamais [clever performer if ever there was]," but Roy also comments on the silence of her peers: "Nous étions trente-cinq élèves dans cette classe, dont trente-quatre muettes comme des carpes [there were thirty-five pupils in that class, thirty-four of whom were as silent as posts]" (D 75; 57). A successful act of individual negotiation, perhaps, as Roy straddles the bicultural divide;[56] but in her view, her peers remain objectified, "carpes [posts (literally 'carp')]" within a system they are failing to master. This comment gives the scene a critical edge by suggesting that retrenchment in a linguistically defined identity is synonymous with defeat, and that bilingualism should be recognized for its strategic value.

Roy's accounts of her schooldays contain clear echoes of the binary divide between anglophones and francophones in Manitoba, and the power relationship that operated on so many levels between Saint-Boniface and Winnipeg. But in her hands, the combative language, the language of religious fervour, guerrilla warfare, and the sacred cause of Catholic education loses its polemical certainty. It becomes tinged with irony, indicating its incongruity with the texts as a whole. The use of this language varies from text to text, of course. In text A, from 1954, the educational context itself is only vaguely outlined, the emphasis being on the privileges that Roy gained from a schooling that posed challenges to the francophone minority but ultimately gave her access to the wider world and her future career. The language of text B gives a much clearer sense of francophone defiance and uses the rhetoric associated with the AECFM. But the piece as a whole rather undermines such zeal, so as to give a much more ambivalent message. Similarly, in text C the representation of the descendants of heroic pioneers being reduced to an oppressed (but fervent) minority feels like a pious rhetorical pose, as the differences between the two sides are subsequently unpicked. The ambivalence hinted at in the first three texts becomes all the more evident in the treatment of education in *La Détresse et l'enchantement*, where the tension mounts between identification with the collective – the Franco-Manitoban people, often personified in the figure of Mélina Roy – and the autobiographical subject. No single rhetoric can contain the ambivalence with which Roy constructs her young self – who identifies nostalgically (or dutifully?) with her fellow Franco-Manitobans and yet desires passionately to distinguish herself from them and their way of life. This ambivalence emerges as well in the themes of academic success and English literature.

Awards and medals

As we know, the AECFM used its annual *concours* both to encourage achievement in French and to raise the status of French in a province where English had a higher status. Once Roy took to studying seriously in Grade VIII, at the age of fourteen, she won the AECFM's top prize each year.[57] Roy's representation of her academic success throws an interesting light on her sense of place within the educational establishment, her institutional biography. In "Souvenirs du Manitoba" there is no mention of her school prizes, but another success is highlighted, that of the amateur French-language theatre group, Le Cercle Molière, with which she acted in her twenties, being a cast member on both occasions when they won the French language trophy in the Dominion Drama Festival. The text both plays this down – "Ce n'est pas que je veuille donner à cet événement une importance exagérée [Not that I wish to give an exaggerated importance to this event]" – and underlines its collective significance – "Il témoigna d'une expression française bien vivante au Manitoba [it testified to the healthy state of French language use in Manitoba]" (A 21). Roy also comments on the pride of anglophone Winnipegers ("nos concitoyens de Winnipeg [our fellow-citizens in Winnipeg]") in the francophone troupe's performance, describing them as "peut-être encore plus fiers que nous l'étions nous-mêmes [perhaps even more proud than we were ourselves]" (A 22). The trophies in a way bridged the divide of the Red River. Roy's personal successes are recounted with a similar mixture of pride and modesty.

In "Mes études à Saint-Boniface," the reference to success is embedded within the account of her teacher relying on her to save the school's reputation by reciting Shakespeare for the anglophone inspector. Roy comments: "Je sauvais déjà l'honneur de la classe au concours en langue française organisée par l'Association d'éducation des Canadiens français du Manitoba. Je trouvais que c'était beaucoup que de la sauver aussi en anglais [I was already saving the honour of the class in the French language competition organized by the Manitoba Association for French-Canadian Education. I thought it was a lot to have to save it in English too]" (B 38). But any unwillingness or inadequacy on her part is then contradicted by a rationalization of her love of success: "Mais j'avais un petit côté cabotin, en partie entretenu par notre complexe d'infériorité collectif, qui me faisait rechercher l'approbation de tous côtés [But I was a bit of a show-off, owing partly to our collective inferiority complex, which led me to seek approval on all sides]" (B 38).

In the third text, "Ma petite rue qui menait autour du monde," the prize winning is also initially presented as the consequence of the passion for education in Saint-Boniface: "Ainsi stimulée, aiguillonnée, je raflai ... tous les prix octroyés par l'Association des Canadiens français du Manitoba [Stimulated and urged on in this way, I ran off with ... all the prizes granted by the Manitoba French-Canadian Association]" (C 48). The form of this statement is particularly interesting. The two past participles with which the sentence opens make Roy the desired product of her education, yet the verbs chosen for the rest of the sentence turn her into a somewhat deviant subject. The formality of "octroyer" emphasizes perhaps the conservatism of the AECFM, while the familiar term "rafler" suggests that there was something excessive, even illegitimate, about her repeated achievements. This is less a show of modesty; rather, it portrays her as immodest, motivated by a zeal for personal success and perhaps by a desire to progress beyond Manitoba, so betraying the principles of the Franco-Manitoban establishment. The following sentence shows a similar shiftiness, the guileless "Mais, sans le faire exprès [But, without doing it intentionally]" being capped by "j'obtins également la première place dans les matières enseignées en anglais [I also took first place in the subjects taught in English]" (C 48).

By the time these prizes reappear in *La Détresse et l'enchantement*, they have become part of a different frame of reference, in two senses. In terms of the autobiography as a whole, they will be the focus of a later episode in Paris, when Roy's trunk is stolen, in it the jewel box containing her medals. But their significance as a symbol of Roy's hunger for success and pleasure in winning prizes is subtly redirected, first to focus on her decision to work hard at her studies, and then to focus on her mother. Roy's initial conversion to study is represented as a response to her mother's despondent state of mind: "Bientôt elle n'en pourrait plus si elle n'était pas épaulée par quelque encouragement [She wouldn't be able to hold on if she didn't soon get some encouragement to brace her]" (D 67; 50). The winning of the first medal "pour je ne sais trop quelle matière [for some subject or other]" (D 67; 50) is at first played down, but her mother's response is dwelt on at length: "Ce que je n'oublierai jamais, c'est le visage de maman [What I'll never forget is Maman's face]"; "elle rayonna [she was radiant]" (D 67; 50). "Je ... fus frappée de l'expression de ses yeux. Ils brillaient comme rarement je les avais vus, deux grands puits de lumière tendre d'où semblait avoir été retirée toute l'eau mauvaise des jours durs [I was struck by the expression in her eyes. They were shining as I'd rarely seen them do, like two deep pools of tender radiance from which all the dark, bitter waters of hardship seemed to have been drained]" (D 68; 50-1). Later in her account, Roy recalls that she had overheard her mother persuading her husband to allow Gabrielle to stay at school for Grade XII, as a result of which she felt obliged to succeed: "Pour dédommager maman des sacrifices sans fin ... il ne fallait pas moins qu'une éclatante réussite de ma part [If I was going to repay Maman for the endless sacrifices she'd imposed on herself, nothing less than dazzling success on my part would do]" (D 77; 58). Similar language is used in the description of Roy's high school graduation ceremony, when she seeks out her mother's gaze. But here the effect on Roy is mixed, showing a dawning awareness of the price of her success: "Levé et tout aimanté vers moi, le pauvre visage gris de fatigue ... brillait néanmoins d'une fierté qui me fit plus de mal que tout ce que j'avais encore vu, tellement il paraissait dur d'en être arrivé là [Her poor face was grey with fatigue ... but was lifted, straining toward me ... It shone with pride, and that hurt more than anything I'd seen before because suddenly I knew how much all this had cost]" (D 79; 60). In *La Détresse et l'enchantement*, then, Roy's mother becomes both cause and ultimate victim of Roy's desire for academic success, a pattern that will resurface in later discussion of Roy's fictional works. The effect of this reframing is to exonerate Roy for the excessive ambition that appeared in earlier accounts and for which she was reprimanded by her teacher after "saving the class" with her *Macbeth* recitation.

The place of English literature within the texts

The third and final theme relating to Roy's characterization of her schooling is the discovery of English literature. It is linked to the two previous themes discussed in that it raises further questions about Roy's sense of identification with the francophone population of Saint-Boniface. The use of the English language for teaching and the study of English literature in Franco-Manitoban schools did not result just from provincial demographic shifts since 1870 or the rise in Anglo-Canadian nationalism; they were part of the enduring legacy of the colonial relationship with Great Britain. As we have seen in our discussion of readers and set texts, the English textbook acted in some ways as a justification of Empire, the great gift to the colonized subjects. Just as the English language was a central tool of assimilation, so was English literature a powerful agent of cultural identification. Roy's response to English literature is perhaps the dominant feature of her representation of her education, and its presence in each pertinent text exerts a curious effect. English literature is represented in the four representative texts either by Shakespeare or by English poetry, or by both, but its place within the structure of the text varies considerably.

In "Souvenirs du Manitoba," English literature takes its time to appear. Much of the article is concerned on the one hand, with an evocation of the similarities between rural Quebec and the oral history and values of Franco-Manitobans, and on the other, with an account of Manitoba's ethnic and cultural diversity, emphasizing the folkloric aspects of other immigrant communities. Then comes Roy's account of a performance in Winnipeg's imposing Walker Theatre (represented thanks to its chronological transposition as a school outing).[58] The structure of what follows is significant. The passage begins with a description of the theatre (one of Canada's largest at the time), presented as the scene of "le premier grand choc esthétique de ma vie [the first great artistic experience of my life]" (A 19). This "choc" is revealed to be a performance of *The Merchant of Venice*, which leads without transition to a recollection of the school curriculum, in which French literature (no authors named) is compared very unfavorably with English literature ("Thomas Hardy, George Eliot, Milton, Shakespeare et, plus tard, Keats, Shelley, Coleridge" (A 20), with Shakespeare centrally placed). There follows a further digression on the good relations sustained by the *directrice* with both francophone and anglophone authorities. Once the digression is concluded, Roy returns to the play, quoting from Shylock's speech "Hath not a Jew eyes? ... Dimensions, senses, affections, passions? If you prick us do we not bleed?" (A 20). She then reflects on the impact these words had on her as an expression of a humanist understanding of the common human condition, which transcends ethnic and linguistic divisions. As if the Shakespearean play symbolized her education as a whole, Roy then concludes in the following paragraph: "Telle était notre éducation, peut-être singulière, pas du tout mauvaise à ce qu'il me semble [Such was our education, odd perhaps, not at all bad as it seems to me]" (A 21). The structure of this passage (and the manipulation of the chronology) emphasizes the centrality of Shakespeare to Roy's memory of her education and the strong sense not just of aesthetic but of moral identification with the play. Roy is reproducing perfectly the position of Shakespeare at the heart of English Studies, his works being, as Robert Morgan writes: "the ultimate sign of English literary-cultural authority, the best distillation of Englishness, and thus all that was sacred to colonial elites."[59] While Roy responds to Shakespeare's "universalism," so revealing the liberal humanist ideology of her education, his place in the curriculum in Canada and throughout the British Empire was much more closely identified with his value as a symbol of the supremacy of England, the English language, and the English race.[60]

In "Mes études à Saint-Boniface," Shakespeare again dominates the section on curriculum, not by surrounding it (as the episode of the theatre production in text A framed the discussion of education) but by placing it at the apogee of her literary education. The text builds up toward Shakespeare, contrasting "nos manuels expurgés [our censored textbooks]" (B 36) – and their omissions – with the "plus hauts génies [the greatest minds]" of English literature, to which, she felt, she had free access ("portes grandes ouvertes [the doors open wide]") (B 36). Praising English novelists and poets, mentioning Daudet as a welcome exception on the French side, she then reaches the climax: "Mais c'est Shakespeare que je rencontrai d'abord [My first encounter was with Shakespeare]" (B 37). Once again, she presents this encounter as a moment of revelation: "J'entendais pour la première fois de ma vie la voix de l'incohérence humaine et, de toutes les voix jusque-là entendues, elle me paraissait la plus vraie [For the first time in my life I heard the voice of human incoherence, and of all the voices I had ever heard, it seemed to me the most truthful]" (B 37). This passage links first to the theatre visit ("c'est là que m'atteignit le délire shakespearien [that is where I was first overwhelmed with passion for Shakespeare]" (B 37) and then carries on to studying *Macbeth* at school and the account of her recitation before the school inspector. Perhaps in the attempt to stress Shakespeare's universalism (and so his transcendence of the Anglo/Franco divide), Roy suggests that his appeal operated despite, not because of, his language: "comme si la magie de Shakespeare pouvait s'exercer sur moi, jusqu'à un certain point, au-delà des mots [as if Shakespeare's magic could work its spell on me, up to a point, at a level beyond the words themselves]" (B 37). But it may also be that Roy was keen to deny the strong appeal of the English language, as her teacher's response to hearing her recite Macbeth's speech suggests: "La sœur n'en revenait pas, peut-être scandalisée, au fond, de me voir tout à coup à ce point anglicisée [The nun could not get over it, perhaps outraged, deep down, to see me anglicized to this degree]" (B 37).

The treatment of Shakespeare in *La Détresse et l'enchantement* both as spectacle and as recitation not only follows the same structure as in B but also reuses many of its phrases, with slight additions and adjustments, as the following comparisons shows:

> Mais c'est Shakespeare que je rencontrai d'abord. Bien sûr, il m'échappa en grande partie, mais pas assez pour que ne me parvienne un peu de cette sauvagerie passionnée alliée parfois à tant de douceur qu'elle fait fondre le cœur, de ce flot d'âme qui nous arrive tout plein de ses tendresses et de son tumulte. (B 37)

> C'est Shakespeare que je rencontrai tout d'abord ... Pour ma part, encore que m'échappât beaucoup de cette grande voix, je fus prise par sa sauvagerie passionnée, alliée parfois à tant de douceur qu'elle ferait fondre le cœur, à ce flot d'âme qui nous arrive tout plein de sa tendresse et de son tumulte. (D 72; 54)

> [But my first literary encounter was with Shakespeare. Certainly there was much I did not grasp, but still I understood a little of his passionate earthiness, joined sometimes to such sensitivity it would melt your heart, the expression of the soul's upwelling, with all its tendernesses and turmoil. (B 37)

> My first literary encounter was with Shakespeare ... As for me, while much of this great voice as yet eluded me, I was enthralled by his passionate earthiness, joined sometimes to such sensitivity it would melt your heart, the expression of the soul's upwelling, with all its tenderness and turmoil.] (D 72; 54)

But text D also includes some details that appeared in text A, written in 1954 and thus much closer to the events recalled:

> A Winnipeg, nous avions, et il y est encore, l'immense théâtre Walker – le plus vaste au Canada, je pense – avec d'énormes lustres, des rampes dorées, d'épais rideaux de scène en velours cramoisi, des loges et balcons sur balcons.

[In Winnipeg we had, and it is still there today, the immense Walker Theatre – the largest in Canada, I think – with enormous chandeliers, golden handrails, thick stage curtains in crimson velvet, boxes, and row upon row of balconies.] (A 19)

In *La Détresse et l'enchantement* the facts are reshaped and tied more closely into the subjective experience (though with an irritating misprint):

C'est au théâtre Walter [sic] de Winnipeg – déjà me disposant au sortilège de la scène avec ses rangs sur rangs de balcons ornés, ses immenses lustres, ses lourds rideaux en velours cramoisi – que commença pour moi l'enchantement.
[The magic began for me at the Walker Theatre in Winnipeg – which in itself predisposed me to the sorcery of the stage, with its rows and rows of ornate balconies, its immense chandeliers, and its heavy crimson velvet curtain.] (D 72; 54)

The link between Shakespeare and "l'enchantement" in the autobiography is supported by the use of several related images in the account of the theatre trip – "sortilège," "ravissement," "fascination," and "mystérieuse" – all of which strengthen the association of Shakespeare, and English literature more generally perhaps, with the title of the autobiography, the opposing pole to the "détresse" that Roy's life also brought her. Just as in B, Roy represents Shakespeare's language both as English and not English, as an ideal metalanguage that transcends linguistic differences. But the desire for such a form of language is explicitly related here to the strictures of the linguistic divide and anglophone domination: "Il ne s'agissait plus enfin de français, d'anglais, de langue proscrite, de langue imposée. Il s'agissait d'une langue au-delà des langues, comme celle de la musique, par exemple [All question of French or English or forbidden or imposed language disappeared. There was only a language that transcended languages, like that of music]" (D 72; 54).[61]

While Shakespeare dominates the references to English literature in texts A, B, and D, English poetry is also present in all four texts in some form; Keats, Shelley, and Coleridge appear in each one by name or by title of poem. The recitation scene in B and D includes Roy's "encore" for the school inspector, "The Ancient Mariner," a line of which is cited in the text: "We were the first that ever burst into that silent sea" (B 39, D 75). But two of the texts include other representations of English poetry as well. In B, after the passage of the recitation, there follows a paragraph that was not incorporated in *La Détresse et l'enchantement* but which gave the article its English title and merits being quoted in full:

> Ces vers, il m'arrive encore de les retrouver dans mon sommeil, émergeant des sables du fond de la mémoire. De ces caches profondes remontent vers moi mes trésors disparates: "Many a flower is born to blush unseen ..." "J'aime le son du cor le soir au fond du bois ..." "Many a gem of purest ray serene ..." "A la très bonne, à la très belle Qui fait ma joie et ma santé ..."
> "Breathes there a soul so dead who never to himself hath said, This is my own, my native land ..."
> [These lines of verse, they some times return to me in my sleep, emerging from the deep sands of memory. From these hidden depths my disparate treasures come back to me.] (B 39)[62]

The passage is striking in particular because of its careful formal arrangement of these "trésors disparates," the English and French quotations alternating, and the lines from Gray's "elegy" being separated by a line from de Vigny. Coming as they do after the account of the recitations from Shakespeare and Coleridge, the quotations continue the sense of a literary education in which English literature was the highlight. Even when Roy quotes French poems, their lines are framed by lines in English, paradoxically concluding with Walter Scott's evocation of "my native land," suggesting perhaps the complexity of Roy's own identification with anglophone culture.[63] While Roy's knowledge of English poetry has clearly come from the official curriculum, with recitation as a highly valued learning objective, the two French poets quoted have a rather different status. While de Vigny's "Le Cor" was included in Edmond Procès's *Modèles français* III, Baudelaire's "Hymne" from *Les Epaves* was not included in Procès at that period. Some of his poems appear in later editions, but the "Notice" on Baudelaire in a later edition is highly critical of his literary style and his moral degeneracy, which makes it likely that teachers would have steered clear of him in the classroom.[64] Indeed, in *La Détresse et l'enchantement* Roy reflects: "Qu'en aurait-il été de moi si, à cet âge, j'avais eu accès à Rimbaud, Verlaine, Baudelaire, Radiguet? [If, at that age, I'd been able to read Rimbaud, Verlaine, Baudelaire, and Radiguet, I can only imagine what it would have done to me]" (D 72; 54). The fact that she did not have access to these poets means that Roy's education in fact provided her with an alternative literary homeland.

In text C ("Ma petite rue qui m'a menée autour du monde") Roy quotes from yet another of her favourite poets, Keats, after a reflection on her deep attraction to Keats, Shelley, and Coleridge. The quotation from *Endymion* comes at the end of a paragraph in which the English language is at once the language of the Manitoban majority and a universal language: "Si mes compatriotes de langue anglaise me traitèrent encore parfois en étrangère, leurs poètes me faisaient me sentir de la famille – et même qu'il n'y en avait qu'une attirant autour d'elle des amis de tous les coins de la terre. [If my English-speaking compatriots still treated me at times like a foreigner, their poets made me feel like one of the family – and even as if there was only one large family, drawing together friends from all corners of the earth]" (C 49) This language of the world-wide family has echoes of the language of Empire, such an integral part of the readers then used in elementary school classrooms, and it reminds us of the rhetoric of universalism that was at the heart of English Studies throughout the British Empire. But the degree to which this literary language had been absorbed to become a fundamental part of Roy's personal bicultural and bilingual identity is stressed as the quotation is presented: "Je récitais avec la même ferveur que si le vers me fût venu à travers ma langue maternelle: "A thing of beauty is a joy forever ..." [I would recite with the same fervour as if the line had come to me in my own mother tongue: "A thing of beauty is a joy forever ..."] (C 49). In this, the least polemical of the four pieces, the overt association of Keats with "la ferveur [fervour]" and "la langue maternelle [mother tongue]" shows the extent to which Roy's identification has shifted toward English literature. The autobiography steps back from such a bold statement, but the quotations that speak out from these four texts, written for quite different occasions and audiences, are evidence enough of the process of acculturation performed by Roy's education and its lasting effect.

The bilingualism needed for a student to succeed academically in Manitoba in the interwar years was more than just a matter of language. Roy's subsequent choice of French as her language of literary expression cannot totally conceal her "ambivalence of placement"[65] in respect to French and English culture as well as language. Snatches of English literature in its original language appear as a recurring element of Roy's representation of her own schooling, just as the Pont Provencher reappears throughout her writings as a marker of the linked yet separate existence of Franco-Manitobans across from the anglophone capital. The presence of these literary elements can be taken as a sign of the depth of Roy's assimilation to the English language and the power of pedagogical methods of memorization and recitation to leave lines imprinted on the mind. As Morgan comments in his related discussion of literary anthologies in use in Ontario in the nineteenth century: "Like many later school anthologies, this text attempts to form the subjectivities of students around an England so haunting it becomes more real than their actual experience of colonial life."[66] But the passages discussed above do more than represent a demonstration of the processes of assimilation and acculturation. They set up a series of tensions between different patterns of identification, so destroying any notion of an authentic, fixed, cultural identity. Figures of performance, recitation, and canny role-play, whether the clever manipulations of the *directrice* or Roy's impressing the inspector in Grade XII, suggest that biculturalism and bilingualism in this context of unequal power could become a game. But Roy's repeated successful playing of the game, winning acclaim from both sides, left her between the two languages and cultures, unable to identify totally with the oppressed francophone minority or with the dominant anglophone establishment. Hence the ambivalence and irony with which these texts abound.

Colonial Legacies and the Clandestine Curriculum

The double process of teacher training that Gabrielle Roy and her fellow Franco-Manitobans experienced in the interwar years, well exemplified Deborah Britzman's statement that: "Teacher education, like any education, is an ideological education."[1] When Roy began her teacher training at the Central Normal School on William Avenue in Winnipeg[2] in September 1928 at the age of nineteen, she was moving from the safe (francophone) cultural environment of the Académie Saint-Joseph to what many Franco-Manitobans felt to be hostile territory. François Ricard describes francophones' view of this most anglophone of establishments: "Not only was the instruction given entirely in English but a good many of the teachers were Scots (McIntosh, McKim, McLeod, McIntyre), who were known among Franco-Manitobans for anti-French fanaticism" (GR 109). Certainly the situation for francophone trainee teachers had changed in Manitoba since Roy's three sisters had trained before 1916.

TEACHING THE TEACHERS: THE PARALLEL FRENCH CURRICULUM

Under the bilingual education system, Saint-Boniface had its own bilingual *Ecole Normale,* and Ukrainian and Polish teacher-training centres were set up in Brandon and Winnipeg in 1907 in recognition of the increasing cultural and linguistic diversity of the province.[3] The immigration and settlement policy of the Laurier government between 1897 and 1915 targeted Central Europeans and resulted in what Henry Johnson refers to as "one of the great migrations of history."[4] But the rapid growth of the population of Manitoba and the other western provinces in the first two decades of the twentieth century put the education system under great strain. The 1916 report on bilingual schools found that standards were uneven and teachers were not all sufficiently well qualified. The quality of spoken English of some trainee teachers was of particular concern: "Some spoke English quite as well as, if not better than, the average student from English-speaking homes. Others were deficient both in speech and ability to read and understand English. They stated that in the schools that they had attended oral English had not been stressed and they had done little reading outside of the prescribed texts. It required a great amount of drill to correct the incorrect language and speech habits formed in early years. Some were unable to come up to the required standard and did not receive certificates."[5]

There is no indication here that the report referred to francophone teachers; indeed, it is likely that the least fluent candidates came from the more recently settled, isolated communities of new Manitobans from Central Europe. However, the response of the Department of Education was to close all bilingual sections in Normal Schools, to make school attendance obligatory from age five to fourteen (Grades I to IX), and to encourage a higher level of qualification within the teaching profession. Before 1916 there had been three classes of qualification, depending on the candidate's level of education on entry to Normal School. Those with only Grade X education could qualify as Third Class teachers, those with Grade XI as Second Class teachers, and those with Grade XII as First Class teachers. In his report of 1915–16, Deputy Minister R.S. Thornton recommended that in future all trainee teachers should have completed at least Grade XI, thereby ending the Third Class qualification.[6] Existing Third Class teachers were encouraged to upgrade their qualifications and non-anglophones were offered summer schools to improve their mastery of English. Non-British citizens were still allowed to teach in Manitoba, but only with an interim, renewable licence. This tightening of control on teacher training aimed to improve standards of education in the province and also enabled Normal Schools to act as powerful tools of assimilation to the English language, culture, and values, which in turn would be mediated by the teaching profession to all pupils in the province.

The emphasis on the English language was still very evident in 1928 when Roy entered Normal School. All candidates were required to pass both a medical test and a test in oral proficiency and silent reading in English. The cohort of 1928 (about four hundred young women students) was divided into five classes. Of these, two were for "Second Class" students and two for "First Class" students like Roy, who had completed Grade XII.[7] The fifth class, for "Graduate" students, was for those who already held a teaching licence but wished to train for secondary teaching. In 1928 the total number of pupils enrolled for Grade XII in Manitoba was 415. The high proportion of female pupils completing Grade XII who then entered Normal School (women representing about 80 percent of trainee teachers) indicates the lack of other career paths open to young women at the time. But as Ricard suggests, the profession offered "undeniable social prestige and ... a certain degree of intellectual life." And to be a woman teacher in Manitoba was very different from being a francophone woman teacher in Quebec: "Whereas in Quebec in those days the lot of teachers verged on pure and simple exploitation, it was different in a province where the educational system was secular and directly controlled by the State (GR 108)." Indeed accounts of the levels of qualification in Quebec at the time show a huge disparity between the (largely anglophone) Protestant and (largely francophone) Catholic sectors. Members of teaching orders (who represented more than 43 percent of the total number of teachers in Quebec in 1929) were not required to hold a formal teaching qualification (this only became obligatory after 1939). Francophones who had completed only the first six years of education could enter Catholic Normal School for a two-year training course, whereas their Protestant peers needed to have completed Grade XI before beginning teacher training at McGill.[8] In this respect, being educated in Manitoba gave Roy a clear advantage over her francophone Quebec contemporaries, even though it meant that she had to learn to teach in English.

Had Roy entered a Catholic *école normale* in Quebec rather than the Winnipeg Normal School, her course would have differed in two key respects in addition to the language of delivery. In Quebec all teachers were trained to teach the catechism, and women teachers followed "some courses more appropriate to the 'nature of the female' ... hymn singing, callisthenics, diction, cutting-out and sewing."[9] From 1926 teacher training for women included compulsory study of household science, reflecting the increased gendering of the curriculum at all levels in Quebec at this time.[10] The curriculum in Manitoba differed markedly from that of the *écoles normales* in Quebec. The Programme of Studies for 1928–29 did not include household science among the subjects studied, which were: Science of Education (Pedagogy and Psychology); History of Education; School Management; Method (in all subjects of curriculum); Academic instruction – subjects plus the School arts of penmanship, reading, speaking, English composition, music, drawing, handwork, physical culture (Phys. Ed.), nature study, and gardening (where possible); First Aid; practice and observation in designated schools;[11] and social work – visits and lectures. Between September and December, First and Second Class students followed a similar course, concentrating on primary grades. From January to June First Class students focused on the senior grades.[12]

However, just as Roy's education at the Académie Saint-Joseph had combined official anglophone and clandestine francophone strands, her teacher training was still indirectly controlled by the AECFM. For the continuation of an unofficial bilingual system, the supply of francophone *institutrices* was imperative. Convents were one source of recruits, but unlike the case in Quebec, Manitoban religious teachers had to be qualified in the normal way. The association advised and encouraged the *directrices* of convents how best to prepare their candidates, recommending in a circular, for example, that Grade XI and XII pupils be allowed to teach classes in English more often in order to prepare them for the English language requirements.[13] The *concours* was also a recruitment tool; prizes for Grade XII were conditional upon the winners (like Roy) taking up places at Normal School, in return for which the fees were paid by the AECFM. A loan system was set up by the AECFM in the early 1920s to encourage more young francophone women to serve "the sacred cause of education."[14] Once recruited, francophone trainee teachers had to continue with a parallel curriculum, being required by the association to take both a monthly course in Catholic pedagogy and a weekly course in apologetics as a condition of the award of a loan.[15] Students sat a separate examination before completing their official course, received a certificate for successful completion, and were reprimanded for non-attendance. The function of the parallel course was clearly to counter certain aspects of anglophone, secular ideology; AECFM circulars reminded the *normaliennes* of their duty to attend these extra classes if they wished to be able "to combat effectively the pernicious tendencies of the materialist philosophy of Normal School."[16] As they did with the school system, the AECFM maintained lines of communication with their counterparts in anglophone institutions, notably through apparently amicable contact with the director, Dr W.A. McIntyre, who features very positively in *La Détresse et l'enchantement*.[17] AECFM Minutes refer to his promise to report on the progress of francophone students at Normal School.[18] The association's monitoring of francophone students' performance led to comments on students' poor pronunciation, their timidity, their appearance, and their lack of fluency, all factors that contribute to underperformance in the classroom.[19] The overall impression that emerges from archival sources is that the AECFM played a clever strategic game, working within the anglophone establishment to subvert its control and also to improve "their" candidates' chances of success. The rhetoric in circulars is unmistakable: "If we are truly committed to what we want and if we want to have some chance of succeeding in the peaceful form of struggle indicated above, it is imperative that we make contact with our opposite numbers in the teaching profession in the province, involve ourselves more closely in their annual debates and make ourselves known."[20]

As Britzman states, prospective teachers all bring to their teacher training "their implicit institutional biographies – the cumulative experience of school lives – which, in turn, inform their knowledge of the students' world, of school structure, and of curriculum."[21] The small number of francophone students within the anglophone institution not only had to negotiate the conflict between their educational past and their present situation, they continued to be caught between two languages, two communities, and two quite different visions of the educational process. It was an education that was both an integrative, assimilating project and a form of resistance to anglophone domination, a resistance grounded in linguistic and religious difference. Clearly some students failed to straddle this divide comfortably. They either became what the AECFM referred to, in the case of one young francophone teacher, as "anglifiée [thoroughly anglicized]"[22] or they lacked the fluency and ease with English language and culture to convince Department of Education inspectors of their ability to represent Canada in the classroom.

Conflicting pedagogies

As if linguistic and religious differences were not already obstacles to success, Franco-Manitoban student teachers had to negotiate their way between conflicting currents of pedagogical thinking. In Winnipeg it was Dr McIntyre who taught the course in pedagogy (a course in which Roy earned an A – which helps to explain the mutual respect of principal and student that came through in her autobiography).[23] His approach to education was, as Roy recalls in *La Détresse et l'enchantement*, progressive and uncompromisingly child-centred: "Bien avant que le mot épanouissement ne devienne à la mode et ne sorte de toutes les bouches, lui, en ce temps lointain, ne parlait déjà que de cela: 'the opening, the blossoming of self' [Long before the notion of self-fulfilment came to be common currency, this man was talking of nothing else, using terms like 'an opening out' and 'a blossoming of self']" (DE 83; ES 63). Roy summarizes McIntyre's pedagogical approach as being based on the view that "l'enfant n'était pas fait pour convenir à l'école, mais que l'école devait convenir à l'enfant [a child is not made to suit a school and so the school must suit the child]" (ibid.). Indeed, it is tempting to detect McIntyre's influence on Roy when one reads about the report of the local parish representative for Cardinal, where she spent her first full year of teaching. The complaint was made that "Mlle Roy does not teach enough French and ... the children do not have lessons to take home."[24] Ricard concludes from the evidence that Roy was quite probably far from being "the ardent activist the association hoped to find in each of the teachers under its 'jurisdiction.'"[25] The Saturday classes led by Père Bourque, which were supposed to inspire such militancy, used as their course book Monseigneur François-Xavier Ross's *Manuel de pédagogie théorique et pratique*, first published in 1916 and the standard teaching manual in Quebec until 1948.[26]

Ross's manual reflects the complex and somewhat contradictory requirements of francophone teachers in Canada throughout Roy's education and teaching career. The discourse of "race" that Ross uses throughout, referring to "the French-Canadian race" and "the French-Canadian child," allows the book to address a wider public than that of Quebec. But it clearly caters primarily to a confessional education system in a province with a francophone majority, not for the clandestine parallel activities of Manitoba. However, the influence of Jesuit teaching, introduced into New France in the seventeenth century and reflected most completely in the *collège classique*, had spread throughout francophone educational establishments.[27] As members of the various teaching orders in Quebec had authored many of the textbooks used at all levels of schooling, so the principles of classical humanism, based on "la culture générale [general culture]," underpinned pedagogical thinking in francophone Canada. Nicole Gagnon explains the notion of general culture as follows: "This culture is general because its sole aim is the education of the man as a human being, that is developing his faculties into a harmonious whole."[28] Francophone pride in the educational principles of classical humanism, product of the Latin spirit, compared with Anglo-Saxon pedagogy was such that it served to justify an assumption of racial superiority. As Gagnon summarizes: "In short, the spirit of humanism is the source of our superiority as a race and the humanist system of education is the reason why we have survived as a race."[29]

But as this quotation suggests – and as Ross's manual shows – onto this apparently abstract, universalist system was grafted a particularist pedagogical theory comprising various strands that emanated from the situation of francophones in Canada. These strands were designed to ensure the militancy of the teaching profession and strengthen ideological resistance to secular, anglophone training. The first of these strands was the Catholic faith. Gagnon argues that, in the interwar years in particular, religious ideology was integrated most closely into humanist pedagogical thinking. Georges Courchesne's 1927 work *Nos Humanités* for example, is cited as the classic exposition of Christian humanist thinking in publications such as *L'Enseignement secondaire*.[30] In Courchesne's view, the Catholic faith gave the overarching unifying principle to humanist education: "We have every interest in spreading sound Catholic thinking in our explanations, for that is the prime means to ensure the consistency of our pedagogical practice."[31] And whereas for the Department of Education in Manitoba, "every lesson should be a language lesson,"[32] francophone Catholic teachers were exhorted: "It is our duty to consider all the truths that we discuss in the classroom, sometimes as an introduction to faith, sometimes as supplementary confirmation of Catholic doctrine."[33] Within this ideology the teacher is constructed as the bearer of a divine mission, responsible not only for children's intellectual and moral development but also for their spiritual welfare (as the AECFM's reference to "the sacred cause of education," cited above, implied).[34] Ross's manual states: "The importance of the role of the schoolmistress can be inferred from her mission. A child's future is in her hands: the State requires her to produce good citizens; the Church, virtuous Christians; parents, rounded human beings. The child has the right to ask her for health and physical strength, intelligence, Christian virtue, the means of developing his character here on earth and an expectation of eternal bliss which is his ultimate purpose."[35]

Throughout the manual, the *institutrice* is constructed both in terms of religion and the family, becoming an ersatz nun/mother figure. As Nadia Fahmy-Eid and Nicole Thivierge point out, the maternal role has an additional association within French-Canadian nationalism, the mother being responsible for the reproduction of the dominant ideology: "In Quebec, this family mission is colored with a nationalist commitment to the preservation of the French-Canadian 'race.'"[36] Indeed, nationalism is the second particularist strand that emerges from French-Canadian pedagogical works at this time, a nationalism most suited to Quebec but which is extended to members of francophone minorities and, as in the following recommendation, interwoven with providentialist thinking: "Teachers of French- Canadian children need to understand how important it is that they form in the soul of their pupils the national feeling which ensures that our race remains faithful to the mission which Providence has entrusted to them in this land."[37] In keeping with the traditionalist nationalism of figures such as l'abbé Lionel Groulx, Ross invokes the colonial past, linking education with evangelization and agriculturalism among the core values of the French-Canadian people: "Colonization and evangelization are still today as in the past the principal duty of its race: The cross and the plough remain its chosen tools."[38]

The third strand, which shifts from the universal to the particular, is that of language. Within classical humanism, both classical languages and the mother tongue were studied above all for their formal interest, as a means of gaining an appreciation of order: "The study of words is everything for well-formed minds, who can gradually be taught to understand the profound harmony of words, ideas and things. In the process the child becomes more human, more able to understand humanity at its highest level."[39] This function of language and literature as providing models of structure and clear thought emerged in the discussion of the school curriculum above. Yet while language remained at the heart of French-Canadian pedagogy in this period, the specific situation of a resistant minority of francophones shifted the message into a more pragmatic mode. Ross's manual resonates with the combative language of the AECFM as he describes the teaching of the French language as "protection against the heretical and materialist infiltration of the foreign tongue which speaks of another faith and other aspirations."[40] Just as the French language acquires moral and political value, so, here it is clear that the English language is considered synonymous with materialism and the undermining of the Catholic faith. The careful interweaving of faith, language, and nationalism is evident throughout Ross's presentation of the particularist interests of French-Canadian pedagogy in the 1920s and 1930s.

As a final example of Ross's very specific (and somewhat idiosyncratic) concern with the corrupting influences to which young French-Canadians were exposed in this period, the manual warns trainee teachers against "the cartoons and the disgusting news items in the gutter press, the movies, sensationalist novels, ridiculous, exaggerated and unedifying fashions, hideous *Teddy Bears* from which babies are never parted, day or night." It concludes: "It is the teacher's duty to maintain her sense of loathing of all these poisonous influences and to inspire the same feeling in her pupils."[41] Whereas the principles of Christian humanist education tended toward the universal and abstract, the specific concerns of French-Canadian pedagogy encouraged the teacher to stand against modernity and seek their justification in a colonial past. This contradiction between the general principles of classical humanism and the particular situation of francophones in Canada compounded the tension between anglophone and francophone views of education. The new generation of francophone teachers thus found itself torn between conflicting images of education and the teacher's role. It is hardly surprising that only a few Franco-Manitobans negotiated their way successfully into the teaching profession. Yet it is possible that the lived experience of the contradictions between systems, and different ideological strands within those systems, enabled Roy and her contemporaries to see teacher training, and education in general, differently from their monolingual, monocultural peers. Doris Lessing writes of education as a self-perpetuating system: "What you are being taught here is an amalgam of current prejudice and the choices of this particular culture. The slightest look at history will show how impermanent these must be. You are being taught by people who have been able to accommodate themselves to a regime of thought laid down by their predecessors."[42] This remains generally true. However, members of the Franco-Manitoban minority, engaged throughout their education in this double game, were constantly alerted to the supposed prejudices of the "other's" system and constantly reminded of the process of accommodation to a regime of thought. Those who mastered the game were potentially more able to maintain some critical distance toward its rules and less likely to perpetuate the system unthinkingly. Equally, successful trainees had already proved themselves to be adept at playing a number of quite different roles within the classroom.

Being a teacher

During the period when Roy was part of the Manitoba education system, the provincial population rose by inward migration and the school system had to spread and consolidate itself. But these were still relatively early days in the history of the province and there were huge discrepancies in educational provision between urban and rural areas. A school inspector recalls the situation in 1914: "Even to learn to read and write was an achievement in many parts of the province until as late as 1914. There was no compulsory education; there was no minimum equipment for a school; text books were difficult to obtain; school furniture was often primitive and handmade; teachers were hard to find and had little training; roads were often mere cow paths across the prairies; child labor was important in the home or on the land. Schooling was a vision present only to those with eyes to see."[43]

While conditions were clearly much better in 1929 when Roy entered the profession, the isolation of many rural districts continued to pose particular problems. The Department of Education Report for the 1927–28 tabulated eighty-one teachers in one-room rural schools, and departmental inspectors commented: "Many of these are fresh from our training classes and have not yet found their bearings ... They are doing as good work as could be expected."[44] While it was rare for a teacher to stay in a one-room school beyond three years, a significant proportion (one in three) by then had four or more years of experience and the inspectors were pleased that this represented a real improvement in continuity. Nevertheless, the one-room school demanded a very particular kind of teacher: "In some of the more isolated districts there is room for the teacher who possesses a real missionary zeal."[45] Even in the secular anglophone system, the colonial model of the rural teacher as evangelist remained bound up with the process of settlement.

If the working conditions were challenging, the pay was relatively good, at least before the effects of the Depression set in. According to the Department of Education Report for 1929–30, rural teachers were paid $875 a year.[46] In fact there were variations between teachers' salaries across the province, as local school commissions had the responsibility for hiring teachers and fixing their salaries. In her first full year of teaching, Roy earned $1,100 in Cardinal, but when she moved to Saint-Boniface in 1930 her salary was a little lower ($1,000) and in the following year, reflecting the deepening economic crisis of the Depression, it went down to $922.[47] A comparison with Quebec in 1929 is once again instructive. There the hierarchy of pay reflected the hierarchy of opportunity, and francophone *institutrices* had a scandalously low status. While a Protestant male schoolteacher was paid $2,351 and his female counterpart $1,068 a year, a Catholic *instituteur* was paid $1,553 and an *institutrice* a mere $387.[48]

Since Manitoba provincial law allowed each school district to appoint its own staff, the AECFM was able to exert considerable influence on the school boards within Catholic francophone districts.[49] They also continued to monitor the performance of francophone teachers both through their unofficial inspections and through intelligence gleaned from local priests, who were given the names of newly qualified *institutrices* and asked to keep a strict eye on their behaviour and contacts.[50] To help keep teachers on message, an annual summer school was held at the Académie Saint-Joseph in Saint-Boniface. It covered both pedagogical and religious topics and was preceded by a five-day retreat, thereby reinforcing Franco-Manitobans' view of teaching as a vocation.

The representation of the teacher and the teaching profession in Roy's work draws largely on the context and experiences of her own teaching career between 1929 and 1937. In May 1929, before officially receiving her teacher's licence, she worked as a temporary supply teacher in the Métis village of Marchand, about fifty miles southeast of Winnipeg. She completed the school year there, the sole teacher in a one-room school covering Grades I to VIII. The final story in *Cet été qui chantait*, "L'enfant morte [The dead child]" draws on an incident that took place there. In September 1929 Roy took up her first full-time post in Cardinal in a largely French-speaking district, about eighty miles southwest of Winnipeg, where once again she taught in a one-room school. This was the setting for two of the stories from *Ces enfants de ma vie*. From the outset her aim had been to acquire a post in Saint-Boniface, and in 1930 she was successful, being appointed to the Institut collégial Provencher, the only francophone school in Saint-Boniface to employ lay school *institutrices*. The school was large (about 1,000 pupils) and covered Grades I to XII. Women teachers taught the elementary and primary classes, while members of the Marianist order who ran the school taught the senior grades. Francophones and non-francophones were taught separately, so that the unofficial bilingual education could best be delivered to French speakers. Roy was given charge of a Grade I "receiving" class of non-francophone boys, many of whom were sons of newly arrived immigrants, to whom she had to teach English. Several stories in *Ces Enfants de ma vie* draw on her experiences in Saint-Boniface. She held this post until June 1937, when she was granted a year's leave to travel to Europe. Before leaving, in order to earn extra money to finance her trip, Roy taught summer school on an isolated island on Waterhen Lake, between Lake Manitoba and Lake Winnipegosis, about two hundred miles northwest of Winnipeg. She lodged with a family and taught their children and some neighbouring Métis children who lived too far from any settlement to receive any official, year-round, primary education. *La Petite Poule d'Eau* includes three linked stories set on the island, the second of which recounts the visits of three such temporary teachers from the perspective of the host mother.

These periods of experience gave Roy a broad insight into Manitoban education in the interwar years, combining as they did both rural and urban schooling, as well as francophone, anglophone, and allophone pupils. While the texts mentioned above deal most fully with the figure of the teacher, and with teaching itself, other texts, such as *La Rivière sans repos, Un Jardin au bout du monde*, and *La Montagne secrète*, include related scenes, as do her autobiographical and non-fictional works.

What follows is not simply an attempt to bring out the biographical elements in Roy's writings and their transposition or formulation in texts. I am interested in the status and process of education, the power relationships that emerge between different cultures and linguistic groups, and the recurring use of images of the teacher and teacher-pupil relationships within a specific historical context of biculturalism and multiculturalism involving anglophone and francophone Canadians, "New Canadians," and First Nations. Biculturalism has been described as "a talent made necessary by the imbalance of power that exists in these boundary situations ... a technique of survival in someone else's world."[51] Franco-Manitobans in the 1920s and 1930s were positioned ambivalently in relation to power; yet the schoolteacher was necessarily in a position of symbolic power within the classroom, acting as a mediator between the dominant culture and a new generation of citizens. Techniques of survival took many forms and involved negotiation at all levels of the educational hierarchy.

REPRESENTATIONS OF EDUCATION IN ROY'S FICTIONAL AND AUTO-FICTIONAL TEXTS

A reading of Gabrielle Roy's work for traces of the institutions and processes of education calls up a wide range of images and references. Older protagonists' recollections of past experiences and the ongoing encounters with education in texts set in the 1940s, 1950s, or 1960s and in different parts of Canada widen the timeframe and the social and geographical scope, and add to the complexity of Roy's treatment of this theme. I discuss brief glimpses of school scenes as well as longer thematic developments in order to analyse the ways in which colonial and neo-colonial power relations resonate in Roy's representation of education in her writing.

It is useful to separate out four different aspects of colonial contact. Historically, the first was the presence of references to French colonialism and to France as a former colonial power. The second aspect of colonial contact was the relationship between Great Britain and Canada after the conquest of New France. The growing domination of the English language and the special role of English literature within the Empire were especially significant. The third aspect relates to patterns of contact and changing power relations between anglophones and francophones from the time of Confederation onward. This aspect comprises not only the role of education within the development of an (Anglo)-Canadian identity but also resistance and counter-moves from the various francophone populations of Canada. Education was central to the strategies of assimilation and resistance that typified this period and exemplified the ambivalent positioning of the settler subjects in relation to their colonial heritage and to new immigrants who did not share this cultural legacy. This period was the setting for many of Roy's texts. A fourth aspect emerges in works set in the 1930s and in the 1960s, the role of education in contacts between Second and Fourth World populations, notably in the case of the Inuit but also among the Métis. Forms of contact here in some cases echoed the patterns of "Canadianization" that typified the post-Confederation period; in other cases they recalled earlier forms of contact between aboriginal populations and White settlers. To complicate the picture further, Roy's texts also make reference to the effects of United States imperialism. Although the following analysis of Roy's texts is structured according to this sequence of subdivisions, a certain amount of slippage between categories is an inevitable result of the very complexity of the processes of colonialism and imperialism. The effects of specific historical periods often continue to shape and colour later periods, sometimes reinforcing later developments, sometimes resisting or undermining official policies and practices. As a result, a complex and conflicted figure of the teacher emerges from Roy's work.

The French colonial legacy

Education in New France was the responsibility of the Catholic Church through its teaching orders. This association between schooling and the propagation of Catholic beliefs was part of the continuing legacy of the French colonial period, particularly in Quebec. Since *Bonheur d'occasion* is set in Quebec in 1940 and deals with family life in the working-class and strongly francophone district of Saint-Henri, the reader might expect there to be references to the Church's involvement in education. In an early description of Saint-Henri the area is evoked simply as "école, église, couvent: bloc séculaire fortement noué au cœur de la jungle citadine, comme au creux des vallons laurentiens [school, church, convent: a close-knit, centuries-old alliance, as strong in the heart of the urban jungle as in the Laurentian valleys]" (BO 35; 33–4).[52] But, despite the fact that the Lacasse family includes many school-age children, Roy makes relatively few references to education either through the characters or through the narrator. One reason for this may be that many passages focus our attention on protagonists who are no longer concerned with education, such as Florentine, Rose-Anna, Emmanuel, and Jean. The little representation there is of Catholic schooling in Saint-Henri is very mixed. At one extreme we have the case of Yvonne, one of the Lacasse daughters, whose discovery of a religious calling is explicitly linked to her experience as a schoolchild. The narrator describes a classroom practice used to inculcate a regular pattern of worship in the pupils: "Au couvent, dans la classe d'Yvonne, il y avait un cœur percé, et chaque petite fille qui assistait à la messe avait le droit en entrant en classe d'aller enlever une de ces épines au cœur transpercé [In Yvonne's classroom there was a sacred heart, and each girl who went to Mass was entitled, as she came into her class, to remove one of the thorns from this suffering heart]" (BO 95; 92). Attendance at mass was associated in the child's mind with the alleviation of Christ's suffering, and non-attendance, clearly, with a sense of guilt.

But this pious child is far from the norm in the novel, many of the young males (such as Yvonne's brother Philippe) prefer to play truant. Their young brother, Daniel, who dies from leukemia toward the end of the novel, also has a more problematic relationship with education. His early memories of learning to write are positive, the process being associated rather traditionally with light. But his memories of the painful experience of falling behind academically because of his absences, whether for illness or for the lack of warm clothing in winter, are all the more traumatic to him because of the strict and punitive figure of the *frère*. This teacher figure is contrasted with the patient and warm anglophone nurse, Jenny, who once again encourages the now-dying child to practise writing in his hospital bed. Emmanuel's school experiences, also in the local Catholic primary school are different again. For him, a bourgeois child in largely working-class Saint-Henri who is seeing others' poverty at close hand, the experience of attending a Catholic primary school was not the source of a religious vocation but rather an inspiration for his socialist humanist values:

Rien dans leur vie ne les liait plus les uns aux autres, sauf le sou-
venir de l'école primaire que tous dans le faubourg
fréquentaient ... sans distinction de classe: fils de bourgeois,
gamins guenilleux des bords du canal, enfants pâles et maladifs
de familles secourues par l'assistance publique. Tous se
côtoyaient sur les bancs de l'école des frères et, pour Emmanuel,
la vision qu'il avait eue, très jeune, de la misère, ne cessait de
l'agiter.
[Nothing in their lives held them together except the memory of
the neighbourhood public school, where everybody went, whatever his class origin. There were sons of middle-class families
along with ragged urchins from the canal side, and the pale,
sickly children of families on relief. They sat side by side on
their benches in the Christian brothers' school, and the glimpse
he had of poverty at that early age never left his mind.] (BO
52–3; 51)

What both Yvonne and Emmanuel share as a result of their Catholic education is seemingly a desire to help the suffering; Yvonne is
shown trying to decide whether to be a "sœur des pauvres [a nun ...
for the poor]" or a "sœur des malades [a nursing sister]" (BO 371;
352). But nowhere does the text suggest that the Catholic system of
education is helping the working class to gain a critical understanding of its own position or any active sense of class solidarity. Even
the representation of Yvonne's vocation is somewhat undermined
by the following description (focalized through her mother, Rose-
Anna) of her developing body constrained by her convent uniform,
suggesting Rose-Anna's misgivings about the girl's convent education: "Rose-Anna l'entendit qui chantonnait des bribes de canti-
ques. Il était surtout question du mois de mai qui était le plus beau.
Enfin, elle apparut dans sa petite robe de couvent, longue, qui lui
battait les jambes, mais qui était trop serrée sur le buste ... Et puis,
raide dans sa vilaine robe malgré son âge gracieux, elle partit
vivement [She was singing snatches of hymns in the next room,
something about the lovely month of May. Soon she appeared in
her convent uniform, the long skirt flapping around her legs but the
bust now too tight ... Then, stiff in her ugly costume despite her
graceful body, she ran off]" (BO 371; 352–3).

In references to education elsewhere in Canada in Roy's work,
the French colonial legacy of Catholicism plays a more peripheral

role. In "La Rivière sans repos," education in Fort Chimo in northern Quebec is delivered in English (and the converted Inuit congregation are Protestant). However, the presence of the two missionaries in the village, one anglophone Protestant and the other francophone Catholic, recalls the parallel missionary efforts of the French and British.

One of the clearest traces of France's colonial past in the classroom is in the teaching of history. In *La Petite Poule d'Eau* the narrative of the second story, "L'école de la Petite Poule d'Eau," is largely focalized through Luzina, the mother who has requested a summer school for her family. A history lesson taught by the young francophone teacher, Mlle Côté, is presented as overheard by Luzina, who eavesdrops on the class as it progresses in the schoolroom, a purpose-built new log cabin. Initially the reader is given an abbreviated version of Mlle Côté's "lesson," which stresses the extent of French penetration into North America and France's colonial possession of those territories:

> Les explorateurs du Nouveau Monde, presque tous étaient des Français: Iberville, de Groseilliers, Pierre Radisson. Le Père Marquette et Louis Joliet [sic] avaient découvert le chemin des grands lacs. Lavérendrye était allé à pied jusqu'aux Rocheuses. Cavalier de La Salle avait navigué jusqu'à l'embouchure du Mississipi. Tout ce pays était à la France.
> [The explorers of the New World, almost all of them, were French: Iberville, De Groseillers [sic], Pierre Radisson. Father Marquette and Louis Joliet [sic] had discovered the water highway of the Great Lakes. La Vérendrye had gone on foot as far as the Rockies. Cavalier de la Salle had traveled by boat to the mouth of the Mississippi. All this country belonged to France.]
> (PPE 70; 63)

The reader is then made aware of Luzina's filtering narrative presence as she responds to rehearing history lessons half forgotten from her own childhood: "Tout en écoutant, Luzina avait même commencé de mener pour son propre compte le récit du passé [Even as she listened, Luzina had begun to spin on her own account the tale of the past]" (ibid.). There follows a history of her family and her husband's family, migrating first from France to Canada, then to Manitoba, and in the final stage continuing this colonizing pattern by settling in northern Manitoba. For Luzina this vicarious rediscovery of school history lessons serves to reaffirm her genealogical relationship to Canada and to reinterpret her current isolation in historical terms, teleologically linking it to the process of colonization. She weaves her personal history into the French-Canadian narrative of history that she refers to as "la belle, vieille, vieille histoire [the lovely, old old story]" (PPE 69; 62) as one might refer to other such familiar yet authoritative tales of origin, from Bible stories to legends, folktales, and oral history.

A number of education scenes draw on the association between France, the French, and their colonial relationship to Canada. For Azarius in *Bonheur d'occasion*, whose decision to join up in 1940 as a volunteer is motivated partly by financial desperation and partly by a desire for individual freedom, the image of France acts as a source of patriotic identity. The text follows Azarius's train of thought, exposing without comment the messy mixture of motives involved in this decision. He does not claim to be fighting for Britain (although, of course, he will be)[53] but to be fighting for France. Something of a sentimental character, he draws his moral and emotional justification from his early education: "Il pensa aux vieux pays, qui l'avaient fait rêver, tout jeune, sur ses livres de classe, à 'France,' ce mot blotti au fond de ses songes comme une nostalgie [He thought of the old countries of which he had dreamed when he was young, the pictures in his schoolbooks, that 'France' lurking in the back of all his dreams like an incurable homesickness]" (BO 393; 372). The common use of "les vieux pays [the old countries]" (in referring to Europe generally but also specifically to France) allows Azarius to see France as a natural, unquestionable place of origin. An attachment to France is lodged deep in his imagination (as the language of dream and nostalgia suggests, in combination with the references to schoolbooks from childhood), the expression of an enduring colonial loyalty rather than any specific political judgment.

If loyalty to France is one attitude that seems to result from the French-language curriculum in Quebec, the learned sense of inferiority of francophone Canadians vis-à-vis the population of metropolitan France emerges in other texts. In *Ces enfants de ma vie* this sentiment is expressed by one of the Franco-Manitoban parents in response to the teacher's decision to visit the home of a recent French immigrant family before visiting any of the other pupils' homes:

– Vous partez pour aller iou comme ça?
– Chez les Badiou.
– On sait ben! On fréquente les Français plutôt que son propre
monde.
– Mais madame!
– Je disais ça pour parler. Vous arrêterez-vous au moins par
chez nous quand vous repasserez?
["Where are you leaving to go, then?"
"To the Badious."
"That's right. Go and see the French, never your own people."
"But madame!"
"I just said that for something to say. Will you drop in at least
on the way back?"] (CEV 115; 87–8)

The pattern of suggestion, protest, and retraction indicates a touch-
iness in relation to Franco-Canadian identity and the cultural status
of the teacher. The reaction of the Franco-Manitoban mother is to
position the teacher between France, the former colonial power,
and its settler populations, as the mediator of France's cultural
values and as such the object of some suspicion. This image of
the French as culturally superior is interestingly modified in *Rue
Deschambault*. In "Gagner ma vie [To earn my living ...]" the
young teacher Christine has among her pupils a family newly
arrived from France. In this case it is Canada that is associated with
literacy, as the parents, both Breton, are illiterate, whereas the children insist on struggling through the snow to attend school, where
they will learn French and English. The text sets up a contrast
between the parents – "ils ne savaient ni lire ni écrire [they did not
know how to read or write]" (RD 256; 157) – and their children –
"les deux petits répétèrent les mots de leur leçon [the two little ones
recited their lessons]" (RD 257; 157). The key to this paradox lies in
another quasi-colonial relationship between the centre and the margins – the relationship between Paris and Brittany and between the
French and Breton languages.

The legacy of the British Empire

The second aspect of colonialism found in Roy's writings concerns
images of Empire in which francophone Canadians become "des

colons colonisés," the colonial subjects of British rule in the
post-1763 era. These scenes are frequently treated with touches of
humour and irony. The second story of *La Petite Poule d'Eau* is
based on the contrasting pedagogical methods and curricula of three
teachers, two francophone and one anglophone, who arrive in the
isolated island to teach summer school for the Tousignant children.
In the case of the anglophone teacher, Roy alludes ironically to the
francophone family's automatic association of anglophones with
Great Britain, referring to Miss O'Rorke as "l'Anglaise," despite her
being from Ontario and of distant Northern Irish extraction. In contrast to Mlle Côté's Franco-Canadian account of the history of Canada, Miss O'Rorke teaches a rigorously British view of Canada's past
and present. Although this middle-aged spinster from Ontario initially seems to be represented as a comic figure, a caricature of the
hard-line Protestant, Luzina comes to appreciate and feel some fondness for her and her teaching. In keeping with the mood of tolerance
and open-mindedness that characterizes this text, Luzina sees it as an
advantage that her children should have been taught both the French
and the British colonial histories.

Love of the British Empire shapes all Miss O'Rorke's lessons, just
as Catholicism pervaded the French language textbooks discussed
earlier. Another scene treated humorously concerns letter writing
(in English). The narrator explains the teacher's motives, making
their ideological nature quite clear:

> Aux fins de créer et de maintenir des relations cordiales entre les
> divers sujets du trône d'Angleterre, Miss O'Rorke, dans chaque
> école où elle passait, imposait aux élèves d'écrire des lettres à
> leurs petits cousins de l'Afrique du Sud, de l'Australie, de
> Terre-Neuve ou de quelque autre partie de l'Empire "sur lequel
> jamais le soleil ne se couchait."
> [In order to create and maintain cordial relations between the
> various subjects of the British throne, Miss O'Rorke required
> the pupils in every school through which she passed to write let-
> ters to their small cousins in South Africa, Australia, Newfound-
> land, or some other portion of the Empire "on which the sun
> never set."] (PPE 108–9; 101)

But despite its humour and the naivety of the child's letter, the scene
makes a serious point about linguistic and ideological assimilation

to the values of British imperialism, a point that is lost on the Tousignant couple, who feel a vague pride at their son's achievement, presented ironically by the narrator: "Que la lettre eût été écrite en anglais, langue pour eux étrangère, tout juste compréhensible, insolite, fut pourtant, en définitive, ce qui leur causa le plus de fierté [That the letter should have been written in English, however – a tongue foreign to them, just barely understandable, far from their normal lives – was what after all gave them the greatest pride]" (PPE 111; 103). The anglophone teacher's language draws on the rhetoric of the Empire as an extended family ("leurs petits cousins") and, in her fierce identification with England and the monarchy, she teaches her pupils to see Britain as the "natural" centre of their world. Indeed this aspect of the story can be read as a reworking of the processes of colonization of Canada, the francophone and then the anglophone teachers writing the remote little northern island and its inhabitants into two opposing colonial narratives.

Rue Deschambault presents a slightly more critical treatment of the rival colonial histories. The narrator, Christine, recalling her first year's teaching in the Prairie village of Cardinal, states her preference for teaching geography rather than history. Geography, she claims rather naively, is safer, because it is based on undisputed facts: "Il n'y a pas moyen de se tromper ... on n'a pas à juger les peuples; il n'est pas question de guerres; on n'a pas à prendre parti [You can't go wrong in teaching it ... you don't have to judge peoples; no wars are involved, no sides need be taken]" (RD 251; 154). The implication is that when teaching history, the francophone teacher is caught between opposing narratives – anglophone and francophone – and would be criticized for delivering the "wrong" one in the wrong context (particularly in Manitoba). Of course one might argue that geography is differently full of signs of authority and ownership, the naming and mapping of Canada, its trading history and its pattern of development also telling an Empire-laden story, but the narrator here is caught within her experience of rival colonial histories and does not herself develop to this level of postcolonial awareness.

Roy's texts also make interesting use of certain key symbols of Empire, notably the Union Jack, which had to be flown outside every Manitoban school, reinforcing the link between education and Empire. The flag itself is humorously treated in *La Petite Poule*

d'Eau as it becomes a symbol of the gap between Luzina's understanding of the world and that of Miss O'Rorke. To Miss O'Rorke,
the new schoolroom cannot be a school without a flag. Luzina's
rapid acceptance of her explanation of the need for the school to be
clearly marked by the British flag is expressed with an ironic echo
of colonial thinking: "Il n'y avait pas de doute qu'il aiderait mieux à
définir un territoire qui, autrement, pouvait passer pour inexploré
[Beyond question it would help to define an area which otherwise
might have passed for unexplored]" (PPE 89; 82).

In "De la truite dans l'eau glacée" in *Ces Enfants de ma vie* the
flagpole outside the school, again explicitly linked with the British
Empire, is the focus of comic undermining. The young teacher
recalls the arrival at the school of her thirteen-year old Métis pupil
with a mixture of admiration and shock:

> Plutôt que d'y pénétrer par le chemin, il éperonna son cheval,
> lui fit franchir au saut le barbelé et continuer sur sa lancée
> jusqu'au grand mât en haut duquel flottait l'*Union Jack*. D'un
> bond il fut à terre, occupé à attacher le cheval qui en secouant
> furieusement la tête ébranla le poteau et fit trembler le drapeau
> comme sous une rafale.
> [Rather than taking the path, he pressed his horse at the barbed
> wire, jumped it, and continued at a gallop to the tall mast where
> the Union Jack was flying. In one leap he was on the ground by
> the flagpole, tying his horse which shook its head so furiously
> that the flag trembled as in a gust of wind.] (CEV 145; 112)

Roy underlines the potentially subversive power of this gesture
through her ironic representation of the teacher's nervous reaction
and the pupil's response, playing on the reference to the British
monarchy:

> L'inspecteur des écoles dont on attendait la visite d'un jour à
> l'autre, me ferait sûrement reproche de permettre ce qui pouvait
> avoir l'air d'un affront au drapeau de Sa Majesté Britannique.
> Médéric avait esquissé une moue, me donnant à entendre que
> pour lui c'était plutôt une marque d'honneur à Sa Très Britanni-
> que Majesté que d'allier son emblème à un si noble animal.
> [The school inspector, who was to visit us any day, would surely
> have something to say about what might seem like an affront to

the flag of His Britannic Majesty. Médéric had made a face, as if to say that as far as he was concerned it was an honour for His Britannic Majesty to have his emblem associated with such a noble beast.] (CEV 153; 119)

Another image that evokes the long association of education with Empire building appears in a brief comment from *Ces Enfants de ma vie*. The narrator (Roy recalling scenes from her teaching career) indicates the importance that the village schoolhouse acquired when seen from afar (as by all pupils on their daily walk to school) by describing it as "un poste, au désert, dans ses sables [like a desert fort amid the sands]" (CEV 121; 92), "poste" evoking an isolated outpost in a military campaign, or, indeed, an outpost of Empire.

Anglophone/francophone relations in the Second World

If we shift our focus from French and British colonial histories and their ongoing connection with the process of education to consider the internal relationships between those two initial settler communities from the post-Confederation period onward, different patterns of power relations come into play. But there are also some continuities. The process of colonization was still taking place across Canada in the interwar years, although the impetus, incentives, and administration were now the responsibility of the Canadian Government. There were two kinds of settlement. New immigrants (such as the Ukrainian protagonists in the title story of *Un Jardin au bout du monde*) often established homogeneous linguistic and cultural communities for a time. And migrant members of the two settler communities (such as the families in *La petite Poule d'Eau*) often built new homesteads on land where Whites had not previously lived. The language of this internal colonization also appears in Roy's representation of education, as do images associated with the pioneer.

In comparison with the autobiographical accounts discussed earlier, Roy's fictional and auto-fictional texts do not always comment specifically on the language of instruction. Signs of the anglicization of non-anglophone pupils sometimes just appear in what can seem like chance references. The stories in *Ces Enfants de ma vie* are based on Roy's time at the Institut Provencher as teacher of the reception class for non-francophone immigrants, who were taught in English. The fact that pupils always address their teacher in English is evident when one pupil visits the teacher and her mother at home on Christmas Day to deliver a gift. He greets her mother with the words "Merry Christmas, Mrs Mother teacher!" (CEV 50). References to "Santa Claus" and "Jack and Jill" illustrate not only the language of instruction but also the process of acculturation to Anglo-Canadian cultural norms that happens even within a nominally francophone school. A number of Roy's works dwell on the gulf that this process creates between immigrant parents and their children. While children who succeed at school are enabled through their education to integrate into the Canadian way of life, their parents experience forms of disempowerment and isolation. In "Le jardin au bout du monde" Martha Yaramko's dispersed, anglicized, children can only write to their Ukrainian mother in English: "Puis l'école du gouvernement les avait pris, leur enseignant l'anglais, les façonnant à sa manière pour une tout autre vie que celle qu'elle aurait pu leur apprendre. Qu'aurait-il fallu faire? ... aller aussi à l'école? [The government had taken them away, teaching them English, shaping them in its own way for a life quite different from the one she could have offered. What should she have done? ... Go to school herself?]" (JBM 137; 145). Martha relies on the Eaton's catalogue – a frequently mentioned tool of a certain kind of acculturation – as her "reader" for learning a little English, but as the narrator points out, this gives her no abstract vocabulary with which to express her sense of dislocation and loss. Newly arrived adult immigrants such as those that figure in *Ces Enfants de ma vie* are often represented as silent when any contact occurs between school and parent; in some cases, however, they pass on beautiful forms of cultural expression in their mother tongue, as when a Ukrainian child sings the songs his mother has taught him (CEV 60–1; 49–51).

When Roy chooses to represent the resistance of the francophone population of the Canadian West to the vigorous process of anglicization, apart from the references back to colonial history discussed above, it is largely signified through a mention of the teaching of grammar. Significantly, when in *La Petite Poule d'Eau* Luzina decides to reopen the schoolroom long after the last teacher, Armand Dubreuil, has left the island, two traces of his teaching remain. The map is still hanging, though now crookedly, on the wall. And the blackboard traces of his last lesson can still just be made out: "les noms ... al ... au pluriel... pendant bal, chacal ... La brosse avait entamé le reste ['Nouns ... *al* ... in the plural ... cept *bal, chacal* ...' The brush had obliterated the rest]" (PPE 107; 99). Roy evokes the teaching of grammar rules again and again as the sign of teaching in French. In "La maison gardée" André, the young pupil who has to stay at home to look after the farm while his father works through the winter in a log camp, is encouraged by his teacher to continue studying at home, leaving him "d'autres problèmes de calcul, quelques règles de grammaire, des repères en somme qui l'aideraient à travailler seul [other arithmetic problems, a few rules of grammar, some guide marks that would help him work alone]" (CEV 133–4; 103). In "De la truite dans l'eau glacée" the narrator makes a pact with Médéric in which his part of the deal involves learning various conjugations. In "Gagner ma vie" in *Rue Deschambault*, when the narrator, Christine, referring to the challenge of making her teaching appeal to the whole age range of pupils, states: "Tout devait être passionnant: l'arithmétique, le caté-chisme, la grammaire [Everything had to be absorbing – arithmetic, catechism, grammar]" (RD 253; 156). Once again, grammar is syn-onymous with the French language. And when Dubreuil asks Joséphine Tousignant what she would like as a gift when he leaves la Petite Poule d'Eau, the girl asks him to give her his grammar book, the symbol of her desire to continue her education.

Teaching aboriginal and Métis children

While relationships between anglophone Canada and its franco-phone minority or its newly arrived immigrants from Europe show the crucial role of language in the processes of assimilation to the dominant culture and resistance to that culture's total domination, it is in Roy's treatment of the schooling of aboriginal and Métis children that education and colonialism are the most intertwined. In *La Montagne secrète* Steve Sigurdsen, friend of the artist protag-onist Pierre Cadorai, sets off in search of supplies across a frozen lake toward an Indian reserve: "Cela voulait dire une mission, par conséquence une école du gouvernement, et par suite quelque Blanc là-bas, maître ou maîtresse d'école, et sans doute quelque petite pharmacie de secours [That meant a mission, consequently a gov-ernment school, and therefore some White or other there, school-master or school mistress, and doubtless some little first aid post]"

(MS 49). The combination of references to the "mission" and the "gouvernement" indicates the coexistence of different stages of colonial contact throughout the Canadian north. Yet despite Sigurdsen's familiarity with the infiltration of White culture in the north, the schoolhouse – complete with desks, map, and stove – is represented through his eyes as incongruous, an improbable mirage from another, southern, world, "aussi fantastique que certains croquis de Pierre [as fantastical as some of Pierre's sketches]" (MS 50).

Attitudes expressed by Roy's protagonists toward educational provision for the aboriginal population range from missionary-like enthusiasm to what can only be read as racism in the case of Luzina in *La Petite Poule d'Eau*. She is shown to feel that her own children's lack of school provision is all the more unjust because a school is provided on an Indian reserve some miles away: "Même les enfants des sauvages étaient mieux partagés que les siens; ils avaient une école, disait Luzina [Even the Indian children had a better portion than her own; they had a school, Luzina would say]" (PPE 36; 30).[54] Equally, it is only when the number of her own children no longer warrants summer teaching that she makes a visit to Métis neighbours to persuade them to send their children to "her" school.[55]

Métis attitudes to education, on the other hand, are explored in some detail. The term "Métis" can be applied to characters in very different circumstances in Roy's work. It can denote an individual born of one First Nations parent and one wealthy White parent – as in the example of Médéric Aymard in "De la truite dans l'eau glacée" – or, in the very different case of Jimmy, to a child born as a result of his Inuit mother's rape by an American GI. It also applies to a community of many generations, such as the Métis population who lived in Manitoba at the time of its entry into Confederation, as in the case of the Métis village in *Cet été qui chantait*. In "L'Enfant morte" the reader is introduced to the population via the school register, in such a way as to emphasize the naivety of the narrator's younger self:

"C'étaient pour la plupart des noms bien français et aujourd'hui encore il m'en revient à la mémoire, comme cela, sans raison: Madeleine Bérubé, Joséphat Brisset, Emilien Dumont, Cécile Lépine ...

Mais les enfants qui se levaient à tour de rôle, leur nom appelé, pour répondre: "Présent, mam'zelle ..." avaient presque tous les yeux légèrement bridés, le teint chaud et les cheveux très noirs qui disent le sang métis.

[The names were for the most part very French and today they still return to my memory, like this, for no reason: Madeleine Bérubé, Josephat Brisset, Emilien Dumont, Cécile Lépine...

But most of the children who rose and answered "Present, mamzelle," when their names were called had the slightly narrowed eyes, warm colouring and jet black hair that told of Métis blood.] (CE 144; 112)[56]

For this village population in southern Manitoba, despite its relative isolation and poverty, school attendance, Catholicism, and the French language are the norm. But further north, the Métis who still live a partly nomadic lifestyle with a number of seasonal lodgings are represented as being far more hostile to compulsory school attendance. As the narrator of *La Petite Poule d'Eau* explains: "Les métis se souciaient d'une école comme d'une prison, d'un cachot muni de barreaux [The half-breeds regarded school as something like prison, a dungeon complete with bars]" (PPE 132; 124).

The association between the Métis figure and the desire for freedom reappears strongly in the representation of Médéric, again expressed in the context of compulsory schooling. Rather as in the case of Jimmy in *La Rivière sans repos,* Médéric is shown to be torn between two cultures. His white father uses the law as a threat against him, relying on an authority above his own parental authority to enforce school attendance – "Il a la loi de son côté [He's got the law on his side]" (CEV 157; 122). But his First Nations mother, who, we are told, has left her husband and son to return to her tribe, symbolizes, by her absence, a freer lifestyle. For the protagonist/narrator, the mother is associated rather stereotypically with "l'innocence primitive [primitive innocence]" (CEV 203; 159). Médéric is represented in the narrator's memory as a challenge to her authority (not wanting to be in school) but also as a temptation. What on one level is a struggle between the teacher (representing the educational institution) and the Métis adolescent becomes on another level a study of the erotic desire between the Métis male and the White woman. The ambivalence of the power relationship between teacher and pupil is played out in a number of classroom scenes in which the teacher first encourages physical and emotional contact and then retreats into her official role. In this light the trip made by the pair on horseback into the hills represents a flight back to nature and a tentative expression of desire. The ending of the story would seem to bring a return to order as the teacher moves on from this post to take up a safer, urban posting, and Médéric, having reached the end of compulsory schooling, moves beyond the pupil-teacher bond. Yet the ambivalence of the text lingers in the reader's mind. On one level the representation of the Métis boy as an object of desire confirms the will of dominant white culture to absorb and control the Other. Yet the strength of that mutual desire and the scenes of flight and erotic fantasy change the terms of the relationship between teacher and pupil, and so subvert the power of the educational system in its neo-colonial role.

It is perhaps in *La Rivière sans repos* that compulsory school attendance is represented most ambivalently. Elsa, the mother of a half-white child, has moved away from the westernized village of Fort Chimo that has grown up around the Hudson's Bay store and government administration. In an attempt to teach her son traditional Inuit ways, Elsa has moved to the old Inuit village where she is teaching him to read English herself. Roch Beaulieu, the local policeman, and husband of her former employer, crosses to the old settlement to remind Elsa of her responsibilities toward the Anglo-Canadian system: "C'est qu'il y avait une loi, finit-il par expliquer, exigeant la fréquentation scolaire dès l'âge qu'avait à présent Jimmy. Il faudrait reprendre logis de l'autre côté de la Koksoak et envoyer l'enfant à l'école régulière [There was a law, he finally explained, requiring attendance at school from the age Jimmy had now reached]" (RSR 177; 88). The narrative shows the change that this effects in the relationship between Beaulieu and Elsa, focalizing on Elsa from a White perspective as she becomes resistant: "Un peu de temps écoulé, il porta de nouveau le regard vers Elsa. Le large visage, toute amabilité et naïve amitié un instant auparavant, était de pierre [When a brief time had slipped by, he looked again at Elsa. The broad face, all amiability and naive friendliness an instant before, was of stone]" (RSR 177; 89). In the journalistic piece that Roy wrote after her trip to Ungava in 1961, she raised the question of the incompatibility between the Canadian school system and the patterns of nomadism in the sub-Arctic zone: "Une école, cela suppose des gens fixes, une sorte de village [a school presupposes people being settled, some sort of a village]."[57] She points out that there are models better adapted to nomadic habits, citing the case of Greenland, where the provision of intensive summer schools allows parents to continue with their nomadic lifestyle throughout the winter months. In the literary representation of Fort Chimo in *La Rivière sans repos,* Elsa attempts to escape from an inflexible system, setting off with her uncle and son to Baffin Island, beyond the reach of the law. But the attempt ends in failure. Quite how we are to read this attempted escape is open to debate. In some ways it expresses a love of freedom, a woman's choice to educate her son as she chooses. But the escape is associated with two developments that seem to undermine such motives. An act of incest takes place between Elsa and her uncle, apparently connected with the return to the more traditional nomadic life, and almost as an act of retribution, Jimmy falls ill. At this point the three of them return to Fort Chimo where "White" medical treatment soon cures Elsa's son. He then begins to attend school. By associating the flight with the incestuous act and with the subsequent illness, is the narrative condemning Elsa's resistance to White Canadian control, or is it testing White readers' taboos?

Roy's representation of schooling in *La Rivière sans repos* is not unrelievedly tragic, but there are other touches of criticism of the system. The absurdity of the curriculum's not being adapted to Inuit pupils is conveyed comically in a scene where a child repeats: "des bribes d'étranges leçons apprises à l'école, comme par exemple: Le chat ronronne. Or de chat, ici, personne n'en avait jamais vu [scraps of strange lessons learned at school, such as: The cat purrs. A cat no one hereabouts had ever seen]" (RSR 103; 10). Alternatively the use of focalization through Elsa allows the exploration of the sense of intimidation she feels when summoned to school to discuss her son's absences: "un large bâtiment superbe ... les salles de classe brillantes derrière leur paroi de verre comme des abris pour la culture de plantes délicates [a splendid spacious building ... classrooms that looked as bright behind their walls of glass as shelters for the nurture of delicate plants]. But the gap between her and the "government" school leaves her feeling "trop craintive et inquiète pour admirer à son gré [too fearful and anxious to admire them as she might have liked]" (RSR 211; 122). Like Luzina, her sense of cultural inferiority means that she is unable to criticize education policy directly, but encourages Jimmy back to school with the words: "une si belle école! Si gaie, si bien éclairée! Qui a coûté si cher au gouvernement qui nous gouverne [Such a lovely school! So gay, so bright! That has cost the great government that governs us so much money!]" (RSR 212; 123). The ambivalence of this narrative allows the reader to see contradictions that result from the application of Second World institutions in the Fourth World. Unlike the journalistic account "Voyage en Ungava," *La Rivière sans repos* offers no route beyond the contradiction, all involved being damaged by the process. Jimmy, educated alongside white pupils until they go south to pursue their education in the higher grades, rejects the school once they leave: "ce n'était qu'une école pour Esquimaux [It was just a school for Eskimos]" (RSR 212; 123).[58] In fact, Elsa's fears are proven right. The school system does indeed separate her son from her and dislocate his sense of identity as he learns only to value White culture and company, and rejects the Inuit part of his heritage.

What is particularly interesting about Roy's exploration of the impact of cultural contact between Whites and Inuit in Ungava is the layering of successive waves of colonial contact in the narrative, which produces contradictory effects within the text. In addition to the assimilationist education policies of postwar Canada, we find clear traces of colonial/missionary contact in the presence of the Catholic and Protestant missions and evidence of United States imperialism, all of which have also become part of Elsa's own story. As seen earlier in this chapter, religion and literacy went hand in hand in early colonial contact. In the case of the Inuit population this happened less through organized schooling than through individual contact. In *La Rivière sans repos* books are the sign of one such form of contact, the relationship between George Black, employee of the Hudson's Bay Company many years earlier, and Elsa's uncle's family, to whom Black left his books. So when Elsa takes her son to live in the old village, although she is retreating from White, Anglo-Canadian culture, she finds her uncle Ian's rich collection of books. Having herself attended school and church while living on the other side of the river, she now has access to these works of English literature and illustrated Bible stories. Elsa reads to her uncle and son:

Dans la cabane ils avaient réussi à faire place à une caisse de bois qui servait de table et autour de laquelle ils s'assemblaient.

Du plafond pendait la lampe. Sa lueur captait le brillant des yeux tout en laissant dans l'ombre la grossièreté du logis ... Elsa entreprit de lire à voix haute *Ivanhoé*.
[They had managed to find space for a wooden crate to serve as a table and around this they used to gather. The lamp hung from the ceiling. Its glow caught the brightness of their eyes while leaving the roughness of the cabin in shadow ... Elsa undertook to read *Ivanhoe* aloud.] (RSR 166; 76)[59]

The scene presents the reading as a ceremony, the "caisse de bois" acting as part teacher's desk, part altar. The positive way in which all three generations respond to their (re-) discovery of English literature can be interpreted as a nostalgic attachment to the first wave of colonial contact, but an attachment that acts out the learned respect for the culture of the British Empire.

Roy's teacher figures

These readings of the representation of education in Roy's texts, fictional and auto-fictional, have tended so far to situate the teacher within the ongoing processes of settlement, assimilation, and acculturation. This is in part because of the choice of settings. Most of Roy's teacher figures (herself included) are shown to be taking education and language to those who are on the margins of the dominant culture, either geographically (in Northern Canada or in rural Manitoba) or in terms of culture or ethnicity (Métis children and allophone immigrants' children in Saint-Boniface). This representation tends to emphasize the teacher's identification with the dominant culture, and the distance between the culture he or she represents and the home culture of the pupils. It also situates the teacher as an agent of the process of acculturation. In *Ces enfants de ma vie* the narrator's reference to her pupils as "mes petits immigrants [my little immigrants]" (CEV 21; 9) echoes the way in which the father of Christine, the narrator in *Rue Deschambault*, while reminiscing about his work as colonizing agent in the Canadian West, refers to *his* immigrant families as "ses 'Petits-Ruthènes' [his 'Little Ruthenians']" (RD 125; 73).

The narrative viewpoint is also a determining factor in the ways the teacher is represented. When the narrative adopts the position of those who are culturally less powerful or marginalized in some

way, the teacher is seen as a figure of authority. So, for example, in
La Petite Poule d'Eau the narrator describes the third teacher,
Armand Dubreuil, from the perspective of Luzina's husband,
Hippolyte: "Il ne se reconnaissait pas le courage lui non plus
d'adresser des réprimandes ouvertes à l'éducation personnifiée [Yet
he couldn't find the courage, either, openly to reprimand education
personified]" (PPE 98). Luzina herself feels intimidated by the presence of all three teachers sent to teach her children, whether
because of her poor grasp of English, her imperfect command of
French grammar, or her level of general knowledge (forgetting the
name of the current Governor General, Lord Tweedsmuir).[60] In *La
Montagne secrète*, Steve Sigurdsen recounts to Pierre Cadorai the
officious behaviour of the schoolmistress, from whom he begs some
coloured pencils for Pierre. Although his account is disrespectful, he
clearly describes her in terms of her position of authority: "La
bougresse de maîtresse d'école avait fait toutes sortes d'histoires
avant de les lui céder ... 'Ses petits Indiens en avaient besoin. Cela ne
se donnait pas sans autorisation. C'était propriété de la mission...
Tout un tralala!' [The damned school mistress had made all kinds
of excuses before letting him have them ... 'Her little Indians needed
them. They could not be handed over without authorization. They
were the property of the mission ... What a fuss!]" (MS 51).

Roy's works also show the psychological process of becoming a
teacher. In some cases a third person narrator comments on the subjective process. In an example from *La Petite Poule d'Eau*, the
narrator, with a touch of ironic detachment points out the transformation that the young Joséphine Tousignant will undergo on her
path to becoming a teacher: "Quelque chose d'étrange poussait
aujourd'hui au cœur de Joséphine. Sa grande amitié pour le monde
allait déjà de préférence aux infortunés, aux ignorants que plus tard
elle aurait la mission d'éduquer [Today something strange was
gnawing at Josephine's heart. Her great affection for all humanity
was already fastening especially on the unfortunate, the ignorant
whom it would later be her mission to teach]" (PPE 124; 115–16).[61]
The use of the phrase "quelque chose d'étrange" in combination
with the word "cœur" suggests that the process of interiorization of
others' values is necessarily a part of the training process. While to
an outsider, the identification of the teacher with the dominant culture that he or she is deemed to represent may seem self-evident, the
teacher, being placed between higher authorities and the pupils in

the classroom, may well experience no such simple identification. Equally, the power relationship between teacher and pupil, rather than being a cultural given, is explored by Roy in different and more complex ways.

Both *La Petite Poule d'Eau* and *Ces enfants de ma vie* look at the way in which a teacher establishes a bond with a class of children. As Mlle Côté arrives on the Tousignants' island, the narrative briefly moves toward her perspective: "Son regard se porta sur les enfants [Her glance fell upon the children]" (PPE 64; 58). What she reads in their eyes is a mixture of emotions: "Tous ces yeux fixés sur la maîtresse montraient en ce moment la même expression d'angoisse amoureuse. Même les plus petits ... hésitaient entre la crainte et la confiance [All these eyes, fastened upon the schoolmistress, displayed at that instant the same expression of loving anguish. Even the smallest of them ... hesitated between fear and trust]" (PPE 65; 58). Similarly in *Ces enfants de ma vie*, a young Italian boy attaches himself passionately to his teacher on the first day of school: "Il tremblait de cet anxieux grand bonheur qui s'était abattu sur lui, bien petit encore pour en supporter l'intensité ... Faute de savoir me dire son sentiment, il s'abîma, comme on dit, à me manger des yeux [He was trembling from this anxious but great happiness that had descended on him and found himself still too small to bear its intensity ... And for lack of ability to tell me what he felt, he gave himself up totally to consuming me with his eyes]" (CEV 30; 17). In both texts Roy uses the verb "apprivoiser [tame]" (CEV 22; 10; PPE 65; 58) in conjunction with animal and bird imagery in her descriptions of pupils. The Tousignant children are likened to "des faons qu'un seul geste peut faire fuir, mais qu'une petite caresse pourrait apprivoiser [fawns which a single movement could put to flight but which the least caress could tame]" (PPE 65; 58), and pupils in *Ces enfants de ma vie* are described by the narrator variously as "cabri [goat]" (CEV 52; 35), "petits animaux à fourrure [furry little animals]" (CEV 43; 27), "de vraies petites pies [real little magpies]" (CEV 115; 87), "un animal ombrageux [a skittish animal]" (CEV 152; 118), or "un lévrier [a greyhound]" (CEV 198; 155). As this use of animal imagery suggests, teacher figures are generally shown as being able both to initiate and to control the feelings of affection of their pupils. The language used to evoke the bond between pupil and teacher constructs the teacher at times as mother figure, seductress, enchantress, or role model. In *Ces enfants de ma vie*, the narrator describes Clair's adoring gaze: "Il restait sagement assis à sa place à me suivre des yeux dans la joie comme si déjà c'était là pour lui une récompense [He would stay quite still in his place and follow me around with his eyes, totally happy, as if that was already his reward]" (CEV 34; 20). In the same story another pupil, Nikolaï, is referred to as "amoureux de moi [in love with me]" (CEV 38; 23). In "Vincento" the narrator describes her class as "enchantée [delighted]" (CEV 27; 14); in "De la truite dans l'eau glacée" she notes: "Mes tout petits élèves me dévoraient de leurs yeux brillants d'amour [My smallest pupils devoured me with their eyes all shining with love]" (CEV 204; 160), commenting that perhaps one has to have been a teacher in a one-room prairie school to understand what she experienced: "le sentiment d'une incroyable emprise sur les enfants [the feeling of having an incredible hold over the children]" (CEV 214; this phrase is omitted in the English translation). While for pupils the teacher may be an object of love – adoration, even – for parents, the teacher can represent a rival who will inevitably distance their child from them as the transfer of identification takes place.

Whereas in Roy's accounts of her own schooling the educative process is driven by desire for academic achievement and a successful transition to a bicultural identity, the motives of her teacher figures vary. In *La Petite Poule d'Eau* the process of education does indeed lead to academic success for most of the children and to a consequent distancing between the children's home culture and their acquired culture, as they move away to follow their careers. In *Ces enfants de ma vie*, the most overtly autobiographical of these texts, the focus is on a rather different kind of influence. Each child, as Agnès Whitfield has argued, undergoes a process of transformation as the teacher reveals and then develops in him or her a special kind of gift. In many cases these are artistic gifts, not strictly related to the process of acculturation to the English language and Anglo-Canadian culture; indeed, in some cases the narrator suggests an association with the home culture of their immigrant parents. In the case of the youngest Demetrioff child, whose gift is for calligraphy, or Nil, the Ukrainian child with a wonderful singing voice, the encouragement of these gifts results not in a distancing between parent and child but in a scene of shared pleasure and pride experienced by parent and teacher as the child performs. However temporary this sense of reconciliation may be, its impact in the narrative is to suggest, at least, the possibility of individual liberation through creativity. Whitfield reads this focus on the teacher's part in the individual transformation and liberation of the young male as a way of addressing obliquely the problematic trajectory of the female artist.[62] It can also be seen as a way of transcending or bypassing the negative aspects of the educative process and the teacher's implication within it, and it represents the positive pole of Roy's representations of the teacher.

Another key aspect of Roy's representation of her schooling was the sense of performance, of role-playing, that both pupil and teacher needed to learn in order to play to their different audiences, notably the anglophone and francophone inspectors and visitors. This sense of the teacher as performer is also present in her fictional works, reminding the reader that the identification between teacher and dominant culture is far from stable. In "Gagner la vie" in *Rue Deschambault*, Christine refers to the need constantly to perform for the class: "Ils me firent monter sur la corde raide, et quand j'y fus, ils ne me permirent plus d'en descendre [They made me mount a tightrope, and once there, they never let me down]" (RD 253; 156). Significantly, it is the older male pupils whom the young female teacher finds the most challenging, as they make her all the more aware of her youth and her gender. In *Ces enfants de ma vie* the final story in the volume, "De la truite dans l'eau glacée" goes the furthest toward upsetting the hierarchical relationship between pupil and teacher. The narrator, as if in justification of her failure to enforce her will on her adolescent pupil, stresses her youth in comparison with his developing maturity: "Et je laissai faire, car que faire! J'avais dix-huit ans, et lui s'en allait sur quatorze. Il me dépassait aisément d'une tête et sans doute dans bien des choses de la vie [And I let him continue; what could I do? I was eighteen and he was going on fourteen. He was easily a head taller than I and no doubt at least that far ahead of me in other aspects of life]" (CEV 146; 114).[63] The effect of the teacher's confusion between her teachering role and her sexual identity is to destabilize the narrator's identification with her official role. When, toward the end of the story, the narrator finally tells Médéric that she cannot go riding with him again in his father's carriage, or return to the Babcock Hills, she speaks as a teacher: "Je m'ennuie nullement à ma tâche, Médéric. Elle est toute ma vie. Toute ma passion. Elle me suffit complètement [I'm not at all bored by my work, Médéric. It's my whole life. The only passion I have. It's quite enough for me]" (CEV 199–200; 157). But the preceding narrative shows that her identification with her role as teacher is in fact far more problematic: "Je me fis aussi maîtresse d'école que possible [I tried to be as schoolmarmish as possible]" (CEV 199; 156). The reason this text is seen by critics to be perhaps the most disturbing of her representations of the pupil-teacher relationship is that both the desire that the teacher inspires in this pupil and her feelings toward him slip into the erotic.

By comparing the female narrator of this text with one of the few male teachers represented in Roy's work, another layer of significance emerges, a layer that suggests a deep ambivalence toward the teacher's social and cultural role. In *La Petite Poule d'Eau*, the third teacher to visit the Tousignant home, Armand Dubreuil, is comically represented through Luzina's eyes as a variation on the colonial figure: "Elle vit en effet s'avancer une curieuse silhouette surmontée d'un casque colonial, en chemise de flanelle à carreaux rouges et grosses bottes huilées, chargée de tout un attirail meurtrier, petites et grandes carabines [She saw advancing toward her an odd silhouette topped with a colonial helmet, wearing a red-checked flannel shirt and heavy oiled boots; he was laden with an armoury of weapons, rifles large and small]" (PPE 93; 86). He sees northern Manitoba as his private game reserve, and neglects his teaching duties because he enjoys shooting and reading. His pedagogical approach contrasts with the formality and routine of his predecessors; he believes that children should learn from nature and enjoy leisure, and leaves them with a wealth of tales of explorers to read aloud in the long evenings. An ambiguous figure, Dubreuil leaves the island early, having been offered a principal's post. Yet as he leaves he tells Luzina she should close her school, privately questioning the point of education: "Qu'est-ce qui sortirait bien de tout cela? Du mécontentement d'abord qui est à la source de tout progrès. Et puis après? [What, indeed, would come of it? Discontent first of all, which lies at the root of all progress. And afterward?]" (PPE 105; 98).

A similar degree of ambivalence emerges from "De la truite dans l'eau glacée," where the Métis figure is used to explore the tension between nature and culture. Médéric is quite explicitly represented as the embodiment of the culture/nature split. His father is portrayed as a sexually crude drunkard determined to mould his son according to White patriarchal culture. He wants Médéric to avoid sexual contact with First Nations girls, whom he labels as "aguichantes et précoces [enticing, know a lot for their age]" (CEV 185; 145), and suggests he wait for "la petite maîtresse d'école, qui nous descend, autant dire, quelque beau jour, du ciel [our little schoolteacher, who drops down from heaven, you might say, one fine day]" (CEV 185; 145). The schoolmistress, as White, educated outsider, is seen by Rodrigue Eymard as the antidote to his own ignorance and lack of sexual control, an antidote, in fact, to métissage. He provided his wife with every material comfort, but, as he phrases it: "Eh bien entre cela et la tribu, c'est la tente, c'est la tribu qu'elle a choisie [Well, between that and the tribe, it was the wigwam, the reservation, she chose]" (CEV 184; 144). Despite the teacher's function in the school to impose patriarchal, White values, her attraction to Médéric and her excursions with him in the surrounding prairie landscape represent a form of resistance as she identifies not with the paternal influence but with the maternal, First Nations figure. While the teacher in her wants to encourage Médéric to read widely and to learn his French grammar, she identifies erotically with his desire for freedom. Just as in *La Petite Poule d'Eau*, however, the nature/culture opposition is resolved by a return to the dominant order, as the narrator leaves the village at the end of the school year to take up a more prestigious post in town. As Médéric appears on horseback to offer her a parting gift of wild flowers, her last image of him, from the train window, frames him against "le vaste pays vide tout autour [the vast country empty all around him]" (CEV 216; 170), as she is carried back to urban civilization.

In contrast to Roy's accounts of her own schooldays, where the tensions and contradictions of her bicultural education are addressed explicitly, these fictional and auto-fictional representations of the teacher figure seem initially to avoid the topic. But a number of these texts do explore the problematic relationship of the teacher to the teacher's role within an ideological climate that sees acculturation to Anglo-Canadian values as the norm. In Roy's case, her success in becoming bilingual and bicultural was arguably more a source of pleasure and a promise of future escape than a handicap. But her writings reveal an awareness of the educational process as a means of inculcating new values and distancing children from their home culture, and a recognition of the power of the teacher to inspire children to admire and imitate the roles that they perform. What appears again and again in her teacher figures is a sense of their operating within a field of opposing ideological currents, between different pedagogical trends, or at the interface between the establishment and marginalized ethnic and cultural groups. Roy's texts both trace the power relations at work within the schoolroom and explore the encounters that result from such cultural diversity. It is the nature of the linguistic encounter, in the school and beyond, that will be the subject of the next chapter.

3

Bilingualism, Diglossia, and the Other's Language

In 1943 Gabrielle Roy wrote, somewhat provocatively: "Le plus grand bien qu'on ait fait aux Canadiens français de l'Ouest, c'est peut-être d'avoir obligé leurs enfants à apprendre l'anglais [Perhaps the greatest favour that has been done to French-Canadians in the west is to have required their children to learn English]."[1] As she explains in her article in the *Bulletin des Agriculteurs*, in her view it was only by mastering English that she and her fellow Franco-Manitobans could avoid remaining in a position of servitude in relation to anglophones. Yet Roy's personal identification with English language and culture was far more complex than this pragmatic argument might suggest. Her bilingualism left a variety of traces in her works and had a profound impact on her relationship to language in general.[2]

BETWEEN LANGUAGES: FRENCH AND ENGLISH IN *LA DÉTRESSE ET L'ENCHANTEMENT*

Roy's bilingual and bicultural education had resulted from the very unequal power relations between French and English language groups, the source of which can be traced back to the secession of French territory to the British after the defeat of 1759. Indeed, the relationships that have developed among languages in Canada in the course of its colonial history and the post-colonial era are a symptom of what Robert Young has termed "the commerce between cultures that map and shadow the complexities of [the] generative and destructive processes [of colonialism]."[3] Although Canada is now officially bilingual, the relationship between the languages spoken by its founding populations retains the marks of inequality.[4] The imbalance in prestige associated with languages has given rise to two quite distinct types of bilingualism – additive and subtractive bilingualism. Additive bilingualism refers to the acquisition by speakers whose first language is a prestigious language of a second, socially relevant language. Subtractive bilingualism, on the other hand, refers to the process whereby members of a minority linguistic group "are forced to shift away from their ethnic language towards a national language, by national educational policies and various social pressures." This type of bilingualism can lead to difficulty in maintaining the minority language.[5]

The efforts of the Association d'Education des Canadiens-Français du Manitoba discussed in chapters 1 and 2 can be understood as a response to the situation of subtractive bilingualism in that province. The relationship between English and French in the period when Roy was being educated and later worked as a teacher in Manitoba is an example of diglossia, which is characterized by Rainier Grutman as follows: "From the moment when a group systematically uses one language to the detriment of another, a conflictual relationship becomes apparent between language varieties, commonly termed *diglossia*."[6] This particular relationship is binary and hierarchical. But as different languages come into play in different linguistic contexts, the binary shifts. In Manitoba in 1930, for example, French was the lower language in the pair English/French, but the higher language in the pair French/Inuktitut or French/Cree. For francophone Canadians the linguistic context is often plurilingual, producing a multi-layered, hierarchical relationship among languages and varieties of language. In a study of language status in nineteenth-century Quebec, Henri Gobard found that Quebec French, metropolitan French, English, and Latin each had a different domain with a different level of prestige (from the domestic, to the public, to the official, and to the ceremonial or religious).[7] This situation, effectively tetraglossia, can be regarded as an archaeological site of the linguistic contact that resulted from the experience of colonization in Quebec.

The impact of such hierarchical relationships on individual language use is evident in territories that have been subject to colonization, whether as colonies of exploitation or colonies of settlement. Writing of the very different colonial situation in Kenya, Ngugi Wa Thiong'o has commented on the way in which colonial subjects have always been measured by their performance against the cultural and linguistic norms of the dominant language: "Any achievement in spoken or written English was highly rewarded; prizes, prestige, applause; the ticket to higher realms. English became the measure of intelligence and ability in the arts, the sciences, and all other branches of learning. English became the main determinant of a child's progress up the ladder of formal education."[8] It is of course important to recognize the difference between Roy's situation as part of a population of "colons colonisés [colonized colonizers]" and that of the colonized indigenous population of Kenya. Nevertheless, the need to perform well in the colonizer's language does link these two cases. Roy experienced similar pressure to excel in English. As a student at the Winnipeg Normal School she was advised by the principal, Dr McIntyre, of the need to excel at both English and French:

Travaillez votre français. Soyez-lui toujours fidèle. Enseignez-le quand l'heure viendra, autant que vous le pourrez ... sans vous faire prendre. Mais n'oubliez pas que vous devez être excellente en anglais aussi. Les minorités ont ceci de tragique, elles doivent être supérieures ... ou disparaître.
[Work at your French. Always be faithful to it. Teach it when you get the chance and as much as you can ... without getting caught. But don't forget, you'll have to excel in English too. The tragic thing about minorities is that they have to be better, or disappear.] (DE 85; 65)

In her late twenties Roy left Manitoba to travel to Europe (both France and Britain, twin centres of Empire) with the intention of studying drama. She then returned to Canada to settle in Quebec in 1939. This itinerary gives an indication of the lasting sense of inferiority that Roy had internalized as a Franco-Manitoban in regard to her own linguistic and cultural formation. The journey to France is a common theme in Franco-Canadian writing; its motivation is often the desire to compensate for a cultural lack by returning to the linguistic and cultural motherland.[9] But significantly in Roy's case, the cultural lack was double; the European trip was a response to her *bi*-cultural, colonial education. As members of former settler communities, both anglophone and francophone Canadians have a relationship to language that is marked by displacement. As

Stephen Slemon explains, Canada's status as a former *settler* colony has resulted in "its ambivalent position within the First-World/Third-World, colonizer/colonized binary."[10] The ambivalence of this position is exemplified in the relationship to language of the ex-colonial settler populations.

In "Unhiding the Hidden" the anglophone Canadian writer Robert Kroetsch writes: "The Canadian writer's particular predicament is that he works with a language, within a literature, that appears to be authentically his own, and not a borrowing."[11] Similarly, for francophone Canadians the French language both is and is not their own; the norms and cultural heritage associated with the French language have been set elsewhere, in France. This means that the language of the francophone minority is doubly marked as inferior: it is inferior in the diglossic relationship between English and French in Canada and it is inferior as a result of the former colonial relationship with France. Lise Gauvin argues that this problematic relationship to language is one of the origins of what she terms "the writer's hyperconsciousness of language."[12] In the case of most francophone Canadian writers, as with Roy, this is a relationship not just with one, but with two or more languages. The complex relationships that are played out between languages, as they come into contact in differing relationships of exchange or of power, heighten the writer's awareness of language. This heightened awareness in turn affects the ways in which bilingual writers then use language, as they are consciously performing in a linguistic context: "Then writing becomes a real 'language act.'"[13]

In Roy's case, her decision to write in her mother tongue, having been immersed in English language and culture, and having lived in both English and French – and in England and France as well as Canada – meant that her relationship to the French language had an element of strangeness or foreignness. As Celia Britton writes in her study of Edouard Glissant: "One's language can no longer be experienced as that naively and unreflectively *single* all-encompassing environment connoted by the expression 'mother tongue.'"[14] Roy's hyper-awareness of language meant that her choice of French as her language of literary expression was perhaps more complex a decision than it might first appear. Her choice of French does not imply an outright rejection of English as the language of assimilation, the language of Empire. Nor is it what Rainier Grutman refers to as "linguistic loyalty," a defensive mechanism that "relates to language as nationalism relates to nationality."[15] Indeed, although she chose to settle in Quebec, Roy was critical of the discourse of Quebec separatism, typified as it was by the equation of language and identity. She remained sympathetic to a federalist Canada and was a speaker, reader, and writer of English until her death in 1983.[16] Her correspondence with Joyce Marshall, written in English, reflects their shared concerns about *Bill 101* and its implications for anglophones in Quebec. Roy's response to the policies of the Parti Québécois is clearly influenced by her Manitoba upbringing, of which she saw an inverse image in Quebec in the late 1970s. She wrote to Marshall: "The madness may pass over. Or deposit hatred on both sides which would last almost forever. I was brought up in much the same atmosphere. I dread it like the worst evil."[17] Her political position reflects both her concern for the francophone minorities outside Quebec, whose future within a Canada minus Quebec seemed terminally threatened, and her identification with anglophones who, like Marshall, were born in Quebec and had no wish to live in a Canada without Quebec.

If Roy's bilingualism and biculturalism meant that she saw some of the cultural and political dangers of equating language with identity, her ability to work with both languages and move between languages also had an impact on her as a writer. Glissant's reflections are pertinent: "Today, even when a writer knows no other language, he takes into account, whether knowingly or not, the existence of these languages around him in the process of writing. One can no longer write a language in a monolingual way."[18] There are some, he continues, who refuse to recognize the plurilingual reality of the modern world "either because they are restricted by the dominant status of their own language: such is the case for citizens of the USA; or because they are asserting their own language in an angry, monolingual manner: this is the case for some defenders of creole. It is also the case for some defenders of the French language in Québec, driven to this by their situation. This blinds them to the real state of the world, what I call chaos-world, these marvelous encounters and clashes between languages."[19]

Roy's underlying suspicion of any definition of identity in purely linguistic terms complicates the ways in which she uses and discusses language in her account of her early life. For a bilingual Franco-Manitoban, a product of a society of *colons colonisés*, identity formation is a double process. In *Peau noire, masques blancs*,

Frantz Fanon states: "To speak a language is to take on a world, a culture."[20] Roy "took on" two worlds. But what does this mean in terms of the way she writes about language and the way she uses language(s)? Since bilingualism and biculturalism were so intetgral to her understanding of who she was and where she was from, how did she write about her bilingual self? Or did her writing in her "mother" tongue erase her bilingual and bicultural cultural identity? And to what extent does her work represent an opening up to the language of the Other? In order to consider these questions from two different angles, I begin this chapter with an analysis of *La Détresse et l'enchantement*, published posthumously in 1984. My aim is to assess the ways in which Roy's bilingualism can be traced both thematically and at the level of the text. I continue by examining the representation of linguistic encounters and linguistic difference in a range of Roy's fictional and auto-fictional works.

Roy devoted much of the last years of her life to her autobiography. According to François Ricard, the two parts that were to constitute *La Détresse et l'enchantement* were written between the end of May 1977 and October 1980.[21] A second, much shorter, piece, *Le Temps qui m'a manqué*, a fragment of a projected continuation but largely complete in itself, was published in 1997, and *Le Pays de* Bonheur d'occasion, a volume including a number of shorter autobiographical pieces, some previously published, appeared in 2000. The discussion that follows draws exclusively on the first and best known of these volumes.

The first part of *La Détresse et l'enchantement* is set in Manitoba before Roy's departure for Europe (this part includes reflections on her family origins, her education, her teaching career, and her involvement in amateur dramatics). The second part recounts the period she spent in France and England between 1937 and 1939 and her ultimate decision to become a writer. Two key moments in the text signal an overriding concern with linguistic identity. The first is positioned at the opening of the autobiography, so flagging a central theme and offering ostensibly the prime motivation for writing: "Quand donc ai-je pris conscience pour la première fois que j'étais, dans mon pays, d'une espèce destinée à être traitée en inférieure? [When did it first dawn on me that I was one of those people destined to be treated as inferiors in their own country?]" The passage continues with references to the shopping excursions she made with her mother to the anglophone capital ("Winnipeg ...

qui jamais ne nous reçut tout à fait autrement qu'en étrangères [Winnipeg ... never really received us otherwise than as foreigners]"), stressing their sense of "dépaysement, de pénétrer, à deux pas seulement de chez nous, dans le lointain [crossing a border and being in a strange place, light years away but right next door to home]" (DE 11; 3).[22] The relationship between language and identity, a relationship that is at once personal, linking Roy with her mother, and collective, extending to include the Franco-Manitoban minority, is placed at the heart of the autobiographical project. The repetition of collective terms and the plural first person pronoun introduces "nous," "les nôtres," "nos gens" [we, our folks, our people] as the apparent "subject" of the autobiography, linking Roy and her mother to a maternal line of descent that has experienced successive periods of displacement, dispossession, and oppression. Yet from the very first few lines the reader can detect a degree of ambivalence, a slight dissociation between the young girl (who found the crossing of the divide between francophone and anglophone territory rather pleasurable) and the entrenched minority on whose behalf she claims to write: "Je crois qu'elle [cette sensation de dépaysement] m'ouvrait les yeux, stimulait mon imagination, m'entraînait à observer [I think it opened my eyes, trained me to observe things and stimulated my imagination]" (DE 11; 3).

A second key moment recalls Roy's realization that she will from now on write only in French:

Or, cette histoire que j'avais découverte m'attendant au réveil et qui venait si bien, elle me venait dans les mots de ma langue française. Pour moi qui avais parfois pensé que j'aurais intérêt à écrire en anglais, qui m'y étais essayée avec un certain succès, qui avais tergiversé, tout à coup il n'y avait plus d'hésitation possible: les mots qui me venaient aux lèvres, au bout de ma plume, étaient de ma lignée, de ma solidarité ancestrale. Ils me remontaient à l'âme comme une eau pure qui trouve son chemin entre des épaisseurs de roc et d'obscurs écueils.
[The story I found waiting when I woke and which flowed so well was coming in my mother tongue, in French. For a time I had thought it might be a good thing to write in English; I had tried with some success and I was torn. Then suddenly there could no longer be any hesitation. The words coming to my lips and from the point of my pen were French, from my lineage, my

ancestral bonds. They rose to my soul like the pure waters of a
spring filtering through layers of rock and hidden obstacles.]
(DE 392; 317)

As if to stress the paradoxical nature of this revelatory moment,
she adds: "Je ne m'étonnais pas d'ailleurs que ce fût en Angleterre
... que je naissais enfin peut-être à ma destination, mais sûrement en
tout cas à mon identité propre que jamais plus je ne remettrais en
question [I wasn't surprised that it was in England, however ... that
I should waken to my destination, perhaps, but certainly to my own
identity, of which I would never again have the slightest doubt]"
(ibid.). Roy's choice of language is firmly linked not only to her
individual identity but through "lignée" and "solidarité ancestrale"
to her collective identity, mediated through the figure of her mother.
This is a point to which the text returns on its final page as the autobiographical subject refers to her future project of writing *Bonheur
d'occasion*, drawing on "la solidarité avec mon peuple retrouvé tel
que ma mère, dans mon enfance, me l'avait donné à connaître et à
aimer [my feeling of having come home, of oneness with my people,
whom my mother had taught me to know and love in my child-
hood]" (DE 505; 410). By identifying the French language both
with her maternal heritage and with nature, "une eau pure," the
narrator represents this awakening to her mother tongue as a pre-
ordained and unquestionable event. Yet despite her repeated references to the opposition between the French and English languages
and the use of a discourse of collective linguistic identity, Roy's
autobiography in many ways unsettles by questioning the very
terms of the choice and identification. As Gayatri Spivak puts it:
"One needs to be vigilant against simple notions of identity which
overlap neatly with language or location."[23]
The division of Roy's autobiography into two parts, the first set
in Manitoba and the second in Europe, highlights the importance of
both language and the colonial context. In the first part language is
frequently cited as a cause of exclusion and inferiority (what Bill
Ashcroft refers to as the "consequences of cultural subjugation")[24]
as experienced by the je/nous Franco-Manitobaines (primarily Roy
and her mother, but by extension a wider, collective – and feminine
– colonial subject). In keeping with the anti-colonial discourse of
the initial quotation, anglophone-francophone relations are repeatedly represented in terms of a binary opposition. When Roy

describes her teacher training year at Normal School, where franco-phones represented only 4 percent of those who completed the course, her words denote open conflict: "Jusqu'ici la tactique à employer contre l'adversaire anglais avait été le tact, la diplomatie, la stratégie fine, la désobéissance polie. Maintenant j'imaginai le temps venu de croiser le fer [Hitherto, the tactics we'd been taught to use against our English adversaries had been tact, diplomacy, cunning, strategy, and polite disobedience. In my imagination, the time had now come to cross swords]" (DE 82; 63).

At other times Roy emphasizes the subordinate position of fran-cophones in Manitoba. The title of the first part of the autobiogra-phy, "Le Bal du Gouverneur [The Governor's Ball]" refers to an episode that took place a few years before Gabrielle's birth. It plays out the power relations between majority and minority linguistic groups, so adding to the reader's sense that the autobiographical subject is this wider Franco-Manitoban collective. Roy's parents had once been invited to attend the provincial governor's ball thanks to Léon Roy's position as a government employee. They arrived at the governor's residence but felt too intimidated and too poor to enter. The narrator recounts her mother's impression of the scene she observed through the window: "'Tu me vois, assistant à travers la fenêtre à l'arrivée des hommes en habit à queue, des femmes en robes à traîne, celles-ci faisant la révérence au gou-verneur, celui-ci inclinant la tête d'un geste un peu hautain, et tout ça en anglais' [Can't you see me watching through the window as the men in tail coats and the women in dresses with trains come for-ward, and then the women curtseying to the lieutenant-governor and the men bending their heads a bit haughtily, and all of it in Eng-lish]" (DE 101; 79). The reference to the English language confirms the source of their feeling of exclusion and so sets up English in a position of dominance. Mélina Roy comes to symbolize the franco-phone minority, whose marginalization is compounded by a poor command of English. Roy quotes her mother's language mistakes with what can be read either as a sense of shared humiliation or as a feeling of being ashamed of her mother: "Parfois survenait une vraie difficulté comme ce jour où elle demanda 'a yard or two of Chinese skin to put under the coat.'" The bilingual daughter/narra-tor proceeds to explain this linguistic blunder to the reader, further emphasizing her mother's lack of fluency: "maman ayant en tête d'acheter une mesure de peau de chamois pour en faire la doublure de manteau [sometimes a real problem arose, like the time she wanted some chamois ('shammy' to the English) to line a coat, and asked for 'a yard or two of Chinese skin to put under the coat']" (DE, 14; 5–6). The narrator adopts an ambivalent stance here, at once empowered by her own superior linguistic knowledge while ostensibly identifying with those who lack the power of language.

Roy's alternation between identification with her community, learned from her mother, and her personal mission to succeed as a bilingual, bicultural Canadian is partly resolved by Roy's representation of herself as a saviour figure called on to avenge the wrongs done to the oppressed minority. The narrative represents this mission as a role imposed on the young Roy by others. After the humiliating scene of the shopping expedition, for instance, the mother is reported as telling the daughter that: "ce serait à moi ... de me mettre à apprendre l'anglais, afin de nous venger tous [I was the one ... who ought to start learning English so I could make up for all the rest of us]" (DE 15). In a later scene, when Roy, star pupil, learns her Shakespeare to impress the anglophone school inspector, it is the teaching nun who urges her: "Sauve la classe, Gabrielle. Lève-toi et saute dans *Is this a dagger...* [Save the class, Gabrielle. Stand up and give him 'Is this a dagger ...']" (DE 73). And on her departure from Manitoba, recounted at the end of the first part of the autobiography, the narrative explains her duty to "mon pauvre peuple dépossédé [my poor dispossessed people]" and her intention to return to "sauver les autres [save the others]" (DE 243; 193).

The representation of Roy's trip to Europe illustrates the anxiety about language that is typical of colonial subjects, who are constantly measured by their degree of fluency against external norms (the king's English, metropolitan French). This frequently produces such a desire for correctness that the subject remains a constant learner of the Other's language, a phenomenon noted also by Selwyn Cudjoe in Trinidadians' concern for "the 'proper' use of classically based English language."[25] Self-criticism of her linguistic performance is a recurrent motif of Roy's text (and links her once more with her mother). Roy recounts the way that a performance of Shakespeare in London reminded her of her own recitation of the dagger speech. A mixture of pride and self-denigration is typical of the colonized subject's obsession with linguistic skills: "Je découvris n'avoir pas été trop mauvaise moi-même, naguère, en Macbeth, par le ton, l'allure, bref par tout sauf par l'accent qui était celui de la rue

Deschambault et devait y être d'un effet éminemment comique [I discovered that I hadn't been too bad a Macbeth way back then, in my tone, delivery, in everything but accent, which was straight out of Deschambault Street and must have been excruciatingly funny]" (DE 74; 56).

Roy's personal sense of linguistic inferiority focuses almost exclusively on her accent, both in French and English. In her accounts she tends to present herself as the object of ridicule, as an anecdote of her time as a drama student at the Guildhall School of Music and Drama illustrates. The diction coach had just spent forty-five minutes working on her pronunciation of the word "little": "'Mais où donc avez-vous appris l'anglais?...' à quoi j'avais répondu distraitement, à bout de fatigue: 'Là où j'aurais dû apprendre plutôt le français' ['Where on earth did you learn your English?' Exhausted by trying, I replied listlessly, 'Where I ought to have learned French instead']" (DE 321; 257). A similar pattern of judgment of Roy as a linguistically inferior colonial subject occurs in the account of her time in Paris, and again in the context of the theatre. An appointment is made for her to see Charles Dullin at the Théâtre de l'Atelier. When she tells him of her acting experience in Manitoba she hears laughter and interprets this as mockery, an expression of metropolitan superiority: "Il m'a semblé que c'était de moi ou peut-être de mon accent. Ou encore de ce 'Saint-Boniface, au Manitoba,' qui avait pu sonner aux oreilles d'ici aussi drôlement que Tombouctou en Mauritanie [At me or perhaps my accent, I had the impression. Or perhaps at 'St-Boniface in Manitoba,' which may have sounded as comical as 'Timbuctu in Mauretania (sic)' to Parisian ears]" (DE 275; 220).[26] The significant addition of "Timbuctu" makes the colonial relationship explicit. Her response is tellingly expressed as a loss of voice: "J'avais la gorge nouée, plus une goutte de salive dans la bouche [My throat was tight and there wasn't a drop of saliva in my mouth]" (DE 276; 220). Physically and psychologically unable to speak, she flees.

In a similar way, Roy's initial arrival in Paris is represented in terms of her exclusion from the language of the colonizer. This scene opens the second half of the autobiography. Interestingly, the placement of the arrival in Paris at the beginning of the second part departs from the chronology of her trip to Europe. The fact that she spent a very happy few days in London en route to France is referred to in an analepsis in a subsequent chapter, so allowing the more traumatic encounter with France and the French language to set the tone. At the station she fails to make herself understood by the railway staff: "Il me paraissait aussi impossible de me faire entendre à Paris que si j'avais été transportée au cœur de la Chine [It seemed as impossible to get anyone to listen to me as if I'd been whisked to the heart of China]" (DE 248; 197). This exoticizing image is then followed by a brief exchange in which she is spoken to in pidginized French, another display of colonial linguistic domination:

> Le contrôleur ne me parlait plus qu'en moitiés de phrases.
> "Ticket de quai ..."
> "Où? "
> Il indiqua une direction.
> "Machine ..."
> [He (the ticket collector) thenceforth addressed me in non-sentences.
> "Platform ticket ..."
> "Where?"
> "Machine ..." He pointed.] (DE 249; 197)

Roy's sense of linguistic displacement is also represented in terms of an inability to *read* the place: "Je me trouvais devant une masse de signes, mots et abréviations à me faire tourner la tête [I was confronted by a forest of symbols, words, and abbreviations that made my head spin]." She is criticized for this: "J'allai à un guichet qui me renvoya à un autre qui, lui, me fit honte de ne pas savoir lire les panneaux où tout, me fut-il dit, était inscrit [I went to a wicket, from which I was sent to another, where I was scolded for not knowing enough to read the signs on which, I was told, everything was indicated]" (DE 248; 197). Her failure to access the codes of the cultural centre is experienced as shame.

Such scenes reinforce the identification of Roy as a colonized subject and bind her identity to the Franco-Manitoban people, who are similarly deprived of agency and voice. However, alongside this anti-colonial discourse we find interferences and contradictions that can be related to Roy's particular interiorization of her bilingualism. A more complex relationship to language emerges. Ashcroft proposes that the relationship of the individual to colonial discourse has dynamic, creative possibilities. To explain the ways in which power operates within various institutions of colonialism, he prefers Gilles Deleuze and Félix Guattari's metaphor of the rhizome to the hierarchical centre–periphery model. "The colonial subject," he contends, "is never simply a *tabula rasa* on which colonial discourse can inscribe its representations: his or her engagement of the culture presented as capital may be extremely subtle ... Post-colonial societies cannot avoid the effects of colonization, but those effects need not necessarily be seen as the tragic consequences of cultural subjugation or as a cultural contamination to be rejected at all costs."[27] In terms of language these more subtle effects can produce a range of colonial exchanges that operate not in a mechanical hierarchical way but in a more active, lateral, intermittent manner. The colonial subject might achieve agency rather than remaining a passive object.

Where does Roy's relationship to language lie on the continuum between these contrasting models of the operation of *la langue dominante* and *la langue dominée*? Perhaps the archetypal colonial linguistic act is the act of naming, a practice that extends even to personal situations. Roy recalls visiting the graves of her aunt and uncle in southern Manitoba:

> Deux hautes pierres analogues me faisaient face, debout, l'une à côté de l'autre, portant en caractères qui me sautèrent aux yeux, l'une *Father*, l'autre *Mother* ... ainsi donc, eux qui n'avaient été *Father* et *Mother* pour personne au cours de leur vie, le seraient à jamais sous le ciel pur, dans ce petit cimetière du bout du monde. Ils m'étaient ravis aujourd'hui plus complètement qu'ils ne l'avaient été le jour de leur mort.
> [Two high, matching stones confronted me, standing on end side by side. In characters that leapt out at me, one bore the word 'Father' and the other one 'Mother.' In English! ... Those two who had never been called Father and Mother in English by anyone while they were living would be identified that way for ever, here in this little cemetery beneath the unsullied sky in the middle of nowhere. They'd been taken from me more surely that day than on the day they died.] (DE 63; 46–7)

This sense of indignation and collective loss contrasts with a later point in the second part where Roy recalls with pleasure how the name that she gives to her elderly host in Essex, and by which he is designated in *La Détresse et l'enchantement*, "Father Perfect," is adopted by all his neighbours: "Au bout de peu de temps personne au village, au manoir et dans les alentours ne le nomma autrement. Je crois même que c'est ce qui est écrit sur sa tombe [Pretty soon no one in the village, at the manor house, or in the countryside around called him anything else. I even believe that this is what is written on his tombstone]" (DE 383; 310). In the first case Roy's relationship to language is that of a colonized passive victim. In the second case Roy takes on the English language for herself, participating as an active subject in the naming process. Throughout the text there are in fact numerous examples of Roy taking on her bilingualism and bicultural capital as an asset. This active stance results not in exclusion and dispossession but inclusion and ownership.

Roy's autobiography also undermines the authority of standard (European) French and English through her interest in regional accents. Her discovery of the accents in southern France or in working-class London, for example, to some extent counterbalances the sense of inferiority that she has internalized about her own Canadian accent. Toward the end of the book there is an account of Roy's trip to France to visit Provence before returning via Britain to Canada. Here she playfully imitates the local accent when giving directions to a passing driver:

> "Mesdames? ... Mesdemoiselles? ... Pardon! Seriez-vous du pays?"
> "Du pays! bien sûr!" dis-je dans ma meilleure imitation de l'accent provençal ... et pour faire encore plus local, je dis avec conviction ce que je m'étais entendu dire mille fois en France: "Pouvez pas le manquer! C'est tout droit devant vous!
> ["*Mesdames?... mesdemoiselles?...* Pardon me, would you be local folk?"
> "Local folk, indeed we are!" said I in my best imitation of the Provençal lilt ...
> Then, to be authentically local, with firm conviction I added something I'd heard a thousand times in France:
> "Can't miss it! It's straight ahead!."] (DE 476; 385–6)

In this exchange, the process of imitation is no longer accompanied by a feeling of humiliating failure to measure up to the required (colonial) standard, but rather by a sense of the pleasure Roy now takes in linguistic difference. The trip to Europe suggests that regional variations within *la francophonie* (and the English-speaking world) might rather be seen as a spectrum of linguistic difference rather than a rigid hierarchy in which Paris/London remain the measure. Such an unpicking of the authority of standard French and English helps to undermine the binary pattern evident in earlier scenes where the colonial subject is a victim within a diglossic system. Equally, the narrator's ability to move between languages and expose the power relations between English and French and between the colonial "centres" and their margins, has the effect of relativizing the two languages and shifting the reader's perspective on both.

Some scenes also suggest that despite her sense of linguistic inferiority in Paris, Roy was able to criticize the cultural and linguistic domination of Parisian standards. She writes mockingly of an actor's rendition of the declamatory style so typical of the Théâtre Français: "Il possède une voix à faire trembler le vieil édifice, et il en joue de façon invariable, entonnant chaque alexandrine du plus bas qu'une voix puisse descendre, pour monter, monter, de palier en palier, jusqu'à une note aiguë donnant l'impression qu'il vous lance du haut d'une tour. Monte ... descend ... monte ... descend [He had a voice that could shake the whole building, however. He used it without the least variation, beginning each alexandrine as deep as a voice can descend and rising from one pitch to the next till he reached such a shrill note it made you imagine he was hurling it at you from the top of a tower. Up ... down ... up ... down]" (DE 273; 218). She also recalls daring to disagree with her hostess over the literary merits of Alain Fournier's *Le Grand Meaulnes*. The hostess clearly considered such an expression of cultural independence to be an act of insubordination against the cultural authority of France on the part of this "jeune Canadienne, tout juste débarquée de sa province natale [young Canadian, just off the boat from her native wilds]" (DE 272; 217).

Despite the discovery that French was her "natural" language of literary expression, Roy works the English language into her autobiography in a variety of ways, both in the representation of dialogue and in the narrative. Her skillful use of English to achieve a desired effect illustrates the creative complexity of the bilingual subject's relationship to language in a colonial/post-colonial context at which Ashcroft hints.

Roy's use of English can be described as a pattern of code-switching at various levels of the text. Defined by Peter Trudgill as "switching from one language variety to another when the situation demands it,"[28] code-switching is characteristic linguistic behaviour of the bilingual speaker. Trudgill refers primarily to the spoken language, and it is indeed in dialogue that one finds English appearing in Roy's text. The majority of conversations with anglophones are naturalized into French, so making the language of exchange invisible, or inaudible. But in some cases the practice of code-switching is explicitly referred to. On arrival in Paris Roy is met by a Canadian contact. The first mention of the fact that this is an anglophone comes after about three pages of text: "Ma payse me suppliait: 'Not so loud! ... Not so loud! ...' car cette payse était de langue anglaise et, quoiqu'elle eût fait en un an à Paris d'énormes progrès en français, il lui arrivait, sous l'effet de la surexcitation, de retomber dans sa langue maternelle ['Not so loud ... not so loud!' my compatriot begged me. She was English-speaking, and although she'd made enormous progress with her French in the year she'd been in Paris she would sometimes lapse into her mother tongue when excited]" (DE 254; 202).

As the narrator's explanation suggests, code-switching is not simply the effect of some linguistic lack or failure. It serves a range of sociolinguistic functions, including the expression of emotion or attitude toward the topic or the interlocutor.[29] Elsewhere, Roy uses English selectively in dialogue, often to frame a conversation, so indicating the language in which it is conducted. In such cases one would expect a number of devices to operate – either the "simultaneous translation" effect of a paraphrase, or the supply by the narrator of a series of clues with which to decode the foreign element. At times Roy does supply such paraphrases and clues; but a non-English speaker would not, for example, follow the precise meaning of sentences like this (when Roy is being helped by a London policeman when lost in the fog): "'Lost miss? And a mean night 'tis to be lost in.' [...] C'est son langage qui me frappe le plus, ancien, pittoresque, extrêmement littéraire ... D'où leur venaient donc ces mots rares, ces termes imagés, cet accent presque shakespearien? ['Lost miss? And a mean night 'tis to be lost in!' ... What struck me instantly and forcefully was his speech: old world, colourful, and extremely literary ... Where could they have found these uncommon words, these metaphoric terms, this almost Shakespearean cadence?]" (DE 307; 246). Here, the author's personal reflection on the differences between British English and Canadian English outweighs any concern for the reader's comprehension of the phrases used.

In many such passages, bilingualism seems to be the author's norm, as if she is forgetting the excluded francophone minority in whose name she claims to be writing. In one instance the pattern of narrative commentary in French on English elements in dialogue is even reversed, as if the narrator has lost her bearings between languages and is addressing an anglophone reader: "'Qu'est-ce qu'il a à être si surexcité?' me demanda Ruby, in English ['What's he so excited about?' Ruby wanted to know]" (DE 477; 386). (Claxton chooses to correct, or omit, this confusion.) In fact the use of English differs considerably between the first and second sections of the text. In the first half, set in Manitoba, the English language tends to signal linguistic domination, as when Roy refers to specific institutions: le Department of Education, Normal School, le Department of Health, and the public arena generally (shopping expeditions in Winnipeg). Similarly, the text of the invitation to the Governor's Ball that Roy's parents receive is given in English as if to prepare the scene of social exclusion that follows. This usage allows anti-colonial critique to be voiced in the text, in keeping with Roy's identification as a colonized Franco-Manitoban.

But in the section set in Britain the usage changes dramatically. Here English is used more frequently and has the effect of suggesting a number of different attitudes. English terms tend to be used above all to refer to the domestic sphere and to literature and culture. The proliferation of words connected with food and the home, such as "porridge," "kippers," "cup of tea," "scones," "un breakfast incroyable," "yorkshire pudding," "crumpets," and other domestic vocabulary such as "scullery," "bow window," indicate Britain's difference; but they also suggest the sense of Roy being at ease in this context, avidly consuming food and culture. The paradoxical effect is that Roy gives the impression of feeling most "at home" among the English urban and rural working classes. This could be seen as a sign of her profound assimilation into the anglophone world, the culture and language of Empire. Or might this degree of ease with everyday British culture be an indication of the range of apparently contradictory subject positions that can be adopted within colonialism?

But what of the reader? Certainly, as the examples cited show, the monolingual francophone reader will to some extent be excluded from this text, which rather contradicts Roy's insistent identification of herself with "nos gens [our people]," "ma lignée [my ancestors]." One might assume that they are not her intended reader. A final few examples will illustrate Roy's pattern of excluding the monolingual francophone reader. In one of the sections set in London, the Shakespeare tutor at drama school, who criticizes all her students harshly, focuses specifically on Roy's accent: "Dommage que vous ayez un accent si barbare car par moments j'ai eu l'impression que quelque chose prenait vie. But child, I could hardly make out a single word of your stupendous accent [It's a pity you've got such a barbaric accent because at times I actually felt something come to life. But child, I could hardly make out a single word with that horrendous accent of yours!]" (DE 323; 259). Here Roy gives no paraphrase of the English. In another case, as Roy is about to return to Canada and is taking leave of an English friend, he asks her to give him have her address in Manitoba:

> Je lui dis … m'efforçant au ton si souvent badin entre nous:
> "If so, will you ever come to visit me in my steppes?"
> Il me posa un léger baiser sur la joue. C'était le premier qu'il me donnait.
> "I shall come and sit on your steps."
> [Trying to keep the tone light between us, I said, "If I do, will you ever come and see me on my steppes?"
> He kissed me lightly on the cheek. It was the first kiss he'd ever given me.
> "I shall come and sit on your steps."] (DE 425–6; 345)

The use of the pun on steps is only partly prepared in the narrative.

In a third example, a number of quite complex and poetic sentences are quoted from letters written by Roy's Essex friend Esther Perfect. Roy gives some of these in their "original" English and translates others, with no comment: "Et c'est vraiment inimaginable tout ce qu'elle trouvait à en dire, surtout du vent qu'elle disait parfois 'soft and balmy, a sweet breath laden with the scent of the hay fields …' ou souvent, à l'automne, 'a nasty vindictive soul shrieking across the land …' [It was really astonishing what she could find to say about this, particularly the wind, which she might say was 'soft and balmy, a sweet breath laden with the scent of the hayfields, or in autumn like 'a nasty vindictive soul shrieking across the land']" (DE 405; 327). Once more, the particular register of the English quoted is there for the bilingual reader to appreciate and the monolingual francophone reader to guess at, thus reproducing the very pattern of linguistic exclusion that elsewhere the text overtly criticizes.

This enjoyment at recounting England in English does perhaps reveal Roy's deep-seated assimilation to the English-speaking world, and the language and culture of the British Empire, as she learned to love them both as a pupil and a teacher in Manitoba's schools. The *Canadian Readers* and then the curriculum for English literature had not only familiarized her at a distance with the rural and urban landscape, seasons, wildlife, and domestic habits of Britain but they had also allowed her to take particular pleasure in the language. If in many ways Roy felt more "at home" in England than in France, it was in large part a result of her colonial education. But perhaps her ability to adapt so readily to life in England is just another sign of the paradoxical and contradictory position of Franco-Manitobans as *colons colonisés*. After all, it was precisely when she felt so completely at home, in the Essex cottage of Esther Perfect, that she awoke, as she writes, to discover her true identity as a French-language writer.

If Gabrielle Roy's autobiography does expose the workings and the effects of the institutional and cultural power of the English language, which had the result of marginalizing the Franco-Manitoban population, that is only one aspect of this complex text. As she examines the origins of her own linguistic identity, Roy uncovers layers of cultural oppression. The result is that the dominant language is at times that of the Anglo-Canadian majority, at times that of the British Empire, and at still other times that of French colonialism, *le français de France*. Yet, despite the apparent certainty of Roy's reclaiming French as her "natural" language of literary expression, secured as it is by the association of "mon identité propre [my own identity]" and "ma solidarité ancestrale [my ancestral bonds]," this is far from the whole story. *La Détresse et l'enchantement* reveals neither a sense of linguistic dispossession nor an essentialist equating of language and individual identity. It manifests a more ambivalent attitude to language.

Roy's writing, in her autobiography as in her other texts, is open to the Other's language and offers examples of linguistic exchanges and the creative use of English alongside the moments of exclusion and humiliation. The representation of a spectrum of language difference begins to unpick any sense of a rigid hierarchy of languages. Above all, this text in French can be read as a bilingual text, in which Roy presents her readers with a range of relationships to language in which speakers and readers can move from being victims of diglossia and colonial power to being active and creative participants in linguistic exchange. Seen from this perspective, her bilingualism seems to be operating as a form of hybridity, a position in between languages and cultures. As Ashcroft proposed, the colonized subject can adopt a range of different positions in relation to the culture of the colonizer, and this variety can be found in the responses to linguistic domination experienced by Franco-Manitobans: "The successful disruption of the territory of the dominant occurs, not only by rejecting or vacating that territory but by inhabiting it differently."[30] Thanks to her ambivalent position as a bilingual/bicultural by-product of colonialism in Canada, Roy is never only the *porte-parole* of her "pauvre peuple dépossédé [poor, dispossessed people]"; nor is she only an assimilated anglophile. To move between languages and cultures is to escape from essentialized notions of identity. In a discussion of hybrid cultural identities that encompasses both Welsh and Jamaican experiences, Stuart Hall characterizes such identities as follows: "They are not and will never be *unified* culturally in the old sense, because they are inevitably the products of several interlocking histories and cultures, belonging at the same time to several 'homes' – and thus to no one particular home."[31] It is just such an ambivalence toward "home" – geographical, cultural, and linguistic – that characterizes *La Détresse et l'enchantement*.

NEGOTIATING THE LANGUAGE DIVIDE: ENCOUNTERS AND DIALOGUES IN ROY'S FICTION

The type of relationship with the English and French languages that emerges from an analysis of Gabrielle Roy's *La Détresse et l'enchantement* exemplifies what Robert Young has termed "the intricate processes of cultural contact, intrusion, fusion and disjunction" that are produced by colonialism.[32] With these "intricate processes of cultural contact" in mind, we now turn to explore a range of Roy's fictional and auto-fictional writing. Roy's bilingualism and biculturalism both required and enabled her to move between languages and to take up a variety of positions within linguistic and cultural hierarchies. In her works encounters with the Other's language tend to arise in a whole range of situations of migration and colonial contact,[33] situations that provoke what Lise Gauvin has termed "a feeling of strangeness in language."[34] For Gauvin this heightened awareness of one's complex relationship to language is commonly felt by writers of minor literatures, according to the categorization of Deleuze and Guattari.[35] In this context Gauvin discusses the work of migrant writers Emile Ollivier, Marco Micone, and Ying Chen and concludes that they represent "many ways of reappropriating and rerouting language, of revealing its otherness, and in so doing of treating it as a porous border, a crossing point and a place of exchange."[36]

Roy's ambivalent position between languages and her heightened awareness of linguistic difference can mainly be discerned in her representations of moments of encounter, dialogue, and exchange within her literary texts. Examples of linguistic encounter between francophones and anglophones, and also with speakers of minority languages, are a frequent phenomenon in Roy's texts, and she handles these moments of contact in various ways and with various effects, as part of a complex network of intercultural relationships. Indeed linguistic encounters illustrate the dynamics of what Mary Louise Pratt refers to as contact zones, "social spaces where disparate cultures meet, clash, and grapple with each other, often in highly asymmetrical relations of domination and subordination – like colonialism, slavery, or their aftermaths as they are lived out across the globe today."[37] A wide range of examples will allow us to gauge the extent to which Roy uses communication to reproduce the power relations inherent in and reinforced by colonialism in its diverse forms. How does Roy signal linguistic difference? And in what ways might her texts be seen as denouncing, erasing, or negotiating the diglossic or heteroglossic hierarchies of the languages concerned?

Estelle Dansereau has written a number of pertinent analyses on the representation of the Other in Roy's work. She has studied the use of narrative slippages and focalization, deictics, free indirect discourse, and questions as ways of creating a space for the Other's voice: "It's about choosing a way of introducing other perspectives which indirectly highlight the discourse of the other without this being directly voiced."[38] She concludes: "By the construction of such mixed, heterogeneous forms of discourse, Gabrielle Roy creates plural voices which help to defuse and diffuse the power of the dominant authority; however these voices encompass and then reveal the contradictions and conflicts which characterise the experience of otherness."[39] To my knowledge, however, Dansereau does not discuss the actual languages used. Yet, in order to appreciate the strategies used in Roy's text to silence or highlight the Other's voice, the status of the specific languages in question must be taken into account. In a discussion of linguistic heterogeneity in the literary text, Grutman defines *hétérolinguisme* [heterolingualism] as follows: "the presence *in a text* of foreign idioms, in whatever form that might be, as well as of varieties (social, regional or chronological) of the principal language."[40] As he points out, it is in most cases both impractical and inappropriate for an individual text to be plurilingual: "The polyphony typical of the world represented could not be reproduced in the world of the representation." Rather, he suggests, the representation of a polylingual reality is more a question of "a few carefully added touches."[41] Excerpts from a selection of Roy's shorter fictional works will allow us to see to what extent they constitute examples of such linguistically hybrid texts. The form of most of these works is that of the volume of linked short stories, a form Roy developed as an alternative to the full-length novel. We shall also look at two scenes from a longer, unfinished work, *La Saga d'Eveline*.[42]

In analysing passages from *La Détresse et l'enchantement* we focused on the interplay between English and French in the text. By turning now to Roy's fictional and auto-fictional works that highlight intercultural contact in the Canadian North and West, we can widen the discussion to include contact with allophone protagonists as well. In the four stories included in *La Rivière sans repos* in which the main protagonists are Inuit from northern Quebec, there are many scenes of contact between Inuit which involve dialogues among them and exchanges with anglophone and francophone characters. *De quoi t'ennuies-tu, Eveline?* recounts a trip south to California during which the central francophone protagonist encounters and engages in conversation with a range of francophone, anglophone, and allophone characters. The other chosen texts all include protagonists at different stages of migration and settlement. The pioneers of the late nineteenth century are represented in *La Saga d'Eveline*; the linguistically and culturally mixed population of Manitoba in the interwar years appear in *La Petite Poule d'Eau, Rue Deschambault*, and *Ces enfants de ma vie*; and various exile figures, products of Chinese, Ukrainian, and Doukhobor immigration to the Canadian West, are the protagonists of the stories in *Un jardin au bout du monde*.

The examples of linguistic encounter in these stories seem to fall into three categories of contact and exchange associated with hybridity. While nowadays the term "hybridity" is applied to many different areas of cultural, social, and political life, in the nineteenth century, as Robert Young demonstrates in *Colonial Desire*, hybridity was a key concept in Western racialism and was intimately connected to the history of colonialism. Young traces the ambivalence of the term back to the taboo status of miscegenation: "In the different theoretical positions woven out of this intercourse, the races and their intermixture circulate around an ambivalent axis of desire and aversion."[43] To Young, the common element in contemporary applications of the term to processes of intercultural mixing appears to be that "wherever it emerges it suggests the impossibility of essentialism."[44] As he states: "There is no single, or correct, concept of hybridity."[45] Susan Stanford Friedmann, in her book *Mappings: Feminism and the Cultural Geographies of Encounter*, finds that three predominant models of hybridity are used by those working in the fields of cultural and postcolonial studies. These models are not mutually exclusive, and writers often weave them together in specific contexts, but in each model the effects of the process of contact are different for those involved. The most relevant aspect here is the way in which hybridity can operate in the context of power relations, given that the linguistic encounters we find in Roy's work can all be related to unequal power relations between languages. Friedmann's first model sees hybridity as an effect of oppression, an imposition resulting in some degree of deculturation or assimilation. "Within this framework, hybridity is more often than not regarded as negative, as a sort of containment, regulation, policing, and control of those whose original cultures pose some sort of threat to hegemonic powers or figure as some sort of forbidden desire."[46] Within such a framework agency is assumed to reside with the dominant power. Friedmann cites a number of

historical cases of such oppressive intercultural contact from the fif-
teenth century onward. In terms of this model, the 1916 Manitoba
provincial legislation on education and the establishment of residential schools for First Nations children are both examples of
hybridity as containment with the aim of assimilation.

Friedmann's second model of hybridity operates as an unsettling,
questioning, transgressive process in which the elements do not
"fit" established categories of power relations. The outcome of this
form of contact is anti-authoritarian, progressive cultural work,
"opening doors of possibility instead of regulating and confin-
ing."[47] Friedmann refers to the work of Homi Bhabha and Salman
Rushdie as examples of this mode of "hybridity-talk." Such progressive interaction assumes human subjectivities that create meanings and act in negotiation with the conditions of the existing social
order. This model of hybridity focuses less on the systems of oppression and more on the agency of the hybridic dissident.

The process of intercultural contact suggested by Friedmann's
third model of hybridity is understood in terms of interaction
between heterogeneous others, as transculturation or negotiation,
and is concerned with what goes on in the common space between
"us" and "them," even if unequal power relations are in operation.
The dynamic of this mode of hybridity is mutual – multidirectional
rather than unidirectional: "Consistent with a Gramscian perspective, hegemony contains within its normative systems contradictions that fuel resistance and change."[48] All the parties have agency,
even though they are in different relationships to power. As S.P.
Mohanty argues: "In understanding the divide between 'us' and
'them,' it is this common space we all share that needs to be elabo-
rated and defined."[49]

The Language of Power

This set of models provides a useful framework for considering the
types of language contact represented within Roy's work, and her
ways of representing language contact.[50] Friedmann's first model
corresponds to an oppressive relationship between languages that
results in, or reinforces, a kind of deculturation. A number of Roy's
scenes represent the situation of diglossia, in which English is recognized as the dominant language of Canada. The experience of being
in an inferior position within a diglossic context appears through-

out Roy's work, in texts set from the turn of the twentieth century
to the 1950s and 1960s, although in the more recent settings, the
characters most marginalized by the dominant language tend to be
allophone rather than francophone. In *La Saga d'Eveline*, an unfinished work set in the late nineteenth and early twentieth centuries,
the narrator recounts the impressions of Bobonne, who has
migrated from Quebec to settle in southern Manitoba some years
earlier and travels to Winnipeg to visit her newly married daughter.
The cultural shock of the rapidly modernizing city, with its automo-
biles, tramway, telephones, and electricity is compounded by the
linguistic alienation she feels in the capital, an alienation first
described but not shown:

> L'anglais, c'était là l'ennui quand on venait en ville. Là-bas, à
> Saint-Léonard et même dans tous les villages environnants, on
> pouvait s'en passer; on était entre gens de parlure semblable.
> Mais arrivant à Winnipeg, aussitôt on se sentait une infime
> petite poignée de gens perdus dans l'étrangeté d'une langue par-
> tout dominante.
> [English, that was the trouble when you came to town. Back
> there, in Saint-Léonard and even in the surrounding villages,
> you could manage without it; you were among people who
> spoke like you. But arriving in Winnipeg, you felt right away
> like a tiny little handful of people lost in the foreignness of a
> language that was dominant everywhere you went.]
> (SE 342–3)

> A la rigueur, Bobonne eût pourtant réussi sans doute à
> demander son chemin en cette langue et quelques autres simples
> renseignements, et peut-être s'y fût-elle risquée, mais à la condi-
> tion de n'avoir pour se gausser de ses efforts aucun témoin
> familier.
> [If need be, however, Bobonne would doubtless have managed
> to ask for directions and for some other basic information in
> that language, and perhaps she might have dared to do so, but
> only as long as there was no one she knew to witness her efforts
> and make fun of her.] (SE 343)

The association between the encounter with the English language,
the feeling of linguistic inferiority, and the fear of ridicule recalls

Roy's account of her mother's linguistic inadequacy in her Winnipeg shopping trips in *La Détresse et l'enchantement*.[51]

The provision of education in rural Manitoba in the 1930s, as we have seen, is a major theme of *La Petite Poule d'Eau*. The three stories that make up that volume reflect the cultural and linguistic diversity of northern Manitoba before processes of linguistic assimilation had had their full effects, the protagonists being francophone Canadian, French, Belgian/Russian, Ukrainian, Métis, and anglophone Canadian. In the second story, "L'Ecole de la Petite Poule d'Eau," Mme Tousignant's efforts to persuade the authorities to provide education for her children reveal the link between education and linguistic assimilation. References to Manitoba's education system appear in English, the italics highlighting their difference while the syntax integrates the words smoothly, as in "les bureaux du *Department of Education* [the offices of the Department of Education]."[52] The francophone mother's ambivalence between her desire for her children to be educated and the fact that their schooling will give them an education that is predominantly English in language and culture is caught by the intrusion of English into the text, as is the mother's own sense of inferiority in the face of the teachers, bilingual and monolingual alike. Once the anglophone Miss O'Rorke arrives, brief passages of English are used in the dialogue. Luzina Tousignant's lack of fluency in English is indicated by her timid questions to the monolingual teacher, the italics highlighting the difficulty with which she forms her phrases in English: "*You not sleep?*" (PPE 80). The link between language and Empire is marked in a combination of form and content in the exchange between Miss O'Rorke and the Tousignant couple concerning the British flag:

> [Miss O'Rorke]: "*Mrs. Tousignant, there must be a flag here.*"
> "Qu'est-ce qu'elle demande?" s'informa Luzina auprès d'Hippolyte.
> "La v'là qui veut un drapeau!" traduisit Hippolyte.
> "Un drapeau!" s'exclama Luzina, fort conciliante. "C'est bien vrai, il faut un drapeau, mais quelle sorte de drapeau?"
> "*The flag of His Majesty the King,*" dit Miss O'Rorke.
> Luzina saisit le mot: majesté. En fait de majesté britannique, Luzina était plutôt en retard sur son temps; elle en était restée pour ainsi dire à la vieille reine Victoria.

["Mrs. Tousignant, there must be a flag here."

"What is she asking?" Luzina sought enlightenment from her husband.

"Now she wants a flag!" Hippolyte interpreted.

"A flag!" Luzina exclaimed with great affability. "True enough, we need a flag. But what sort of flag?"

"The flag of His Majesty the King," said Miss O'Rorke.

Luzina fastened on the word majesty. As far as British majesty was concerned, Luzina was rather behind the times; in this matter she had progressed no further than the old Queen Victoria.] (PPE 88; 80–1)

The italicization here both highlights the problems of communication and perhaps suggests the natural response of the anglophone – to speak more loudly. The position of the narrator is to move between the two languages while indicating through moments of coincidence with Luzina's viewpoint ("Luzina saisit le mot: majesté") the latter's lack of familiarity with the language and with the institutions of the British Empire. Equally, the register of the French narrative is distinguished from the Tousignants' vernacular (indicated phonetically and syntactically in Hippolyte's "translation" of Miss O'Rorke's command ("La v'là qui veut un drapeau"). As the confrontation moves on to the issue of a flagpole from which to fly the flag, the narrator summarizes Luzina's patchy comprehension, inserting the British symbol into the French narrative: "Apparemment, il ne suffisait pas d'avoir l'Union Jack [Seemingly it was not enough to have a Union Jack]" (PPE 89; 81).

In linguistic encounters between the francophone family and teacher figures, the burden of comprehension/communication all lies on the side of the francophones, defined by their lack of fluency in English or *educated* French (whether metropolitan or urban Manitoban). They are shown to lack appropriate language in both English and French, their vernacular clearly being portrayed as inferior to the vehicular language of the teachers, and in time, to the learned French and English of their children. But in the next example, which occurs towards the end of the story, Roy gives another angle on the linguistic hierarchies at play in switching to Luzina's view of the Métis on a different occasion. As her older children leave home to further their education on the mainland, Luzina needs to find more pupils to warrant having a teacher to educate her remaining children and she approaches the Métis family on the island. In contrast to the way the educated French- and English-speaking teachers had all given Luzina the sense of being linguistically inferior, the power relationship she has experienced between linguistically dominant and dominated is temporarily reversed, as the Métis family enters the equation. Through the focalization of Luzina, the narrative describes the children as follows: "Presque des petits sauvages, demi-nus, barbouillés, qui parlaient on ne savait quelle langue: un peu d'anglais, du français très approximatif et sans doute un peu de saulteux mêlé avec quelques mots cris peut- être [They were almost wholly wild, half-naked, grimy, speaking the Lord knew what language – a little English, a smattering of French, and probably some Saultais mingled perhaps with a few words of Cree]" (PPE 132; 123). The use here of "presque," "on ne savait quelle langue," "un peu," "peut-être" emphasizes Luzina's rather uneasy sense of superiority over these linguistically incomplete others. She can find no words to label their linguistic hybridity, all the parts ("un peu de saulteux," "quelques mots cris peut-être," "du français très approximatif") adding up to something unknown, or unnameable ("on ne savait quelle langue").

In a further example, the position of the protagonists in relation to the dominant language indicates a quite different response to the processes of linguistic assimilation. *Rue Deschambault* is a collection of linked short stories about the linguistically and ethnically diverse inhabitants of Saint-Boniface. The central protagonist of the short story "Wilhelm" is a young Dutchman who is lodging with Irish neighbours of the narrator/protagonist Christine, a fictional (francophone) counterpart of Gabrielle Roy. The narrator introduces Wilhelm as typical of the many foreign workers who come to Manitoba: "C'était venir de loin pour faire comme tout le monde en somme; gagner sa vie, tâcher de se faire des amis, apprendre notre langue [A far journey to have come merely to behave, in the end, like everyone else – earn your living, try to make friends, learn our language]."[53] Only later, when the exchange of love letters between Wilhelm and Christine is mentioned, does the exact implication of "notre langue" emerge. The language they communicate in and that he has come to learn in the Canadian West is English not French. This is significant both thematically and at the level of the narrative. The fact that both protagonists, as French- and Dutch-speakers, accept English as the natural language for communication indicates that their acquisition of English represents a subtractive form of bilingualism. But it is also significant that when the language of their correspondence is clarified, the English language cited in the text is of a highly literary register, reinforcing the sense that English is the language of cultural prestige for both users: "Wilhelm avait fait de grands progrès en anglais. Il m'envoya de très belles lettres qui commençaient par: '*My own beloved child ...*'. Ou bien: '*Sweet little maid ...*'. Pour ne pas être dépassée, je répondais: '*My own dearest heart ...*' [Wilhelm had made great progress in English. He sent me very beautiful epistles which began with: 'My own beloved child ...' or else 'Sweet little maid ...' Not to be outdone, I replied: 'My own dearest heart ...']"(RD 202). The narrator admits that her model for her first love letters was a copy of Tennyson, so linking her own fluency in the language with the literary English studied in Manitoban schools. Within the narrative the non-equivalence between "notre langue" and the subsequent use of English by both protagonists would seem to be too normal to be signalled. In this case the text is not concerned with the potential deculturation that such an unquestioning acceptance of English as the dominant language implies. Indeed, the narrator, as we saw in the case of *La Détresse et l'enchantement*, assumes a degree of reading ability in English on the part of the reader.

In the final example of a hierarchical model of hybridity, the treatment of diglossia focuses not on francophones in a position of inferiority but on allophone migrants who have settled in the north of Alberta. The title story of *Un jardin au bout du monde* concerns an elderly first-generation immigrant couple from the Ukraine, Martha and Stépan Yaramko. While the story is usually discussed in general terms of the loss of cultural identity of Ukrainian immigrants, it can also be read as a dramatization of the couple's differing reactions to the process of assimilation. The narrative highlights the evident hostility between the couple and the breakdown in communication between them. In the case of Stépan, his refusal to assimilate culturally or linguistically and his fierce identification with his language of origin have led to his breaking off the contact between Martha and their children, whose assimilation into Canadian society has made them English speakers. The loss of contact is traced back to a final letter, which Stépan secretly destroyed in his rage at being excluded from the circle of communication. In this text the threat of English is described within the French narrative, not articulated in English, with one telling exception:

> Griffonnés en anglais au dos de cartes postales, on recevait d'eux de petits messages, avec "leurs amitiés et bons souvenirs," et, de temps en temps encore, une vraie lettre qu'ils n'adressaient plus qu'à Mrs Yaramko. La dernière, Stépan l'avait interceptée, jetée au feu – ça leur apprendrait à se liguer contre lui avec Mrs Yaramko.
> [There'd be messages scribbled in English on a postcard, with "Best regards, happy memories," and even from time to time a real letter addressed only to Mrs. Yaramko. Stepan had intercepted the last one, thrown it in the fire. That would teach them to take sides against him with Mrs. Yaramko.][54]

The couple's differences literally silence them – they cease to communicate, retreating into a kind of prelinguistic state, using only occasional grunts and calls. The sympathetic representation of the now dying woman, for whom language only operates inside her own head, and the portrayal of the inflexibility and selfishness of the husband's attitude toward language at once confirm the absolute domination of English and suggest that a rigid adherence to a language-based identity is damaging and bigoted.

In these examples of Friedmann's first model of linguistic contact, the encounters all function within the context of a hierarchical relationship between dominant language and dominated language. The scenes offer a range of responses to the position of linguistic inferiority, responses of shame, anger, silence, or in some cases recognition of the desirability of eventual assimilation to the dominant language. But despite the variety of responses to hybridity, existing power relationships between languages are not challenged and the status quo is confirmed.

Disruptive Encounters

In the second of the three models proposed by Friedmann, hybridity is understood as "a liberatory, anti-authoritarian force for good."[55] Within Roy's works there are a number of scenes that unsettle or question the positions of marginalization, exclusion and disempowerment in which her protagonists find themselves. While as individuals the protagonist may not be transformed into agents of change, their words, actions, or representation in some way subvert or disrupt the status quo.

The first example, from *La Petite Poule d'Eau*, acts as a bridge between the first and second models of hybridity. Like examples of the first, it too concerns the use of English by a new generation and reflects parents' mixed response to the evidence of their children's acculturation. The ambivalence of the acquisition of the dominant language is matched in the text by the inclusion of the Tousignant parents' reading of a letter written in English by one of their sons. Despite, or because of their difficulty in reading the letter, their response is one of pride by association with the status of English, the language of Empire: "Que la lettre eût été écrite en anglais, langue pour eux étrangère, tout juste compréhensible, insolite, fut pourtant, en définitive, ce qui leur causa le plus de fierté [That the letter should have been written in English, however – a tongue foreign to them, just barely understandable, far from their normal lives – was what after all gave them the greatest pride]" (PPE 111; 103). The paradoxical nature of their response is captured in the series of qualifications that disrupt the flow of the sentence. The letter is then "quoted" at some length, naturalized into French, so creating a French imitation of a francophone child's writing in English:

Je suis à la Petite Poule d'Eau. Ma mère est Mrs. Tousignant. Mon père garde les moutons de Bessette. On a quarante-neuf moutons. On est loin des gros chars. J'ai jamais dans toute ma vie pris les gros chars. Mais ma mère prend les gros chars. Elle achète des bébés. Et comment est-ce tu aimes le New-Zealand, toi, mon petit ami de New-Zealand?
[I am at the Little Water Hen. My mother is Mrs. Tousignant. My father keeps Bessette's sheep. One has a hundred and forty-nine sheep. One is far from the big train. Never in all my life have I taken the big train. But my mother takes the big train. She gets babies. And how do you like New Zealand, you, my little New Zealand friend?] (PPE 109; 101–2)

The use here of English terms of address and place names (Mrs. Tousignant; New Zealand), together with Canadianisms ("les gros chars") and the imitation of a child's view of the world and a young learner's grasp of sentence structure result in a mixed linguistic form that indicates the child's position in the process of acculturation. On one level, the letter is a symbol of the very process of acculturation, and so of linguistic domination. Yet within Roy's text the linguistically hybrid letter, in its artificially naturalized form, alerts us as readers to the play between languages that typifies the hyperconsciousness of language of many francophone writers for whom, in Gauvin's words, "écrire devient ... un véritable 'acte de langage' [writing becomes a real 'language act'].">[56] It is this level of playfulness that tips the force of hybridity into a more subversive mode.

When Roy does indicate language difference explicitly in her texts, the languages used are almost exclusively French and English, with only touches of or allusions to other minority languages belonging further down the language hierarchy. A sense of the multiple layers of linguistic domination and the changing dynamic that these introduce nevertheless appears through Roy's representation of migrant and First Nation protagonists. W.H. New highlights the difficulties of writing about a place using a language that comes from elsewhere, a practice intimately associated with linguistic domination under colonial and neo-colonial expansions, and also implicated in travel writing, post-colonial writing, and migrant writing. As White writers attempt to write the Canadian North, for example, the foreignness of their language to the landscape and cultures it represents can produce a range of effects: "If a language (together with the values it encodes) has been brought from somewhere else, and is being used to describe a new environment and to voice another culture's inevitably changing values, the old terms might no longer conventionally apply."[57] But what might be seen as a mismatch between language and place can have creative and productive effects, as New points out: "Under these conditions, the language is at once an impediment to communication and the very means of communication, a site of paradox, a ground at once of exhaustion and creativity."[58]

The short stories of *La Rivière sans repos* include a number of scenes of linguistic and cultural contact between Inuit protagonists and representatives of White institutions and economic interests, including the Church, medical services, the police, and the Hudson's Bay Company. The very titles of the three short stories, "Les satellites," "Le téléphone," and "Le fauteuil roulant," by their reference to products of White, southern culture, introduce a degree of foreignness into the Ungava setting.

"Le téléphone" focuses on the acquisition of a telephone by Barnaby, an Inuit in Northern Quebec, the telephone being used to symbolize the way in which the north is being penetrated by Canadian and U.S. consumerism, capitalism, and lifestyle. However, rather than simply exposing the Inuit as passive receivers of the new technology, Roy portrays its Inuit owner using the telephone to mimic and question the codes of communication between whites. In a series of telephone calls Barnaby defamiliarizes the linguistic and cultural etiquette associated with the telephone as he practises and plays with the new tool. He is shown to be learning the spoken codes: "'Je suis là,' dit-il, et tout amabilité soudain, comme il avait vu faire chez les Blancs, il se donna un air pieux et s'informa: 'Comment ça va?' ['I'm still here,' he answered. And then in a sudden burst of kindness, he took on a pious sort of air, in the way he had often seen whites do, and asked, 'How are you?']"[59] A later call adds another element of the code of communication: "Quelque chose cependant l'avait ravi. C'était le bye-bye. Enfin il connaissait la manière polie de clore un entretien au téléphone [Something had delighted him nevertheless. It was the 'bye-bye.' He finally knew the polite way of ending a telephone conversation]" (RSR 58; 64).[60] Rather than remaining a naïve victim, Barnaby proceeds to bombard the local White, anglophone companies (notably the Hudson's Bay Company, the original tool of anglophone colonization in the North) with calls, causing irritation and wasting of time. This is all narrated in French, other than the use of the terms "âllo" and "bye-bye." But the dialogue clearly suggests that Barnaby is both imitating and questioning the English he has heard all his life, from the Hudson's Bay Company traders or from the Anglican pastor, as the following example makes clear:

> "C'est la Compagnie? Elle-même? En personne? Elle va bien?"
> "Comment ça, en personne?" lui fut-il demandé sur un ton où perçait franchement l'irritation.
>   Barnaby pensa à l'explication que donnait le pasteur anglican de Dieu en trois personnes, et il faillit pouffer. Savoir combien de personnes la Compagnie, elle, se résumait!
> ["Is it really the Company? In *person*? Is it well?"
> "What do you mean, in person?" he was asked in a tone of voice which made it clear that the man at the other end was getting irritated.

Barnaby thought how the Anglican pastor had explained that God was really three persons, and he almost snickered. Goodness knows how many persons the Company was!] (RSR 58–9; 65)

Barnaby's playing with the codes and values of the south destabilizes for a moment the neo-colonial power relationship between White and Inuit. Roy's representation in French of Barnaby's imitation of the English of the Anglican pastor and of the code of polite telephone conversation creates a humorous and mildly subversive effect in the text.

In "Les satellites" the defamiliarization process works in a different direction, as Deborah, an Inuit woman, is flown south for medical treatment and experiences scenes and objects and feelings for which she has no words in her own language, Inuktitut.[61] Two examples illustrate how Roy uses focalization to distance the reader from their (probable) familiarity with the "southern" culture of Quebec. In the first quotation, the focalized narrative represents Deborah's first sight of trees: "Laissée à elle-même pour un instant, elle aperçut à peu de distance, au bord de la piste d'envol, quelque chose de fascinant. C'étaient des espèces de petites créatures vertes qui ployaient avec le vent, s'agitant presque sans arrêt. Sans doute étaient-ce ce qu'elle avait entendu nommer des arbres [Left by herself for a moment ... she noticed something fascinating on the edge of the runway a short distance away. This was a species of small creatures that bowed with the wind, quivering almost without cessation. Doubtless these were what she had heard called trees]" (RSR 24; 13).

Roy's technique of describing before naming has the effect of stressing the subjective response to the "petites creatures" and suggesting the newness of the visual impact. Once Deborah has spent some time at the hospital where she is being treated for cancer, her emotional state changes in response to this cultural dislocation:

Alors un jour le gouvernement revint auprès d'elle et dit: "Tu t'ennuies donc tant que cela! Voyons, ce n'est pas raisonnable, Deborah!"

Ainsi, c'était cela, l'ennui! Il lui avait fallu être entourée de soins, comblée d'oranges et de visites, aimée comme jamais, traitée comme une reine, pour le connaître, l'ennui. Quelle drôle de maladie c'était!

"Oui, ça doit être que je m'ennuie," avoua Deborah.
[Then one day the government came back to her again and said, "So you're as lonesome as that! Come, this isn't reasonable, Deborah."

So that's what it was – lonesomeness. She had needed to be surrounded with attention, showered with oranges and visits, loved as never before and treated like a queen to know lonesomeness. What a curious illness it was.

"Yes, it must be that I'm lonesome," Deborah admitted.]
(RSR 33–4; 20)[62]

In this excerpt, it is abstract language that is shown to be culturally specific, and foreign to Deborah. The narrative follows the protagonist across the border that is the treeline in the sub-Arctic and back again as she returns home to die. Symbolically, her journey to and fro between cultures represents what Ashcroft, Griffiths, and Tiffin have termed the "continual reminder of the separation, and yet of the hybrid interpenetration of the coloniser and colonised."[63] Roy's use of shifting perspective throws an ironic light on the exchanges across cultures and highlights the ways in which the world is constructed differently by different languages. Her reversal of the flow of meaning has the effect of questioning the fixity of the relationship between dominant and dominated cultures.

A final example of Friedmann's second model of hybridity occurs in the story "Où iras-tu, Sam Lee Wong?" which is included in the volume *Un jardin au bout du monde*. Its central protagonist is a Chinese immigrant to Saskatchewan who, like Martha and Stépan Yaramko, illustrates the dislocation experienced by many immigrants to the Canadian West, who are marginalized and rendered second class by their imperfect mastery of the English language and the absence of any opportunity to use their own native language. After twenty-five years working as a chef in the Prairie village of Horizon, Wong is forced out of his rented premises as oil companies move into the West bringing wealth and transforming the labour market. He moves on to a less affluent village, where he will have to build up another business from scratch. In this story, however, two factors give a slightly different twist to the scenes of linguistic encounter. The community, though largely English speaking, is represented as composed of many first and second generation migrants – from Iceland, the Isle of Man, Quebec, and the French Pyrenees.

Wong's customers are a cross-section of other solitary people and together they develop a kind of contact and exchange. He forms a mutually supportive friendship with one regular client who, like him, is marked as being linguistically Other – a Basque from the French Pyrenees whose strong accent and speech impediment are enough to deter anglophones from communicating with him, even though he and Wong find no problem communicating with each other in their second language.[64] In addition, Wong's relationship to the English language is shown to be subtle and tactical. The White community accepts him among them on their terms, that is, as a stereotypical Chinese worker whose grasp of their ways and their language will always be wanting. And Wong plays their game. The following scene exemplifies this interaction. Farrell, one of Wong's customers, is bitter after his wife has left him:

> Un soir qu'il était plus éméché que d'habitude Jim Farrell apostrophe directement le Chink.
> "Toi, Chinois, bien chanceux au fond de n'avoir pas femme!"
> Sans posséder encore un vocabulaire étendu, Sam Lee Wong serait parvenu à s'exprimer très convenablement, si on l'y avait un peu aidé. Il apprenait vite. Mais on continuait de lui parler comme à un déficient. Et lui, par politesse, pour ne pas faire honte à ceux qui lui parlaient ainsi, répondait à peu près sur le même ton.
> "Toi, chanceux en diable de n'avoir pas femme!" reprit Farrell.
> "Oui, Wong chanceux pas femme!" acquiesça le cafetier.
> [But one evening when Farrell was more dishevelled than usual, he addressed himself directly to the Chink.
> "You Chinaman, darn lucky not have woman!"
> Though he didn't have a big vocabulary, Sam Lee Wong would have learned to express himself quite well if people had only helped a little. He learned quickly. But they went on talking to him as if he were retarded. And he, out of politeness, so as not to shame those who spoke in this way, would answer in much the same style.
> "Yes, Wong lucky no woman!" he acquiesced.] (JM 65–6; 70)

The placement of the word "Chink," previously attributed to Farrell, prepares the reader for this scene of conscious mimicry, in

which the Chinese immigrant reflects the customer's racist discourse back on himself, in an act which the narrator explains to the
reader as being quite conscious on Wong's part. As with the earlier
example from *La Petite Poule d'Eau*, the double layer of linguistic
imitation (in this case the imitation in French both of a non-anglophone's use of English and of an anglophone's use of pidginized
English) draws attention to the strangeness of the language, and to
the power relations underlying this particular exchange.

Linguistic exchange and beyond

In the examples discussed above, the linguistic and cultural exchanges
can be seen as moments in which the terms of the exchange are
exposed and destabilized by strategies of decentring or defamil-
iarizing. In regard to her third model of hybridity, Friedmann
writes: "Power flows multidirectionally in the contact zone instead
of unidirectionally."[65] Roy's texts also contain scenes that represent
this third kind of encounter, which validate what goes on in the
common space between "us" and "them." These scenes tend to be
literally encounters or meetings, often the result of travel or social
events that bring diverse groups together. They portray a very
strong desire to communicate with the other across the language
barriers that are the legacy of colonization and migration.

One of Roy's last texts to be published in her lifetime, *De quoi
t'ennuies-tu, Eveline?* gives an update on the now elderly Eveline,
who is travelling by bus from Manitoba to California to attend
what turns out to be her brother's wake. As she travels south she
meets a variety of other North Americans, who speak different languages and come from a wide range of cultural backgrounds but
find ways to communicate. As travellers join and leave the bus and
different voices enter the dialogue, linguistic differences are negotiated either by translator figures or by the protagonists' sheer will
to exchange stories. At the end of the road, on the California coast,
Eveline learns that her brother has now died, but she is greeted
warmly by his unknown, culturally diverse, and apparently
English-speaking family. A moment of communication between
Eveline and her great-nephew gives the tone of their exchanges and
stresses the role of empathy and gesture in the process of intercultural contact:

"Je te raconterai aussi," dit Frank, "toutes les histoires que Grandpa racontait sur toi, quand tu étais une petite fille."

"Oh vraiment!" dit Eveline en s'emparant des mains de l'enfant, "il t'a parlé de moi?"

"En échange," dit Frank, "tu me conteras *some other fine stories about the old people ...*"

"Mais je ne sais pas raconter en anglais."

"*It's all right*," dit Frank. "Tu conteras comme tu peux, dans ton français, et je guetterai tes petits yeux qui rient, je guetterai ton visage, et je pense que je comprendrai."

["I shall also tell you," said Frank, "all the stories that Grandpa told me about you when you were a little girl."

"Oh really!" said Eveline, grabbing hold of the child's hands, "did he talk to you about me?"

"In return," said Frank, "you will tell me *some other fine stories about the old people ...*"

"But I can't tell stories in English."

"*It's all right*," said Frank. "You will tell them the way you can, in your French, and I shall watch your little eyes laughing, I shall watch your face, and I think I'll understand."][66]

Similarly, in "Le capucin de Toutes-Aides" the third story of *La Petite Poule d'Eau*, Roy represents a positive contact between speakers of a number of different languages. By means of what Grutman speaks of as "a few carefully added touches,"[67] the text hints at the plurilingual world of northern Manitoba. We hear a brief snatch of Ukrainian speech – "*toc, toc*" (PPE 155; 146) – and, through phonetic representation, the accent of a francophone Métis: "Quelqu'un le salua dans le français roulant, chantant des métis: 'Soirre, mon Perre' [Someone saluted him in the singing, rolling French of the half-breeds, 'Evening, Father']" (PPE 156; 147). Roy also creates scenes of bilingual and polylingual performance by the Métis trapper, Tom Mackenzie, and the polyglot travelling missionary. Tom Mackenzie organizes a dance for a multilingual gathering of neighbours and visitors, including speakers of English, French, and Ukrainian. His opening words of welcome acknowledge the linguistic, ethnic, and cultural mix:

"Nous avons avec nous *to-night*, une demoiselle de la ville," avait débité Tom, du haut de la petite plate-forme, "une

demoiselle diplômée, maîtresse d'école, school teacher dans les
deux langues, bilingue et tout le tralala; Miss Côté. C'est un
grand honor, je vous demanderai à tout un chacun de bien vous
conduire, on account of this little lady from Saint-Agathe,
Manitoba, very nice little lady, et allons donc, entrez dans la
danse. Demandez votre dame, formez votre company ..."
["We have with us tonight a young city lady," Tom had recited,
looking down from the small platform, "a young lady with
diploma, *maîtresse d'école*, schoolteacher in both languages,
bilingual and what have you: Miss Côté. It is a great honour,
and I'll ask every one of you to behave, on account of this nice
little lady from Saint Agathe, Manitoba, very nice little lady,
and come now, begin the dance. Ask your lady, form your company ..."] (PPE 230–1; 221)

While Mackenzie is shown (particularly in the original text) to
move effectively between the two (dominant) languages, the focalized narrative makes the position of the Métis clear within power
relations old and new, as we see in the following reference to
France's colonial prestige:

Si quelqu'un pouvait convenir à Miss Côté, c'était bien le
représentant parmi eux de la France, pays par excellence des
grands saluts, de la galanterie et de tout ce qui s'ensuit. Ils se
sentirent donc très fiers de disposer de lui, en cette occasion de
gala. Tom, par égard pour ce beau pays du Français, essaya
même de franciser sa vieille ritournelle.
[If anyone could be suitable for Miss Côté, it was surely the
representative of France among them, the country above all
others for ceremonious greetings, gallantry, and everything they
involved. So they felt very proud to have him on hand for this
gala occasion. Tom, out of regard for the Frenchman's beautiful
native land, even tried to give a Gallic feeling to his monoto-
nous old jigs.] (PPE 234; 225)

The polyglot priest's polylingual performance in the text is described
but not reproduced in the text, his lengthy digression in Ukrainian
for the benefit of a couple of first generation immigrants being summarized by the narrator. Yet the general point is made that for
Father Joseph-Marie, as for other missionary figures in Roy's

works, polylingualism is more than a pragmatic necessity; the transcendence of linguistic barriers has a spiritual value:

> Il était à l'aise en mettant pied dans cette petite Babel ...
> N'était-ce pas à tout prendre dans une petite foule de races bien brassées telle qu'il en avait sous les yeux que se révélait d'une exécution toute simple, toute naturelle, l'"Aimez-vous les uns les autres!"
> [He was at ease as he stepped through this tiny Babel ... On the whole, was it not in a small crowd of well-mixed races, such as he then saw before him, that stood revealed, in its most simple, natural fulfillment, the precept "Love one another!"] (PPE 156–7; 147–8)

The polyglot priest and the Métis trapper act as agents of linguistic and cultural contact, and are both linguistically creative. The priest manages to transcend the divisions of heteroglossia thanks to his linguistic range, whereas the Métis performs a verbal negotiation among the various languages of his audience. Both are represented as ambivalent figures, identifiable with the forms of contact typical of colonialism – evangelism and *métissage* – yet able to adopt a mobile hybrid position between languages.

In other cases, the desire to communicate verbally across language barriers is frustrated and other forms of exchange or contact come into play. An episode from *La Saga d'Eveline*, for example, recounts the chance meeting of two pioneer families in southern Manitoba, one migrating from Quebec and one from Scotland, on the trail to their new homesteads. Their relative equality as migrants and the Scottish origins of the Protestants attenuate the potential inequality between anglophone and francophone. Dialogue is presented in both English and French. None of the protagonists understands all the dialogue, which initially sets up a pattern of partial communication and misunderstanding. Since the narrator does not summarize or comment on all the dialogue, the monolingual francophone reader is placed in a position similar to that of the francophone protagonists. The expression of mutual good will is achieved through the giving of help (repairing a wheel on the Scottish family's wagon, sharing of food) and by the Quebec mother acting as midwife when the Scottish woman goes into labour. Against this background of generosity between migrant groups, the narrative recounts the mutual attraction between the young Scottish son and Eveline. The dialogue comically suggests the hit-and-miss nature of their linguistic exchange:

> Il dit avec autorité:
> "I'm a good head taller than you."
> "Peut-être," dit-elle, à tout hasard, n'ayant pas compris un mot.
> "Tu viens de loin, toi? De Scotland?"
> "From Inverness."
> "Inverness. Vous en avez-t-y des mots curieux dans votre langue."
> [He said with authority:
> "*I'm a good head taller than you*"
> "Perhaps," she said at random, not having understood a word.
> "Do you come from far away? From Scotland?"
> "*From Inverness.*"
> "Inverness. You've got some odd words in your language."]
> (SE 129)[68]

When the son gives Eveline a gift of a young puppy, her imperfect comprehension is again underlined: "'Be most kind to him ... His name is Tom' ... Eveline serrait dans ses bras le petit chien. Elle avait compris qu'il se nommait Tamme, – un curieux nom – mais Tamme elle l'appellerait [" '*Be most kind to him ... His name is Tom*' ... Eveline held the little dog tightly in her arms. She had understood that his name was Tamme, – an odd name – but Tamme she would call him]" (SE 136).

In these exchanges the inability to communicate in a common language is represented as a lack that can be filled by other means, here by the exchange of practical help and the giving of a gift, tokens of the desire to transcend the barriers of difference. The setting of this nostalgic image of pioneer days in the late nineteenth century, prior to the banning of bilingual education, and in rural Manitoba, helps to explain the idealized view of relationships between anglophone and francophone new Manitobans. But a similarly optimistic view of the possibility of transcending language difference through alternative modes of expression and creativity, such as art or music, appears in *Ces Enfants de ma vie*. As we have seen in the previous chapter, the encounters between teacher and pupil in *Ces Enfants de ma vie* all involve some degree of cross-cultural contact, whether the pupil is francophone, as in the case of immigrant children from France and Métis Manitoban pupils, or allophone, from Ukraine, Italy, or Flemish-speaking Belgium. Each story focuses on building a contact between teacher and pupil, and often between teacher and parent. The process of contact is frequently problematic and requires some negotiation on the part of the teacher/narrator, through which teacher, pupil, and parent can achieve understanding or mutual respect across the divide of culture and language. Typically, language is represented as an obstacle to communication, but the exchange that is eventually achieved transcends difference, rather in the way that the gift of the puppy as a token of love in *La Saga d'Eveline* transcended the language barrier.

In the stories of *Ces enfants de ma vie*, while the teacher initiates the process of contact (going to visit the parents at home, encouraging the child to develop a particular gift), the transcendent moment in the process usually comes from the child and his or her parents. One final example will illustrate the way in which incomplete verbal communication can be overcome by some other form of expression. In "L'alouette," Nil, a Ukrainian child with a wonderful singing voice, is asked by the teacher on several occasions to perform for others. The story closes with a scene of the teacher visiting the boy's mother, in which the evident difficulties of spoken communication are transcended by mutual good will: "Je tentai, par l'intermédiaire de Nil, d'exprimer à Paraskovia Galaïda quelque chose de la joie que les chants de son petit garçon avaient apportée à tant de gens déjà, et elle, à travers lui, chercha à me dire ses remerciements pour je ne compris pas trop quoi au juste. Bientôt nous avons renoncé à épancher nos sentiments à l'aide des mots, écoutant plutôt la nuit [With Nil's help, I tried to express to Paraskovia Galaïda something of the joy her small son's singing had brought to so many people; and she, with his help, tried to thank me for I wasn't quite sure what. Soon we had given up trying to pour out our feelings by means of words, listening instead to the night]" (CEV 73; 52–3). The final paragraphs of the story describe the moment when mother and son begin to sing together, the music and their voices transcending the gap in linguistic comprehension: "Alors [leurs voix] montèrent et s'accordèrent en plein vol dans un chant étrangement beau qui était celui de la vie vécue et de la vie de rêve. [Then (their voices) flew upward, harmonizing as they rose in a strangely lovely song, one of life as it is lived and life as it is dreamed]" (CEV 73–4; 53).

These scenes recognize linguistic divisions between individuals (and acknowledge the relative power of the languages concerned), and they also show a way of transcending the language divide. But as examples of what goes on between "them" and "us," they are rather utopian and do not represent strategies of linguistic interaction. Usually Roy uses English or French, or a combination of both, and brings allophones or assimilated groups into an Anglo-Franco dialogue. While plurilingualism may seem to become more a reality than a concept within the text, Roy's utopian scenes of exchange arguably do little to unsettle the linguistic division in Canada between the two dominant languages and the speakers of minority languages. Yet language scenes in Roy's work are more than what Margaret Steffler has referred to in her analysis of postcolonial Canadian writing in English as "separations and collisions of languages, drawing attention both orally and visually to the coexistence of two types of language – that of the colonizer and that of the colonized."[69] In fact the second model of linguistic encounter, the type that Roy treats with mimicry and subversion in her texts, is potentially more far-reaching in the way in which these tactics defamiliarize and denaturalize language. Significantly, it is when Roy looks at English or French from outside the binary divide of English/French that "all language becomes denaturalized, distanced"[70] and the real effects of linguistic domination become clear. Through the more subversive encounters (and to a lesser extent through utopian exchanges), Roy makes an attempt to unpick or transcend the hierarchy and move beyond the colonial binary to represent a more fluid relationship between languages.

Roy's position as a bilingual, bicultural francophone and the traces of this bilingual, bicultural voice in her texts, produce for the reader the sense of an ambivalent relationship toward language, an ambivalence that destabilizes any identification with a single language position within the hierarchy of encounters and exchanges. This ambivalence is further complicated when Roy, writing in French, includes encounters not only between English and French, but also between French and other languages and between English and other languages (minority, migrant, and indigenous). The fact that these encounters are narrated in French accentuates the complexity of the relationships between languages and their users, and highlights the various forms of negotiation and tactics possible in any confrontation with the other's language. In trying to conceptualize such an ambivalence of emplacement, Michael Cronin's understanding of the "entre-deux," or the in-between, is useful. In a discussion of the temporal and spatial interpretations of this figure that have arisen in response to Bhabha's essentially temporal use of the notion of the "Third Space,"[71] Cronin offers the following model: "The 'entre-deux' ... should be conceived of less as a space, a reified entity tending towards stasis than as a constant movement backwards and forwards in which there is no fixed identification with either of the poles."[72]

The analysis of Roy's position between languages in this chapter has offered a reading of her work that reveals just such a sense of oscillation between French and English, majority and minority languages. Roy's texts display a fascination with the language or subjectivity of members of the First Nations and other linguistic minority subjects. This awareness both indicates the space for their voice and leaves it to a certain extent unattainable. From this perspective, the representation of the Other's language, in dialogue or in other modes within the text, can be likened to the process of translation. Indeed, if, as Joyce Marshall has written, "all dialogue is an exercise in translation," then what the writing of dialogue and the creation of a literary translation have in common is the recognition that the representation of the Other's voice will never be unproblematic.[73] For Cronin, the work of a translator exemplifies the movement of the "entre-deux": "The continuous oscillation between source text and target text, between home culture and foreign culture, native language and foreign language, define both translator and traveler as figures in motion."[74] In the following chapter the notion of translation as movement between languages and cultures will be examined with specific reference to the translation of Roy's work into English.

4

Translating Differences: Conveying Context

The previous chapter explored the ways in which Roy used linguistic encounters and exchanges to represent the Other's language, and considered the extent to which such scenes demonstrate a sense of "hyperconsciousness of language." In it I also suggested how representations of the Other's language may have been related to Roy's experiences of and responses to her bicultural and bilingual formation. We observed that Roy's references to, and use of, elements of languages other than French in her autobiographical and fictional works can both highlight and problematize the status of the languages concerned, and alert the reader to the difficulties and contradictions inherent in all communication with the Other. This chapter considers translation as a process that necessarily involves, and tries to convey, the encounter with the Other's language.

As Henry Schogt points out in a general discussion of issues in literary translation: "There is some loss when a bilingual situation is presented in only one language."[1] In the process of translation into English, Roy's texts are rewritten in the Other's language. But how are scenes of linguistic encounter and the signs of linguistic difference – often marked in the French text by the use of English – affected once the texts are translated into English, the dominant language in the Canadian context? When a translator is faced with a heterolingual text, technical and strategic issues also arise, issues that have been addressed on the methodological and theoretical level by those working in Translation Studies and Postcolonial

Studies. We begin with comments on the relevance of translation and Translation Studies to an understanding of Roy's work. After brief remarks on the importance of translations in Roy's literary career, and her attitudes toward the translation process, we examine some issues salient to the translation of Roy's works, to establish a conceptual framework for analysing selected translations. We then turn our attention to aspects of Roy's participation in the translation process as they have emerged from the recently published correspondence between Roy and Joyce Marshall.[2] In the final section of the chapter we look at translations of *Alexandre Chenevert* and *Bonheur d'occasion* in order to discover what happens to the "bilingualism" of Roy's texts when they are translated into English.

ROY IN ENGLISH

Translation has been of immense strategic importance in the career of Gabrielle Roy. Francophone readers identify Roy primarily as the author of *Bonheur d'occasion*, yet it was the English translation, *The Tin Flute*, selected in 1947 as the Literary Guild of America book of the month, that established her international recognition and gave her the financial security to pursue a literary career. William Arthur Deacon, literary critic of the *Globe and Mail* between 1936 and 1960, has estimated that whereas in Quebec the revenue from *Bonheur d'occasion* was about $5,000 (with sales of about 1,000 copies a month, this made it a bestseller in Quebec), the English translation earned Roy about $250,000.[3]

Translations of Roy's works have had a strong impact not only on sales figures but also on her status as a *Canadian* writer. In an analysis of the reception of Quebec women writers in Anglo-Canada, Barbara Godard recalls that "Gabrielle Roy was named best Canadian woman novelist (in English) in a poll carried out amongst professors of English in Canadian universities in 1978." In a footnote she comments: "This nomination reveals that Roy has been completely integrated into the Anglo-Canadian literary system."[4] She cites the findings of Jane Koustas's analysis of the index of *Canadian Translation*, which revealed that the Quebec authors with the highest percentage of their works translated into English were Anne Hébert (90%), Gabrielle Roy (75%), and Marie-Claire Blais (60%).[5] As Godard points out, this rate of translation is part of a cycle of interrelated phenomena within the literary system: "The more translations, the more reviews by literary critics, the more symbolic capital, the more translations."[6]

It is evident from the published correspondence between Roy and Deacon – who from 1946 onward advised Roy and promoted her work in Anglo-Canada – that from their earliest contact, Deacon was working for Roy's eventual integration into the Anglo-Canadian literary system and that the translation of her work served this purpose. In April 1946 he wrote to Roy: "Certainly you must write in French. (They told me in Montreal that a reader of your novel could *smell* St. Henri.) But you are a writer of the world, not just Quebec; and it is most important of all that your novels shall be known and read in English Canada. The translation route is correct."[7] This appeal to universalism would have resonated with Roy's own humanistic thinking, as expressed in a later letter she wrote to Deacon in which she admits her disappointment about the French-language reception of *Alexandre Chenevert*: "My dear Bill, I begin to see that this chord I'm always trying to touch – this theme of human love regardless of nationality, of religion, of tongue, this essential truth doesn't mean much to my people."[8] The conflict that emerges here – between Roy's ideological attachment to universal values and her dutiful attachment to "her" people – recalls the contradictory positions that her parallel education instilled in her. Yet just as Roy's humanistic universalism was a product of her very specific background, so Deacon's support for Roy was part of a particular view of Canada's future. His letter of 24 March 1946 continues: "The United States is a big, rich country, but English Canada is going to love and honor you because you are one of us ... We shall be proud of you, more glad of your success than if you wrote originally in English. And making the French-Canadian mind known to English-speakers will be the most important work you can ever do in your life."[9]

The interesting ambiguity of the phrase "one of us" and the mediating role of "making the French-Canadian mind known to English speakers" seem to place Roy somewhere *between* English and French Canada. Mariel O'Neill-Karch goes further: "In William Arthur Deacon's thinking, Gabrielle Roy is part of Anglo-Canadian literary history ... She can therefore be considered legitimately within the framework of the dominant ideology of the literary institution in Anglo-Canada, which explains the importance that Deacon accords to her as a figure whom he cultivates and to her work which he encourages enthusiastically and with unfailing belief."[10]

Deacon's advice on Roy's publication in English, while making sound economic sense, was grounded in his belief that as a francophone Canadian writer, Roy needed anglophone Canada. His view of Canadian literary history, as expounded in a lecture course delivered at the Ryerson Institute of Technology in 1951–52, was that Anglo-Canadian culture would gradually assimilate the best talents among Canada's francophone writers and that any separate Franco-Canadian culture would eventually disappear in the natural course of the eventual assimilation of the francophone population of Canada.[11] As O'Neill-Karch astutely observes, Deacon's motivation in championing Roy can be understood in terms of an ideology of "quiet assimilation."[12]

One of the measures of success of the Canadian writer is of course the annual announcement of the prestigious Governor General's Awards.[13] Roy's name appeared three times on the list of winners: in 1947 for her first novel, *The Tin Flute*, in 1957 for *Street of Riches*, and in 1977 for *Ces enfants de ma vie*.[14] The reason the first two titles are given in English is that prior to 1959 only works published in English were eligible for consideration. So, for Roy to gain recognition as a *Canadian* writer in the 1940s and 1950s, she had first to be translated into English, a fact that confirms the very different status of the French and English languages in the eyes of the Canadian literary establishment at the time.[15] Yet, despite the importance of the "translation route" in Canada, the absence of any reference to the names of the translators of Roy's two prize-winning texts (Hannah Josephson in the case of *The Tin Flute* and Harry Binsse in the case of *Street of Riches*) suggests that in the 1940s–50s the translating process was felt to be a necessary formality, an anonymous and low-status task.[16]

Translation studies

A lack of awareness of the transformation that any text undergoes as it is rewritten in another language was, indeed, symptomatic of the position of the study of translation, in Canada and elsewhere, prior to the 1970s. Looking back to the 1970s, Susan Bassnett recalls: "Translation was the Cinderella subject, not taken seriously at all, and the language used to discuss work in translation was astonishingly antiquated when set against the new critical vocabularies that were dominating literary studies in general. To pass from a seminar on literary theory to a seminar on translation in those days was to move from the end of the twentieth century to the 1930s."[17]

Different forms of translation had been essential to European colonial expansion. Given Canada's double colonization, translation was all the more crucial. E.D. Blodgett asserts: "Because Canada is officially bilingual, translation is more than a mere craft; it is, and has been for generations, a political necessity."[18] Nevertheless, despite the long history of contact between Canada's anglophone and francophone settler populations, Philip Stratford remarked in his 1977 *Bibliography of Canadian Books in Translation: French to English and English to French / Bibliographie de livres canadiens traduits de l'anglais au français et du français à l'anglais*: "Canada has as yet no tradition in literary translation."[19] This lack of tradition doubtless has many causes, but among them, the unequal power relations between the two linguistic groups are key. The political importance of translation in Canada became particularly salient in the 1970s, with the growth of Quebec nationalism. As Jacques Brault declared in 1975: "The keys to translation are in the hands of the powerful and we are painfully aware of that every day."[20] Sherry Simon explains why translation has long been such a sensitive political issue in Quebec: "Too closely linked with the liberal, humanist discourse of official bilingualism, too closely associated with the virtues of tolerance and transparency which care little for the abuse of power, translation has always had negative connotations in public discourse in Quebec."[21] The history of translation as a form of cultural exchange between anglophone and francophone Canada opens up a range of issues that are now widely discussed in the increasingly interdisciplinary fields of Translation Studies, Postcolonial Studies, and Cultural Studies. Translation in Canada is at once a product of, and a vector of, the relationships between colonial centres and their margins, the successive waves of colonization and post-colonial migration, and the cultural heterogeneity resulting from the cohabitation of linguistic and cultural minorities.

Perhaps the most significant development in the field of Translation Studies in the last thirty years is the so-called cultural turn, described by Godard as "a recent paradigm shift in translation theory ... concerned with historical and cultural difference as these inflect power dynamics in the production of meaning."[22] Whether one is dealing with the relationship between French and English in Manitoba in the 1920s, between Haitian Creole and French, or between Russian and French in nineteenth-century Russia, relationships between languages are increasingly conceptualized not in terms of "an abstract ideal of cosmopolitan communicability," but rather "under conflicting and changing socio-historical contingencies."[23] Lawrence Venuti argues that translators have tended in the past to hide cultural difference in the interests of what he terms a "fluent" strategy: "A translated text is judged successful – by most editors, publishers, reviewers, readers, by translators themselves – when it reads fluently, when it gives the appearance that it is not translated."[24] As he develops this notion, the link between a strategy of fluency and colonialism emerges from his choice of terminology: "A fluent strategy performs a labor of acculturation which domesticates the foreign text, making it intelligible and even familiar to the target-language reader, providing him or her with the narcissistic experience of recognising his or her own culture in a cultural other, enacting an imperialism that extends the dominion of transparency with other ideological discourses over a different culture."[25]

Nor is this "imperialistic" power restricted to the past. In a Canadian context such erasure may happen whenever a text is translated from a lower into a higher language within a diglossic system (between French and English, or from the language of an allophone culture into one of the two "official" languages of Canada). The fluent strategy of translation attempts to rewrite the text in the codes of the receiving culture and can result in the effacement of the cultural and linguistic difference of the source text. An illustration of the prevalence of such thinking about translation occurs in the 1967 introduction to the translation of *Rue Deschambault*, in which, as Brandon Conron writes: "One of the achievements ... is that most English-Canadian readers will scarcely be conscious that it deals primarily with French-Canadians. Such an impression, although perhaps contradictory to the author's purpose, is a tribute to the breadth of humanity expressed."[26] (Interestingly, Conron's hesitation about Roy's intentions reveals some awareness that what he likes to see as universal humanism might equally be understood as the reduction of the cultural difference to sameness.) Given the effects of the fluent strategy, the universalism attributed to any literary work in translation may be as much a product of the translation as the text. Maria Tymoczko reminds us: "In judging a translation, a reader may be deceived into overreading a text as 'universal' by a translator's assimilative strategies of rendering the text."[27]

Assimilation practices take many forms and are often not the result of a conscious decision on the translator's part but a product of deeply rooted cultural and ideological attitudes. In an influential essay in 1985, Antoine Berman listed twelve "deforming tendencies" found in literary translation which act to prevent the translation from being a "trial of the foreign" and instead work together to produce a text that is "more 'clear,' more 'elegant,' more 'fluent,' more 'pure' than the original," but which represents "the destruction of the letter in favour of meaning."[28] His method, termed the "analytic of translation," was intended to operate both on the rational and the psychoanalytical levels, "insofar as the system is largely unconscious, present as a series of tendencies or *forces* that cause translation to deviate from its essential aim."[29] Of the tendencies discussed by Berman, the following are particularly relevant for the translation of francophone Canadian literature into English: "the destruction of vernacular networks or their exoticization"; "the destruction of expressions and idioms"; and "the effacement of the superimposition of languages."[30] Berman then discusses ways in which such deformation can be limited ("a sort of counter-system destined to neutralize, or attenuate, the negative tendencies").[31] Berman's preferred translation strategy is that of literal translation, arguing that: "It is through this labor that translation, on the one hand, restores the particular signifying process of works (which is more than their meaning) and, on the other hand, transforms the translating language."[32]

Godard, while welcoming what is termed the "ethical turn" in translation theory, seeks a more politicized model of ethical translation, aligning herself with Henri Meschonnic, Venuti, and Gayatri Spivak rather than Berman: "For them [Venuti and Spivak] the ethical dimension concerns hierarchical relationships between languages and cultures: by means of attempting to transform these into reciprocal recognition, ethics positions itself in the political domain."[33] Clearly this stress on "hierarchical relationships between languages" is highly relevant to the work of translators in Canada's multilingual society. Simon similarly accepts the ethical parameters of translation, while emphasizing the role of historical context: "In the Canadian experience ... the ethical dimensions of translation are anything but accessory. Translation brings into play concepts of cultural difference which result in the construction of implicit (sometimes explicit) relations of alterity through language. These relationships are far from static and come to materialize the changing values with which language is invested."[34] It is precisely such a concern with cultural difference that requires that translation not eliminate the grounds of specificity of the source text, an elimination that Conron, in his previously cited preface to *Street of Riches*, clearly welcomed.[35]

The widespread recognition in recent translation theory of these opposing models of "foreignizing" and "domesticating" translation has been reflected in critical analysis of translation practices in Canada, and a number of translation strategies have emerged as being conducive to preserving the "foreignness" of the text. If, as Simon argues, "translation ... is the materialization of our relationship to otherness, to the experience – through language – of what is different," how have translations of francophone texts attempted to recognize the difference of Canada's Others?[36] Blodgett's well-known article, appropriately titled "How do you say 'Gabrielle Roy'" reflects on the effects of domesticating translation in the diglossic context of Canada: "To find an equivalent is to make the Other mine, to practise a kind of assimilation. Hence we have both an anglophone and a francophone Gabrielle Roy."[37] But if Canadian translation becomes more self-reflexive, then, he argues, the translator's position becomes more ambiguous, "neither within nor outside his language, steeping equivocation with a particular significance."[38]

A reference to Roy features in the title of another key article from the 1980s, "'Pas *lonely* pantoute?',," in Schogt draws on Berman's notion of "foreignness of the text" to discuss the translation of four highly distinctive francophone Canadian texts – W.H. Blake's translation of Hémon's *Maria Chapdelaine*, Hannah Josephson's translation of Roy's *Bonheur d'occasion*, Sheila Fischman's translation of Carrier's *La Guerre, Yes Sir!* and Luis de Céspedes's translation of Maillet's *La Sagouine*. Across this corpus Schogt finds two traits that he judges to be characteristic of francophone Canadian writing – the deliberate use of regionalisms and the presence of the English language. Both, he concludes, are untranslateable: "The English element because the target language is English, regionalisms because the extra-linguistic reality that they evoke is unique."[39] Translation strategies vary. In Josephson's case, for example, the "hybrid character"[40] of Alphonse's language is erased, whereas Fischman makes attempts to mark the tensions between English and French at key points in her translation of *La Guerre, Yes Sir!*

The publication of Nicole Deschamps's edition of *Maria Chapdelaine* in 1980 provides an instructive coda to Schogt's article. Schogt uses a 1970 edition of Hémon's work for his comparisons between the English translation and the "original" text. But as Deschamps's introduction establishes, the 1970s edition and its predecessors were based on a censored text: the original manuscript, corrected by Hémon before his accidental death in 1913, underwent significant editorial work for the serialization published in Paris by *Le Temps* and again when Louvigny de Montigny prepared it for publication in book form in Montreal in 1916.[41] In addition to introducing mistakes and substituting French terms for unrecognized Canadian usages, the version in *Le Temps* treated the Canadianisms it retained differently from Hémon. Whereas Hémon incorporated regionalisms "without affectation, as the appropriate elements of the language that he recreates in his story,"[42] the Parisian editors chose to exoticize these signs, separating out regionalisms with inverted commas. As Deschamps argues, this is a form of rewriting according to external norms: "The use of inverted commas for the language of Quebec has since then become part of Hémon's text. In a way this practice has begun to colonize it."[43] Turning to the changes introduced by Louvigny de Montigny, Deschamps writes: "Paradoxically, the Canadian edition is the one which conforms the most closely to standard French,"[44] a paradox which she explains by the enduring position of France as a cultural model for Quebec society in the early twentieth century. Clearly, the strategies of exoticization, normalization, and assimilation that are part of the cultural exchange between centres and their margins operate at all stages of the rewriting process, from editing to marketing to translation. Equally, as this case illustrates, revised editions and retranslations can in some cases, and to some extent, reverse the flow.

In "Speaking White: Literary Translation as a Vehicle of Assimilation in Quebec," Kathy Mezei includes a larger corpus of texts (including works by Hébert, Renaud, Ferron, Tremblay, and Marchessault in translation) and focuses specifically on the transla-

tion of the English language elements in the source texts. Most of
the examples discussed reveal the mistranslation or the nontrans-
lation of English, a phenomenon that Mezei attributes both to the
focus on the target audience – "desire is directed towards creating a
readable pleasurable text for the English reader"[45] – and on editorial intervention. But she reflects on the alternatives "in which the
target text, instead of assimilating, absorbing the original Quebec
text, effecting a form of closure as the English text firmly closes its
jaws upon the French original, tries to and does create an open target text, open to differences, open to varieties of meanings, open to
both the original cultural referential system and the one in the process of being created."[46] Pragmatic suggestions for an open model
of translation include "textual devices such as italics, parentheses,
translator's notes, additions, conscious alterations, and explanatory
phrases."[47] All these features would add to the reader's awareness
not only of the linguistic and cultural difference of the source text,
but also of the translation's status as translation, as an example of a
process, incomplete and non-definitive.

Simon's work has ranged widely over the field of literary translation, including the comparison of different translations of the same
work and a more recent exploration of questions of cultural
hybridity.[48] In "The True Quebec as Revealed to English Canada:
Translated Novels 1864–1950," Simon compares two translations
of Philippe Aubert de Gaspé's *Les anciens Canadiens* and Louis
Hémon's *Maria Chapdelaine* in order to analyse the strategies
employed for the translation of dialect. She finds wide variation
between translations, with accordingly diverse effects: "Though
explicitly motivated by the needs of national reconciliation, translations offer different versions of that 'other society' and its people.
Affirmations of essential identity (most clearly typified by Roberts's
translation of *Les anciens Canadiens*) coexist with declarations of
fundamental difference (the examples of both W.H. Blake and T.G.
Marquis)."[49] Simon's article also raises a further issue of relevance
to our analysis of Roy – that of *re*translations. She argues that
retranslations are of extra significance both because of their role as
rewritings within the literary polysystem (enhancing and maybe
reorienting the text's reception) and because of the opportunity for
stylistic revision, which can give the translation the status of a literary work.[50]

The notion of rewriting is further explored with reference to Roy's work in a recent volume of essays edited by Jane Everett and François Ricard. In a jointly authored article, "How do you translate 'regard'? Rewriting Gabrielle Roy," Lorna Hutchinson and Nathalie Cooke apply Lefevere's notion of rewriting to three categories of rewriting (translations, re-editions, and posthumous critical editions), which "all serve to guide and shape particular responses to Roy's authorial persona."[51] They conclude that Roy was not a mere object of, but rather an active participant in, the various modes of rewriting discussed.

A final example of analyses of the translation of francophone Canadian literature offers a comparativist perspective that draws on postcolonial theory. In a jointly authored article comparing literary translation in India and Canada, Simon and Vanamal Viswanatha argue that "translation practice is always grounded in a theory of culture, in a set of assumptions about the ways in which linguistic forms carry cultural meanings."[52] Constrasting the conceptualization of cultural difference in operation in Quebec in the translations from the 1920s, the 1970s, and the 1990s, the article argues that postcolonial theory alerts us to "the need to restore complexity to our understanding of relations of alterity, of oppositional identities created through struggle."[53] In the discussion that follows, we focus on the extent to which translations of Roy's works have carried out assimilative cultural work, and the extent to which they might reflect a more pluralistic conceptualization in keeping with what Viswanatha and Simon refer to as "the dramas of hybridity and self-doubt characteristic of much cultural expression today."[54]

Roy and her translators

If Roy had not left the Canadian West to travel to Europe but had established herself as a writer in Manitoba, it is quite conceivable that she might have written in English. In a letter to Deacon in 1946 she stated: "Before leaving Canada, I had a few stories published in English and a few in French."[55] Ricard's bibliography lists only two publications in English prior to Roy's departure for Europe, but it is possible that some have not yet been traced or were published under pseudonyms, as were some of her short stories in the early

1940s.[56] Yet once she had made the decision to write in French, she published only in French, and her work was translated by a variety of named and unnamed translators.[57]

Roy's command of English and her wide reading of literature in English – both English-language literature and foreign literature translated into English – meant, however, that she was able to take an active part in the translation process. Her letters written in English to William Arthur Deacon (1946–61), to Jack McClelland (1957–1980), to Joyce Marshall (1959–80), and to Margaret Laurence (1976–80) testify to her ease and effectiveness in the language throughout her literary career.[58] Yet, despite an impressive degree of fluency, Roy clearly felt hampered by not being able to write to Deacon in French, and a recurrent tone of self-criticism appeared in the letters. In 1946 she wrote: "I know this is poorly expressed; I haven't written in English for a long time and I'm full of misgivings concerning the propositions."[59] Her correspondence with Joyce Marshall, conducted entirely in English, shows similar dissatisfaction. Roy writes, perhaps with an eye to posterity: "Sometime I feel that our letters (I have kept all of yours) would make a book, if only mine were worth, partly worth yours. Perhaps, if I had written in French from the beginning, we would now have an exchange of some value to others. But I so needed the exercise in English, that I plunged, no matter what the consequences."[60] Marshall, who knew Roy's English not only through their lengthy correspondence but also through their close collaboration on translations, gave Roy the reassurance she needed: "I think the way you express yourself in English has a very particular charm, very often poetic and with just the occasional oddity (not quite a mistake) that adds something quite delightful."[61] In a letter to Margaret Laurence (6 March 1978), Roy once more compares her English unfavourably with that of her correspondent: "You write to me in your superb English, so alive and rich. If only I could write to you in French. Still, never mind! We have been able to reach to [one] another beautifully across what is called the language barrier and which is not such a barrier after all."[62]

This desire to perform in English (her letter writing in both languages can be regarded as a form of performance), coupled with a degree of self-deprecation, recalls Roy's internalized sense of cultural inferiority both as a schoolgirl in Saint-Boniface and as a student at the Guildhall School of Music and Drama in London in

1937–38. Yet this self-doubt disappears when she is dealing with the translation of her own work. Joan Hind-Smith, in her study of Roy, Laurence, and Frederick Philip Grove, describes the working relationship of Roy and Marshall as follows: "The relationship between Gabrielle Roy and Joyce Marshall is distinguished by mutual respect and many arguments. Each accuses the other of being exacting; each takes a passionate interest in language."[63] Marshall has given a number of accounts of her work as Roy's translator and these confirm that Roy was both passionate and sometimes wrong: "I was made to turn the meaning and connotation of words ... up and down and sideways as I'd never had to before. Some rare old rows took place. Gabrielle's knowledge of English grammar was no longer as complete as she believed it was and she sometimes considered me *exigeante* (fussy) in my insistence on strict word-order and usage."[64]

As editor of the volume of correspondence between the two women, Jane Everett has a close knowledge of Roy's (hand)written English. She comments on the apparent confidence with which Roy writes, but adds: "But she does make errors, and even when her English is technically correct, it is not always idiomatic."[65] The errors are of different types – some confusion of English and French spellings, tense errors, lack of capitalization (months, nationalities), some old-fashioned hyphenation ("to-day"), the wrong choice of prepositions after verbs, and incorrect use of the possessive. This is not to say that her contribution to the translation process was not significant. Marshall praises "her excellent ear, her sense of the nuances and subtleties as well as the sound and rhythm of language." She adds: "I owe her a great deal as a writer and translator."[66] Indeed, Roy's familiarity with the translation process and confidence in evaluating literary translation between English and French is clear in a letter she wrote to Margaret Laurence in 1980 commenting on the quality of the translation into French of *The Diviners* (*Les Oracles*). Roy's close knowledge of Laurence's novel in its original English allows her to test the translation by comparing certain distinctive passages, including the opening page, Piquette's song (included with the music and text of three other songs at the end of the narrative), and a passage in which the translator transposes a section of colloquial language. Her first impressions are good: "I have the feeling that the work has been done with love and a flair for the right kind of transposition which is after all

very near creative talent itself."[67] The emotive and instinctive terms
used here characterize her approach to translation, as does her recognition that the translator's work is far from a mechanical transposition, but "very near creative talent itself."[68] Everett, in her
Introduction to the Marshall-Roy correspondence, reflects on what
the letters reveal about Roy's criteria for judging a translation. She
points out that evaluative terms such as "smoothness" and "clarity" used in the correspondence are never defined, but she concludes: "Scattered remarks ... suggest that for her, a successful
translation was (at least in part) a stylistic reconstitution of the
original, and a good translator was one who paid particular attention to sentence rhythm and to the expressive values of the words
Roy considered most important in a sentence."[69] The fact that
issues commonly discussed in translation theory do not seem to figure in Roy and Marshall's remarks on translation should not sur-
prise us, for, as Schogt observes: "The solutions translators choose
do not depend on theoretical considerations, but on practical abili-
ties."[70] But as we consider a number of cases of translation practice,
certain practical choices will have theoretical implications, and
they might also be related to particular political, social, or historical contexts.

Five translators have been responsible for the English translations
of Roy's major works. The degree of collaboration between author
and translator seems to have varied (according to Roy's own circumstances and to the working practices of her translators) but the
closest was with Joyce Marshall. Hannah Josephson, an American,
translated *Bonheur d'occasion*, published in 1947 with the title *The
Tin Flute*, but was unavailable to translate Roy's second work.[71]
Unlike Josephson, Harry Binsse, Roy's second translator, was a
Canadian with a house in La Malbaie on the St Lawrence.[72] Binsse
worked as Roy's translator from 1951 till 1962. His expertise was
appreciated, but Roy's correspondence reveals some irritation with
Binsse's working patterns. In a letter to Deacon, Roy writes about
the slow progress of the translation of *Alexandre Chenevert*: "I
begin to foresee endless delays as my translator, Mr. Binsse, is I'm
afraid, a terrible procrastinator."[73] As her letters to Joyce Marshall
reveal, it was Roy who decided to terminate the arrangement.[74]
When the roles of McClelland & Stewart and Harcourt Brace
changed to give priority to the Canadian publication for the translation of *La Route d'Altamont*, Binsse was sacked.[75] On Roy's

recommendation, Joyce Marshall, who had already translated the short story "Grand-mère et la poupée" for publication in *Chatelaine* in 1960,[76] replaced him, and *The Road Past Altamont* appeared in 1966 – the last of Roy's works to be separately published in the United States.[77] When Marshall decided to devote more time to her own literary work, Alan Brown was commissioned for the translation of *Un jardin au bout du monde*, and he remained Roy's official translator until her death.[78] In a letter to Roy in 1976 Marshall reacted very positively to news of her successor, describing him as "most skilful and, of course, very sympathetic to your work."[79] In the following year, when work on the translation of *Un jardin au bout du monde* was completed, Roy wrote to Marshall and mentioned Brown, "who did a very fine translation by the way."[80] It is his *retranslation* of *Bonheur d'occasion* that will be discussed alongside Josephson's original translation later in this chapter. The translation of Roy's posthumous publications, including the award-winning translation of Roy's autobiography, has been the work of Patricia Claxton.[81]

We now turn to consider in more detail the collaborative work on translation between Joyce Marshall and Gabrielle Roy. The fact that this is possible is in large part thanks to the work of Jane Everett, whose edition of the correspondence between the two women has recently been published. Everett's work on the Roy-Marshall correspondence, on Marshall as translator, and on Roy's attitudes toward the process of translation offers a much fuller discussion of this working relationship than can be envisaged in this context.[82] Here, we can only consider the question of the treatment of aspects of cultural and linguistic difference as they arise in their correspondence.

Translating together: the collaboration between Joyce Marshall and Gabrielle Roy

The existence of the Roy-Marshall correspondence puts this particular working relationship into a unique category. As the editor of the correspondence, Jane Everett, comments: "Although this correspondence cannot provide a complete portrait of Joyce Marshall's and Gabrielle Roy's personal and professional relationship, the letters do offer thought-provoking glimpses of this partnership, as well as of the creative process and of the writerly life more generally."[83] For Sophie Montreuil the letters throw new light on our understanding of Roy: "Like Gabrielle Roy's other sets of correspondence, the Roy-Marshall correspondence is precious because it allows ... us to capture her as a woman and an author in a different relationship to language from that which is at the heart of her published work."[84] While accepting the point on a general level, I would suggest that this particular correspondence is *un*like any of the others precisely in the way that it reveals Roy's relationship to language(s). For it was perhaps in this correspondence, written *in English*, that Roy displayed most vividly her position between the two languages, engaged as she and Marshall often were in discussions about the possibilities of transposing French text into English text.

For both women, bilingualism was a source of fun. The pleasure that both took in their command of two languages and the range of cultural references (European and North American) that these languages open up occasionally emerges in the correspondence. A letter from Marshall to Roy, after a particularly annoying experience with the publication of the French and English versions of Roy's essay "Terre des hommes" (written as part of the celebration of Montreal's hosting of Expo '67) gives an insight into this sense of shared pleasure: "If we were together, we could perhaps soothe ourselves by repeating those comforting (and bilingual) words, '*Je suis le presbytère* of Mesopotamia.'"[85] Another example of the kind of bilingual wordplay that amused the two women appears in a letter by Roy to Marshall in which she imagines a whole series of unlikely French/English hybrid names, such as Ivanhoe Beaulieu.[86] This more playful side of their correspondence allows a glimpse of the kind of exchange they might have had in conversation – by telephone and on the occasional visits to work on the final stages of a translation. Their shared views of bilingualism and biculturalism also informed their responses to the issue of Quebec separatism, to which Marshall was particularly hostile, and to the question of a continuing place for the English language in Quebec. After the 1970 election in Quebec, for example, in which the Liberals gained 45.4% to the Parti Québécois's 23.1%, Roy wrote: "Now it seems that we can breathe in peace for a while, which is not saying that we are through with the ills and dangers of fanaticism ... Dear Joyce, always, I hope, you will feel that you can tread in freedom and joy the soil of your native province."[87]

Roy's view of her own involvement in the translation of her work into English emerges strongly from her correspondence with Marshall. The letters from both women use terms that stress this collaborative process. Referring to the mixed responses of readers to the translation of *La Rivière sans repos*, Roy wrote: "Well, you and I have done our best. What else can one do."[88] Marshall's correspondence echoes this sense of joint ownership of the translations. In one letter she reflects on the potential interest to an academic audience of the drafts, proofs, and corrections of the translations, referring to the "manuscripts of our translations as annotated by you, the corrected galleys etc etc."[89] Marshall referred to the translation of *Cet été qui chantait* as "our book," a term that Roy picked up in her reply.[90] When the finished translation, *Enchanted Summer*, was awarded the Canada Council Translation Prize for 1976,[91] Marshall wrote delightedly to Roy about "our translation" winning the prize.[92] Even after Marshall had stopped acting as Roy's translator, the closeness of the relationship meant that their collaboration continued in other ways, as when Marshall gave an interview for Bill Whitehead's CBC production on Roy and Blais. Writing to Roy after the program had been televised, she referred to it as "'our' program."[93] This sense of joint production seems at times to unsettle the fixed divide between translator and author, and indeed the divide between anglophone and francophone.

Because of the varied ways in which the women decided to work together, their correspondence throws more light on the translation process of some texts than of others. Their collaboration on the translation of *La Route d'Altamont*, for example, was largely carried out when Marshall visited Roy at Petite Rivière, whereas their collaboration on the translation of *La Rivière sans repos* and *Cet été qui chantait* was conducted by correspondence and telephone. The differences between the structure, style, and setting, of the latter texts raise questions of cultural and linguistic difference that require a range of translation strategies. The correspondence allows us to follow a few of those distinctive responses as the dialogue progresses.

What is striking about the way in which the translation of *La Rivière sans repos* features in the correspondence is the lengthy discussion between Roy, Marshall, and their publisher about the English title. Clearly, a title plays a part in the promotion of the work, as do its cover design, publisher's blurb, and many other features of the marketing strategy. But the search for the right title dominates the correspondence, and Roy was particularly active in making new suggestions. Here too issues of linguistic and cultural difference are at issue. The consultation of drafts and proofs of works reveals the number of changes that many titles undergo on their way to permanence. So, the corrected title page of Brown's translation of *Un jardin au bout du monde* still displays the title *Exiles* rather than the eventual title, *Garden in the Wind*.[94]

Roy's working title for *La Rivière sans repos* was *Elsa*[95] and Roy tells Marshall that another alternative title had been *Fleur boréale*.[96] In a letter to Marshall concerning a planned visit to Toronto for the last joint revision of the translation, Roy writes: "We shall have to set our minds on finding an appropriate title – in English – for *La rivière*."[97] The matter was clearly not decided then, as she returns to the topic in January 1970, saying that she does not like *River beyond Time* and that *Windflower* is her favourite, or something using "River to ..." She mentions that Jack McClelland favoured a title that included the word "River." Roy then suggests to Marshall: "How about using the name of the river Koksoak? Is it too wild? Too hard to pronounce?"[98] Roy clearly senses that this word with its non-English and indeed non-French appearance would have signalled the text's linguistic and cultural foreignness. But as her questions suggest, it might have alienated her potential readers, who might be brought more easily to her Inuit setting with a less "wild" title. In her next letter Roy reported that Jack did not like *Windflower* but that the variations on "River" do not work. She plays with other options: "*River to the Source* (there is a slight hint there, perhaps, of light) ... *River to Beginning*; *River from Time*; *River to Sea*; *River to Intent*."[99] In February Marshall wrote to say that an editorial meeting would take place that day to discuss the case for *Windflower*, which the editor was very keen to support.[100] But the issue did not seem to have been resolved at that meeting, as Roy continued to try out more possibilities in her letters. *Windflower*, she says, does not convey the turbulence, though it is pleasant. She explores ideas connected with journeys – "As a long fluid voyage"; "Voyage along the sky" – and then considers the literal translation, "Restless River."[101] A few weeks later, Marshall replies, rejecting the word "restless" as part of a title: "It's quite all right as a word but, as part of a title, I'm afraid the two identical vowel sounds have an unfortunate effect."[102] This is where the correspondence leaves the issue, at least for the time being. But there is a follow-up. In 1974 Marshall, doing corrections for a reprint of *Windflower*, tells Roy that a fellow literary translator at a conference in the Gaspé had commented on how good a title it was.[103]

When Marshall was translating *La Rivière sans repos* she worked on the full text, including the three short stories. These were not included in the eventual volume. Jack McClelland did envisage publishing them at a later stage, but this never happened. Nevertheless, Roy and Marshall did discuss potential titles, nearly ten years after the publication of *Windflower*, Roy writing: "Could it be *Eskimo Tales*? Or *Stories*? Nowadays one hear [sic] only of the *Inuit* people. Eskimo will look old-fashioned, no doubt!"[104] Clearly Roy was aware of the changing attitudes to cultural difference and the possible need for later translations to choose between the ideological context of the setting (and the writing) of a work and the expectations of a new generation of readers. Had the volume ever appeared, it would indeed have been interesting to see what decision the women would have reached.

The correspondence raises two other specific problems of translation that are revealing in regard to Roy's attitudes to the language used in her works and her translations. Roy refers to the translation of the word "mamelon," used to describe the rounded hills typical of the landscape of Ungava. She writes to Marshall: "I did not hear of a special English word there, having been only five days in all at Fort-Chimo, but if you find out such a word so much the better. Specially if it seems to fit in well with the narrative."[105] The phrase "so much the better" shows the extent to which Roy is interested in signalling the physical distinctiveness of Ungava. In order to help Marshall find the most appropriate word, she explains that she could have used "tertre" or "butte" in French, but that "mamelon" had conveyed the particular form better (rather than suggesting that she chose the word for reasons of style or balance in the sentence).

A second point that leads to a detailed discussion between Roy and Marshall is raised in an undated letter written after Roy's visit to Toronto. It concerns the translation of the word "désaxé," as applied to Elsa's mixed-race son.[106] The two women considered a range of possibilities, Roy giving a detailed explanation of the word's significance in relation to Jimmy's life and Marshall sending a list of options from Roget's *Thesaurus*, a reference book that they both use. Marshall is apparently giving Roy the choice, but adds: "I do not like the psychological jargon such as 'disturbed' etc." What is at issue is Jimmy's state of cultural hybridity and its effect on his identity, so it is interesting to see what choices were discussed long before the notion of hybridity became commonly applied. Marshall's preferred options for the phrase are: "a youth become cynical and twisted" or "cynical and emotionally wounded," failing which she asks, "What about 'rootless' or something else in that area?"[107] Roy states her preference for "twisted" – "It's the perfect word"[108] – and that is what appears in the translation. As meanings, connotations, and concepts change over the years, it is likely that Jimmy's state of mind would be rendered differently were the text to be retranslated today.

As Roy's official translator, Marshall not only worked on her own translations of Roy's works but she also gave a range of advice on the revision of existing translations. In August and September 1973, Roy and Marshall collaborated on modifications to the late Harry Binsse's translation of *The Hidden Mountain* prior to its re-issue in the New Canadian Library collection. The control that Roy imposed on Marshall's participation is carefully analysed by Sophie Montreuil, who notes the contradiction between the respect each woman expresses towards the other and "the subterranean manoeuvres of what is in fact a power relationship between the two women."[109] Roy took the lead in this process in a letter of 7 August 1973, pointing out passages to "mend" and offering her own suggestions, which she says Marshall is free to correct (a strange reversal of the author-translator roles).[110] Marshall's memory of Binsse's version was that "there were some little stiffnesses, even French rather than English word-order."[111] Having reread the translation she praises it as "a good translation, in fact excellent," but adds: "Every now and then, however, he slips into a syntax or phrasing that isn't English. (I do not criticize, having noticed that when you work long in French, you begin to think in French)." She points out a few problems of French usage ("rejoiced him," modelled on "réjouir") and "a few rather serious problems of unEnglishness – these may involve turning a sentence around."[112]

Equally, Roy would ask Marshall to read through her works in French as she revised them for a new edition. This might be a question of picking up typographical errors by the publisher; or Marshall might spot a stylistic point. When Marshall had the manuscript of *La Rivière sans repos* so that she could begin working on the translation before the French text was published, Roy wrote: "It would be wise to look for too many 'petite' or 'peut-être' or, in this book it may be another word which I have used too frequently, in a sort of 'tic.'"[113] Occasionally Marshall comments on a more substantive point such as whether Roy's text adequately explains Elsa's decision to return to Fort Chimo. To this last point, Roy replied: "Anyway we will consider that together, the two of us."[114] It is fair to suggest that the collaborative work between Roy and Marshall in some ways blurs the boundaries between author and translator, between source text and target text, and between French and English.

Marshall's final translation for Roy, that of *Cet été qui chantait* (the award-winning *Enchanted Summer*), in many ways reflects a significant stage in the professionalization of literary translation in Canada. In 1975 Marshall became one of the founding members of the Literary Translators' Association of Canada.[115] The availability of government funding now meant that Roy's publisher, Jack McClelland, was able to apply to the Canada Council for a grant to fund two working visits for Marshall to work with Roy.[116] These structures, together with the recently introduced Canada Council awards for literary translation, supported and promoted literary translation in Canada. Roy's praise for Marshall's work on *Enchanted Summer* was perhaps more positive than for any other of the translations of her work. In her letter of 28 September 1976 she quoted the review from the *Montreal Star* ten days earlier, which declared the work to be "exquisitely translated," and added her own view: "All the simplicity, the transparency, the liquid flow I longed for is there."[117] If this translation was the highpoint of the collaboration, it also marked its end, as Marshall had decided to devote more time to her own writing.[118] Roy felt a keen sense of loss. She wrote to Marshall: "I feel an emptiness and the sentiment that it will never be the same again for me, no matter how good a translator I may have. But I understand and approve your decision."[119]

The correspondence covering this final collaboration shows some interesting developments. Ricard describes *Cet été qui chantait* as being marked by "a profoundly religious, even mystic spirit that is completely detached from everything preoccupying the contemporary era."[120] If Marshall initially saw the text as particularly challenging, it was because "the material is so delicate and so poetic, so much a question of balance and tone."[121] Yet despite its mixture of innocent marvelling at nature and pervasive sense of loss and death, the discussion over the translation posed some very specific issues of linguistic and cultural difference. The two women met in late 1975, with a prepared list of alterations and problems for discussion.[122] In addition to the issue of finding appropriate terms for very specific plants and objects (such as "laitue panache," "cerises de France," "bouleau à sabot de cheval," "loche"), Marshall reported that she found the opening page very difficult.[123] When they were later working on the proofs, Roy wrote to Marshall noting a few errors, and also answering a query concerning the inclusion in the text of a Quebecism. Roy responded that it should be there and added: "It could be in italics if the editor preferred. *You* decide."[124] The women also discussed the translation or non-translation of French terms on the book's dust jacket. At proof stage Marshall picked up the anglicized forms "French Academy" and "French-Canadian Academy," and restored them to their French forms. Informing Roy of this decision she wrote: "Having these in English looks ridiculous and most insular as I'm sure you'll agree."[125] The correspondence on this final translation by Marshall shows a shared desire to highlight the specificity of references to Quebec's linguistic difference. Indeed, when the translation was published, this is an aspect that was picked up in a review by Shirley Gibson in the *Globe and Mail* that Marshall refers to in a later letter: "Marshall appears to be completely at ease in both languages and she has the good sense to leave words in French – *gatte, chaloupe, carillonneur* – when she thinks English can't do the job as well."[126] Interestingly, the reviewer chose to italicize these words, so rewriting the translation in which (Marshall's?) decision had been to leave the words in French without any additional sign of foreignness. Clearly in this case Marshall's strategy (of retaining certain words in French) can be seen as an effective way of resisting the process of assimilation that translation into English represents. It is interesting to speculate what would have happened had Marshall been commissioned to retranslate *Bonheur d'occasion* (as Roy seems to have hoped) and whether she would have used similar, selective techniques to foreignize the text.

ROY: LOST IN TRANSLATION?

It would be a major undertaking to attempt an analysis of all the translations into English of Roy's works, and the following analyses can be no more than a partial consideration of some of the issues they raise. But in order to indicate a range of possible lines of approach, I shall consider examples of the work of three of Roy's translators. My analysis is based upon the published translations, with occasional references to the manuscript of the translation at proof stage, where available, and to other archival material relevant to the specific translation.[127] Alan Binsse's translation of *Alexandre Chenevert* allows us to examine the ways in which traces of the power relationship between languages in postwar Montreal are treated, bearing in mind Schogt's warning that "English translations of French-Canadian works in which English plays some role will have great trouble maintaining the effects of the bilingual situation prevailing in the original texts."[128] We will then return to *Bonheur d'occasion*, the only one of Roy's book-length works so far to have been *re*translated. The point of comparing its translations is not to pass some qualitative evaluative judgment on their literary merits, nor to see how "faithful" the two versions are to their respective originals.[129] Rather, the translations by Hannah Josephson and Alan Brown will be put beside the current edition of the text in French to compare the extent to which linguistic difference, denoting cultural alterity, emerges in the three texts.

Alexandre Chenevert/The Cashier: *the diglossic city in translation*

Alexandre Chenevert (*The Cashier*, 1955) was the second of Roy's works to be translated by her second translator, Harry Binsse. In *Alexandre Chenevert* linguistic diversity is written into the text not only in encounters and conversations but also in representation of the urban environment. Parts One and Three are set in Montreal and Part Two describes Alexandre's brief rural retreat to the countryside near Rawdon. Although the novel does give significant glimpses of Montreal's ethnically and culturally diverse population, linguistic diversity in the text is largely centred on the dominant presence of the English language in the life of the francophone protagonist – at the workplace, in the media, in the urban environment, and in his domestic life. If the oppositions between French and English in this representation of a diglossic urban society were erased, not only would the thematic strand of the linguistic hierarchy be weakened, but the novel would also lose an important element of its distinctive texture.

Roy's second Montreal novel represents the city primarily as a place in which the English and French languages coexist. English is used in brief references to transport and medical services, advertising and news media, business and product names. The text reproduces in capitals two charity appeals on hoardings, one in French one in English, the lack of comment or explanation in the text indicating the normality of this situation: "OBJECTIF À ATTEINDRE POUR L'HÔPITAL SAINT-JOSEPH: DIX MILLIONS. Alexandre lut le chiffre une deuxième fois, s'arrêta sur place, effaré. Autrefois, il n'y avait que la guerre à exiger des millions ... DRIVE FOR THE JEWISH HOSPITAL ... Encore des millions! [CAMPAIGN GOAL FOR SAINT JOSEPH'S HOSPITAL: TEN MILLIONS. Alexandre read the figure a second time and stopped in his tracks, bewildered. In days gone by only war had demanded millions ... DRIVE FOR THE JEWISH HOSPITAL ... Still more millions!]" (AC 111; C 80).[130] As Vincent Schonberger points out, the effect of the slogans and other verbal messages in the text, in bilingual or hybridized form can be seen as a dramatization of Chenevert's cultural alienation. But by foregrounding these verbal messages, he argues, "these linguistic signs become de-automatized and defamiliarized,"[131] alerting the reader to the problematic nature of linguistic communication. In the French text the representation of the working environment of the bank, and the world of commerce in general, similarly highlights through the use of English phrases, both the need for employees to speak English and the status of English as the dominant language. As Chenevert calls the next customer, the formula is given in bilingual form, italics marking out the English: "*Next* ... au suivant ... " (AC 55). His job status is given in both languages: "Il était devenu *caissier-payeur*, en français; *teller* en anglais" (AC 48). But when he fantasizes about being promoted, his elevation is expressed only in English, reflecting the relative status of the two languages: "Mr Alexandre Chenevert, *Manager of the Bank of Economy* ... " (AC 48).[132] The fact that in the French text the name of the bank has been given in French within the narrative makes this sudden appearance of the name in English, within Alexandre's fantasy, all the more striking.

The connection between the English language and positions of power in the financial sector is confirmed with the linguistic representation of his boss, whose relationship with English confirms Frantz Fanon's comment: "To speak a language – is to take on a particular world, a culture."[133] M. Fontaine is francophone, but while his conversation with Alexandre takes place in French, he uses the occasional phrase in English, marked by italics in the text: "Vous allez diminuer un peu votre travail, n'est-ce pas? *Slow down*, ajouta M. Fontaine comme pour accentuer le ton de la bonne camaraderie ['Now you're not going to take things so hard, eh? Slow down a bit!' added Monsieur Fontaine, as though to emphasize the tone of good-fellowship." (AC 100; C 73). Fontaine's pity for Chenevert is the only sign that this francophone has anything other than positive thoughts about his personal attraction toward, and gradual assimilation into, the language and values of the Anglophone bourgeoisie. The association of these values with the English language in Roy's text points to their two complementary sources – the British Empire, represented by the portrait of the dour Presbyterian founder of the bank and by the notion of *"fair play"* (AC 102), and the business ethos of Anglophone North America, reflected in Fontaine's favourite slogan, *"Play hard ... work hard"* (AC 90) and his choice of bedside reading, *Comment réussir dans la vie et se faire des amis.*[134] The description of Fontaine's domestic life reveals the all-pervasive effects of the lifestyle of affluence, also marked as being anglophone by the text: "Son intérieur ressemblait au living-room célébré par des magazines, le *Home Ideal* ou le *Perfect Housekeeping*. Suzanne Fontaine s'inspirait de ces publications pour le choix de draperies à dessins futuristes [It at once reminded you of the living-rooms set up as models in the magazines, in *Ideal Home* or *Perfect Housekeeping*. Suzanne Fontaine found in these publications her inspiration for choosing her curtain materials of modern design]" (AC 91; C 66).[135]

Turning now to examine the translation into English, it is interesting to recall Lawrence Venuti's criticism of "fluent translations" into English – that they "invisibly inscribe foreign texts with English language values and provide readers with the narcissistic experience of recognizing their own culture in a cultural other."[136] Given that this text is explicitly concerned with the inscription of English language values in francophone Canadians, the issue is all the more acute. There are two aspects to bear in mind. To what extent does the translation retain a sense of the source language and its cultural references? And in what ways does the text reproduce the bilingual features of the original? For, as Godard remarks with reference to Claxton's translation of *La Détresse et l'enchantement*, anglophone Canadian translation practice often silences the different meanings and values of bilingualism for francophones in Canada, so confirming the "hegemonic position of English within this multilingual culture."[137] The first thing to note is the change of title for the English-speaking market from *Alexandre Chenevert* to *The Cashier*. This has the effect of erasing from the cover the Frenchness of its protagonist, although arguably it does a better job of indicating the social setting for the potential reader. In fact the change was already introduced in part for the 1955 Paris edition, which added the term in apposition in the title *Alexandre Chenevert, caissier*. However, inside the book, French language names and titles are used throughout (Mademoiselle Leduc, Madame Chenevert, Monsieur Fontaine), as are the polite forms of address where used in the original ("'Take care of yourself, Mademoiselle'") (C 34). References to anglophones are indicated, as in the French original, by English titles (Mrs Roosevelt). A rather whimsical reference to Stalin in Alexandre's interior monologue retains the French term of address of the original: "But had God ratified the Yalta agreement? Did He concede that His earth be divided into zones of influence: 'To you, Monsieur Stalin, goes Poland. To me, South Korea ... '" (C 205–6). The effect of this is to remind the reader subtly of the language in which Alexandre muses, and also, perhaps, of the source language of the text. The treatment of street names varies, there being some integration of French names, as in the reference to "the Rue de la Visitation" (C 33), but the references to better-known streets in Montreal are generally anglicized, giving Saint Denis Street and Saint Louis Square (rather than the distinctively named "carré Saint-Louis"). As for other place names, the text retains the francophone Canadian style of hyphenated forms such as Sainte- Thérèse and Saint-Donat (C 132) (but the hyphen is omitted, presumably in a typographical error, for Sainte Geneviève on the same page).

Roy's effective representation of the bilingual urban environment is somewhat weakened in the translation, either because French is naturalized into English or because the original English is no longer marked. Thus, signs and announcements lose their distinctive bilingual mode, "*track number one; traque* numéro un ... " (AC 188) becoming "Platform Number One ... Platform Number Six" (C 136);[138] billboard charity appeals are only given in English, naturalizing the linguistic and cultural difference by referring to "SAINT JOSEPH'S HOSPITAL" and "THE JEWISH HOSPITAL" (C 80). At the workplace Chenevert's spoken language is only given in English: "Next, please" (c 40). In certain cases the translation removes the visible bilingual markers but retains the narratorial comment that appeared in the French text, as in the following passage:

SILENCE

HOSPITAL ZONE

The car was approaching the sign ... in French and English, as always, and as must needs be, for you are in a city which thinks and suffers in two languages. (c 221)

In French the Canadian pattern of bilingual signage is reproduced:

HÔPITAL

SILENCE

HOSPITAL ZONE

La voiture approchait de l'indication ... en français, en anglais, toujours, il faut bien, car on est dans une ville qui pense et souffre en deux langues. (AC 307)

In the case of the bilingual performance of the bus conductor, the translation again retains the comment, telling the reader about linguistic difference rather than preserving it in the dialogue: "'Use both entrances! Step forward!' the conductor shouted exasperatedly in French. Then, in English, 'Step inside if you please.' He was instinctively more polite when he spoke in English" (c 195). In French this reads as follows, the italics highlighting the bilingual form of address: "'Embarquez des deux bords ... Avancez en arrière ... *Step inside if you please ...* ' répétait la voix exaspérée du receveur. Il était plus poli, d'instinct, quand il parlait anglais" (AC 272).

The treatment of M. Fontaine and his fondness for the English language also demonstrates the effects of different translation choices. The use of italicized English to inscribe without comment the ideological framework of Fontaine's worldview in the original (*"Play hard ... work hard"*; *"fair play"*) is still emphasized in the English version, the former with italics, the latter with question marks, showing their status as slogans, but not their original linguistic difference. The title of Fontaine's reading matter is given in its English form, *How to Win Friends and Influence People*, doubtless familiar to the contemporary anglophone reader. At another point in the chapter, the translation does insert an additional comment in the narrative, giving a rather different slant to Fontaine's use of English, as the comparison below shows:

> "What about the old employees?" wondered Monsieur Fontaine, thinking in English, as he often loved to do – or, to be more accurate, thinking bilingually, as he had every right to. "Those are the people you should have talked about; what are we to do with them, old boy?" ... "Poor old devil!" he reflected charitably about Alexandre. (C 70–1).

> "*What about the old employees?*" demanda M. Fontaine qui aimait souvent penser en anglais. "C'est de ceux-là qu'il aurait fallu parler; qu'en faire, *old boy?*" ... "*Poor old devil!*" pensa-t-il charitablement d'Alexandre. (AC 97)

In the translation the loss of italicization makes M. Fontaine's switch to English less visible, but the comment in the narrative compensates for this loss of emphasis: "thinking in English, as he often loved to do – or, to be more accurate, thinking bilingually, as he had every right to." In the French version the following sentence in its linguistically hybrid form – "C'est de ceux-là qu'il aurait fallu parler; qu'en faire, *old boy?*" ... "*Poor old devil!* [Those are the people you should have talked about; what are we to do with them, old boy?]" – demonstrates ironically M. Fontaine's smooth glide toward the anglophone world. This bilingual sentence is lost in translation and the additional comment, "or to be more accurate, thinking bilingually, as he had every right to do," changes the impact of the scene to focus not on the unequal power relations between the French and English languages, but, with an additional layer of irony, on bilingualism as an individual's right.

The comparison of a final scene gives a sense of how the signs of the diglossic city function differently in the English translation. The final chapter of Part Two of the novel is devoted to an account of Alexandre's return, by bus and then tram, from his brief holiday at Lac Vert in the Laurentians. The narrative intersperses Alexandre's growing despair with descriptions of what he sees through the window, the return to urbanization being signalled by a return of English language elements in the text:

Les cartons-réclames se multipliaient, à la louange du *Seven-Up*
... Madame Aludude servait des *light lunch: hot dogs, hamburgers*, patates frites ... Jos Latendresse était Entrepreneur de
Pompes Funèbres ... et il n'y avait pas de meilleur talon que
l'inusable *Cat's Paw* ...

De hautes cheminées d'usine venaient à la rencontre du
regard, des clochers noircis, des panneaux-réclames qui dès lors
prenaient appui sur les toits. Ils proposaient deux cents
chambres avec eau courante ... soixante chambres avec bain ...
des matelas *beauty-rest* ... Six cents autres chambres ...
fire-proof ... Vulcanisation ... des parties usagées ... le garage Pie
IX Enrg. (AC 264–6)

More and more posters, now, in praise of Seven-Up ... Madame
Aldude served LIGHT LUNCHES, HOT DOGS, HAMBURGERS, and
FRENCH FRIES ... Joe Latendresse was a Funeral Director ... And
there was no better heel than the long-wearing Cat's Paw ...

High chimney factories caught the eye, blackened spires, bill-
boards which, from now on, were propped on roofs. They
prated of two hundred rooms with running water ... sixty rooms
with private baths ... Beauty-Rest mattresses ... six hundred
other rooms ... fireproof ... Vulcanizing ... used parts ... The
Pius XI Garage, Regd. (C 189–90)

In the English translation all italicization is removed from the
advertising hoardings and all products and services are naturalized
into English, Madame Aludude's offerings thereby losing their
bilingual texture to read "LIGHT LUNCHES, HOT DOGS, HAMBURG-
ERS, and FRENCH FRIES ... (C 189)." The only remaining signs of linguistic difference are the names of Madame Aldude [sic] and the
hybrid form Joe Latendresse. Given that no narrative comment is
added, this results in the erasure of this particular aspect of linguistic difference.

While the linguistic encounters in *Alexandre Chenevert* are the
main indicators of the diglossic relationship between English and
French, the text also represents a Hungarian Jew in terms of linguistic difference:

"Mon ami Chinevert," l'appelait-il. "Pourquoi que ti restes à la
banque?" lui demanda-t-il. "Ti ferais mieux ta vie à préparer les

> rapports pour le Receveur général ... Je t'y trouverai trois ou
> quatre autres marchands qui font pas d'assi grosses affaires
> pour garder un comptable à l'année, et ça ti fera de bons clients
> ... Laisse-moi faire," disait Markhous, "j'y ferai ton fortune."
> (AC 122)

This representation relies on selective phonetic imitation (mainly of
vowel shifts as in "Chinevert"; "ti"; "assi"), low register ("qui font
pas") and gender mistakes ("ton fortune") to convey the Otherness
of Markhous.[139] In the translation Markhous is given a much more
pronounced accent in English dialogue:

> "Mine friend, Shinvert," he called him. "Why you stay at de
> benk?" he would ask. "You should make yet a better liffing fix-
> ing reports for collector, income tax ... I dig you up tree, four
> oder businessmen" not big enough to afford an accountant the
> year round, and Alexandre would have all the clients he needed.
> "Leaf it to me," said Markhous, "I mek you rich." (C 88–9)

Here the phonetic shifts affect a higher proportion of vowels and
consonants and the English syntax deviates more from the norm
that did the French. The narrator summarizes more of the dialogue
than in the French version, leaving the reader with a glimpse of
Markhous as a reified Jewish Other.[140] Because elsewhere in the
translation, linguistic difference in dialogue tends to be described to
us rather than shown, the effect of these strategies is that the Hungarian Jew remains the only figure whose *language* marks him as
strikingly Other in the text.

So, can it be argued here that literary translation serves as a vehicle of assimilation? Some markers of linguistic alterity are retained,
enough for the reader to be aware that the setting is Montreal and
not Toronto or Boston. But the reader in English is given little sense
of the problematic nature of linguistic exchange in 1940s Montreal,
nor of the ramifications of the power relations that underlie all linguistic exchange within the city. Perhaps above all, the translation
loses much of the visible evidence of a diglossic city, of those parts
of the urban fabric that shape Chenevert's experience of Montreal,
making the text itself far less open to linguistic difference. Nevertheless, the comparison between the French and English versions
shows that the translation does use some of the strategies of com-

mentary suggested by Mezei which to some extent counter the domesticating effects of translating into the dominant language.

The translation(s) of Bonheur d'occasion

If Hannah Josephson's translation of *Bonheur d'occasion* (*The Tin Flute*, 1947) has acquired an unusual level of notoriety, it is largely as a result of a striking mistranslation of one short sentence. The French text reads: "Vers huit heures du soir, la poudrerie se déchaîna."[141] Presumably unfamiliar with this Quebec term for drifting snow, Josephson chose the standard French meaning of "la poudrerie" and inserted the line: "Towards eight o'clock in the evening the powderworks exploded."[142] Roy herself had very little time to correct the proofs of the translation, but did read them and made a fair number of corrections by hand.[143] She also passed the translation to Hugh MacLennan for his opinion.[144] Neither Roy nor MacLennan had spotted the mistake. Yet, probably because the mistranslation concerned a Quebecism and was committed by an American, and perhaps because of the association of Quebec with snow, it has never been forgotten. In W.H. New's *Encyclopaedia of Literature in Canada*, the entry on translation includes a reference to "*The Tin Flute* (1947), Hannah Josephson's notoriously poor translation of Roy's *Bonheur d'occasion*," commenting that: "Josephson's translation suffered primarily from the translator's unfamiliarity with Québec."[145] Yet this notoriety is probably an overreaction and demonstrates the power of the literary system to construct and manipulate images of both authors and translators. When Eugène Reynal informed Roy that, after some searching, they had secured Hannah Josephson for the job, he declared himself overjoyed with having found such a good translator.[146] The decision to engage Harry Binsse for the translation of Roy's second text, *La Petite Poule d'Eau*, was not made because of the quality of Josephson's work, but rather because she was unavailable at the time.[147] But a number of broader misgivings were expressed about the translation. Indeed, MacLennan himself later admitted to Deacon: "In retrospect I'm disappointed in the translation. I saw Gabrielle while I was half through the English galleys and told her then I thought she needn't worry about it, but by the end I had changed my opinion. The prose went dead to me by the end. It's true that BONHEUR was weaker at the end than the beginning, but this seemed to me purely a matter of prose. The translator seemed tired. But then, no translator could have preserved the peculiar savour of Gabrielle's St. Henry dialect."[148]

Ricard's view is a little more positive, although he too picks up on the handling of the dialect: "The sound of the local speech is not well conveyed, but all in all the translation is not bad."[149] Yet both the handling of the vernacular and the mistranslation of "poudrerie" can be seen as an illustration of the need for a translation to retain what Sherry Simon termed "the grounds of specificity," without which a work loses its cultural difference.[150] It was in the early 1970s that Roy's Canadian publisher, McClelland & Stewart, first began thinking about commissioning a new translation of *Bonheur d'occasion*. Referring to "la poudrerie," with which the text has clearly become associated, Roy mentioned to Joyce Marshall that her publishers had raised the question of whether the translation needed a "face-lifting."[151] A few weeks later Marshall wrote to Roy, saying that Jack McClelland had sounded her out on retranslating the text. She asked Roy for her opinion before responding to McClelland: "apart from obvious boners like '*poudrerie*,' do you feel it needs a fresh go? I'm inclined to think it does. 'Fixing' can be a very tricky business."[152] In fact the job of retranslating *Bonheur d'occasion* was finally offered to Alan Brown, Marshall's successor as official translator, and the new version appeared only in 1980.

In the last part of this chapter we take a close look at some passages from *Bonheur d'occasion* and their translations by Josephson and Brown.[153] Reference will also be made to Roy's comments and corrections to the proofs of each translation. Since Roy revised her texts for each new edition, and also made cuts or revisions in the original or the translated text during the various phases of translation, we must keep in mind that the translators were working with slightly different source texts. In addition, Brown's *re*translation of the novel more than thirty years after the publication of Josephson's translation may reveal a different pattern of choices because of that distance in time, and a different attitude on the part of Roy as she worked with Brown on the translation. My interest in the comparisons that follow is not, therefore, in finding the "better" translation, but rather in considering the strategies the author and her translators used to highlight or neutralize linguistic and cultural difference, and the possible effects on the reader of these different strategies. Before examining specific aspects of linguistic difference, a few general points will help indicate where Roy makes use of both Quebec French and English to suggest the cultural difference of working-class Montreal in the early 1940s and show how the two translators handle this.

Perhaps the most immediate indicator to a reader of the specificity of a text's setting is the use of names – proper names, terms of address, and place-names. Since almost all the named protagonists are francophone and the great majority of conversations take place in French, the text contains a high frequency of French names and nicknames. When referring to francophone protagonists by name, both translators use French forms of address (though capitalizing them in keeping with English practice), monsieur Lévesque (R 187) becoming Monsieur Lévesque (J 124, B 179), but some cases are less clear-cut. The first conversation in the novel is that between Jean Lévesque and Florentine. Jean introduces himself and then says: "Et toi, je sais toujours bien pour commencer que c'est Florentine ... Mais tu es mademoiselle qui?" (R 10). Josephson had translated this last sentence as: "But you're Miss what?" but in the correction of the proofs, Roy changes this to "But you're Mademoiselle who?" (J 2).[154] This helps establish the language used between the two, but in Brown's translation the French form disappears to give: "But if I call you miss, miss who?" (B 8).

The forms adopted for certain place-names also show different degrees of normalization. As in Binsse's translation of *Alexandre Chenevert*, street names are given an anglicized form, although the high incidence of saints' names reminds the reader of the Catholic, if not always the French Catholic traditions of Montreal. While Roy seems to have agreed with this pattern of normalization – she comments in the proofs on the abbreviation of Saint to St. for use in street names (so Saint-Henri for the area, but St. Catherine for a street name) – she does recommend one or two exceptions. So, while Josephson translates rue du Couvent (R 35) as Convent Street (J 19), in Brown's translation this form is corrected to reappear as rue du Couvent, so reinserting the French term for a small street known only to the local population (B 33).[155]

Other signs of Montreal's distinctive cultural and linguistic situation include references to institutions associated with Catholicism (and the status of Latin within the Catholic Church), to the workplace, to consumerism, and to popular culture, each of which is marked by specific French and English-language connotations and influences. The following examples illustrate Roy's representation of Catholicism in the novel. As Florentine attends mass with Emmanuel after attending a party at his house, she prays to the Virgin Mary to let her see Jean Lévesque again. Roy uses the terms "le prie-Dieu" and "une neuvaine," and Florentine addresses her prayers to the "bonne sainte Vierge" (R 147). Here the term "prie-dieu" (lower case for dieu) and the latinized form "novena" are used by both translators and have the effect of suggesting the "foreignness" of the Catholic ritual. A common feature in the description of family life in Quebec prior to the Révolution Tranquille is some reference to popular religious iconography.[156] Roy's description of the Lacasse home mentions an image of Christ on the cross.

Passage 1
(Bonheur d'occasion/The Tin Flute)

Gabrielle Roy original	Hannah Josephson translation	Alan Brown translation
Dans l'ombre, directement au pied du lit, la figure ensanglantée d'un Ecce Homo meublait la muraille d'une vague tache sombre. À côté, faisant pendant, une Mère des Douleurs offrait son cœur transpercé au rayon blafard qui se jouait entre les rideaux. (R 76)	At the foot of the bed, a darker shadow marked the place where an Ecce Homo hung framed on the wall. Beside it there was a lithograph of Our Lady of Sorrows offering her bleeding heart to a pale ray of light from between the window curtains. (J 48)	In the shadows, at the foot of the bed, the bleeding face of a Christ with his crown of thorns darkened a patch of the wall. Beside it, completing it, a *mater dolorosa* offered her transpierced heart to the ghostly light that flickered through the window. (B 73)

In Roy's text the status of Latin as the language of sacred ritual and of the highest social prestige is reflected in the reference to *Ecce homo*. Whereas Josephson's translation reproduces the Latin phrase ("Ecce Homo") and gives a close equivalent of the French in "Our Lady of Sorrows," Brown's translation transfers the use of Latin to the latter and offers an extended description for the former. The effect is that in all three texts the religious references introduce a further layer of language into the text, and so create a parallel to the heteroglossia of Quebec, with its distinct domains of Latin, English, standard French, and Québécois French.

Whereas toponomy and religion both signal Saint-Henri's French language and its Catholic traditions, the representation of the workplace, commercial life and popular culture is associated more with Montreal's anglophone influences, which Roy's text indicates with the selective use of English. When, in chapter 14, Florentine goes in search of Jean Lévesque at the foundry, the juxtaposition of English and French and the use of italics reminds the reader of the power of anglophone capitalists over francophone workers.

Passage 2:
(*Bonheur d'occasion/The Tin Flute*)

Gabrielle Roy original	Hannah Josephson translation	Alan Brown translation
Une clarté vive incendiait les carreaux de la *Montreal Metal Works*, rue Saint-Jacques. (R 187)	The windows of the Montreal Metal Works on St. Jacques Street seemed to be on fire. (J 124)	The windows of the Montreal Metal Works on St. James Street were brightly lit. (B 178)

In both English translations this tension is erased. In fact Josephson's hybrid form of street names is the only remaining sign of the language of origin here. The juxtaposition of English and French also occurs in Roy's representation of Florentine's workplace, the restaurant of the *Quinze-Cents* (which is translated as "the five-and-ten" (J) and "the Five and Ten" (B)).[157] References to menu items include the terms "*sundae special*" (R 16), "Hot dog," "Coca cola" (R 340), "Banana custard pie" (R 110), "des *mixers* de lait malté" (R 15). Both translations remove the italics, and the combination of English and French in the original becomes invisible.

This survey of the treatment of distinctive cultural references would seem so far to indicate the extent to which both translations, with occasional exceptions, fit into the mode of translation as cultural assimilation, as analysed by Mezei, in which "desire is directed towards creating a readable pleasurable text for the English reader."[158] Roy's text seems far more able to suggest the polylingual reality of the modern world than is either translation, and this is at least in part because the translations are into the dominant language, with its associations both with the former Empire and the United States. Yet it is not sufficient to focus solely on the translation of isolated words and phrases. Might the translators not have found other strategies that allow the reader to glimpse what Mezei calls "an open target text, open to differences, open to varieties of meanings, open to both the original cultural referential system and the one in the process of being created"?[159]

In order to compare the ways in which the three texts deal with broader questions of linguistic heterogeneity, I have selected a few brief passages in which language difference is central to the style, theme, or situation. The specific problems of translating Canadian texts from French to English relate to the use of distinctive Quebec or Canadian French forms and the inclusion of English words in the French original. Translators have a range of options: "regionalisms" can be left in their original form (possibly being highlighted or commented on by the translator in the text or in a note); an "equivalent" form in English can be chosen; or the terms can be neutralized. In the case of English words in the original, the problem is different. Such words will automatically lose their "visibility" in the text when it is translated into English, unless the translator either highlights them in some way, as for regionalisms, or recreates the linguistic heterogeneity by some other means. Schogt points out that the translator may choose to signal linguistic difference at particular points where the linguistic, social, or stylistic tension requires or suggests it, rather than consistently. In his view, Josephson's translation of *Bonheur d'occasion* tends to neutralize the linguistic heterogeneity of Roy's work: "The English translation does not keep the dialect features, Quebec peculiarities being treated in the same way as standard French, and the English of the original fusing with the English of the translation."[160]

It does seem that Roy was perfectly aware of the issue, even with this first translation, but at that time preferred the route of neutralization to that of equivalence. An article in *Le Devoir* in February 1947 reported Roy as having urged her translator "to feel free to use her own judgment concerning the rendering of the typically French-Canadian style." The article continues: "The result is, says Mlle Roy, that the translator has remained faithful to the French text, only modifying the dialogues, so as to give them a tone which sounds more universal, particularly for the English-speaking readers. It is particularly fortunate that there has been no attempt to introduce American slang as an equivalent of the spoken French of working-class Montreal (which would have been a false equivalent, by the way). So there is no risk of the work being read as an expression of working-class life in the United States."[161] This suggests that Roy's aim was to preserve the cultural, if not linguistic, difference of working-class Montreal in the translation, so avoiding one variation of Venuti's "fluent strategy," whereby American readers would be given "the narcissistic experience of recognizing their own culture in a cultural other."[162] But Roy's text uses a variety of strategies to represent the diversity of the spoken language of Saint-Henri in terms of lexis and register, and the range of linguistic situations that can arise in Montreal. The following scenes give a taste of what happens to Roy's text in translation.

Passage 3:
(*Bonheur d'occasion/The Tin Flute*)

Gabrielle Roy original	Hannah Josephson translation	Alan Brown translation
Tout ce que j'ai vu de beau dans ma vie, à traîner la patte su la rue Sainte-Catherine, ça pourrait quasiment pas se dire! Je sais pas, moi, des Packard, des Buick, j'en ai vu des autos faits pour le speed pis pour le fun … Ouvrez le radio un petit brin; et qu'est-ce que vous entendez? Des fois, c'est un monsieur du Loan qui vous propose d'emprunter cinq cents piasses. *Boy*, de quoi s'acheter une vieille Buick! D'aut' fois, c'est un billboard qui vous offre de ben nettoyer vos guenilles. (R 58–9)	I can hardly describe all the fine things I've seen while tramping up and down St. Catherine Street! Packards, Buicks, racing cars, sport cars … Turn on the radio and what do you hear? A bigwig from the loan company who wants to lend you five hundred bucks! Boy, you could buy a secondhand Buick with five hundred bucks! Or a fellow begs you to let him clean your old rags. (J 35–6)	The great things I've seen, just bummin' along St. Catherine, you couldn't make a list of it. Packards, Buicks, cars for speed, cars for fun … Turn on your radio a minute and what do you hear? Sometimes a gent from the loan company, he wants to lend you five hundred bucks. Boy! That's enough to buy an old Buick! Or you see a billboard that says how well they're goin' to dry-clean these rags you've got on. (B 57)

The first passage, from chapter 4, is an example of what Schogt has termed "the hybrid character" of Alphonse's language.[163] Alphonse is holding forth in la mère Philibert's restaurant about the way the poor are exposed to the temptations of consumerism. His language is marked by a mixture of Quebec spoken French (expressions such as "traîner la patte," "piasses"), phonetic representation of pronunciation ("su la rue," "d'aut' fois," "pis"), the low register of spoken language ("je sais pas, moi"), English borrowings ("pour le speed pis pour le fun," "un billboard"), brands and phrases in English ("des Packard, des Buick," "un monsieur du Loan," "*Boy*!"). The high frequency of English language items stresses the link between consumerism and anglophone wealth. Neither translation leaves any trace of the language of origin, nor of the linguistic diversity of the original, other than finding some way of suggesting the register used. Josephson omits phrases typical of oral performance such as "je sais pas, moi," using occasional colloquial terms such as "bigwig" and some North American vernacular ("bucks"), but otherwise she adopts a more standard language, and more standard syntax than the French text. Brown keeps more closely to Roy's syntax (as in the first sentence), and gives some phonetic indication of pronunciation for the nasals ("bummin'," "goin'"), which helps make the register a little less formal, though with no real indication of the linguistic heterogeneity of Alphonse's speech in this passage.

Roy not only uses touches of phonetic representation to indicate the Québécois accent but she also individualizes the speech of her protagonists, whether to show how they change register in different contexts (Emmanuel talking to his working-class friends or to his middle-class family and friends)[164] or to show their mispronunciations. These mispronunciations are usually of words that the protagonists are unfamiliar with, or might have heard only recently and are still unsure of. In the proofs Brown queries the inclusion of Azarius's mistakes and Roy marks the proof "stet," adding: "he makes mistakes in pronunciation. But if you think people will think *we* made a mistake ..."[165] This degree of linguistic individuality is picked up by both translators to some extent, as shown in the examples below.

Passage 4:
(*Bonheur d'occasion*/*The Tin Flute*)

Gabrielle Roy original	Hannah Josephson translation	Alan Brown translation
La ligne Imaginot! (R 43)	The Imaginot Line! (J 25)	That there Imaginot line! (B 42)
Astérologues (R 310)	Astrologers (J 209)	asterologists (B 295)
Anguelterre	England (J 25)	Ingle-land (B 42)
Palogne	Poland	Po-land
l'Autriche et la Tchécoslaquie (R 44)	Austria and Czechia – Czechiaslavia (J 26)	Austria and Czechoslovakia (B 43)

Although elements of the English language are present in the speech used by Roy's francophone protagonists, the novel makes very little reference to the anglophone population of Montreal. But the scene in which Rose-Anna goes to visit her son Daniel, dying from leukemia in hospital in the anglophone area on the slopes of Mont-Royal, shows the language divide from Rose-Anna's viewpoint. It represents the English of the anglophone nurse in the text with no paraphrase or comment, but marks it with italics.[166]

Passage 5:
(*Bonheur d'occasion/The Tin Flute*)

Gabrielle Roy original	Hannah Josephson translation	Alan Brown translation
elle lui demanda comme d'une grande personne à une autre: – *All right now, Danny?* (R 232)	she asked him in English, as one grownup to another: "All right now, Danny?" (J 156)	and, as if she were speaking to another grown-up, asked: "All right now, Danny?" (B 223)
– *He's getting tired. Maybe, tomorrow, you can stay longer.* Les paupières de Rose-Anna papillotèrent. Elle comprit vaguement qu'on la congédiait. (R 236)	"He's getting tired," she said in English. "Maybe tomorrow you can stay longer." Rose-Anna screwed up her eyes as she grasped that she was being dismissed. (J 159)	"He's getting tired," she said in English. "Maybe you can stay longer tomorrow." Rose-Anna blinked. She understood vaguely that she was being dismissed. (B 227)

Both translations add the information "in English," but in the case of Brown, this only appears in the second case, as in the first case the narrative lets us follow Rose-Anna's gradual realization that the nurse speaks no French. In Brown's translation this reads:

> When the nurse had left she leaned over toward the bed. She had a fear that her child couldn't make himself understood in this place. And another sentiment made itself felt, as cold as steel.
> "Does she only speak English?" she asked with a touch of unfriendliness. "When you need something, can you ask for it?'
> "Yes," said Daniel. (B 223)

Although the narrative alone might have conveyed the language used, in both translations the additional reminder serves to highlight the language of dialogue and by implication to remind the reader of the language of the original text.

Brief snatches of spoken English also appear in Roy's text in the form of code-switching within dialogues between francophones in specific contexts. In Schogt's analysis of the translation of Roy's use of English, he suggests: "English often seems to be used to express very strong emotions which would be difficult to control without the distance established by the use of the foreign language." He qualifies this by adding: "Sometimes it is not so much emotion, but rather showing off that is emphasized by the use of English."[167] What Schogt does not mention is that male characters frequently associate words and phrases spoken in English with the army, which in turn recalls the former colonial relationship with England. Both Pitou and Alphonse decide to follow Emmanuel's example and apply to join up as volunteers as an alternative to continuing unemployment. Emmanuel happens to see Pitou on patrol outside the barracks. In the following dialogue Roy's use of phrases in English acts as a sign of Pitou's transformation and of his naivety:

Passage 6:
(*Bonheur d'occasion/The Tin Flute*)

Gabrielle Roy original	Hannah Josephson translation	Alan Brown translation
C'était Pitou qui faisait les cent pas devant la caserne, se retournait carrément, claquait les talons, seul dans la nuit, l'arme sur l'épaule, et repartait d'un pas mesuré et agile	Pitou it was who patrolled the barracks, clicking his heels as he turned to retrace his steps, alone in the night with his gun on his shoulder.	It was Pitou, marching up and down in front of the armouries, stomping, clicking his heels, about turn, quick march, all alone in the night, rifle at the slope.
... Pitou se retourna brusquement, frappa les talons, et ses yeux s'allumèrent un instant de l'espièglerie de l'enfance.	... Then Pitou turned about smartly and clicked his heels, his eyes lighting up with the old mischief.	... Then Pitou turned abruptly, stomped to a halt. His eyes lit up with mischief.
–*Thumbs up*! dit-il.	"Thumbs up!" he said in English.	"Thumbs up," he said in English.
–*Thumbs up*! reprit Emmanuel.	"Thumbs up!" repeated Emmanuel.	"Thumbs up!" said Emmanuel.
Et pour la première fois, il prononça les mots avec une hésitation, comme s'il avait eu un arrêt dans sa pensée.	And for the first time he said the words hesitantly, as if his mind were not quite made up.	For the first time he uttered these words with a shade of hesitation, as if his thoughts had refused to follow.
–T'aimes ça? demanda-t-il.	"D'you like this?" he asked.	"D'you like it?" he asked.
–*You bet*, dit Pitou. ...	"You bet," said Pitou ...	"You bet," said Pitou, again in English ...
–On se reverra, promit Emmanuel.	"We'll be seeing each other," promised Emmanuel.	"We'll get together," Emmanuel promised.
-*You bet* ... en Angleterre!	"You bet... in England!"	"You bet! In England!"
(R 333)	(J 225)	(B 316)

Pitou's use of these short, morale-boosting phrases indicates his apparent acceptance of the army's values and goal, the defence of "England." Italics used in Roy's text show instantly where the language switch takes place. Josephson's translation comments on the first use of English for "Thumbs up!" but not the second when Pitou alone continues in English. Brown does mark this second occurrence, but the code-switching of Pitou's "*You bet* ... en Angleterre!" is lost in both cases.

Passage 7:
(*Bonheur d'occasion/The Tin Flute*)

Gabrielle Roy original	Hannah Josephson translation	Alan Brown translation
"Il s'en trouvait un, au ras moi, qui m'a fait un clin d'œil. J'y ai répondu. J'aime pas gros les familiarités, moi, mais dans un cas comme ça, quand tu pars pour une walk qui pourrait ben finir au bout du monde, faut ben que tu fasses un peu la parlette avec ceux qui se grouillent à côté de toi ...	"There was one little chap in my rank who gave me a wink. I'm not inclined to be familiar with strangers, but in a case like this, when you start off on a walk that may take you to the end of the world, you may as well exchange a word or two with the fellows crawling along beside you, because it'd be a hell of a long walk if you had to do it all alone ...	"There was one guy right beside me and he winks at me, eh? Well, I winked right back. I don't like a guy that makes friends all that fast, but what the heck, when you're takin' a stroll that could end up God knows where, you've gotta be a bit sociable with the guys swarmin' alongside, right?
C'est encore drôle aussi quand j'y pense, comme ça se fait vite les bargains entre les gars ferme-la-gueule et traîne-la-patte..."	It always makes me laugh to think how fast bargains are struck between bums."	Funny when I think about it, how fast you can make a bargain with guys that don't give a damn."
—Continue donc, fit Emmanuel vivement. —O.K.! J'arrive betôt au plus beau de l'histoire, ricana Alphonse. J'étais pas aussitôt greillé d'un compagnon de route qu'on s'est mis à lever la patte drette pis la patte gauche et, left, right, le gars d'en avant nous gueulait left, right, on faisait comme lui, on se démenait que le 'iable, left, right, c'est une affaire que	"Go on," said Emmanuel sharply. "Okay, I'm coming to the best part of the story," chortled Alphonse. "I was no sooner all rigged out with a partner than someone ahead began bawling left, right, and we began to move – forward march, left, right, left, right. We did the best we could, imitating him – you catch on quick as the devil – left, right, and so it went	"Go on," said Emmanuel. "I'm just getting to the best part. No sooner have I got this buddy in the army, but they get us liftin' one foot, then the other, and left, right, you catch on fast. Then away we go like the devil as far as the barracks. What a bunch of nuts!" (B 310)

Passage 7 continued

tu poignes vite ça, pis en avant la patte, on a marché comme ça jusqu'à la caserne, une saprée bande de fous! (R 326-7)	until we reached the barracks, a fine bunch of fools!" (J 220-1)

Whereas Pitou is recruited and shown as being rapidly assimilated to the mindset of the army, Alphonse's attempt to volunteer ends in failure. He gives a lengthy account of this, at once comic and bitter (Passage 7). The language he uses is again marked by its heterogeneity, as he apes the military language of the recruiting soldiers within his narrative in the spoken vernacular of Montreal. The excerpt below includes anglicisms ("une walk," "les bargains"), quebecisms ("ben, parlette" – his pronunciation of parlotte – "se grouillent," "greillé," "le 'iable," "la patte drette," "betôt," "poignes," "saprée"), idioms ("les gars ferme-la-gueule et traîne-la-patte"), spoken register syntax ("au ras moi," "j'y ai répondu"), and a case of code-switching ("left, right"). As with the example of Pitou's language, English is connected to a military context. The translators use different strategies to render this narrative. Josephson's syntax and register are more formal throughout ("I'm not inclined to be familiar with strangers"), and the informality of spoken language is conveyed with a few touches, such as "one little chap," "a hell of a long walk," and "all rigged out." Brown's translation is marked throughout with features of informal spoken language, in terms of vocabulary ("one guy," "this buddy") the frequent use of mild profanities or euphemisms ("God knows where," "like the devil," "what the heck"), phonetic imitation of spoken forms such as "gotta," and, particularly, in the informal syntax. However, his translation does not indicate the code-switching; nor does it imitate the vernacular effect of distinctive phrases like "les gars ferme-la-gueule et traîne-la-patte," using an approximate equivalent with "guys that don't give a damn." In this instance too, Josephson adopts a much more neutral approach, translating both those phrases with the term "bums," an all-purpose colloquialism that she had used a few lines earlier to translate "les chômeux." Brown's version, in its attempt to convey the register and flow of Alphonse's narrative, does go some way to marking out his distinctive linguistic identity within the novel as a whole. Yet the translation into English does erase the specific roles of anglicisms and code-switching, and also, by increasing the number of mild swear words, relies on a different, and culturally specific method of indicating informal register.

Roy's novel ends with a scene at Bonaventure Station (Passage 8) where Emmanuel is setting off to rejoin his regiment for active service in Europe. Once more the text uses snatches of English in its representation of the patriotic mood shared by many Canadians. Given the fact that conscription was such a divisive issue between francophones and anglophones in Canada in both world wars, it is clear that the use of English in this chapter is loaded with

Passage 8:
(*Bonheur d'occasion/The Tin Flute*)

Gabrielle Roy *original*	Hannah Josephson *translation*	Alan Brown *translation*
Plus loin, un autre, la voix avinée, s'avançait en criant: *"W're* [sic] *going to see the world! You bet that we are going to see the world!"* (R 395)	Behind them came another, shouting drunkenly: "We're going to see the world! We're going to see the world!" (J 267)	Another, his tongue thickened by drink, came by shouting in English, "We're going to see the world! You bet we're going to see the world!" (B 373)
Soudain, Emmanuel entendit dans la foule une voix aux accents métalliques et impérieux: *-We'll fight to the last man for the British Empire.* "L'Empire! songea Emmanuel. Pour qu'un territoire garde ses limites! Pour que la richesse reste d'un côté plutôt que de l'autre!" Maintenant un groupe tout entier chantait: *-There'll always be an England.* "Oui, mais moi, mais Pitou, mais Azarius! pensa Emmanuel. Est-ce pour merry England, est-ce pour l'Empire que nous allons nous battre?" (R 399)	Suddenly Emmanuel heard rising above the uproar a metallic, arrogant voice in English: "We'll fight to the last man for the British Empire!" The Empire! thought Emmanuel. Are we fighting to hold on to territory? To keep the world's wealth for ourselves and bar the others out? Now a whole group was singing: "There'll always be an England." Yes, but how about me and Pitou and Azarius? wondered Emmanuel. Are we to fight for Merry England and the Empire? (J 270)	Suddenly Emmanuel heard a voice from the crowd, metallic and imperious, a voice in English shouting: "We'll fight to the last man for the British Empire!" The Empire, he thought. For the Empire, so that a territory can keep its old boundaries. So that wealth stays on one side rather than the other. A whole group had started to sing: There'll always be an England... Yes, but what about Pitou, what about Azarius? Is it for merry England and the Empire we're going to fight? (B 377)

significance. In the passages below, Roy once more uses italics for dialogue in English, including the line from the patriotic song "There'll always be an England." The narrative inserts these sentences of English with no comment, either assuming the readers' familiarity with them or leaving them literally excluded from the discourse of Empire. But Emmanuel's interior monologue returns at the end to pick up the imperial rhetoric and question it. His use of the familiar cliché "merry England" has an ironic effect, subverting the triumphalism of the crowd and underlining the contradictions in Emmanuel's relationship to this war. Josephson and Brown both correct and edit the form of the English in the first excerpt, but only Brown adds the comment "in English." In the second section, both translators point out the language of the first English voice, and Brown marks the line of song with italics. Emmanuel's ironic reference to "merry England" is not highlighted in any way in Brown's translation, whereas Josephson's use of capitalization does alert the reader to the myth of Englishness, which the phrase evokes.

The translations also differ slightly in the way they position Emmanuel in respect to the troops. In Roy's text, Emmanuel responds to the cry "*We'll fight to the last man for the British Empire*" with general reflection on the imperial nature of this war: "Pour qu'un territoire garde ses limites!" Josephson implicates Emmanuel personally in the process with the use of the first person plural, continuing the rhetoric of "We'll fight" with "Are we fighting ...," so placing him, somewhat uncomfortably, in the British camp – "To keep the world's wealth for ourselves." In Brown's version, the impersonal tone is restored – "So that wealth stays on one side rather than the other."

Roy's interventions in the translation process show no consistent line in regard to the marking of Englishness in text. Indeed, on a few occasions she rejects the suggestion that the English of the original be highlighted. The proofs of Brown's translation include a footnote to comment on the use of the word "speeches" in the French text: "The second 'speeches' is in English in the original." This footnote is deleted at proof stage, presumably by Roy, and so the original language difference is lost.[168] In another example Brown's translation draws attention to Florentine's use of English in conversation with Emmanuel: "And in English she threatened 'You better!'" Roy cuts the words "in English."[169] There is of course a point where such additional comments can overload the translation and a selective use of indicators can be just as effective, but Roy's choice here does seem to confirm that the visibility of English as a foreign language was not a high priority for her.

The discussion of the scenes above does suggest, however, that both author and translators felt the marking of the original English to be more significant in passages that draw attention to the contradictory position of francophone Canadians as British subjects, whether in the case of Rose-Anna's feelings of linguistic disempowerment at the hospital or in the case of francophone recruits risking their lives for the British Empire. In the ways that they handle language difference, both translators acknowledge, at least partially, the power relations between English and French. Brown also makes an attempt to create a sense of the linguistic heterogeneity in terms of register in some parts of his translation. But whereas Marshall, in her translation of *Cet été qui chantait*, retained certain distinctive Quebecisms as a sign of the specificity of the language of origin, neither Josephson nor Brown attempts this. In Berman's terms, this means that the vernacular networks and the use of Quebec expressions and idioms are largely effaced in translation. Given the effect of the linguistic heterogeneity in the monologues of Alphonse and Pitou, the inclusion of some Quebecisms might have been an excellent strategy for the retranslation of *Bonheur d'occasion*. Indeed it would probably have been well received, since a greater interest in linguistic heterogeneity was present in Canada in the late 1970s and early 1980s than in late 1940s, when Josephson was preparing her translation for the lucrative anglophone market.

We have focused particularly on Roy's two Montreal-centred texts, and close examination of other texts by Roy would reveal different issues of translating difference. By highlighting the translation strategies adopted by the three translators to render linguistic and cultural difference in those two texts, we have inevitably emphasized the extent to which the translations into English carry out the work of cultural assimilation. In Venuti's terms, the "fluent" translation strategy is in itself assimilationist, "presenting to domestic readers a realistic representation inflected with their own codes and ideologies as if it were an immediate encounter with a foreign text and culture."[170] Within the Canadian context, or indeed the North American context, the specific work of assimilation takes on an extra weight, given the relative positions of the two languages. Translations take place within very specific linguistic, political, and cultural contexts and each translation will bear traces of those contexts. While assimilation may well be the underlying motive of many, whether in the Anglo-Canadian literary world or the increasingly globalized English-speaking world, and while translations may in many ways erase difference or alter the value of differences, I would argue that the comparison of translations one with another and of both with a text in French can reveal not only the assimilationist aspects of individual translations, but also the obstacles to translation. As Simon declares: "Translation is not always the confident, complete transfer of a message from its place of origin to a new cultural home. Translation often reveals difference, nonequivalence, the impossibility of total transfer, and so it often remains incomplete."[171]

5

Writing Canada: Finding a Place Between

In the preceding chapters on education and language I attempted to trace the origins and effects of Roy's ambivalent position between languages and cultures. Close examination of the curricula that Roy followed as a student and subsequently taught as an elementary school teacher in Manitoba revealed a complex pattern of sources and influences. The strands that fed into the parallel anglophone and francophone curricula in Manitoba in the interwar years ranged from the "universalism" of the British Empire to elements of an emerging Western Canadian identity, and a traditionalist, Catholic ideology drawn variously from France, Belgium, and Quebec. This plurality of sources produced a culture of contradictory elements each with its own claim of universality, a claim that was undermined by the existence of the others.

I have argued that Roy's bilingualism and biculturalism, the result of her exceptional ability to succeed within the Manitoba education system, precluded any sense of stable or exclusive identification with one language community or the other. Rather, her texts, while attesting to her choice of French as her language of literary expression, display a heightened awareness of the problematic and creative potential of all language in scenes of confrontation, encounter, and exchange. We have also explored the implications and difficulties of translating Roy's work, marked as it is with traces of bilingualism, into English, the language of the majority. In this concluding chapter the discussion will broaden to focus on ways in which Roy's work can be understood as part of a project of "writing Canada," with all the ambivalences and contradictions that such an endeavour implies.

MAPPING THE PEOPLE

As I have suggested throughout, Roy's own complex sense of identity was, at least in part, one specific case of a much wider issue of identity construction common to former invader-settler colonies. Eva Mackey analyses the interplay between national identity and cultural pluralism in *The House of Difference* as follows: "The complex patterns of colonisation and cultural and economic development that created Canada have resulted in a situation in which the multiple identities which make up the nation are constantly at battle with each other, and in which the boundaries, inclusions and exclusions of identity are unstable and constantly changing."[1] Roy's work, from the earliest days of her career as a professional writer, explored Canada's cultural pluralism, "the multiple identities which make up the nation." It may seem paradoxical, at this stage of the book, to return to the beginning of Roy's writing career. Yet I hope to show that her journalistic work of 1940–45 can be read as an early working-through of her relationship to Canada, and also as an attempt to shape Canada in language, both of which enterprises are implicated in the colonial and neocolonial activities that she had encountered in Manitoba and are repeated in different ways throughout her *œuvre*. Just as in our discussion of linguistic encounters and exchanges it was important to see what happened when Roy's texts confronted languages outside the English/French axis, so here our focus will shift away from the two dominant populations. The second part of the chapter will turn to discuss two later texts inspired by Roy's visit to an Inuit community in the Ungava Bay region of northern Quebec, the 1961 reportage "Voyage en Ungava" and *La Rivière sans repos* (1970), to examine the place of the indigenous peoples in Roy's journalistic and literary representations of Canada.

Although Roy had been submitting short texts, both fiction and non-fiction, to a range of newspapers and magazines since the mid-1930s, it was only in the years 1939–45 that she earned her living through journalism.[2] During this period her work for the *Bulletin des Agriculteurs* stands out, not only in terms of its volume (a total of fifty substantial pieces, published between October 1940 and November 1946, consisting of forty-one reportages and nine short stories), but also in terms of its range, its quality, and the insight it provides into the whole of Roy's *œuvre*.[3] As François

Ricard points out in his discussion of Roy's association with the *Bulletin des Agriculteurs*, the political and intellectual climate in Montreal in 1940 could not have been more propitious. In October 1939 Adélard Godbout defeated Maurice Duplessis's Union nationale, bringing in a reforming liberal government in Quebec, which was in turn strengthened by a liberal victory in Ottawa in March 1940. Ricard describes Godbout's government of 1939–44 as ushering in "a kind of foretaste of the Quiet Revolution"[4] that was evident in such measures as the long overdue law giving the vote to women in Quebec (1940), the law on obligatory schooling (1942), and the improved recognition of the rights of trades unions (1944). Both the domestic and international climate gave an impetus to the periodical press, which, in order to cater to its expanding readership in an age of modernization and economic growth, needed new writers with new ideas.[5]

Thanks to her contacts in the progressive liberal press, notably Henri Girard, literary editor of the *Revue moderne*, who became her intimate friend and mentor, Roy established herself remarkably quickly in journalism. By May 1943 she had progressed from being paid as a freelance contributor to the *Bulletin des Agriculteurs* to securing a contract with a monthly salary of $275, with all travel and expenses for her research trips paid.[6] Although the *Bulletin* did have some other women contributors, Roy was a rare example of a female features reporter who travelled widely researching her stories.[7] To my knowledge, little attention has been paid to the composition of the readership of the *Bulletin des Agriculteurs*, but Ricard suggests that Roy's new target audience was composed of "readers who were both attentive and more varied than those she had previously had (who had been almost exclusively women)."[8] The readership was largely rural (though published in Montreal, the *Bulletin* was distributed throughout rural Quebec) and likely to have had a very different experience of Canada from that of its new Franco-Manitoban features writer.

Apart from the section in Ricard's biography that situates Roy's journalism in the context of her career as a whole, and in the precise cultural, political, and economic context of Montreal in the early 1940s, critical studies have tended to focus on two different aspects. For René Labonté the interest of Roy's journalism is primarily thematic. His study of her reportages gives a detailed description of the work published between 1939 and 1945. He finds that its originality lies in its character of "empathy-report-age," a style that he defines in the following terms: "Miles away from the simple statement of facts, a style of writing which draws on documentation, interviews, observation and reflection, but which demands that the writer sees people and things from the inside."[9] Labonté's article is also useful in its comments on the ways in which those early texts, later incorporated in the 1978 collection *Fragiles lumières de la terre*, were edited or modified.[10] While most changes were minor, he also draws attention to some more significant changes: "Many passages, almost always at the end of an article, have been revised, which indicates a close attention to the ending of a text at the same time as the need to modify nuances of meaning."[11] Among these, he cites the ending of the reportage on the Hutterites: "That of *Le Bulletin des Agriculteurs* is more positive and serene, that of *Fragiles Lumières de la terre* lets a certain degree of scepticism and uneasiness show through."[12]

In "Gabrielle Roy: portraits d'une voix en formation," Cynthia Hahn also points out the exceptional thematic interest of Roy's journalistic writing: "There is perhaps no other writer in Canada who has articulated the Canadian mosaic so well in the gallery of characters in her early writing."[13] Hahn goes on, however, to concentrate on the second aspect of their interest, the light they can throw on the apprenticeship of the future writer, drawing particular attention to the emergence of Roy's distinctive narrative style, including the use of shifts in physical, temporal, and emotional distance, movement among multiple perspectives, and the use of antitheses and juxtaposition.[14]

Almost all the critics who have written on Roy's journalism, Labonté and Ricard included, point out that these early writings contain glimpses of scenes and characters that reappear, often, but not always, revised or reworked, in her later fiction. Labonté cites a number of these, from the passage on "la dompe" at the Pointe Saint-Charles in "Les deux Saint-Laurent" (BA, June 1941), and the description of the sound of the Transcontinental as it passes through Saint-Henri in "Du Port aux Banques" (BA, August 1941), both of which reappear in *Bonheur d'occasion*, to the brief appearance of a woman called Masha in a reportage on the Doukhobors, (BA, December 1942), who prefigures the character Martha Yaramko in "Un jardin au bout du monde." The transformation of these early sketches in different stages of rewriting have been a rich source of critical study, particularly since the archive of Roy's unpublished work has become available to researchers.[15]

Roy's own evaluation of her journalism was somewhat ambivalent. In a radio interview with Judith Jasmin for the Radio-Canada series *Premier Plan* (30 January 1961) she refers to her early writing as "de petites choses pour me faire une main [little exercises to teach me how to write]."[16] But elsewhere she acknowledges the demanding nature of the genre, describing the writing of reportage as "tout aussi difficile, peut-être, que d'écrire un roman [just as difficult, perhaps, as writing a novel]."[17] Labonté recalls Sartre's view of reportage, which in *Situations II* he classifies as a distinct literary form, albeit a minor genre: "The qualities that the reporter most needs are the ability to grasp the significance of things intuitively and instantly and the skill to assemble them in such a way as to offer the reader an overall picture that is immediately comprehensible."[18] Sartre's terms here indicate the need for the individual reporter to respond intuitively to facts and synthesize them in order to communicate a message. Certainly this interaction of the observing subject with the world does not exclude subjectivity. At the end of *La Détresse et l'enchantement* Roy mentions that it was the *Bulletin des Agriculteurs* that gave her the chance to "traiter de sujets me rapprochant des faits, de la réalité, de l'observation serrée des choses [write on subjects involving fact, reality, close observation]" (DE 505; 410). Yet Roy's reportages are highly personal and recognizable writings, as Labonté's phrase "empathy-reportage" suggests. This sense of recognition comes not only from the stylistic and linguistic features that appear elsewhere in her work but also from the autobiographical references, judgments, and preferences expressed, and the desire of the reporter to enter into the lived experience of her subjects. Indeed the porous boundary between Roy's fictional and autobiographical works extends to her journalistic writing, in which imagination and invention are at work alongside the assembling of facts.[19] Roy adopts no single tone, and experiments with a variety of styles and viewpoints, some apparently more nostalgic than others, some more campaigning; yet a thread runs through them that evokes a desire for exchange and contact. At the same time they construct for their readers in Quebec a series of images of Canada that take them beyond the world of the rural *paroisse*.

Mapping the nation

In April 1939 Gabrielle Roy arrived back in Canada after spending a year and a half in Europe, a trip that had both marked the symbolic break with Manitoba (and with her mother)[20] and reaffirmed the importance of Britain and France as twin poles of her cultural identity. Rather than returning to her teaching post in Saint-Boniface, she made the bold decision to settle in Quebec and make her living as a writer. In the closing pages of *La Détresse et l'enchantement* Roy describes the sense of foreignness and dislocation that she felt on her arrival in Montreal: "Ce pays, que je n'allais pas être longue à aimer de toute mon âme dans sa détresse, dans sa solitude, je m'y sentais, ce premier jour, étrangère com[m]e si je n'y avais jamais encore mis les pieds [I soon learned to love this forlorn, lonesome urban landscape with all my soul, yet on this first day I felt as foreign as if I'd never set foot here]" (DE 498; 404). Having been identified, and identifying herself in Europe as "la Canadienne" (DE 259), and having identified fellow (mostly anglophone) Canadians whom she met on her travels in terms of a shared national identity ("ma payse [my compatriot]") (DE 251; 200), she returns to find she does not feel at home in Canada, and certainly not in Quebec.

One can understand Roy's journalistic writing partly as a response to this feeling of non-belonging. Other texts confirm this association. In the title article of *Le Pays de* Bonheur d'occasion, originally published in *Le Devoir* in 1974, Roy describes her exploration of Quebec as follows: "Je me découvrais un pays. A l'heure où j'en avais le plus grand besoin, pauvre, errante, solitaire, et peut-être précisément parce que j'en avais un tel besoin, il se révélait à moi [I was discovering a country. At the time when I most needed it, poor, rootless, alone, and perhaps precisely because I did so need it, it was revealing itself to me]." As for Montreal, she discovered it on foot: "En pèlerin, émue, éreintée, je l'ai traversée en entier [as a pilgrim, emotional, weary, I explored every corner of it]."[21] This passage suggests the contradictory nature of Roy's relationship to Quebec (and perhaps to Canada). On the one hand the positive, active statements – "je me découvrais un pays"; "je l'ai traversée en entier" – evoke the image of an explorer, a colonial adventurer or voyageur.[22] Yet the rather self-pitying tone of "pauvre, errante, solitaire," coupled with the reference to "le plus grand besoin," is elevated with the reference to pilgrimage to suggest that her quest was motivated by an inner, spiritual lack. This relationship between an inner need and an outer world reappears in the form and content of the reportages. Also significant is the tense usage in the phrase "je me découvrais un pays," the imperfect stressing as it does the nature of this discovery as a process, continuous and incomplete. As such, the discovering of the country, like the writing of the reportages, is represented as an unfinished act of taking possession, of positioning herself within her country, territory, or homeland of choice, be it Montreal, Quebec, or Canada. For, of course, the word "pays" is a remarkably slippery word, meaning different things in different contexts and to different users. Within the article cited, Roy uses "le pays" to refer to the immediate locality around her parents' respective native villages ("le pays de ma mère en haut de Saint-Jacques-de-l'Achigan, celui de mon père aux alentours de Beaumont [my mother's country up above Saint-Jacques-de-l'Achigan, that of my father around Beaumont]")[23] as well as to Montreal and to Quebec. More broadly, the "pays" that Roy will construct in her reportages goes well beyond the provincial border to encompass a vast swathe of Canadian space.

If Roy constructs her relationship to Quebec as a return home (to her parents' native province), in fact this is only part of a much more complex process. In "Cultural Identity and Disapora," Stuart Hall argues that cultural identity is a matter of "becoming" as well as of "being": "Cultural identities come from somewhere, have histories. But, like everything which is historical, they undergo constant transformation. Far from being eternally fixed in some essentialized past, they are subject to the continuous 'play' of history, culture and power."[24] While cultural identities, in Hall's words, "come from somewhere, have histories," they are also constructed as part of a future project, that is to say, they are going somewhere. Indeed, in Roy's reportages, "Canada" is more about the future than the past, and a future imagined through a number of privileged spatial relationships. In imagining, constructing her country, Roy is reassessing her position within Canada and choosing the elements of a personal and a shared identity. In this light the statement "je me découvrais un pays" takes on its full significance. It is not a return to origins as such, having more in common with the experience of migration. Salman Rushdie suggests: "Migrants must, of necessity, make a new imaginative relationship with the world, because of the loss of familiar habitats."[25] It is in this light that Roy's exploration of urban and rural Canada can be understood: an imaginative process that generates a number of key preoccupations, such as colonization, migration, forms of cooperative action, work, and cultural difference and freedom, which recur in a variety of guises in her later literary work.

Roy's articles for the *Bulletin des Agriculteurs* constitute a huge body of work. As a rough estimate, each article was about 4,000 words long. If collected into one volume, the fifty reportages and short stories published between 1940 and 1946 would constitute a work of about 200,000 words, comparable in length to *La Détresse et l'enchantement*.[26] The reportages include a number of individual studies, usually of diverse areas of Quebec, with a focus not only on agriculture but also on a range of economic activities from the primary and secondary sectors. But what characterizes her journalism most strongly is the special series of linked articles, each the result of information-gathering trips, interviews, and extended visits to a variety of communities across Canada. The first series of four articles, published from June to September 1941 under the heading "Tout Montréal," is the product of Roy's own process of familiarization with the city in 1939 and 1940 and covers the topography, population, working world, and history of the city. The second major series, "Ici l'Abitibi," comprises seven articles that appear between November 1941 and May 1942. They study different aspects of the process of colonization of this western corner of Quebec. The seven articles of the third series, "Peuples du Canada" (November 1942–May 1943), are the best-known, six of them having been selected for republication in the collection *Fragiles Lumières de la terre* (1978).[27] These take Roy on a long journey throughout the Prairie provinces, from Manitoba to western Alberta, where she finds her subject matter among a range of ethnic and cultural minorities, immigrants, or migrants, who have settled in small communities across Canada and are an immensely significant part of what Canada means to her.[28] The final series, with the umbrella title "Horizons du Québec" (January 1944–May 1945), is less a coherent body of articles than a series of investigations of further regions of Quebec (including the Saguenay and the Cantons de l'Est), their resources (timber, fishing, mining, asbestos, aluminium), and the working lives of those they employ. By this time, of course, Roy's life was more and more dominated by the completion of *Bonheur d'occasion*. Once the book was published, her professional life took a new turn, and while she continued to publish occasional reportages, essays, and short stories throughout her career, her association with the *Bulletin des Agriculteurs* effectively ended in 1946.

What emerges even from this brief overview of Roy's contributions is its geographical sweep. These articles are a working-through of the project of discovering a country. As the articles move first across Montreal, then outward through the province of Quebec to the newest regions of colonization in Abitibi, to the tip of Gaspésie, to the Côte Nord, and then westward, following the route of the railway line from Winnipeg through scattered communities up to the north-west of Alberta, they are mapping out Roy's vision of Canada. The series' titles ("Tout Montréal," "Ici l'Abitibi," "Peuples du Canada," "Horizons du Québec") suggest this desire to discover, know, and name the country for her readers. The metaphor of mapping cannot fail to raise echoes of French and British colonial history, and Gayatri Spivak's image of a solitary British soldier walking across India in the nineteenth century, "effectively and violently sliding one discourse under another."[29] Roy's relationship to the process of mapping is at once more ambivalent and subtler than this, but the colonial dimension remains pertinent. Bill Ashcroft reflects: "The discourse of mapping, even though it may proceed in a fragmentary and intermittent way, is a formal strategy for bringing colonized territory under control by knowing it in language."[30]

Roy's mapping of Canada explicitly places her in some ways in the role of an outsider. The act of visiting and interviewing often involves the use of contacts (the missionary, a government administrator, an interpreter, an "expert" advisor), many of whom are placed at the interface between the local inhabitant and an institution – such as the Catholic or Protestant churches, government departments, social, educational, or welfare services, or scientific research bodies. This role reinforces the reporter's position as a cultural outsider, and the observed as her object of study, often accessible only through the mediation of figures of authority. In other cases the contact is apparently more direct, more spontaneous, as Roy turns up unannounced in a village to find lodging at one of the farms (as in her visits to the Hutterites, to the Jewish colony in Saskatchewan, or to the refugees from the Nazi annexation of the Sudetenland).[31] Nevertheless her position as a reporter places her in an ambiguous relationship, in which her desire to know, and then to represent her impressions of, the lives and thoughts of her diverse subjects is in part an act of appropriation. However much Roy might try to see her subjects' lives from the inside, her stance remains problematic. As Laurie Kruk has written about the pedagogical issues related to the discussion of Native identity: "Whether we are insiders or outsiders, we realize that we are tangled in a web of cultural stereotypes, positive *and* negative, and gaps in knowledge of the Other that we struggle to evade."[32] The problematic issue of Roy's relationship to her subject matter is perhaps most intriguingly posed in the case of the representation (or non-representation) of indigenous subjects in her texts, in her early journalism, and also in her later accounts, both fictional and non-fictional. This is a question to which we shall return.

The hybrid city

If we look at Roy's reportages as a mapping activity, what is striking is the way that her journalistic writing re-enacts the history of colonization, following the course of the St. Lawrence inland to the rapids of Lachine, crossing Montreal from east to west, seeking out the successive waves of colonization, from that of the French, with its traces of the seigneurial system, to the new settlements under Quebec's colonization program, and then following the railroad west (the railroad, which both served British needs to people and secure the west and helped create the Canadian Federation). Yet there is something perverse and interesting in Roy's focus. She takes her readers away from the beaten track, by focusing on peripheral areas, isolated and marginal communities, often those who are fighting to retain their ethnic and cultural difference in defiance of assimilatory pressures.[33] Even the first special series of articles devoted to Montreal offers unexpected perspectives on the city. While the title "Tout Montréal" suggests a bird's eye view of the whole, and individual articles promise a representation of the city in terms of twin poles – "Les deux Saint-Laurent," "Est-Ouest," and "Du Port aux Banques" – what emerges is a narrative of the city that is marked by mobility, flexibility, shifting boundaries, and interactions rather than by a binary division between its anglophone and francophone territories.[34] This narrative is reinforced by

Roy's use of personification, as in the following passage from the description of the route of the boulevard Saint-Laurent:

> Dans sa carrière tumultueuse, il s'est fait à l'image du monde: boutiques de tatouage, refuges de matelots, antres crasseux des diseuses de bonne aventure avec leurs vitrines tapissées de mains géantes et de tentures grossières, maisons de gros, débits à l'once ou à la verge, voitures ambulantes, brasseries, syna-gogues, théâtres, halles et tavernes.
> [In the course of its tumultuous career, it has adapted itself to the changing world: tattoo shops, shelters for sailors, fortune-tellers' squalid dens, their windows covered with giant hands and rough hangings, wholesale businesses, shops that sell by the ounce or the yard, hawkers' carts, restaurant-bars, synagogues, theatres, covered markets and beer taverns.] ("Les deux Saint-Laurent," BA, June 1941, 8)

The use of the list suggests an ever-changing scene, the boulevard taking on a multiplicity of faces but never resting as it hurtles along: "Partant des bas quartiers, il monte jusqu'à côtoyer la montagne. Il regarde les signes de conquête qu'on a dressés aux deux pôles de la ville: la croix sur les hauteurs, les élévateurs sur les quais. En haut, les châteaux; en bas, les taudis [Starting from the low-lying part of the city, it climbs up to skirt the mountain. It looks at the signs of conquest erected at the twin poles of the city: the cross up on high, the grain elevators down on the waterfront. Up above, the castles; down below, the slums]" (ibid.). At this point the allusion to the contrasting histories of the French and British in Canada is clear, but the description flows on, complicating the picture:

> Âme vagabonde, il connaît la senteur du blé, du cambouis, du poisson, de l'ail, de la bière, du blé-d'Inde soufflé, des frites et du *smoked* meat ...
> Il connaît les cotonnades fleuries, les calicos, le tabac canadien, les melons, les concombres, les laitues, les aubergines, les friperies, les olives. Il voit des visages turcs, grecs, annamites, français, anglais, irlandais, slaves.
> Le cri de la sirène assiste à son départ et le tumulte d'un cou-rant rapide et dangereux l'accueille au terme de ses fantaisies.

[Roaming spirit, it knows the smell of wheat, engine grease, fish, garlic, beer, popcorn, fries and smoked meat ...

It knows flowered cotton fabrics, calicos, Canadian tobacco, melons, cucumbers, lettuces, aubergines, second-hand clothes, olives. It sees all kinds of faces – Turkish, Greek, Annamite, French, English, Irish, Slav.

The siren sounds as it sets off and at the end of its wild imaginings it is greeted by the tumult of a swift and dangerous current.] (Ibid.)

While references are made to anglophone and francophone influences, these are either part of a greater list of diverse parts, as in the second paragraph above, or, in some cases, brought together in new hybrid ways, as in the following passage from "Est-Ouest" referring to the (personified) rue Sainte-Catherine:

Elle n'est ni française, ni anglaise, ni même américaine. Elle reste une rue hybride mêlant les enseignes et les affiches dans un charabia d'anglais et de français.

Elle dira: "Venez au roi du chien chaud," ou "Sauvez vos rebuts," ou encore elle parlera d'un certain tabac "dispendieux." Elle insistera sur la qualité de cent breuvages. "Buvez 7 up. Essayez Flirt; c'est un amour." Et elle plonge les gens dans l'abîme même de l'incompréhension lorsqu'elle assure: "Vous aimerez it."

[It is neither French nor English, nor even American. It remains a hybrid road, mixing together signs and advertisements in a jumbled combination of English and French.

It will say: "Visit the king of the chien chaud," or "Sauvez your cast-offs," or again it will refer to a particular tobacco as "dispendieux [expensive]." It will stress the quality of a hundred different drinks. "Drink 7 up. Try Flirt; c'est adorable." And it plunges people into the depths of confusion when it guarantees: "Vous aimerez it."] ("Est-Ouest," BA, July 1941, 9)

If this particular account of linguistic hybridity is relatively light-hearted, the final article in the series, in which Roy surveys the history of Montreal, explores the legacy of French and British colonialism in more depth.[35] As Montreal entered the industrial

age, Roy suggests, a new relationship developed between anglophones and francophones:

> Montréal découvre peu à peu qu'il n'est pas plus français
> qu'anglais, mais bien une ville du Nouveau-Monde, avec une
> destinée toute neuve à suivre. Il fait cette découverte longtemps
> après New-York et s'en émeut étrangement. Sa tâche est plus
> complexe. Il s'agit de préserver et de combiner ses éléments
> divers plutôt que de les fonder et de les amalgamer.
> [Gradually Montreal discovers that she is no more French than
> English, but really a city in the New World, with a completely
> new destiny to follow. She makes this discovery long after New
> York and is strangely upset by it. Her task is more complex. It's
> a case of preserving and combining the different elements rather
> than blending and merging them.] ("Après trois cents ans," BA,
> September 1941, 38)

The article builds up toward a lengthy analysis of modern-day
Montreal in terms of its linguistic and cultural duality. But while
Roy recognizes the existence of divisions (between Westmount and
Outremont, between east and west), she tries to unpick the binary
stereotype:

> Montréal a des paroisses distinctes; il n'a pas de quartier
> complètement homogène. Westmount s'affirme anglais; de
> nombreuses familles canadiennes-françaises y habitent.
> Notre-Dame de Grâce, que l'on considère généralement anglais,
> est 18 pour 100 français. Le district Delorimier d'atmosphère si
> française est 14 pour 100 anglais. Aucune particularité
> marquante ne distingue l'habitation canadienne-française du
> home anglais. Canadiens français et anglais vivent de façon à
> peu près identique. Ils achètent aux mêmes magasins, prennent
> le même tramway, travaillent souvent aux mêmes bureaux. Ils
> ne se séparent que pour aller à l'école et à l'église.
> [Montreal has distinct parishes; no neighbourhood is completely
> homogeneous. Westmount declares itself to be Anglophone;
> many French-Canadian families live there. Notre-Dame de
> Grâce, which is generally considered to be English speaking, is
> 18 percent Francophone. The De Lorimier district with such a

French atmosphere is 14 percent English. No distinguishing
characteristic marks out the French-Canadian residence from
the English home. The way of life of French- and Anglo-Canadians is more or less identical. They shop in the same stores, take
the same trams, often work in the same offices. They only separate to go to school and to church.] ("Après trois cents ans," BA,
September 1941, 39)[36]

At times Roy's analysis reinforces certain stereotypes, such as the
gendering of French and British difference: "L'apport masculin lui
fut donné par l'élément anglo-saxon; l'influence féminine, en
nuances et en caprices, par la France [Its masculine side came from
the anglo-saxon heritage; the feminine influence, in its subtlety and
its whimsicality, from France]" ("Après trois cents ans," BA, September 1941, 39). At other times more fluid notions of identity
apply. As for Roy herself, bilingualism and biculturalism seem to
emerge in these articles as an advantage, not a problem:

> Montréal se dit la deuxième ville française du monde. En vérité,
> il est bien trop de choses pour se définir ainsi. Il parle français et
> anglais dans le même souffle ... Deux de ses rues honorent la
> victoire du vainqueur et du vaincu des Plaines d'Abraham. Il y a
> de la place pour eux deux dans le cœur généreux de la ville.
> [Montreal calls itself the second French-speaking city in the
> world. In fact it is far too complicated a place to be defined in
> that way. The city speaks French and English in the same breath
> ... Two of its streets honour the victory of the conqueror and the
> conquered at the Plains of Abraham. There is room for both in
> the generous heart of the city.] (Ibid.)

She concludes that Montreal's duality is at once its weakness and its
strength, and it is with the positive combination of elements that
she closes the article and the series: "Dans la dualité de Montréal
réside le principe de sa durée et de son caractère [Montreal's duality
is the key to her long life and her character] (ibid.)." Whereas the
earlier three articles shaped the city in terms of its dynamic heterogeneity, this final article, perhaps because of its historical approach,
concentrates on a dualistic view. Yet because of the way Roy qualifies and tests the relationship between the two traditions, she gives
the effect of a reflection on negotiation and interaction rather than

on the hierarchical power relations that tend to predominate in both *Bonheur d'occasion* and *Alexandre Chenevert*.

Settlers, Travellers, and Migrants

In the second series of reportages, "Ici l'Abitibi," we move from the representation of modern, urban space to the latest generation of *habitants* and *colons*, and a way of life that has more in common with Roy's father's work with immigrants to the Canadian West between 1897 and 1915 than with agricultural life elsewhere in 1940s Quebec. Given the fact that her father's career was ended rather abruptly by his dismissal when Roy was only six and a half years old, it is remarkable how strongly his involvement with the process of colonization remained imprinted on her imagination.[37] Here, of course, the focus is on modern-day colonization policies, given a new urgency in Quebec in the Depression years and aimed at resettling groups of urban unemployed and rural poor.[38] Roy's series follows the migration of a group of familes who had been recruited for resettlement from the Iles de la Madeleine to the île Nepawa in Abitibi, on the border between Ontario and Quebec. At first sight the reportages seem to idealize both the aims of the colonization program and its recruits. In the view of the district manager, Louis Simard, the articles were certainly a glowing vindication of the colonization program. Simard had acted as informer and guide for Roy and was the subject of the third of Roy's seven articles, "Le chef de district," published in January 1942.[39] In a letter sent in response to the first three articles he thanked her for what he saw as her work on behalf of the colonization program: "You have done much for the cause of Colonisation and rest assured that your pen is worth more than our work here, for publicity is needed for the true value of Colonisation to be recognised in our Province." His letter makes it clear that he sees the colonization program as a project in which the provincial government and the Catholic Church are equally involved: "In colonisation there are many things to do and the most important of these is deciding on the site and building a church where mass will be said or sung until the end of time."[40]

It is interesting to speculate whether Simard's gratitude was tempered by the remaining four articles, which expressed a number of criticisms of government policy and the attitudes of the settlers.

Roy later restated her admiration for Simard's devotion to the cause, but she distanced herself from his optimism:

> Ce n'est pas avec les yeux d'un voyageur qu'il faut visiter cette campagne, mais bien avec ceux d'un croyant. Ou plutôt avec les yeux d'un chef colonisateur, d'un M. Simard par exemple, qui arrêtait hier son regard sur des forêts intactes, qui voit aujourd'hui naître les maisons dans les clairières et qui sait que tout progrès arrive à son heure.
> [When you visit this countryside you have to see it not with the eyes of a traveller, but really with the eyes of a believer. Or rather with the eyes of a chief colonizer, of someone like Monsieur Simard, for example, who yesterday was looking at uninterrupted forest, who today is seeing houses appear in the clearings and who knows that progress always comes when the time is right.] ("Bourgs d'Amérique I," BA, April 1942, 45)

While Ricard finds it difficult to read the series "as a plea in favour of colonization and a return to the land,"[41] nevertheless he is still struck by Roy's enduring attraction to what he calls "the myth of the colony."[42] In fact the articles do not adopt a consistent attitude toward colonization efforts in Abitibi. In "La terre secourable" (BA, November 1941) and "Le pain et le feu" (BA, December 1941) the Madelinots are held up as model pioneers: "Le père Azade, c'est le voyageur né [Old Azade Poirier is the born traveller]" (BA, November 1941, 11). Indeed, when Roy returns to monitor their progress she reports: "Je retrouve chez eux les vieilles vertus françaises: l'extrême propreté, l'économie, la belle humeur et le don de solidarité qui n'est peut-être autre chose que la véritable charité chrétienne [I find in them the old French virtues: extreme cleanliness, thrift, good nature and the gift of solidarity which is perhaps nothing other than genuine Christian charity]" (BA, December 1941, 30). This line echoes the values of traditionalist Quebec, even raising an echo of their representation in the famous "voix du Québec" of Hémon's *Maria Chapdelaine*. The explicit reference to Christianity supports the association, but as the articles unfold, Roy's particular "myth of the colony" acquires a more political slant. She praises the communal spirit of the Madelinots: "Je n'ai jamais encore rencontré au Canada un groupement qui fît preuve d'un tel sens social. Je me rappelle maintenant ne jamais les avoir entendu parler de leurs maigres biens en terme de possessifs singuliers [Never before in Canada have I met a group who displayed such a collective spirit. I remember now that I never heard them using the singular form of the possessive to refer to their meager belongings]" (ibid., 30). This attitude suits them to the principles of the colonization program in Abitibi which, in the conclusion to the article "Le chef de district," she compares with Soviet models of organization:

> Une chose me frappe: c'est que dans cet étatisme de la colonisation qui tend à gérer la construction des maisons, la tenue de la ferme, la rotation des récoltes, on a emprunté beaucoup aux Soviets, mais que, par contre, on a définitivement respecté le droit à la petite propriété et qu'on a jusqu'à un certain point, en autant qu'il fut possible, secondé l'initiative individuelle. Ne serait-ce pas là un premier pas vers un socialisme chrétien? [One thing strikes me: it is that in this state control of colonization which tends to manage the building of houses, the running of the farm, the rotation of crops, a great deal has been borrowed from the Soviets, but that, on the other hand, the right to own small property has definitely been respected and, up to a certain point, as far as it was possible, individual initiative has been supported. Would that not be the first step towards a Christian socialism?] (BA, January 1942, 29)

And while the Madelinots are the focus of the first two reportages, Roy also mentions a number of other new settlers in Abitibi who are immigrants from Finland or Ukraine, making this example of colonization more a case of creating a new community than of simply preserving Quebec traditionalism. Read in this light, her articles are not so much a rewriting of the "roman de la terre" as a call for an alternative future society that would combine socialist economics and Christian ethics with a diverse population of migrants.

This series of articles is probably the most ambivalent, as if Roy is torn between a deep-seated belief in the figure of the *colon* and a troubling, critical response. Despite Roy's admiration for the migrants, ever ready to move on to find new land and pursue new dreams, a critical edge soon surfaces, with a degree of irony piercing the stereotype of the simple pioneer:

Chacun, la brise aidant, le soleil aidant, commence à bâtir une image de cet Abitibi dont le nom est venu les troubler jusqu'au fond de leurs îles. Ceux qui jamais ne sont sortis de ces îles éprouvent quelque mal à imaginer un pays de souches et de forêts. Mais, naïvement, ils le construisent avec des souvenirs de cartes postales, des comparaisons enfantines, de vagues besoins de bonheur. La terre promise prend des contours des choses que l'on transforme à sa fantaisie.

[Everyone, with the help of a good breeze and some sunshine, begins to build an image of Abitibi, this place whose name came to unsettle them back there on their islands. Those who have never left those islands have some difficulty imagining a land of tree stumps and forests. But, naïvely, they build it up with memories of postcards, childlike comparisons, vague longings for happiness. The promised land takes on the form of things that each changes as the fancy takes them.] (BA, November 1941, 11)

But Roy shifts her ground again, suggesting that the migrants' apparent naïvety is in fact a strategy for bridging the void between desire and action:

Les émigrants sont toujours des gens qu'on leurre un peu, oh pas toujours sans le vouloir. Ce sont des gens qui se leurrent, peut-être, aussi eux-mêmes. Car entre les mots et l'interprétation de chacun, il y a souvent un abîme. Et il est bien qu'il en soit ainsi, car qui donc prendrait son fardeau et se mettrait en marche, si le mirage n'était venu s'interposer entre la vie quotidienne et les lendemains toujours pareils?

[Migrants are always people who are being slightly deceived, oh, not always against their will. They are people who also, perhaps, deceive themselves. For there is often a gulf between words and people's interpretation of them. And it is good that it should be so, for who would take up their load and set out if the mirage had not come to stand between everyday life and a future of endless repetition?] (Ibid., 59)

In later articles Roy moves from this speculative mode to make a number of serious criticisms of what she has seen, whether the exploitation of schoolmistresses within the province of Quebec, the mentality of some of settlers and their lack of moral, spiritual, or political vision, or the imposition of uniformity in planning and construction. Two examples demonstrate the tone of Roy's criticisms. The article "Pitié pour les institutrices" focuses on the case of one schoolmistress, but makes a general attack on denominational school boards for their treatment of underqualified rural schoolmistresses.[43] Not only is the schoolmistress underpaid but she is allowed little personal or moral freedom: "Il ne fallait pas seulement qu'elle fût soumise à la pauvreté, mais encore à la tyrannie [Not only did she have to be subjected to poverty but also to tyranny]" (BA, March 1942, 7); as a general rule schoolmistresses tend to be underqualified, to be given no incentive to expand their cultural horizons, and to have poor French and no English: "on leur avait fait croire que c'était superflu dans ce pays que d'apprendre l'anglais [they had been made to believe that it was unnecessary in this country to learn English]" (ibid., 45). In this highly critical account of Quebec's education provision, Roy draws a telling parallel with "other provinces":[44]

> En d'autres provinces, on a vu des jeunes filles ambitieuses travailler comme domestiques pendant quelques années pour gagner leur cours à l'Ecole Normale et devenir institutrices. Ici, on voit des institutrices devenir domestiques, car en cet emploi déjà elles trouvaient une amélioration matérielle
> [In other provinces ambitious young women have worked as domestic servants for a few years in order to pay for their course at the Teacher Training College and become schoolmistresses. Here you see schoolmistresses becoming domestic servants, for even in this job they found themselves financially better off.]" (Ibid., 45)

Given the fact that in Quebec education was largely under church control, through the denominational school boards, this was an outspoken attack on the Catholic Church.

In the second example, "Plus que le pain" (BA, February 1942), Roy ends with a direct appeal to settlers, with the aim of encouraging them to work together collectively, finding strength in solidarity rather than being divided by envy and suspicion. She claims to have found a general lack of initiative among the settlers to do things for themselves, citing a widespread dissatisfaction with the state of roads in the region. Roy challenges the settlers to take responsibility for their community:

> "Cela est l'affaire du gouvernement," dites-vous. Mais le gouvernement, c'est vous, c'est nous, c'est toute la société humaine dans laquelle chacun reçoit et donne.
>
> La terre vous donne; la forêt vous donne; le gouvernement vous donne. Que donnez-vous en retour?
>
> Le pain et le feu s'achètent, vous le savez bien; mais la paix, le calme, la joie aussi s'achètent. Personne ne vient les porter à domicile. C'est en donnant et non pas en recevant qu'on acquiert la clarté qui inonde le cœur ...
>
> Il vous reste, si vous le voulez bien, à donner au monde le plus grand des exemples: l'exemple de la bonne entente, du vrai courage, de l'union.
> ["That is a matter for the government," you say. But the government is you, it is us, it is human society as a whole in which each of us gives and receives.
>
> The land gives; the forest gives; the government gives. What do you give in return?
>
> Bread and fire have to be bought, as you know; but peace, calm, joy, also have to be bought. Nobody delivers them to your door. It is in giving and not in receiving that you gain the light that fills your heart ...
>
> It remains for you, if you are willing, to give the world the finest of examples: the example of good understanding, of true courage, of unity.] (Ibid., 35)

After this article the moralizing tone fades and the series closes with a vision of the region not in terms of individuals or communities of rural settlers, but rather in terms of its industrial development and the effects of capitalist interests on the shape of its growth. For, of course, the settlement of new areas of Quebec was only viable if profit could be made from the various industrial opportunities, from mining mineral resources or processing primary materials such as timber. Roy criticizes the lack of aesthetic appeal of the series of new towns, including La Sarre, Duparquet, and Amos. Where the landscape is already so unvaried, she argues, could the architecture and planning not be less uniform? Abitibi compares poorly with other regions of Quebec:

Je pense qu'il nous arrive tous de nous rappeler les pays visités
en terme de couleur. Ainsi, je me rappellerai toujours la Baie des
Chaleurs en terme d'ocre, de blanc et de rouge; la Côte Nord,
en terme de bleu clair et d'or; et l'Abitibi, en terme de gris. Oui
le gris est bien la couleur de ce pays. Grises les maisons sans
peinture, grises les étables, grises les fermes de glaise.
[I think we all find that we remember countries we have visited
in terms of colour. So I shall always remember the Baie des
Chaleurs in terms of ochre, white and red; the Côte Nord in
terms of light blue and gold; and Abitibi, in terms of grey. Yes
grey really is the colour of this country. Grey the unpainted
houses, grey the stables, grey the clay soil of the farms.]
("Bourgs d'Amérique I," BA, April 1942, 44)

The two articles entitled "Bourgs d'Amérique" create a fluid picture of towns springing up over the last thirty years for specific economic reasons (gold mines, timber, woodpulp), flourishing in a
burst of capital investment, and attracting a wave of labour, a
mobile population of latter-day nomads:

Les mineurs, gens nomades, quittent les villes finissantes pour
les commençantes. Une nuée de petits marchands suivent là où
mène la troupe hardie. Et d'autres encore viennent de loin, de
partout, vers la ville nouvelle. La population de l'une devient
celle des autres ... Et la plus belle ville est toujours celle où l'on
fait fortune.
[The miners, nomadic people, leave the towns as they are nearly
completed for new towns. A cloud of small traders follow wherever the brave troop leads. And still more come from far away,
from everywhere, to the new town. The population from one
place moves to the next ... And the loveliest town is always the
one where you make your fortune.] ("Bourgs d'Amérique, II,"
BA, May 1942, 37)

As the hunt for new resources shifts elsewhere so the towns are left
to decline, disappear, or diversify. If there are traces in Roy's earlier
articles of her own nostalgic identification with the figure of the
colon, by the end of this series it is clearly Roy the "voyageur"
rather than Roy the "croyante [believer]" whose impressions predominate. The image of Roy as a traveller who is constructing a

"pays" made up of the variety of figures and landscapes encountered on her journey helps the reader to grasp what is distinctive –
and challenging – about the vision of Canada that her journalism
offers. In "Tout Montréal," "Ici l'Abitibi," and the final series,
"Horizons du Québec," the great majority of central protagonists
or actors are Québécois. But in the series "Peuples du Canada,"
Roy takes the reader on a very different journey in search
of Canada.

Travel and Roy as a travelling subject

Journeys of different types recur throughout Roy's work in all its
genres. *La Détresse et l'enchantement*, for instance, is structured in
two parts, the first in Manitoba, the second in Europe, and within
each part the narrative can be divided into a series of journeys
(Roy's various teaching posts, visits to rural cousins, references to
her father's journeys as *agent colonisateur*, memories of travelling
through rural Manitoba with her fellow amateur performers, walks
in London, excursions to Epping Forest, the West of England, the
walking tour of Provence). The published edition of Roy's correspondence with her husband, "*Mon cher grand fou ... ": Lettres à
Marcel Carbotte 1947–1979*, records journeys by car and on foot,
the discovery of new places and encounters with strangers, in
Florida, in Arizona, Provence, or Brittany.[45] Lori Saint-Martin
highlights the symbolic value of the journey in Roy's work as follows: "Incarnation des plus hautes valeurs spirituelles, philosophi-
ques, humaines, le voyage représente la découverte, l'ouverture à
autrui, l'élan passionné vers les inconnus qui annonce l'avènement
de la grande fraternité humaine [Incarnation of the highest spiritual, philosophical, human values, the journey represents discovery,
openness to the Other, the goodwill toward strangers that prefigures the coming of an age of true fraternity]."[46] Saint-Martin's
feminist analysis develops the opposition between traveller and
prisoner to trace the desire for liberation and the critique of the con-
straints of patriarchy in Roy's published and unpublished work.
Reading this work from the perspective of colonialism and postcolonialism opens up a further dimension on the significance of the
journey, a significance that complements rather than contradicts
Saint-Martin's approach. It is as a journalist that Roy develops her
own practice as a writer (and finds a degree of liberation), travelling

physically in search of her subject matter and engaged in a series of encounters and exchanges in the attempt to cross borders between her and others. As her travels take her further afield, her encounters become more diverse and she seeks out subjects from different cultural and ethnic groups.

Roy's years in Europe and Quebec meant that, as she returned to western Canada in summer 1942, she was bringing a new perspective on the West, both repositioning herself in relation to her past and perhaps offering her Quebec readers a new angle from which to see their own place in Canada. As Stuart Hall observes: "Identities are the names we give to the different ways we are positioned by, and position ourselves within, the narratives of the past."[47] As an independent woman journalist writing for Montreal-based papers, she is neither required nor expected to write from the perspective of the minority francophone community of Saint-Boniface that she has left behind. Nor does she become a spokesperson for Quebec, traditional or liberal. Roy shapes the Canadian West in the image of her own values, as a land of migration, of minorities, a land where the diverse population is a positive alternative to the identity politics of either Saint-Boniface in the 1920s and 1930s or Quebec in the 1940s.

In *Routes: Travel and Translation in the Late Twentieth Century*, James Clifford states that "travels and contacts are crucial sites for an unfinished modernity" and that travel facilitates "a view of human location as constituted by displacement as much as by stasis."[48] Roy's role as a journalist makes her a literal traveller, a mobile "actor" to join Clifford's list of figures such as missionaries, translators, government officers, pilgrims, servants, explorers, tourists, migrant labourers, and new immigrants. Her articles tend to seek out subjects who fall within this list of mobile actors, particularly in the Abitibi series (settlers, new immigrants, government representatives, travelling priests, seasonal workers), as well as in "Peuples du Canada." If Abitibi proved to be something of a disappointment for Roy, then "Peuples du Canada" can be read as a renewed search for communities that still exemplify the experience of the migrant, those seeking new land, and whose relationship to the land, and to the country in which they live, is founded on the process of migration. As with the settlers in Abitibi, Roy's fascination with these figures is not simply a nostalgic longing for a past way of life. While the series allows her to return to find for herself the migrant communities to whom her father dedicated himself so fully, Roy also seems to be searching for her own ideal of a (future) community that is able to live in freedom on the land, in Canada. Indeed, in the auto-fictional account "Le puits de Dunrea" the narrator/protagonist, Christine, assesses her father's view of the colony of Petits-Ruthènes in Saskatchewan in terms that could be applied to Roy:

> Sûrement le passé comptait dans leur vie, un passé de profonde misère, mais l'avenir, un merveilleux et solide avenir, voilà surtout à quoi crurent les Petits-Ruthènes en arrivant au Canada. Et c'est ainsi que papa aimait les colons: tournés vers l'avant et non pas geignant tout le temps sur ce qu'ils avaient dû abandonner.
> [Certainly the past counted for something in their lives – a past deeply wretched – but it was in the future, a wonderful and well-founded future, that the Little Ruthenians above all had faith when they came to Canada. And that was the sort of settler Papa liked: people facing forward, and not everlastingly whining over what they had had to leave behind.] (RD 126; 73)[49]

Not only does Roy's series include visits to communities of migrants who settled in the late nineteenth and early twentieth century in the west, such as the Doukhobors and Mennonites, but she also meets much more recent arrivals – the latest being refugees from the Sudetenland who fled after the Munich agreement in 1938 to escape Nazism. The series follows Roy's route from Winnipeg across Manitoba to visit the Hutterites in Iberville, then across Saskatchewan where she visits the Doukhobors, the Mennonites, a settlement of German and Russian Jews, and the Sudeten Czech refugees in northwest Saskatchewan, before crossing to Alberta to visit Ukrainian and Franco-Canadian communities. The different communities have various reasons for migration. For some such as the Doukhobors, Mennonites, and Hutterites, Canada represented the chance of freedom from religious persecution and the possibility of living according to their pacifist principles (the Hutterites who settled in Canada in 1918, for instance, were granted exemption from conscription). For others, such as the Sudeten Czechs and Ukrainian peasants, Canada offered freedom from political or economic oppression. In many cases it was the chance to own and cultivate land that attracted them, but others, including many second-generation migrants, came for educational opportunities. Roy's accounts of these diverse peoples are at times ethnographic, characterizing the groups in terms of their dress, their food, their domestic and church architecture, or their cultural differences. Given the interests of her readers, she also gives some details of their style of farming (the strains of wheat and rye grown by Jewish farmers, the range of modern agricultural machinery owned by the Hutterite community).

These portraits of the different "Peuples du Canada" raise fascinating questions about the relationship between these "peoples" and Canada, and reveal Roy's own ambivalence toward questions of assimilation and cultural difference. She both welcomes and fears signs of the communities' cultural and linguistic openness toward "Canada." At the end of the article on the Hutterites, the most ascetic and least integrated of the groups she visits, Roy recounts the request of a young girl that Roy send her a copy of the photograph she has taken and some books about Canada and Quebec:

> Je continuai mon chemin, rassurée du moins sur la curiosité des jeunes Huttérites qui les mènera sûrement hors de leur isolement. Mais en même temps une crainte m'assaillait.
> "Dieu veuille que, se rapprochant de nous, ce ne soit pas eux, les perdants!"
> [I went on my way, reassured about the curiosity of the young Hutterites, which will surely lead them out of their isolation. But at the same time I was afraid.
> "Please God they do not lose because of coming to us!"]
> (FL 26; 29)[50]

Yet in most cases Roy writes very positively about contact and interaction with these different "peoples," recognizing that it is through the medium of English that this contact between linguistic groups will happen. In her article on Franco-Canadians, in a passage that prefigures a similar scene in *La Petite Poule d'Eau*, she describes a Catholic church service in Alberta:

> Le curé fait son prône en français, puis tirant un petit paquet de notes, il toussote, s'éclaircit la voix, rougit un peu et dans un anglais trébuchant s'adresse aux paysans à figure de moujiks et

aux femmes slaves, quelques-uns seulement au fond de l'église
[The priest gives his sermon in French, then taking out a little
pack of notes, he clears his throat, turns slightly red and in a
halting English speaks to the peasants who look like moujiks
and the Slav women, just a few of them at the back of the
church. ("Les Gens de Chez-Nous," BA (May 1943): 36)

The article on the new arrivals from the Sudetenland closes with a
scene in which Elfrieda, a young Czech woman, struggles to express
herself to Roy, a scene that confirms the importance of learning
English as a means of survival and communication:

Nous possédions peu de mots pour alimenter la conversation ...
mais entre nous, sur la table, il y avait un petit dictionnaire. Elle
y pigeait des mots anglais, à mon tour j'y pigeais des mots
tchèques et nous arrivions à faire des bouts de phrase ... A la
fin, je réussis à lui faire comprendre que j'admirais beaucoup sa
persévérance ... Et elle arriva, après de pénibles recherches, à
m'expliquer à peu près sa pensée ...
    "Ce que j'apprends, ça personne, au moins, peut ôter à moi."
[Elfrieda Wagner and I had little to stoke our conversation ...
But between us was a little dictionary. She would look for an
English word, I would look up mine in Czech, and we managed
to make up bits of sentences ... At last I managed to tell her how
much I admired her perseverance. After more painful research,
she too succeeded in expressing her thought ...
    "At least, what I learn, no one can take that from me."]
(FL 73; 73–4)

This image of linguistic adaptation and the effort required for
two-way communication shows us what Roy finds most interesting
in the migrant communities and what she seems to favour as a
model of becoming Canadian. The history of the Mennonites, a
group whose religious beliefs have caused them to uproot themselves and move on many times, exemplifies the cultural hybridity
that results from the experience of migration: "Ni complètement
allemands, ni complètement russes, ils se réclament un peu de tous
les pays qui les virent passer à la recherche de la liberté [Neither
quite German nor quite Russian, they have taken over something
of all the countries through which they passed in search of free-

dom]" (FL 40; 44). This hybrid identity is not an obstacle to the Mennonites' belonging in Canada; rather the reverse, as the following self-correction in the final paragraph of the article suggests: "un peuple content d'être chez nous, que dis-je, chez lui [a people glad to be in our country – what am I saying? In their country!]" (FL 48; 51).

Roy's article on Ukrainian-Canadians, a widely scattered population of 600,000 in the 1940s, focuses on a diverse group, divided by religious differences between the Catholic and the Orthodox faiths, between the older and the younger generations. They are an example of an ethnic group that has migrated at different times and has largely assimilated itself to an Anglo-Canadian way of life. But assimilation, for Roy, is not a one-way process that erases difference. Rather, she presents it in dialectical terms:

> Etrange chose: ce peuple le plus féru de nationalisme, celui qui aurait pu le plus facilement résister à l'assimilation, est quand même celui qui s'est le plus complètement adapté au pays, qui, non seulement s'y est adapté, mais a contribué à façonner le visage de l'Ouest du Canada. Ses traditions passent, ont passé à l'héritage national. Ses danses, ses costumes pittoresques, ses chants, nous les tenons pour nôtres.
> [A strange thing: this people, so fiercely nationalist, the one which could most easily have resisted assimilation, is in fact the one that has most completely adapted to the country, and not only adapted but contributed to fashioning the features of Canada's West. Its traditions have passed into our national heritage. Its dances, costumes, and songs have become our own.]" (FL 84; 84)

Roy's use of "nous" in this instance and throughout her articles on Canada has an interesting status. Her rural Quebec readers were unlikely to share her personal familiarity with Ukrainian culture.[51] Careful reading of the articles makes it clear that Roy was writing above all as a francophone, but bilingual, Canadian, and with a very particular understanding of what that meant in terms of being part of a land of many migrant peoples, not just two founding peoples.

The series "Peuples du Canada" ends with what might seem like an anomaly. The seventh article in the series, "Les Gens de Chez-Nous," is devoted to the Franco-Canadians of Western Canada. But far from being represented in terms of Canada's two "founding nations," the Franco-Canadians are treated as another minority, a diasporic minority dispersed across the vast Canadian West, establishing small communities or living in towns and villages alongside migrants of Irish, Polish, or Ukrainian extraction. While Roy's account does indicate some cultural and spiritual bond between the Franco-Canadians of the West and Quebec, notably through family links, domestic architecture, and a fondness for the familiar iconography of Quebec Catholicism, she emphasizes the way Franco-Canadians have embraced the openness and diversity of the West. It is the individual, mobile figure of the explorer La Vérendrye that provides the role model rather than the anonymous, collective "colons," or indeed the Catholic priest.

Evidence of this openness to other influences and other cultures can be seen in Roy's description of schooling in the West. The article stresses the positive attitude of Franco-Canadians toward an inclusive, bicultural, and bilingual education. Roy paints an idealized picture of education in the West, failing to mention the effects of laws such as the 1916 Thornton Legislation on education in Manitoba. Rather, she praises the way in which schoolteachers in the West (in Alberta in this instance) give their pupils equal access to English and French: "Ces enfants n'étaient privés ni de leur langue ni de ces contes rimés, de ces poésies enfantines, qui ont enchanté les petits Anglais depuis des siècles [These children were deprived neither of their language nor of those nursery rhymes, those poems for children, which have delighted English children for centuries]" ("Les Gens de Chez-Nous," BA, May 1943, 39).[52] For Quebec readers this would have constituted an implicit criticism of the confessional education system and its defensive, partisan spirit. But for Roy, the same spirit of openness expresses itself in the relationships that Franco-Canadians in the West form with other migrant groups, a quality that she contrasts with the attitudes of some Anglo-Canadians: "Partout où les Canadiens français vivent dans le voisinage des Ruthènes, des Galiciens, des Sudètes et des Doukhobors, ils se montrent leurs amis. C'est plus que j'en pourrais dire des fermiers anglais qui ont encore pour désigner ces gens-là le terme de *foreigner* [Wherever French-Canadians live near to Ruthenians, Galicians, Sudetenlanders, and Doukhobors, they become their friends. That is more than I could say for the English farmers who still use the term *foreigner* to refer to those people]" (ibid., 39). Indeed, it is in the final paragraphs of the article on Franco-Canadians that Roy's reasons for including them among the "Peuples du Canada" become clear. Salman Rushdie's discussion of the migrant includes the following point: "To be a migrant is, perhaps, to be the only species of human being free of the shackles of nationalism (to say nothing of its ugly sister, patriotism)."[53] Speculating on the likely reactions of Franco-Canadians and Ukrainians to a discovery of arable land at the North Pole, Roy comments: "Ni l'un ni l'autre ne s'y rendraient pour planter un drapeau et marquer des frontières, mais pour y voir, naïvement, pousser du blé [Neither of them would go there in order to put up a flag and mark out frontiers, but, innocently, to see wheat growing there]" ("Les Gens de Chez-Nous," BA, May 1943, 39). If, as Rushdie argues, the migrant has to make a new imaginative relationship with the world, so too must migrants reevaluate the basis of their identity, rejecting nationalistic forms of identity in order to recognize their place within a space shared by many different minorities, groups of exiles, travellers, the "Peuples du Canada." It is with this notion of identity that Roy concludes her article on the Franco-Canadian: "En définitive, il aime par-dessus tout la grande variété que lui offre sa vie nouvelle. Il est peut-être déjà plus simplement canadien que canadien-français. Il ne s'est pas fondu dans la mêlée canadienne, mais il y appartient [When all is said and done, what he loves above all is the great variety that his new life offers him. He is already perhaps more simply Canadian than French-Canadian. He has not blended into the Canadian mix, but he is one part of it]" (ibid.).

So, what initially appeared somewhat anomalous, the inclusion of one of the two colonizing peoples of Canada in a series of articles apparently devoted to the various minorities who have settled in Western Canada from the late nineteenth century now seems more logical. Roy is reclaiming the Franco-Canadians of the West as a migrant people. In the 1940s Roy needed to look beyond Quebec, and indeed, beyond Saint-Boniface, Manitoba, to find this alternative model of francophone identity. Since 1980, of course, it has become much more common to redefine Québécois identity in terms of notions such as *américanité*. With reference to Jean Morisset's *L'Identité usurpée: l'Amérique écartée* (1985), Bill Marshall writes: "His work, invokes the alternative mapping of *Américanité*, of the vast spaces of hybridity traversed by the original, racially 'impure' *canadien*, who, crucially for Morisset's argument, was bereft of a state, escaping as he did the hierarchies and boundaries of French absolutism."[54] In Roy's case, I would argue that she is in fact offering a model of *franco-canadienneté* that marks a break with rigid definitions such as those invoked by phrases such as "le Québécois de souche [Québécois of French origin]" or "le Québécois pure laine [100 percent Québécois (literally 'pure wool')]," and in so doing her journalism prefigures a much more fluid and hybrid understanding of identity. Seen in this light, the decision not to include "Les Gens de Chez-Nous" in the selection that appeared in *Fragiles Lumières de la terre*, and to substitute an article about a Gaspé fisherman, changed the balance of the section.[55] The effect was to destroy the coherence of the original series, which arose from the distinctive Western perspective of the articles and the consequent decentring of notions of identity.

The image of Canada that emerges from "Peuples du Canada" is an alternative Canada, a Canada of the margins, minorities, and peripheries, which offers a *pays* composed of many peoples that resembles neither the *pays* of the dominant Anglo-Canadian population nor that of Quebec. It largely escapes the polarization between the anglophone and francophone "founding cultures," looking rather to another kind of myth of the *pays* – that of a nation of migrants, of cultural difference that does not assimilate to a uniform model (even in the case of the sizeable Ukrainian population) but contributes something distinctive.

What is at times a euphoric sense of a series of communities, migrants, and displaced groups of exiles living in differing degrees of exchange and reciprocity with others has its attraction as an antidote to the hierarchical relationships of linguistic and cultural domination that have been studied elsewhere in this book. Yet in Roy's concentration on the diverse groups of migrants in the West, does she replace the colonial vision of two "founding nations" with another model (of a land of predominantly White, predominantly European immigrants) which erases just as completely the place of the indigenous peoples? Roy's representation of Canada's minorities can be seen as a working-through of the ambivalent position that she herself assumed as a *colon colonisé*, between two cultures and two languages, fully at home with neither the one nor the other, but seeing each from a place in between. How, then, will this ambivalent gaze of the Second World writer perceive the First Nation and Inuit populations?

IMAGINING THE INDIGENE

In Roy's series of articles on Montreal, there are occasional references to the presence of Native Peoples in the historical account of the establishment of Ville Marie, and also as part of the daily life of the city, notably in "Les deux Saint-Laurent," which, as seen earlier, stresses the cultural and ethnic diversity of its population. The reference to women from the reserve just outside Montreal stresses not so much their difference as their unknowability, suggested by the term "mystère": "Cauteleuses et encore imprégnées de mystère, les Indiennes de Caughnawaga y rôdent avec leurs paniers d'osier et leur bric-à-brac en série [Cunning and still deeply mysterious, the Indian women from Caughnawaga hang around there with their wicker baskets and their cheap mass-produced goods]" (BA, June 1941, 37).[56] In one article, however, the First Nations are the central subject of the piece. After a trip to Sept-Iles in summer 1941, Roy wrote two articles, the second of which is devoted to the life of the Montagnais Indians who spent the summer months on the reserve there. But the title of the article, "Heureux les nomades," refers not to the Montagnais's lifestyle on the reserve, which Roy represents at times as bleak and pitiful, at times as comic, but to their nomadic life away from the reserve and their freedom from material ties. The article is framed by positive images of the Montagnais's annual cycle of migration: "L'hiver, dans les bois, l'été, à la mer, les nomades ont une loi qui les apparente aux oiseaux migrateurs [Winter in the forest, summer by the sea, the nomads obey the same kind of laws as birds in migration]" ("Heureux les nomades," BA, November 1941, 7). The closing section describes their departure from the coast as autumn approaches: "Légère, la tribu errante s'en va vers la liberté. Elle retrouvera avec joie ce qu'elle a laissé avec joie. La migration lui assure le renouveau. Et son âme est satisfaite parce qu'elle ne cherche nulle part la durée [With no ties, the wandering tribe sets off back to freedom. They will be happy to return to what they were happy to leave behind. Migration assures them of renewal. And their soul is satisfied because they do not seek permanence anywhere]" (ibid., 49).

But in contrast to this euphoric vision of the nomadic life, Roy's description of life on the reserve reflects the real power relationships between the First Nations and the Canadian government. The bulk of the article focuses on the Montagnais's life during the summer, that is, the way of life Roy was able to observe as a visitor to the reserve near Sept-Iles. As in the accompanying article on the white community of Sept-Iles, Roy sets up a superficial, "southern," even colonialist view, before proceeding to probe, question, and reassess her subject. The first part of the article on the Montagnais constructs Native Peoples as childlike:

> Dans les réserves, on les retrouvera vivant de ruses et d'expédients, habiles à soutirer du secours et à appeler la pitié. Leur vie y laissera tomber son caractère d'individualité. Ils descendront à un degré d'imitation puérile, parfois comique, souvent pitoyable. Doux, dociles, espiègles comme des enfants. [On the reserve, you will find them once more living by their wits, by cunning, cleverly getting themselves benefits, appealing to others' compassion. While there, their life will lose its individual character. They will stoop to a level of child-like imitation, at times comical, often pitiful. Gentle, docile, mischievous like children.]" (Ibid., 7)

Childlike too is how Roy describes the Montagnais's taste for the cheap mass-produced merchandise sold by white traders on the reserve: "Tout ce qui brille dans la vitrine, tout ce qui s'amoncelle sur le comptoir le tente comme un nouveau jouet tenterait un enfant [Anything that glitters in the shop window, anything that is heaped up on the counter tempts him as a new toy would tempt a child]" (ibid., 47).

Yet while many of Roy's observations of her subjects on the reserve seem to reinforce stereotypes of the First Nations as naive, even willing victims of white neo-colonialist exploitation, at moments a certain ambivalence appears. Roy describes, apparently patronizingly, the Montagnais's adoption of southern styles of dress. One of the photographs that illustrate the piece shows a young Montagnais man in Royal Air Force uniform. The article explains:

> L'ancien costume de la R.A.F. don de l'Etat, habille plusieurs hommes de la réserve. Naïvement, l'Indien se croit investi des

pouvoirs des Blancs lorsqu'il a endossé leur costume, même
démodé et usagé. Une cigarette entre les doigts, un képi sur la
tête, et ce comédien né oublie qu'il est habillé par la charité au
point de scander le pas, de renfler le buste, de redresser la tête,
gravement émerveillé de lui-même
[The old RAF uniform, provided by the state, clothes many men
on the reserve. Naively the Indian believes himself to be invested
with the white man's powers when he has donned his dress,
even when it is old-fashioned and worn. A cigarette between his
fingers, a cap on his head, and this born actor forgets that he
has been clothed by charity to the extent that he falls into step,
swells his chest, holds his head high, solemnly marveling at himself.] (Ibid., 48)

Here the "comédien" seems to be taken in by his own act, or so
Roy's description implies, but in another case there is perhaps a
glimpse of self-awareness in the amused, ironic gaze of a young
woman:

J'ai bien aperçu, l'autre jour, une jeune madame montagnaise en
grande toilette. Chapeau-jardin, aigrette, rubans, jupe circulaire,
elle s'en allait dans un frou-frou de soie et dans un bizarre
claquement de quincaillerie. Mais de son visage, je n'ai aperçu
vaguement que deux grands yeux qui paraissaient rieurs sous
une véritable voilette de veuve.
[The other day I did see a young Montagnais woman in formal
dress. Garden hat, decorated with a feather plume, ribbons, circular skirt, she went off in a rustle of silk and a strange clatter
of jewellery. But of her face I only caught a vague glimpse of
two big eyes which seemed merry beneath a genuine widow's
veil.] (Ibid., 47)

A similar touch of irony occurs after a lengthy account of the process by which the Montagnais elect their new chief each year, in
what Roy suggests is little more than a symbolic exercise, the First
Nations being at the time still classified as "pupilles d'Etat [qui]
n'ont aucune part dans le gouvernement du pays [wards of the State
[who] play no role in the government of the country]" (ibid., 48).
She refers to their election of a chief in rather dismissive terms:
"Les Montagnais prennent encore très sérieusement leur élection

annuelle, peuple d'enfants qui vivra toujours d'illusions [The
Montagnais still take their annual election very seriously, a childlike people who will always live on illusions]" (ibid.). Yet moments
of hesitation pierce the surface of the text, as when Roy wonders
about the winning candidate's real feelings: "Rage-t-il intérieure-
ment contre ceux de sa tribu qui se prononcent contre lui? Reste-t-il
profondément amusé de tout ce décor? Nous ne le savons pas plus
l'un que l'autre. Impossible de lire sur ce visage d'un Indien qui se
sent surveillé [Is he raging inwardly against those of his tribe who
vote against him? Does he remain profoundly amused by all this
set-up? None of us can tell. Impossible to read anything on the face
of an Indian who senses he is being watched]" (ibid.). But in
response to Roy's "félicitations d'usage [customary congratula-
tions]" he reveals a wry awareness of his people's status within
Canada, which undermines the stereotypes of naïve, or inscrutable
Indian:

> Un sourire non sans humour souligne les petites rides de ses
> yeux.
>   Par l'interprète me revient sa réflexion: "Les pouvoirs d'un
> chef montagnais ne sont pas grands!"
> [A smile not lacking in humour emphasizes the little wrinkles
> around his eyes.
>   His remark is relayed to me by the interpreter: "The powers
> of a Montagnais chief are not great!"] (Ibid.)

As Arun Mukherjee writes, irony is a discursive strategy commonly
used by non-White-Canadian writers: "As long as the right of
non-white people to get 'human behaviour from the other' [this
being a reference to Frantz Fanon] is not granted, as long as
non-white skin is a caste maker, as long as Canadian society's image
of the norm remains 'white,' the ironies of non-white-Canadians
will continue to parody the assumptions of 'Canadian' culture, literature, and social order."[57] While Roy's use of irony and her inclusion of the ironic voice of the new Montagnais chief do alert the
reader to the assumptions of Canadian culture, they do not pretend
to cover up the distance between the journalist and her subject. Roy
is invited to attend the *macoucham*, the celebration of the new
chief's election. But her description is accompanied by brief, comic
reminders of her sense of cultural disorientation: "Nous songeons

déjà à nous esquiver lorsque le chef nous aperçoit à travers la buée des bouches haletantes. Il vient nous chercher pour nous attirer en pleine fournaise [We are already thinking of slipping away when the chief spots us through the mist of hot panting breath. He comes to draw us back into the furnace]" (ibid). The distance between Roy and her subject is perhaps greater here than in other articles. Whereas in her visits to the other migrant groups of the "Peuples du Canada" series Roy's accounts gave the impression of her seeing their lives at least to some extent from the inside, as she was usually lodged and fed by members of the community, her contact with the Montagnais is limited to observing only one part of their life, the summer months on the reserve, that is, in the space that the Canadian government has allocated them and which it controls. An additional barrier is that, whereas in her dealings with other migrant groups she used English to communicate, on the reserve she uses the services of an interpreter. She is, in Mary Louise Pratt's terms, caught within the "contact zone," a space "where disparate cultures meet, clash, and grapple with each other, often in highly asymmetrical relations of domination and subordination – like colonialism, slavery, or their aftermaths as they are lived out across the globe today."[58] But it is the Montagnais's life beyond the reserve that Roy admires and evokes in the title of her piece. That way of life remains beyond reach, imagined, but still apparently mediated by a White source: "Dans le grand nord, il devient le maître. Le Blanc qui s'y aventure surprend tout à coup une nouvelle expression dans le regard de son guide et de ses porteurs indigènes. Une métamorphose subtile l'avertit que les rôles sont renversés, inutile de feindre l'autorité [In the Far North he becomes the master. The White man who ventures up there suddenly spots a new expression in the eyes of his indigenous guide and porters. A subtle transformation alerts him to the fact that the roles are reversed and that it is no use pretending to be in charge]" (BA, November 1941, 49). Within the framework of her reporting, it is as if Roy can go no closer to approach the indigenous subject, from whom her colour, her gender, her language, and the nature of neo-colonial power relations all create a barrier, despite those moments in the article in which the indigenous subject emerges from the stereotype, as if to gaze back at the reporter.

It is perhaps no coincidence that twenty years later Roy refers to the subject of indigenous people in what is one of her most fascinating pieces of reportage. In 1961 Roy took the opportunity of accompanying a geologist friend on a trip to the subarctic zone of northern Quebec, where, in what can be seen as a continuing search for the "peuples du Canada," she met the Inuit population of Ungava Bay. What resulted was a lengthy article, which has much in common with the series published in the *Bulletin des Agriculteurs*. The original intention had been to publish the article illustrated with photographs taken by the telephone salesman whom she met at Fort Chimo, modern-day Kuujuuaq.[59] "Voyage en Ungava" was eventually published posthumously in *Le Pays de Bonheur d'occasion*, without illustrations, along with eight other autobiographically inspired texts.[60]

Like many of her articles for the *Bulletin des Agriculteurs*, this account relates a journey, apparently in chronological order, framed by arrival and departure. It, like them, includes interviews, factual information, references to other sources, and some more impressionistic accounts of individuals encountered. As with our discussion of her 1940s journalism, our interest here will be to gauge how Roy represents Canada's minorities in the text, and specifically here how she, as a representative of the Second World, approaches her Fourth World subjects. In the final part of this concluding section we will then turn to examine the fictional transformation of that material in *La Rivière sans repos* to see what light this text throws on Roy's ambivalent positioning as a *Canadian* writer.

Throughout "Voyage en Ungava" the first-person narrating voice constructs itself insistently as outsider, as White, as southern (that is, from southern Canada), particularly through the use of "nous [we]," "notre gouvernement [our government]," "notre civilisation [our culture]," even though these terms are often used in a critical mode. Comparisons are made between the northern landscape and that of southwest Ontario, with which it is assumed the reader will be familiar.[61] The range of sources quoted strengthens the sense of this being a White account of the North. Roy's interlocutors are the Catholic and Anglican missionaries (the three Catholic priests are all European), the policeman, and a telephone salesman, who represent categories of external influence or power, and typify certain encounters within a "contact zone."

Ungava itself is represented as being on the periphery, described as "cette terre au bout du monde [that land at the end of the world]" (VU 102) or "l'Arctique [the Arctic]" (VU 128).[62] Roy's judgment of the Ungavan landscape is framed in negatives, confirming W.H. New's comment on the representation of landscape in Canadian writing: "The language of apparent description is also a language of coded evaluation."[63] With rare exceptions Roy constructs Ungava as a non-place.[64] It is empty: "La terre apparaissait, mais non plus de terre; de roc seulement, de plateaux dénudés, une immense étendue stérile, un paysage comme hors de ce monde [The earth was becoming visible, but there was not any earth; just rock, bare plateaus, an immense sterile expanse, a landscape from out of this world]." It is static: "Des lacs aussi apparaissaient, sans doute des milliers de lacs, mais sans liens entre eux, presque tous figés dans les creux, les plis et les dépressions de l'étonnante plaine [Lakes were also coming into view, doubtless thousands of lakes, but with no water flowing between them, almost all contained in the hollows, the folds and the depressions of the astounding plain]" (VU 101). The place is unnamed and dead: "Ici, ce sont les lacs qui forment à la surface de l'aride pays des îlots si foisonnants que bien peu d'entre eux ont encore reçu une appellation. Beaux lacs inconnus, sauvages, oubliés ou jamais repérés, ils éclairaient de leur eau morte ma première image de l'Ungava [Here it is the lakes which form on the surface of the arid land such a multitude of small islands that very few of them have been named yet. Beautiful unknown lakes, wild, forgotten or undiscovered, with their stagnant water they lit up my first impression of Ungava]" (ibid.). To her southern gaze, the trees are barely recognizable as such: "ces frêles arbrisseaux, ces enfants-arbres ... de petites épinettes squelettiques [these frail shrubs, these infant trees ... skeletal little spruces]" (VU 107). Despite the fact that Roy's visit took place in the short summer season, when vegetation briefly flourishes, she saw only sterility and death. To counter this pattern of description of the north as absence and sterility, the account does describe some strange beauty in the landscape. But even here a southern sensibility emerges, as the view is described as being "d'une beauté tragique [tragically beautiful]" (VU 101). Roy admires the colours of the North, "ce jeu inimitable de tendres coloris [this unique interplay of delicate shades]," but undermines the positive: "A un certain degré de dénuement, nous apprend Camus, le moindre don, la moindre douceur apparaît comme une grâce [At a certain level of deprivation, Camus tells us, the smallest gift, the slightest act of kindness seems like a blessing]" (vu 102). The use here of a European frame of reference (Camus's philosophy) both highlights and explains Roy's sense of alienation from the landscape she is observing.

Roy's descriptions of the Inuit are coloured by the frustration of her desire to know or understand the Other. She learns from her White sources about the history and the current situation of the Inuit, but no communication with the indigenous population is recorded other than through the summaries of an interpreter. She observes the Inuit, individually and collectively, and finds them either slightly comic, as when dressing their children in "southern" clothes, or inscrutable (a regular feature of Second World descriptions of the Fourth World indigene, as came out in our discussion of "Heureux les nomades"). Roy's desire to understand is evident in her repeated attempts to imagine or guess the thoughts of the people she describes. But perhaps out of a desire not to impose her assumptions on others, she resists speaking for them: "Assis au bord du lit, le vieil Esquimau aveugle doit se rappeler des temps durs, se demander peut-être pourquoi maintenant on le laisse vivre, pourquoi ce changement, ces choses compliquées. Peut-être le reste de sa vie s'écoulera-t-il à sonder ce mystère [Seated on the edge of the bed, the old blind Inuit must be recalling hard times, wondering perhaps why nowadays they let him live, why this change, these complicated things. Perhaps the rest of his life will be spent fathoming this mystery]" (vu 111). This mode of qualification ("peut-être [perhaps]") is applied consistently to Inuit but not to White interlocutors, who tend to speak for themselves. The emphasis on the language barrier, cited as a cause of this lack of communication, seems excessive, given that Roy might easily have spoken in English to some of the Inuit she met. Whatever the reason for her reticence, Roy remains very much outside the scenes she reports – a southern, colonial observer, if not a voyeur. The Inuit of "Voyage en Ungava" remain Other, at times essentialized as innocents, at times simply unknowable.

Roy's account of Fort Chimo may not escape the rigid opposition of White "Self" and Inuit "Other" that characterizes colonial discourse, despite her well-intentioned, liberal views on the need for the Inuit to preserve their own language and learn to help themselves. Nevertheless, by the use of the first person plural, Roy acknowledges a historical complicity with the White colonial presence. Her account proceeds to denounce the actions not only of successive Canadian governments but also of the United States, builders of the army base in 1942 and source of many of the cultural forms and economic pressures at work in Fort Chimo. While this could be seen as Roy's shifting her focus from Canada to American economic imperialism, it is perhaps more a case of Canada being identified as part of North America, exploiting a wide range of minorities across the continent in a post-colonial age. In fact the account draws parallels between the power of the American market with that of the Hudson's Bay Company, past and present. The effects of ongoing domination are exposed in examples at once cruel and faintly ridiculous (from the legacy of refuse from the American bases to the cynical creation of a market for top-of-the-range telephones for the Inuit to call each other from one end of the village to the other). This didactic aspect makes the general thrust of Roy's account anti-colonial. It questions the situation in terms of justice, freedom, and self-determination, but does not quite manage to unsettle the opposition between White and Inuit. There are, however a few features in "Voyage en Ungava" that begin to ruffle the waters.

The first of these is Roy's description of a Métis[65] woman with her child, whose father was White. (This brief scene will become the starting point of *La Rivière sans repos*.) The figures of the Métis clearly destabilizes any pattern of binary opposition and offers the potential for analysis in terms of postcolonial notions of *métissage,* or hybridity. In mentioning the two Métis, Roy refers to the history of *métissage* in the area, which resulted from the long period of contact between White and Inuit. In her description, one feels the tension of a pattern of persistent stereotyping. The mother is described as looking perplexed (perhaps by her very existence?), but she remains silent. The child in her care is described as "le plus bel enfant du monde [the most beautiful child in the world]" (vu 118), marked by his beauty and his whiteness. Roy's comment on this case of *métissage* would seem to be shaped by essentialist and deterministic thinking. Rather than the Métis being something new (and one thinks here of Poulin's Métisse figure in *Volkswagen Blues*), here they are more an unhappy mixture of two essential beings:

Pauvres gens: de race pure, ils sont gais, enfantins, insouciants, serviables et accueillants. Mais une goutte de notre sang

coule-t-elle dans leurs veines, et on les dirait déjà moins heureux
de vivre. Et cette chose-ci encore tout à coup m'étonne: alors
que nous rarement à leur contact apprenons leur douce insouci-
ance, eux, au nôtre, nous prennent notre mélancolie, un peu de
notre nature plus compliquée – tout ce qui en des âmes simples
devient pénible à voir.
[Poor people: those of the Inuit race are gay, childlike, carefree,
obliging, and welcoming. But if a drop of our blood flows in
their veins then it is as if they are already less happy to be alive.
And what still suddenly astonishes me is this: whereas we rarely
acquire any of their carefree nature in our contact with them,
they, in contact with us, take on our melancholy, a bit of our
more complex nature – everything that becomes painful to see
in simple souls.] (VU 118–19)

Another feature in Roy's piece that might seem to allow a brief
reversal of the colonial/White view of the North is the moment
when the narrator records her awareness of being the object of the
Inuit gaze, a spectacle both for them and the White male inhabitants of Fort Chimo. This moment of self-consciousness is described
as pleasurable. The narrator's subsequent comment at once recognizes this reversal, but reasserts a sense of White perspective:
"Après tout, c'est bien leur tour d'être curieux de nous, depuis le
temps que nous allons les scruter, les peindre, les fouiller [After all,
it is certainly their turn to be curious about us, given the length of
time that we have been examining them, depicting them, delving
into their lives]" (VU 103). Yet, as if understanding the potential
here for undermining relations of power, Roy then recounts an episode when the Inuit bought a camera and began taking their own
pictures of the astonished GIs arriving in the "primitive" North. As
the narrator returns south, the South/North relationship is again
briefly reversed as she is hit by the shock of the South's lushness,
modernity, and luxury. As at the film show she attended in Fort
Chimo, she tries to imagine the Inuit point of view, but even here
can only conceptualize the south in terms of superiority: "Les
Esquimaux se penchent-ils pour regarder notre terre ... la voyant
apparaître si riche, si comblée, se croient-ils arrivés en un monde
trop doux, trop généreux pour qu'il puisse leur sembler réel? [If the
Inuit take a close look at our world ... seeing it appear to be so rich,

so well-provided, do they believe they have arrived in a world that is too pleasant, too generous to seem real to them?]" (VU 127). The text closes on the enigma of the Inuit Other, as if Roy is fascinated and frustrated by their opacity to her. She imagines a sick Inuit patient transported to a southern hospital weeping silently at the sight of snow as she lies in her hospital bed, a scene that is reworked as the story of Deborah in "Les satellites." Imagination and identification are perhaps better routes than journalistic observation to an attempt to see the world differently. And in *La Rivière sans repos* Roy revisits the scenes of "Voyage en Ungava" as if attempting to approach that subjectivity which the original encounter and this earlier writing project had precluded.

Entering the Contact Zone? "La Rivière sans repos"

Whereas in "Les satellites" the glimpse of the Inuit woman travelling south for hospital treatment, and in "Le téléphone" the consequences of the telephone salesman's visit are imagined and developed, in the title story of *La Rivière sans repos* it is the scene of the Métisse and her son that is at the core of the narrative. The fictional account follows the relationship between Elsa (an Inuit, not of mixed race) and her Métis son Jimmy, from his conception during World War II as a result of her rape by a young GI stationed at Fort Chimo to the late 1960s during the Vietnam War. At the end of the novel Elsa is alone, prematurely aged, having devoted her life to bringing up her son, only to lose him when he runs away to the south at the age of sixteen. In the journalistic "Voyage en Ungava" Roy declared herself as the source of the first-person narration, but in "La Rivière sans repos," as in all of her fiction, she employs an elusive, shifting narrative voice. Indeed, Ellen Babby goes as far as to claim that the narrative voice allows the adoption of "their [Inuit] subjective vision."[66] She argues that Roy's narrative engages in a process of defamiliarization, and that its phenomenological method highlights the signifier rather than the signified, so taking readers away from their habitual frame of reference. Nevertheless, she argues, the (White) reader remains in the realm of the knowing, which is the source of the text's irony and pathos. Estelle Dansereau also analyses the narrative techniques of the novel and finds a subtle shifting of focus, signalled in particular by the use of deictics, slippages from the past to the present, near to far, and so on.[67] But do such techniques of defamiliarization and shifting focalization really constitute the adoption of Inuit subjectivity?

The question of who is speaking is central to much debate in postcolonial studies.[68] When compared with "Voyage en Ungava," where Roy as a journalist repeatedly came up against cultural and linguistic barriers to communication that the presence of an interpreter/mediator accentuated rather than removed, the narrator in "La Rivière sans repos" does indeed seek to enter the subjectivity of a number of central protagonists. Dialogue (presented in French in the text) includes the voices of Inuit characters, young and old. Interior monologue and less direct forms of focalization also give the impression of interiority. So the reader does not simply receive images of the inscrutable, objectified Other. Shifts in focus allow for others' judgments to be described or voiced (for example, Winnie, in free indirect discourse, comments on the eccentricities of her daughter Elsa's behaviour,[69] and Jimmy experiences their attempted escape to Baffin Island through the disorienting effects of a growing fever). But the source of narrative authority periodically reasserts itself as that of an outsider moving beyond the different focalizations. As the following examples illustrate, this type of shift could happen through the occasional explanation for the White reader, or through judgment or omniscience:

> ... une pâte à *bannock* qu'elle mit à cuire sur la surface d'une roche chauffée d'avance. Le pain dur sans levain commença à répandre une bonne odeur
> [... some bannock dough which she placed to cook on a rock she had heated in advance. The hard unleavened bread began to give off a pleasant odour] (RSR 163; 73);

> ... ces pauvres huttes éparses
> [these scattered rickety huts] (RSR 98; 6);

> ... une difficulté, sans grande importance, sembla-t-il, qui devait cependant avoir sur sa vie une influence décisive
> [a difficulty ... which though seemingly of no great importance would have a decisive effect upon her life to come.] (RSR 194; 104)

In the Afterword to the English translation, Phyllis Webb wonders who might be supposed to be narrating Elsa's story and adds: "surely not an Inuit."[70] The question of voice and authority is problematized within the novel in a number of ways. At Elsa's mother's funeral, for example, the Reverend Hugh Paterson reflects on Winnie's life of struggling toward a better, more modern way of life, to the amazement of the small congregation of Inuit: "Eberlué, Archibald avait l'air de se demander de qui le Pasteur parlait avec tant de considération [Archibald, astounded, looking as if he were wondering whom the pastor was discussing with so much respect]" (RSR 204; 114). This response to the pastor's words can be read as an ironic *mise en abyme* of the narrative voice itself.

The final chapter also plays on questions of voice, authority, and ambiguity. In Fort Chimo short-band radios can pick up conversations between crewmembers on aircraft passing overhead. One day a few local inhabitants hear a voice addressing them directly, naming members of Elsa's family and asking for news. Different listeners hear different phrases, the voice fading and breaking up at times. At no point does the aviator identify himself other than as "un aviateur américain ami [an American airman come in peace]" (RSR 235; 146). However, it seemed to the villagers that the voice from the skies is that of Jimmy. Different accounts circulate and are passed on to Elsa. She in turn nurtures and elaborates on the stray phrases to construct a fiction that acquires its own life in her mind. This closing episode, with its fragments of fact and fiction, once more unsettles the reader's grasp of the whole and reminds us of the ambiguities and ultimate uncertainty of "telling" the Other's story.

Clearly as a member of the White majority, (albeit doubly *minoritaire* within that group – as francophone and non-Québécoise) Roy cannot speak as a member of an aboriginal minority. Yet the complex and shifting position within the Second World of sub-groups, minorities, reminds us of the artificiality and imposed nature of all binary divisions. The representation of people and place in "La Rivière sans repos" seems to challenge essentializing categorization. Roy both uses and exposes stereotypes. In order to appreciate the process, it is useful to look at Abdul R. JanMohamed's distinction between two forms of colonialist literature – the imaginary and the symbolic.[71] In JanMohamed's categorization, the "imaginary" text represents the Other through a fetishized and non-dialectical

opposition between self and nature. The aboriginal Other is identified with nature. Difference is understood as natural, generic, in the
blood. In Roy's text the Inuit are frequently objectified, essentialized, referred to generically, or identified with nature, with the land,
as the following examples show:

> Winnie, tâchant tout juste de s'en cacher, triomphait, le visage
> creusé par le bonheur à en paraître fendillé à l'égal des vieilles
> pierres de la toundra.
> [Winnie scarcely tried to conceal her triumph, her face so
> creased with happiness that it looked cracked – as cracked and
> fissured as one of the ancient stones of the tundra.] (RSR 127;
> 36)

> Madame Beaulieu voyait bondir ... une vague forme si bien
> ramassée sur elle-même pour aller vite qu'elle faisait penser à
> quelque objet roulé, emporté par les rafales.
> [Madame Beaulieu watched a little shape bounding ..., so gath-
> ered in on itself in its efforts to go quickly that it looked like
> some vague, rolled-up object carried by the wind.] (RSR 120; 28)

> Le bon visage un peu confus d'Elsa paraissait de la couleur de
> certains bois à demi calcinés.
> [Elsa's pleasant, slightly troubled face was the colour of
> half-charred wood.] (RSR 187–8; 99)

Significantly, though viewed respectively from the perspective of
an Inuit, a White, and then a Métis, the object in each case is an
Inuit woman. This process is almost exclusively one way. White
characters are occasionally described by means of a natural image,
the pastor being likened to a bird, for instance: "son singulier
regard d'oiseau seul [his singular bird's glance]" (RSR 139; 49), but
White characters are not likened to the land, rock, or wood. As
Albert Memmi points out, another sign of objectification typical of
colonial discourse is the use of collective designations.[72] Here, the
Inuit are referred to as "eux [them]" (RSR 178; 89), as "les pauvres
gens éberlués [the bewildered Eskimos]" (RSR 230; 141). General-
izations are used: "leur âme placide [their gentle and placid souls]"
(RSR 97; 6), and Elsa becomes a type: "L'Esquimaude [Eskimo
woman]" (RSR 194; 104). The Otherness of the Inuit is also evident

in the way they seemingly conform to stereotypes – notably their frequent designation as non-rational, non-logical beings: "A la longue, la leçon du Pasteur pénétra son esprit, et quand elle eut quelque peu compris ... [The pastor's lesson finally penetrated her mind and, when she had somewhat understood ...] " (RSR 140; 50). Yet this stereotype, which recurs a number of times, can be double-edged, acting as an ironic comment on the *il*logicality, even absurdity, of the opinions and advice given to Elsa by Whites (the pastor, the wife of the Hudson's Bay Company representative, or the local policeman).

The figure of the Métis clearly presents a challenge to any essentialist understanding of the world. In "Voyage en Ungava" Roy comments on the relative frequency of mixed race births, which is explained in part by the liberal attitudes of Inuit parents towards sex. Roy has chosen to make Elsa an Inuit, not a Métisse, yet her dress, habits, working life, and upbringing of her son do constitute her as a hybrid figure who escapes fixed cultural categorization. Her representation seems variously comic, grotesque, alienated, or tragic. In Elsa, Roy unpicks the process of acculturation represented in the assimilation of the indigenous group to the dominant culture.[73] Elsa adopts a series of learned behaviour patterns, but they serve only as temporary roles or gestures. She remains caught between a number of competing cultural and economic systems, not sufficiently autonomous to move beyond the contradictions of which she is the focus. At the end of the text, she is represented physically in essentialized images, becoming ever less distinguishable from her mother. Yet her thoughts are concerned with the imagined afterlife of her son in his latest transformation as an American pilot and with her hope that while in Vietnam he may have fathered a child, so widening the circle of *métissage*.

In postcolonial studies the notions of hybridity and *métissage* have of course been used metaphorically to refer to a range of forms of cultural contact. What models of cultural contact does Roy explore by making the Métis child central to her text? The figure of Jimmy operates strangely, in ways that seem both to confirm essentializing notions of race and to confound them. Since he is the only mixed-race child in Fort Chimo mentioned, his treatment as "cet être unique [this unique little being]" (RSR 112; 20), a miraculous being, is more plausible. In fact the text represents Jimmy precisely as miraculous – the White child of an Inuit woman whose darkness is stressed: "sa jeune maman au visage foncé [his young mother of the dark face]" (RSR 110; 17); "elle, la noiraude [herself, so swarthy]" (RSR 109; 17). His singularity is conceptualized in terms of (White) Christian traditions, his golden halo of curls recalling much Eurocentric iconography of the infant Jesus. The bath scene, repeated daily before a crowd of worshippers, is celebrated with all the ritual and spectacle of a baptism or a communion service. Jimmy's elevation as "White" confirms the perceived inferior status and self-image of Inuit women. His eventual escape from Fort Chimo to enlist, apparently, in the U.S. Air Force, and his final "appearance" as a disembodied voice from above can be read as parodies of Christ's ascension to a higher place.

But if Jimmy's Whiteness seems excessive, that is perhaps the point. His singularity allows him to be represented not realistically as a sociological and ethnic type (the Métis), but rather as the signifier of a more abstract process of *métissage*.[74] In the bath-time scene he is the symbolic White Other, object of his mother's – and the other Inuit women's – desire. When his mother takes him to Old Chimo to live with Ian and adopt the traditional Inuit lifestyle, he adapts rapidly to indigenous ways, as it were, briefly becoming Inuit. On his return to Fort Chimo, this place of contact between White and Inuit, he is repossessed by White authority, in hospital, at school, and among his White peers. In fact the Métis figure is not essentialized in any fixed identity, but rather is constructed as a process, a process that results from contact between different cultures. This process is not unidirectional, in that Jimmy "becomes" both Inuit and White, but it clearly operates within specific contexts and under differing power relationships.

Seen from this perspective, if Jimmy is the locus of a variety of types of cultural contact in Roy's text, Fort Chimo functions in a similar way. The encounter between Inuit and White (colonial) Other takes different forms, and these are inscribed on the landscape of the settlement. The divide between White and Inuit territory is not absolutely clear-cut (not, by comparison, as rigidly delineated as Fanon's distinction between "la ville du colon [the colonizer's town]" and "la ville du colonisé [the colonized's town]").[75] There are indeed many signs of colonial domination: the implantation of the Hudson's Bay Company store and its predecessor from the 1830s, the trading post; the presence of church missions, a school, medical services, the police; the arrival of the U.S. military base, and the Inuit village's move from the east to the west bank of the Koksoak River. While Fort Chimo has remained at the margins of power, a number of centres (Britain, the Vatican, Ottawa, Quebec, Washington) have imposed signs of their influence in pursuit of their colonial, and neo-colonial interests. All these factors have changed the movement patterns and behaviour of the indigenous population, sometimes by economic strategies, sometimes by legal or religious practice. Roy's references to the community's preoccupation with the Vietnamese War bring Fort Chimo into an ongoing struggle against imperialism. And some contact blurs the border between Inuit and White, so alerting the reader that place acts as "continual reminder of the separation, and yet of the hybrid interpenetration of the coloniser and colonised."[76] The cemetery in Old Chimo has White and Inuit graves side by side. Ian, the traditional Inuit, resistant to acculturation, nevertheless has positive memories of collaboration with the mission and the Hudson's Bay Company. The Catholic mission has no Inuit converts, but is full of Inuit villagers who use the space for their own social purposes, exemplifying Michael de Certeau's notion of tactics through which the dominated can act subversively:

La tactique n'a pour lieu que celui de l'autre. Aussi doit-elle jouer avec le terrain qui lui est imposé tel que l'organise la loi d'une force étrangère ... Elle profite des "occasions" et en dépend, sans base où stocker des bénéfices, augmenter un propre et prévoir des sorties. Ce qu'elle gagne ne se garde pas. Ce non-lieu lui permet sans doute la mobilité, mais dans une docilité aux aléas du temps, pour saisir au vol les possibilités qu'offre un instant.
[The tactic can only take place on the other's territory. Thus it must play with the space which has been imposed on it, organized as that is by the law of a foreign power ... It profits from "chances" and depends upon them, having no base in which to store its assets, increase its own holdings and plan sorties. Whatever is won cannot be kept. This lack of a place doubtless allows for freedom of movement, but only as allowed by the comings and goings of the time, to seize in flight the possibilities offered at any one moment.][77]

Similarly, the road built by the U.S. Air Force for transportation and drill becomes a play space and a promenade for the local population, Inuit and White, when the base closes. In this way the different layers of contact explicitly construct Fort Chimo *in history*, subverting the stereotype of the North as timeless and unchanging.

Finally, reading Roy's text in French adds a crucial layer to this Second World writing of a Fourth World borderland. Within the French text, English phrases stand out as signals of anglophone or American presence in a way that is lost in the English translation. In the French original they need no commentary. But in the translation this differentiation disappears. "*Bannock*" (RSR 163; 73), italicized in the French text, loses the italics in English; English lexis in phrases such as "Bye-bye" (RSR 98), "left right" (RSR 106), "unbelievable" (RSR 153), "study" (RSR 226), "*tea parties*" (RSR 123), also lose their italics in English; and "Hello baby!" (RSR 99) appears "natural," and the hybrid form "Hello soldat!" (RSR 99) is lost in its translation to "Hello soldier!". The language(s) of colonial power are normalized and in both "Voyage en Ungava" and "La Rivière sans repos" a triple language situation is simplified to a double language situation. In contrast, Roy's use of English in the French text explicitly draws attention to the role of language in the acculturation of the indigenous peoples and confirms the status of "La Rivière sans repos" as a (minority) Second World account of the North.

Despite the authoritative and sometimes didactic voice of the Second World journalist, "Voyage en Ungava" acknowledges the impossibility of speaking *for* the Inuit. In a text that has elements of both colonial and anti-colonial understanding the focus shifts from complicity to denunciation, in keeping with the moral and conceptual dilemmas of Second World writing. Turning to the fictional writing of Fort Chimo in "La Rivière sans repos," the unsettling effects of Roy's shifting focalization give a dynamic quality to the relationships between Second and Fourth World. Power relationships are not reversed but they are destabilized. By bringing Fort Chimo into history, by exploring the figure of the Métis not simply as sociological fact but rather as a symbol of ongoing processes of cultural contact and mutual influence, the text allows the reader to think beyond the colonial and the anti-colonial. The very uncertainty and openness of the ending takes us beyond the circularity of Elsa's story to imagine other forms of contact that might combine Inuit and White, Métis and Vietnamese.

Conclusions

In the year in which *La Rivière sans repos* was published in Montreal and Marshall's translation, *Windflower*, was published in Toronto, Roy published a short autobiographical piece in French in the Winnipeg-based journal *Mosaic* entitled "Mon héritage du Manitoba [My Manitoba heritage]." To this Western readership she declares (in French): "Je me sens Canadienne jusqu'à la moëlle [I feel Canadian to the core]."[78] She attributes her identification with "Canada," and her "âme canadienne [Canadian soul]" to the geographical position of her native province, sited as it is at the geographical centre of the country. The language used ("Canadienne jusqu'à la moëlle," "âme canadienne") sounds every bit as essentialist in inspiration as terms such as "Québécois de souche [Québécois of French origin]" or "pure laine [pure wool]." Yet the picture is more complex. When the article was later included in *Fragiles Lumières de la terre* in 1978, significantly, Roy edited out those statements, perhaps as part of an ongoing process of self-censorship as her text was reissued for a wider readership nearly a decade later. But even in the 1970 version, there is a tension between what seems initially to be an essentializing notion of identity and a more fluid understanding of Canada. She refers to the formative memory of waves of migrants arriving in Winnipeg, and the way in which this familiarity with foreigners ("étrangers") shaped her sense of self and Other: "Il n'y avait plus d'étrangers dans la vie; ou alors c'est que nous l'étions tous [There were no more foreigners in life; or rather it's just that we were all foreigners]."[79] Once again, the image of the migrant seems central to Roy's own sense of being/becoming Canadian, and allows her to resist the official Canadian narrative of two "founding" peoples.

This chapter has suggested that Roy's journalism can be read as a search for her "pays," which involves imagining Canada differently, from the position of an outsider, or at least from the position of its minority populations. If being Canadian or indeed Franco-Canadian was problematic for Roy, it was so for very specific reasons that originated in her education and her ambivalent positioning between the two dominant, yet unequal, languages and cultures of Canada. Hers was a very particular case of the ambivalent position of the "colon colonisé [colonized colonizer]," partly complicit in and partly resistant to the processes of assimilation exemplified in the double education she experienced in Manitoba. In writing about Quebec and about Canada for a Montreal-based paper in the early 1940s, she confronted the impossibility of applying one model, or even two models of Canadianness to the individuals and groups she encountered (or sought out). What she wrote of was a series of individuals and groups in different relationships to Canada, some on the geographical peripheries, some minorities within a dominant majority, some the hybrid result of historical contact between peoples. More "at home" with the model of Western Canada, a land of migration where distinctive groups could share the space without losing their differences in the inevitable process of assimilation, Roy nevertheless chose Quebec as her home once she returned with her husband, Marcel Carbotte, from her second prolonged stay in France in 1950. But Roy's sense of belonging, and of non-belonging, was not resolved by living in Quebec for more than thirty years. Her writings can be read as a working-through of a relationship to Canada that does not coincide with the federalist or nationalist label. Distrustful of language-based models of identity, Roy explores modes of belonging that have more in common with models of migration and cultural hybridity, so pointing forward to postcolonial notions of identity construction.

For Salman Rushdie, the migrant figure is emblematic of the widespread displacement of communities and individuals in the twentieth century, through processes of exile, colonization and decolonization, flow of capital to new areas of economic exploitation, migration, and dispersion. Such processes destabilize and render untenable any notions of fixity and essentialism. Yet they also help to create new ways of seeing and new ways of relating to the world and to others in the world: "Migrants must, of necessity, make a new imaginative relationship with the world, because of the loss of familiar habitats."[80] Roy's identification with migrant communities can be explained in part as the recognition of a common bond with them, her decision to leave Manitoba having made her not just the child of migrant parents and grandparents but a migrant herself. But this is not to say that Roy's experience of migration can be likened in real terms to that of the Chinese immigrant to the Canadian West whom she encountered in Canora, Saskatchewan,[81] or that of the Czechs fleeing from Hitler's occupation of the Sudetenland after the Munich Agreement. Arun Mukherjee, in *Oppositional Aesthetics*, criticizes the rhetoric of identification used by writers as diverse as Northrop Frye and Margaret Atwood whereby "we are all immigrants to this land and, therefore, all Canadian literature can be classified as immigrant literature."[82] I want to argue a rather different point. What I understand to be Roy's fascination with – and indeed partial identification with – migrants of many kinds is not a mere generalization of her family's history of various migrations from France to Acadie, to Quebec, to the United States, to Manitoba, and, in her case, back to Quebec, but rather the result of the split consciousness that her Franco-Manitoban upbringing opened up for her and which made her acutely sensitive both to the inadequacy of any essentialized notion of identity and to the marginalized position of other linguistic, racial, and cultural minorities. This is what she shares with the migrants, who, in Rushdie's terms, "have been obliged to define themselves – because they are so defined by others – by their otherness; people in whose deepest selves strange fusions occur, unprecedented unions between what they were and where they find themselves. The migrant suspects reality: having experienced several ways of being, he understands their illusory nature."[83]

The desire to speak from the perspective of the migrant, the indigene, or the marginalized, to see the world from outside the gaze of the dominant culture, informs Roy's reportage and colours her subsequent writings. In "Voyage en Ungava" Roy finds just such a perspective through the Métis woman and her child. In "La Rivière sans repos" Roy is able to carry through her project of looking at her culture from a decentred angle, with a series of shifts and reversals, and above all through her attempt to imagine both the Inuit and the Métis, an attempt that leads her to a new understanding of identity as shifting, plural, problematic, and unfinished. She can, of course never speak with the voice of those most dispossessed in the processes of colonialism and neo-colonialism, the migrants or the indigenes. But as Bill Ashcroft suggests, to look from the position of the least powerful is a valid tactic for seeing the shape of domination: "The successful disruption of the territory of the dominant occurs, not only by rejecting or vacating that territory but by inhabiting it differently."[84] Thanks to Roy's ambivalent position as a bilingual/bicultural product of colonialism in Canada, she is never only the *porte-parole* of the Franco-Manitoban population; nor is she only an assimilated anglophile; nor does she identify fully with the ideology of Quebec nationalism in the 1960s and 1970s. It is in this sense that Roy emerges as a bilingual and bicultural Canadian writer, writing in French and translated into English, a writer whose texts open up a place *between* languages, cultures, and allegiances.

Notes

INTRODUCTION

1 Gabrielle Roy, *La Détresse et l'enchantement*, 74; *Enchantment and Sorrow*, 56. English translations will follow all quotations in French, these being taken from the published translation. The page references to the original and the translation will be indicated thus: (DE 74; 56). Non-referenced translations are my own. The Bibliography lists the original edition of Roy's cited works, the edition to which page references refer, the abbreviated form of the title used for page references, and the edition of the translation used for quotations.

2 Bill Ashcroft, Gareth Griffiths, and Helen Tiffin, eds., *The Post-Colonial Studies Reader*, 426.

3 David Cobb, "Seasons in the Life of a Novelist: Gabrielle Roy," *The Canadian* (1 May 1976): 12 (my emphasis).

4 Ibid., 13.

5 Lori Saint-Martin, *Lectures contemporaines de Gabrielle Roy: Bibliographie analytique des études critiques (1978–97)*, 16. Where quotations appear in the text in my English translations, the note supplies the reference to the original source.

6 John Willinsky, *Learning to Divide the World: Education at Empire's End*, 13.

7 Thomas Macaulay, "Minute on Indian Education," in Ashcroft, Griffiths, and Tiffin, eds., *The Post-Colonial Studies Reader*, 430.

8 For a discussion of the complexities of these terms see Anna Johnston and Alan Lawson, "Settler Colonies," in Henry Schwarz and Sangeeta Ray, eds., *A Companion to Postcolonial Studies*, 360–76.

9 See Diana Brydon, "Introduction: Reading Postcoloniality, Reading Canada," *Essays on Canadian Literature* 56 (fall 1995): 1–19. Brydon uses invader-settler rather than settler or settler-invader to stress that "the narrative of settlement in itself occludes and denies the prior fact of invasion," footnote 1, 16–17.

10 Alan Lawson, "Postcolonial Theory and the 'Settler' Subject," *Essays in Canadian Writing* 56 (fall, 1995): 29.

11 Ibid., 24.

12 The issue has been discussed in a number of recent studies. See, for example, Laura Moss, ed., *Is Canada Postcolonial? Unsettling Canadian Literature*; Marc Maufort and Franca Bellarsi, *Reconfigurations: Canadian Literatures and Postcolonial Identities/Littératures canadiennes et identités postcoloniales*; "Quebec and Postcolonial Theory," *Québec Studies* 35 (2003), special issue edited by Vincent Desroches.

13 Ashcroft, Griffiths, and Tiffin, eds., *The Post-Colonial Studies Reader*, 425.

14 Robert Morgan, "The 'Englishness' of English Teaching," in Ivor Goodson and Peter Medway, eds., *Bringing English to Order*, 210.

15 Ibid. The quotation is from Rev. J. George, "The Mission of Great Britain to the World, Or some of the Lessons which she is now Teaching," lecture delivered at Stratford, Ontario, in 1867.

16 R. Phillipson, *Linguistic Imperialism*, 47. Phillipson adopts the term "linguicism" to denote this practice.

17 Gauri Viswanathan, "The Beginnings of English Literary Study in British India," in Ashcroft, Griffiths, and Tiffin, eds., *The Post-Colonial Studies Reader*, 434.

18 C.E. Trevelyan, *On the Education of the People of India* (London: Longman, Orme, Brown, Green, and Longmans, 1838), 176.

19 Morgan, "The 'Englishness' of English Teaching," 203.

20 Heather Murray, "English Studies in Canada and the Case of Postcolonial Culture," *Essays on Canadian Writing* 56 (fall, 1995): 58.

21 Ibid., 73.

22 The details of the Manitoba Schools question are explored in detail in W.L. Morton, "Manitoba schools and Canadian nationality, 1890–1923," in David Jones, Nancy Sheehan, and Robert Stamp, eds., *Shaping the Schools of the Canadian West*, 3–13; C.J. Jaenen, "Le français au Manitoba: fruit de l'histoire ou d'une contrainte extérieure?" 3–16; J. Blay, *L'Article 23: les péripéties législatives et juridiques du fait français au Manitoba 1870–1986*; Jean-Marie Taillefer, "Les

Franco-manitobains et l'éducation, 1870–1970: une étude quantitative,"
unpublished PhD dissertation, University of Manitoba, 1988.

23 Jaenen, "Le français au Manitoba," 8.

24 Lionel Groulx, *L'Enseignement français au Canada. Vol. 2. Les écoles des minorités*, 84.

25 Ibid., 75.

26 Johnston and Lawson, "Settler Colonies," 360–76.

27 For details of the migration of the family of Roy's mother to Manitoba see François Ricard, *Gabrielle Roy: A Life*, 19–21. Roy gives a fictionalized account of her mother's journey in the unpublished *Saga d'Eveline*.

28 Jaenen, "Le français au Manitoba," 10–11.

29 See Ricard, *Gabrielle Roy*, 124. It is interesting to speculate on whether the fact that the village was Métis contributed to what Roy recalls as a very hostile response from her mother to the news of her month's supply teaching assignment (in *La Détresse et l'enchantement*).

30 Taillefer, "Les Franco-manitobains et l'éducation 1870–1970," 284.

31 The figures for 1981, given as a point of comparison, show that those of French or English origin count for only 44% of the population, whereas those of Ukrainian and German origin stood at 9.8% and 10.7% respectively.

32 Manitoba Debates, 1916, 53, quoted in Jones, Sheehan, and Stamp, eds., *Shaping the Schools of the Canadian West*, 10.

33 W.L. Morton, "Manitoba schools and Canadian nationality, 1890–1923," in Jones, Sheehan, and Stamp, *Shaping the Schools of the Canadian West*, 9.

34 Ibid.

35 For a full discussion of the 1967 legislation see Taillefer, "Les Franco-manitobains et l'éducation 1870–1970." Since then the bilingual principle has extended to include aboriginal and Ukrainian programs of study in the province's schools.

36 Provincial Archives of Manitoba, Winnipeg, Department of Education: Half-yearly returns of attendance, 1930–31, District 1188.

37 Groulx, *L'Enseignement français au Canada*, 242.

38 Blay, *L'Article 23*, 46.

39 Minutes of the meeting of the *comité du fonctionnement scolaire*, 31.3.1925, AECFM 42/232/58. Interestingly, this kind of competitive examination is a feature today for students of French as a second language in the United States, doubtless with the same aim of raising the status and profile of the French language.

40 AECFM 42/279/1108–1112.

41 The association relied on grassroots support from its members in the form of annual donations and a small levy on each pupil.

42 AECFM 42/279/1108.

43 Minutes of the *comité du fonctionnement scolaire* of 31.8.1926, AECFM 42/232/59.

CHAPTER ONE

1 Robert Morgan, "The 'Englishness' of English Teaching," in Ivor Goodson and Peter Medway, eds., *Bringing English to Order*, 222.

2 For postcolonial analyses of the function of the curriculum see: Homi K. Bhabha (1985); Ania Loomba (1991); Wa Thiong'o Ngugi (1993) in relation to India and Africa; J. Docker (1978) and Stephen Slemon (1990) in relation to settler colonies; and Arun Mukherjee (1986), Robert Morgan (1990), and Cynthia Sugars (2004) with reference to Canada.

3 *Bulletin des Institutrices Catholiques de l'Ouest*, March–April, 1935, 88–9.

4 Letter from J.H. Daignault (secrétaire) to M C.J. Magnan, président de l'Association St Jean-Baptiste, Quebec City, 1927: "In our schools we set, in addition to the official curriculum, which does not allow it, a French curriculum modelled on the curriculum followed in primary schools in Quebec" (AECFM 42/279/1109). (All translations of archival sources are my own unless otherwise stated.)

5 Quoted in Jean-Marie Taillefer, "Les Franco-manitobains et l'éducation, 1870–1970: une étude quantitative," unpublished PhD dissertation, University of Manitoba, 1988, 282.

6 Ibid., 283.

7 Ibid., 284–5.

8 Ibid., 282.

9 Minutes of the comité du fonctionnement scolaire, 1.08.1924, AECFM 42/232/58.

10 Taillefer, "Les Franco-manitobains et l'éducation, 1870–1970," 284.

11 In 1930 a teaching nun in Saint-Malo, Manitoba, who for years had been using the *Petit catéchisme du Québec*, complained that her pupils were disadvantaged in the *concours* because questions were now based on a new version. The response from the association's secretary is clear: Lasfargues's *Catéchisme des trois provinces* was the recommended text and had been since 1926. The school were therefore at fault for not

heeding AECFM guidelines. See letters dated 6.6.1930 and 7.6.1930, AECFM 42/279/1112.

12 Circular dated 15.01.1930, AECFM 42/234/118.

13 AECFM 42/279/1108.

14 For a clear description of the history, aims, and methods of the *collège classique* see Norbert Renaud, "Le collège classique: la maison d'enseignement, le milieu d'études, les fins et les moyens," *Etudes Littéraires* (December 1981). For a critical analysis of their legacy in Quebec see André Lemelin and Claude Marcil, *Le Purgatoire de l'ignorance: l'éducation au Québec jusqu'à la Grande réforme.*

15 For further details see Gérard Filteau, *Organisation scolaire de la province de Québec: historique, législation et règlements.*

16 Renaud, "Le collège classique," 424.

17 On the notion of "minor literature" see Gilles Deleuze and Félix Guattari, *Kafka. Pour une littérature mineure.*

18 Renaud, "Le collège classique," 424.

19 Edmond Procès, *Modèles français: extraits des meilleurs écrivains, avec notices*, II, 1935, 316.

20 Ibid., 6.

21 Procès, *Modèles français: extraits des meilleurs écrivains, avec notices*, III, 1928, 646.

22 Gérard Tougas, *La Littérature canadienne-française*, 67–8.

23 Manitoba Programme of Studies, July 1925, 44.

24 Ibid.

25 Annual Report of the Department of Education, 1929–30, 95.

26 Diana Brydon, "Postcolonial Pedagogy and Curricular Reform."

27 John George Lambton Durham, Charles Buller, and Edward Gibbon Wakefield, *The Report and Despatches of the Earl of Durham*, 218.

28 See Nancy Sheehan, "Indoctrination: Moral Education in the Early Prairie School House," in David Jones, Nancy Sheehan, and Robert Stamp, *Shaping the Schools of the Canadian West*, 223.

29 Quoted in Morgan, "The 'Englishness' of English Teaching," 219.

30 On the ideological function of animal stories see Kathleen Marie Connor, "Cornering the Triangle: Understanding the 'Dominion-itive' Role of the Realistic Animal Tale in Early Twentieth-Century Canadian Children's Literature," in Cynthia Sugars, ed., *Home-Work: Postcolonialism, Pedagogy and Canadian Literature*, 487–501.

31 *Handbook to the Canadian Readers, Books II–III–IV–V*, 57.

32 Morgan, "The 'Englishness' of English Teaching," 221.

33 The abuse of the notion of the "universal" to refer to Western culture and values is expressed by Chinua Achebe, who describes the term as "a synonym for the narrow, self-serving parochialism of Europe." See Chinua Achebe, "Colonialist Criticism," in Bill Ashcroft, Gareth Griffiths, and Helen Tiffin, eds., *The Post-Colonial Studies Reader*, 60.

34 *Handbook to the Canadian Readers*, 53.

35 Ibid., 424.

36 I'm adapting here the term "nation-tinged" coined by Lauren Berlant in *The Queen of America Goes to Washington City*, 45.

37 Charles Reade, "The Lark at the Diggings," *The Canadian Readers*, Book v, 223.

38 Morgan, "The 'Englishness' of English Teaching," 220.

39 The extract is not included in my 1926 edition of Book v, but an entry on it in the 1928 copy of the *Handbook to the Canadian Readers*, 415, suggests that it may well have been in the editions used by Roy in the early 1930s. All other extracts discussed are written by anglophone authors.

40 "The Coureur-de-bois," *The Canadian Readers*, Book v, 42.

41 *Handbook to the Canadian Readers*, 355.

42 Ibid., 356.

43 As stated in the Elementary School Programme of Study for 1927–28, 2.

44 "The Rescue," *The Canadian Readers*, Book v, 277.

45 Heather Murray, "English Studies in Canada and the Case of Postcolonial Culture," *Essays on Canadian Writing* 56 (fall, 1995), 73.

46 The Royal Society of Canada, founded in 1882, elects its members mainly from the academic world, but has admitted a number of eminent Canadian writers, including Antonine Maillet, Marie-Claire Blais, Jacques Godbout, Germaine Guèvremont, Naim Kattan, and Roch Carrier. Among its academic members are François Ricard, Antoine Sirois, and Patricia Smart.

47 The English quotation is taken from Patricia Claxton's 1999 translation of Ricard's biography, *Gabrielle Roy: A Life*, 284. All future references will be to this edition and given as follows: (GR 284).

48 The article was published in *Mémoires de la Société royale du Canada*, XLVIII, 3, June 1954, *Revue de Paris*, 1955, *Les Cloches de Saint-Boniface*, 1955, and *Le Devoir*, Montreal, 1955. References here will be to the reprinted version in *Le Pays de* Bonheur d'occasion, 13–22.

49 The article was first published as "The Disparate Treasures of a Young Girl Who Came from Deschambault Street," *Globe and Mail*, 18 December 1976, 6. The French original, "Mes études à Saint-Boniface,"

appeared in *Le Pays de* Bonheur d'occasion, 35–9. Suggested translations are my own.

50 *Le Pays de* Bonheur d'occasion, 139. Indeed, Sophie Marcotte subsequently published a comparison between the two texts, including details drawn from the study of earlier drafts of *La Détresse et l'enchantement* in "Réécritures de l'enfance dans 'Mes études à Saint-Boniface' et *La Détresse et l'enchantement* de Gabrielle Roy," *Voix et images* 86 (winter 2004): 99–113.

51 Roy began work on *La Détresse et l'enchantement* in about 1977.

52 The text was published posthumously in *Littératures*, (Montreal), 14 (1996): 135–63, and in J.R. Léveillé, *Les Editions du Blé: 25 ans d'édition*. Saint-Boniface: Editions du Blé, 1999, 164–83. The version consulted here is that from *Le Pays de* Bonheur d'occasion, 41–61.

53 *Le Pays de* Bonheur d'occasion, 141.

54 Roy, *La Détresse et l'enchantement*. Montreal: Boréal, 1984. References throughout will be to the 1996 edition.

55 Marcotte, "Réécritures de l'enfance," 111.

56 The phrase is borrowed from J.J. Healy, "The Melting of the Mosaic: Landscape, Power and Ethnicity in Post-Confederation Canada," in Jean Burnet, Danielle Juteau, Enoch Padolsky, Anthony Raspovich, and Antoine Sirois, eds., *Migration and the Transformation of Cultures*, 70.

57 For details of the prizes and their donors see Ricard, *Gabrielle Roy*, 92–3; and see *La Détresse et l'enchantement*, chapter 5 for Roy's account of her decision to excel in academic work.

58 As Ricard has pointed out, this production took place in October 1928, and thus after Roy had left school and during her year at Normal School. It may well be that the nuns took her to a different play in 1926 or 1927, but it is interesting that Roy transposes this key theatrical experience, so associating it with her schooling in Saint-Boniface and representing herself as one of a group of francophone *fillettes* in the audience. See Ricard, *Gabrielle Roy*, 97.

59 Morgan, "The 'Englishness' of English Teaching," 212.

60 See comments by Canadian prime minister Arthur Meighen on Shakespeare as "the Greatest Englishman of History" expressing "the genius of his race" ... "a champion of the Reign of Law," quoted in Morgan, "The 'Englishness' of English Teaching," 214.

61 As will be seen in chapter 3, this desire to find a language "au-delà des langues" haunts Roy's work, but can be related both to her Manitoban origins and to her love of Shakespeare.

62 The quotations are from the following poems: Thomas Gray, "Elegy Written in a Country Churchyard"; Alfred de Vigny, "Le Cor"; Gray, "Elegy" (bis); Charles Baudelaire, "Hymne," from *Les Epaves*; and Walter Scott, *The Lay of the Last Minstrel*, Canto vi, Stanza 1.

63 In its source, *The Lay of the Last Minstrel*, this refers to the border country between Scotland and England, which has interesting resonances for Saint-Boniface as a borderland.

64 The "Notice" states, for example: "Il est vicieux et faux de ne voir dans l'humanité que ce qu'elle a de mauvais, et de tout rapporter à soi comme à un centre, dont toute l'activité n'aurait pour objet que la recherche de la sensation ... [Baudelaire] s'est créé une originalité factice, et c'est pourquoi certains n'hésitent pas à l'appeler tout simplement un mystificateur [It is perverse and incorrect only to see in humanity its faults, and to relate everything back to oneself as the centre of all things, all of whose actions have no other object than the pursuit of sensations ... Baudelaire's self-proclaimed originality is a sham and that is why some people do not hesitate to call him quite simply a charlatan]." See Procès, *Modèles français*, iv, 1936, 517.

65 See Stephen Slemon, "Unsettling the Empire: Resistance Theory for the Second World," 40.

66 Morgan, "The 'Englishness' of English Teaching," 211.

CHAPTER TWO

1 Deborah Britzman, "Cultural Myths in the Making of a Teacher: Biography and Social Structure in Teacher Education," 443.

2 Normal Schools in Manitoba date back to 1882 (for Protestant students) and 1883 (for Catholic students). The Central Normal School in Winnipeg was built in 1905–06 and served as the headquarters for teacher training for more than forty years.

3 Henry Johnson, *A Brief History of Canadian Education*, 96.

4 "Between 1896 and 1912 immigration totaled over 2,500,000. In the peak year of 1913 it was 400,870." See Johnson, *A Brief History of Canadian Education*, 95.

5 See the Department of Education Report, Winnipeg, 1916, 74.

6 R.S. Thornton, Report on Curriculum, Department of Education Report, Winnipeg, 1916.

7 Given the cost of staying in school, it was quite a rare achievement to complete Grade xii at the time (and all the more so for francophone

pupils). (See Department of Education Reports, Year Ending 30 June 1928.)

8 See André Lemelin and Claude Marcil, *Le Purgatoire de l'ignorance: l'éducation au Québec jusqu'à la Grande réforme* for these and further details of Quebec's education system.

9 Nadia Fahmy-Eid and Nicole Thivierge, "L'enseignement au Québec et en France: 1880–1930," in Nadia Fahmy-Eid and Micheline Dumont, eds., *Maîtresses de maison, maîtresses d'école: femmes, famille et éducation dans l'histoire du Québec*, 210.

10 Ibid., 208. In their comparative study of education in France and Quebec between 1880 and 1930 Fahmy-Eid and Thivierge stress the way in which traditional gender roles became embedded in the curriculum in France and Quebec in the 1920s, despite the evident differences between the two education systems.

11 Teaching observation and practice took place exclusively in anglophone schools (see François Ricard, *Gabrielle Roy*, 109).

12 Programme of Studies, Department of Education, Manitoba, 1928–9.

13 Circular to *Directrices* of convents 24.4.1925 (AECFM 44/234/117).

14 Circular to *Directrices* 20.5.1926 (AECFM 44/234/117).

15 See circular 20.01.1927 (AECFM 44/234/117).

16 Ibid.

17 In *La Détresse et l'enchantement* Roy refers to the principal as "le docteur Mackintyre."

18 Minutes of the *Comité du fonctionnement scolaire* 15.1.30 and 20.2.30 (AECFM 42/232/60). This would seem to confirm Roy's own positive portrayal of Dr McIntyre, although Ricard quotes a rather different assessment of him from a fellow student, Léonie Guyot: "I never felt that Dr. McIntyre had a remarkably 'open mind' about things to do with French." Letter of 1.02.1994 to the author, Ricard, *Gabrielle Roy*, 512, fn. 11.

19 Letter to High Schools, 1.09.1929 (AECFM 44/234.117).

20 Circular 13.2.28, p. 2 (AECFM 44/234/117).

21 Britzman, "Cultural Myths in the Making of a Teacher," 443.

22 See Minutes of the *Comité du fonctionnement scolaire*, 15.5.1930 (AECFM 42/232/60).

23 Roy received an A for Writing, Seatwork, and Pedagogy and B+ for Reading, Speaking, School Management, and PE, and an overall score of 24 points, placing her thirteenth in the First Class cohort. See Ricard, *Gabrielle Roy*, 123.

24 Ibid., 114.

25 Ibid.

26 This is confirmed in Minutes of the *Comité du fonctionnement scolaire*, 18.6.1930 (AECFM 42/232/60). For a detailed comparison of the five manuals used in Quebec between 1835 and 1965 see Vincent Ross, "La structure idéologique des manuels de pédagogie québécois."

27 For a description of the *collège classique*, see Norbert Renaud, "Le collège classique: la maison d'enseignement, le milieu d'études, les fins et les moyens."

28 Nicole Gagnon, "L'idéologie humaniste dans la revue *L'Enseignement secondaire*," 172.

29 Ibid., 176.

30 Georges Courchesne, *Nos Humanités*.

31 Ibid., 377.

32 Introduction to the Program of Studies 1927–28, Department of Education, Winnipeg, 2.

33 Courchesne, *Nos Humanités*, 392.

34 Circular to *Directrices* 20.5.1926 (AECFM 44/234/117).

35 Monseigneur François-Xavier Ross, *Manuel de pédagogie théorique et pratique*, 3ᵉ édition, 11.

36 Fahmy-Eid and Thivierge, "L'éducation des filles au Québec et en France (1880–1930)," 200.

37 Ross, *Manuel de pédagogie théorique et pratique*, 3ᵉ édition, 90.

38 Ibid., 323. In the late 1920s in Quebec there was in fact a modernizing counter-current to this traditionalist pedagogy, in which a number of the teaching orders developed a scientific strand in secondary schools to parallel the *cours classique*. For further information see Pierre-André Turcotte, "Sécularisation et modernité: les frères éducateurs et l'enseignement secondaire public, 1920–1970."

39 Courchesne, *Nos Humanités*, 283.

40 Ross, *Manuel de pédagogie théorique et pratique*, 3ᵉ édition, 170.

41 Ibid., 71–2. Teddy Bears were a relatively recent phenomenon, appearing almost simultaneously in Germany and the United States in 1902–03. For Ross, as his use of the American name indicates, they are part of a wider cultural threat from the United States.

42 Doris Lessing, *The Golden Notebooks*, quoted in Peter McLaren, *Schooling as a Ritual Performance: Towards a Political Economy of Educational Symbols and Gestures*, xvii–xviii.

43 A.A. Herriot, "School Inspectors of the Early Days in Manitoba," *MHS Transactions*, series 3 (1947–48) (online version).

44 Department of Education Report 1927–28, Winnipeg, 13.

45 The words of H. Connolly, quoted in Department of Education Report 1927–28, Winnipeg, 17.

46 Department of Education report, 1928–29, Winnipeg, 29.

47 Ricard, *Gabrielle Roy*, 132. In the depths of the Depression many teachers were far less fortunate than Roy, some being paid as little as $35 a month for an eight-month contract.

48 Lemelin and Marcil, *Le Purgatoire de l'ignorance*, 102. In 1942 Roy wrote an article, "Pitié pour les institutrices," *Bulletin des agriculteurs*, 38, no. 3 (March 1942), 7, 45–6, which drew attention to the poverty of the *institutrices* in areas of new colonization such as Abitibi, on the western borders of Quebec.

49 Ricard argues that the AECFM "thus controlled the placing of virtually all francophone teaching personnel in the province," Ricard, *Gabrielle Roy*, 112.

50 See references to letters to local *curés*, Minutes of the Comité du fonctionnement scolaire, 24.09.27, 17.03.1927 (AECFM 42/232/59).

51 J.J. Healy, "The Melting of the Mosaic: Landscape, Power and Ethnicity in Post-Confederation Canada," in Jean Burnet et al., eds., *Migration and the Transformation of Cultures*, 70.

52 This familiar description of Saint-Henri is reminiscent of the descriptions of Saint-Boniface in Roy's autobiographical writing, where the close association between education and the church is read into the urban landscape.

53 Canadian citizenship was not introduced until 1947, so Azarius and all "Canadian" soldiers were British citizens in World War II.

54 While this degree of prejudice is consistent with some of Luzina's other references to the Métis, she is at other points in the text shown as being very close to them, so the representation is rather problematic. Luzina's racist comments are not condemned within the narrative, but they are highlighted by the narrator's use of the terms "la tribu saulteux [the Saultais tribe]" and "la réserve indienne [the Indian reservation]" and the addition of a footnote giving information about the hunting and fishing rights of the Saultais tribe (PPE 35; 29).

55 When Roy herself taught summer school in Little Waterhen in 1937, her class was in fact composed of both White and Métis children.

56 In *La Détresse et l'enchantement*, when Roy informs her mother that she has a supply post in a Métis village, her mother responds with a violent outburst of anger, the cause of which remains unexplained, but which the reader might connect with the poverty of either the village or its Métis population: "Pas à Marchand. Jamais! C'est un trou! J'en ai entendu

parler. Un vrai trou! Tu n'iras pas là [Not Marchand ... Never! It's a dreadful place! I've heard about it. The boondocks! You're not going there!]" (*DE* 107; 83).

57 Roy, "Voyage en Ungava," in *Le Pays de* Bonheur d'occasion *et autres récits autobiographiques épars et inédits,* 121. This text was written after the 1961 visit, but Roy abandoned her plans for publishing the piece.

58 Roy uses the term "Esquimaux" throughout the text, but in discussion with Joyce Marshall about the translation into English acknowledges that the term will sound old-fashioned in the late 1960s. The working title for the translation of the three accompanying short stories, which in fact were not included in the translated volume, was "Inuit Tales."

59 *Ivanhoe,* a tale of chivalry set in the age of Richard the Lion-Hearted, depicted the rivalry between the king and his wicked brother John.

60 Incidentally, this reference to Lord Tweedsmuir helps to confirm the setting of *La Petite Poule d'Eau* in the late 1930s, as his period in office was short. Sworn in in November 1935, he died in office in February 1940. Encouraged by his wife, also a writer, Lord Tweedsmuir was responsible for creating the Governor General's Awards in 1936.

61 While the reference to the teacher's "mission" here recalls the pedagogical views of Monseigneur Ross's manual, Joséphine, like the majority of Roy's teacher figures, seems to be motivated by cultural rather than explicitly religious fervour.

62 See Agnès Whitfield, "Gabrielle Roy's *Children of My Heart* or Portrait of the Artist as a Young Woman," in Janice Morgan and Colette Hall, eds., *Redefining Autobiography in Twentieth-Century Women's Fiction,* 209–25; and Whitfield, "Altérité et identité: tensions narratives dans *Ces Enfants de ma vie* de Gabrielle Roy," in Louise Milot and Jaap Lintvelt, eds., *Le Roman québécois depuis 1960,* 167–80.

63 Significantly Roy's auto-fictional persona here, at eighteen years old, is a year younger than she herself was when she took up her teaching post in Cardinal.

CHAPTER THREE

1 Gabrielle Roy, "Les gens de chez nous," *Bulletin des Agriculteurs* (May 1943), 38.

2 An earlier version of the first part of this chapter has appeared in article form as: "French and English in Gabrielle Roy's Autobiographical Work." *The French Review,* special issue, "Le Québec et le Canada francophone," 78, no. 6 (May 2005): 1127–37.

3 Robert Young, *Colonial Desire*, 5.

4 In 1969 the *Official Languages Act* adopted bilingualism as official policy in Canada after the recommendations of the Commission on Bilingualism and Biculturalism. In 1988 a new *Official Languages Act* came into force. Among its stated objectives was that of supporting the development of anglophone and francophone minority populations across Canada and moving further toward equality of status between the two official languages within Canadian society.

5 René Appel and Pieter Muysken, *Language Contact and Bilingualism*, 102.

6 Rainier Grutman, *Des Langues qui résonnent: l'hétérolinguisme au Québec au XIXe siècle*, 29.

7 See Henri Gobard, *L'Aliénation linguistique. Analyse tétraglossique.*

8 Ngugi Wa Thiong'o, "The Language of African Literature," in Patrick Williams and Laura Chrisman, eds., *Colonial Discourse and Post-Colonial Theory: A Reader*, 438.

9 The return to France is often represented as a failed rite of passage, as in Michel Tremblay, *Des Nouvelles d'Edouard*, or Marie-Claire Blais, *Une liaison parisienne*. For further analysis see my article "The Colony Hits Back: the French Experience in Quebec Literature," in Yvette Rocheron and Christopher Rolfe, eds., *Shifting Frontiers of France and Francophonie*, 235–53.

10 Stephen Slemon, "Unsettling the Empire: Resistance Theory for the Second World," in Ajay Heble, Donna Palmateer Pennee, and Tim Struthers, eds., *New Contexts of Canadian Criticism*, 236.

11 Robert Kroetsch, "Unhiding the Hidden," in Bill Ashcroft, Gareth Griffiths and Helen Tiffin, eds., *The Post-Colonial Studies Reader*, 394.

12 Lise Gauvin, ed., *L'Ecrivain francophone à la croisée des langues*, 6.

13 Ibid., 7.

14 Celia Britton, *Edouard Glissant and Postcolonial Theory: Strategies of Language and Resistance*, 182.

15 Grutman, *Des Langues qui résonnent*, 32.

16 Roy was therefore much more in sympathy with Pierre Elliot Trudeau's vision of a bilingual Canada than with René Lévesque's Parti Québécois. In this respect she was similar to her father, whose loyalty to the Liberal Laurier and his bilingual model of Canada aroused the hostility of conservative Franco-Manitobans.

17 Letter to Joyce Marshall, 7 September 1977, in Jane Everett, ed., *In Translation*, 200.

18 Edouard Glissant, *Introduction à une Poétique du Divers*, 112.

19 Ibid., 113–14.

20 Frantz Fanon, *Peau noire, masques blancs*, 30.

21 For details of the genesis of the published text see François Ricard, *Gabrielle Roy*, 481–8 and Sophie Marcotte, "Réécritures de l'enfance dans 'Mes études à Saint-Boniface' et *La Détresse et l'enchantement* de Gabrielle Roy," *Voix et images*, 86 (winter 2004): 99–113.

22 Full publication details of the other two autobiographical works can be found in the Bibliography.

23 Gayatri Spivak, *The Post-Colonial Critic*, 38.

24 Bill Ashcroft, *Post-Colonial Transformation*, 44.

25 Selwyn Cudjoe, *Eric Williams Speaks: Essays on Colonialism and Independence*, 43.

26 I am grateful to David Diop of the Université de Pau et des Pays de l'Adour for pointing out that Timbuctoo is in fact not in Mauritania but in Mali.

27 Ashcroft, *Post-Colonial Transformation*, 44.

28 Peter Trudgill, *Sociolinguistics: An Introduction to Language and Society*, 10.

29 On the range of possible social motivations for the use of code-switching in the spoken language see Richard Skiba, *Internet TESL Journal*, 3, 10 (October 1997).

30 Ashcroft, *Post-Colonial Transformation*, 53.

31 Stuart Hall, "Culture, Community, Nation," *Cultural Studies*, 7, no. 3 (1993), 362.

32 Young, *Colonial Desire*, 5.

33 On the connection between notions of alterity and colonial discourse see Sylvia Söderlind, *Margin/Alias: Language and Colonization in Canadian and Québécois Fiction*.

34 Lise Gauvin, "Passages de langues," in Robert Dion, Hans-Jürgen Lüsenbrink, and James Riesz, eds., *Ecrire en langue étrangère: interférences de langues et de cultures dans le monde francophone*, 25.

35 Gilles Deleuze and Félix Guattari, *Kafka. Pour une littérature mineure*, 33.

36 Gauvin, "Passages de langues," 40.

37 Mary Louise Pratt, *Imperial Eyes: Travel Writing and Transculturation*, 4.

38 Estelle Dansereau, "Narrer l'autre: la représentation des marginaux dans *La Rivière sans repos* et *Un jardin au bout du monde*," in André Fauchon, ed., *Colloque international "Gabrielle Roy,"* 471.

39 Ibid., 472.

40 Grutman, *Des Langues qui résonnent*, 37.

41 Ibid., 42.

42 *La Saga d'Eveline*, édition critique établie par Christine Robinson (microfiche, Library and Archives Canada, 1998). Future references to this edition will be given in the text as (SE).

43 Young, *Colonial Desire*, 19.

44 Ibid., 26.

45 Ibid.

46 Susan Stanford Friedmann, *Mappings: Feminism and the Cultural Geographies of Encounter*, 89.

47 Ibid., 90.

48 Ibid.

49 S.P. Mohanty, "'Us and Them': On the Philosophical Bases of Political Criticism," *New Formations* 8 (summer, 1989), 71.

50 Friedmann recognizes the criticisms of some cultural theorists of the widespread use of "hybridity-talk," arguing that: "Much of the attack on the spread of hybridity discourse comes from those who remain committed to the epistemological and political imperatives of difference discourse, particularly in its most binarist forms (e.g., the West/the Rest, First World/Third World, white/other)" (*Mappings*, 92). While recognizing the strategic importance of invoking difference (for organized political opposition, for example), her personal conclusion is to advocate what she terms "a dialogic relation between the two, allowing each approach to rein in the excesses of the other" (ibid., 103).

51 See Roy, *La Détresse et l'enchantement*, 14.

52 Roy, *La Petite Poule d'Eau*, 40. Future quotations from the text will be to this edition and will appear after the quotation, followed by the reference to the published translation, thus: (PPE 40; 34).

53 Roy, *Rue Deschambault*, 111. Future quotations from the text will appear after the quotation, thus: (RD 199).

54 Roy, *Un jardin au bout du monde*, 149, 156. Future quotations from this text will appear after the quotation, thus: (JM 149; 156)

55 Friedmann, *Mappings*, 90.

56 Gauvin, ed., *L'Écrivain francophone à la croisée des langues*, 7.

57 W.H. New, *Land Sliding: Imaginary Space, Presence and Power in Canadian Writing*, 11.

58 Ibid.

59 Roy, *La Rivière sans repos*, 56. Future quotations from this text will appear after the quotation, thus: (RSR 56).

60 See the Bibliography for full details of the translations used.

61 Roy's journalistic piece "Voyage en Ungava," written after her brief visit to Fort Chimo in 1961, includes a passage in which she tries to imagine the culture shock experienced by Inuit patients being flown south for medical treatment. "Les satellites" and the figure of Deborah are clearly inspired by the questions she raised in that earlier text (see "Voyage en Ungava," in Roy, *Le pays de* Bonheur d'occasion, 101–28).

62 Roy uses the term "le gouvernement" on several occasions in the dialogue of Inuit and other members of linguistic minorities to refer to individual representations of various government institutions, so indicating the sense of alienation that such characters feel from the provincial or federal layers of Canadian government.

63 Ashcroft, Griffiths, and Tiffin, *The Post-Colonial Studies Reader*, 391.

64 In the text Roy represents this encounter by including Wong's dialogue in English marked by Chinese pronunciation – "Good molnin! Nice molnin!" (JM 60) – or by grammatical errors – "Nice days to days" (JM 60). Smouillya's dialogue is, however, naturalized in French, his accent not being phonetically indicated.

65 Friedmann, *Mappings*, 90.

66 *De quoi t'ennuies-tu, Eveline?* and *Ely! Ely! Ely!*, 83, [my translation]. Future quotations from this text will appear after the quotation, thus: (DQ 83).

67 Grutman, *Des Langues qui résonnent*, 42.

68 The underlining used by Christine Robinson in the critical edition would probably have appeared as italics in a published form, so stressing the linguistic difference between English and French; hence my use of italics in the proposed translation.

69 Margaret Steffler, "Postcolonial Collisions of Language: Teaching and Using Tensions in the Text," in Sylvia Sugars, ed., *Home-Work: Postcolonialism, Pedagogy, and Canadian Literature*, 353.

70 Sherry Simon, in Susan Bassnett and Harish Trivedi, eds., *Post-colonial Translation: Theory and Practice*, 70.

71 On the "Third Space," see Homi Bhabha, *The Location of Culture*.

72 Michael Cronin, *Across the Lines: Travel, Language, Translation*, 106.

73 Joyce Marshall, "The Writer as Translator. A Personal View," 28.

74 Ibid.

CHAPTER FOUR

1 Henry Schogt, *Linguistics, Literary Analysis, and Literary Translation*, 115.

2 See Jane Everett, ed., *In Translation: The Gabrielle Roy–Joyce Marshall Correspondence*.

3 The figures were included in the notes for Deacon's lecture on French-Canadian writers prepared for an evening course at Ryerson Institute of Technology, Toronto, in 1951–52. (For details see Mariel O'Neill-Karch, "Gabrielle Roy et William Arthur Deacon: une amitié littéraire," 94–5.) The English translation was commissioned by Reynal and Hitchcock, the deal being signed by Roy's legal advisor and literary agent, Jean-Marie Nadeau, on 4 December 1945.

4 Barbara Godard, "La traduction comme réception: les écrivaines québécoises au Canada anglais," 66–7.

5 Ibid., 66.

6 Ibid. See André Lefevere, *Translation, Rewriting and the Manipulation of Literary Fame*. Lefevere argues that translation is one of a whole series of linked forms of rewriting (including anthologization, interpretation, editing), all of which act together to make or break a writer's reception in a receiving culture.

7 Letter to Gabrielle Roy, 24 March 1946, in John Lennox and Michèle Lacombe, eds., *Dear Bill: The Correspondence of William Arthur Deacon*, 214. The correspondence was initiated by Deacon in February 1946 and consists of forty-one letters, fourteen of which are reproduced in full in Lennox and Lacombe's edition. Further extracts appear in Clara Thomas and John Lennox, *William Arthur Deacon: A Canadian Literary Life* and Mariel O'Neill-Karch, "Gabrielle Roy et William Arthur Deacon: une amitié littéraire," *Cultures du Canada français* 9 (1992), 75–97.

8 Letter to William Arthur Deacon, 16 March 1954, in Lennox and Lacombe, eds., *Dear Bill*, 305–6.

9 Letter to Gabrielle Roy, 24 March 1946, in Lennox and Lacombe, eds., *Dear Bill*, 214.

10 O'Neill-Karch, "Gabrielle Roy et William Arthur Deacon: une amitié littéraire," 97. For further consideration of Roy's relationship with Anglo-Canada see François Ricard, "La métamorphose d'un écrivain: essai biographique," 441–55 and Antoine Sirois, "Gabrielle Roy et le Canada anglais," *Etudes littéraires* 17, no. 3 (winter, 1984), 469–79.

11 An account of the notes for this lecture, held in the Deacon archive at the University of Toronto, Thomas Fischer Rare Books Library, can be found in O'Neill-Karch's article, cited above.

12 O'Neill-Karch, "Gabrielle Roy et William Arthur Deacon: une amitié littéraire," 95.

13 Deacon, who served as chairman of the Governor General's Award Board until 1949, had been associated with these awards since their introduction in 1936.

14 See the Council of Canada website for a full list of past winners: www.canadacouncil.ca.

15 Equally, for Roy to gain recognition in France, her works needed to be published by Parisian, not Montreal-based publishers. The French edition of *Bonheur d'occasion*, published by Flammarion, won the Prix Femina in 1947.

16 Another sign of the increased recognition of literary translation is the existence of the Canada Council Translation Prize (established in 1973–74), which was awarded in 1976 to Joyce Marshall for her translation of Roy's *Cet été qui chantait* (*Enchanted Summer*). In 1987 the Governor General's Awards included for the first time a category for translation (French to English and English to French). The first winner in the former category was Patricia Claxton for her translation of *La Détresse et l'enchantement* (*Enchantment and Sorrow*).

17 Susan Bassnett, "The Translation Turn in Cultural Studies," in Susan Bassnett and André Lefevere, *Constructing Cultures: Essays on Literary Translation*, 124.

18 E.D. Blodgett, "Towards a Model of Literary Translation in Canada," 199.

19 Quoted in E.D. Blodgett, "How do you say 'Gabrielle Roy'?" in Camille La Bossière, ed., *Translation in Canadian Literature. Reappraisals: Canadian Writers*, 13. See Blodgett's article for an assessment of the history of literary translation in Canada prior to 1982.

20 Jacques Brault, *Poèmes des quatre côtés*, 16.

21 Sherry Simon, "Traduction et représentation identitaire," in Duchet and Vachon, eds., *La Recherche littéraire: objets et méthodes*, 315.

22 Barbara Godard, "Between Performative and Performance: Translation and Theatre in the Canadian/Quebec Context," 5.

23 Ibid.

24 Lawrence Venuti, ed., *Rethinking Translation: Discourse, Subjectivity, Ideology*, 4.

25 Ibid., 5.

26 *Street of Riches*, trans. by Harry Binsse (Toronto: McLelland & Stewart, 1957). Introduction to the 1967 edition by Brandon Conron, xi.

27 Maria Tymoczko, "Post-colonial Writing and Literary Translation," in Susan Bassnett and Harish Trivedi, eds., *Post-colonial Translation: Theory and Practice*, 38.

28 Ibid., 297.

29 Antoine Berman, "Translation and the Trials of the Foreign," translated by Lawrence Venuti, in Venuti ed., *The Translation Studies Reader*, 286. The article was originally published as "La Traduction comme épreuve de l'étranger," *Texte* 4 (1985): 67–81.

30 Ibid., 294–5.

31 Ibid., 286.

32 Ibid., 297.

33 Barbara Godard, "L'Éthique du traduire: Antoine Berman et le 'virage éthique' en traduction," 77–8. Godard analyses Berman's shifts of position on ethical translation and concludes that he ends up with a universalist, metaphysical model of translation rather than a materialist, historicized view of translation's function. See Henri Meschonnic, *Poétique du traduire*. Lawrence Venuti, *The Scandals of Translation: Towards an Ethic of Difference*; Gayatri Spivak, "The Politics of Translation," *Outside in the Teaching Machine*, 179–200.

34 Sherry Simon, "The Language of Cultural Difference: Figures of Alterity in Canadian Translation," in Venuti, ed., *Rethinking Translation*, 162.

35 Ibid., 159.

36 Ibid., 161.

37 Blodgett, "How do you say 'Gabrielle Roy'?", 33.

38 Ibid., 34.

39 Schogt, "'Pas *lonely* pantoute?'," in Cécile Cloutier-Wojechewska and Réjean Robidoux, eds., *Solitude rompue*, 344.

40 Ibid., 348.

41 *Maria Chapdelaine* was published in *Le Temps* between 27 January and 19 February 1914. It was then published in 1916 in Montreal by LeFebvre, and in Paris in 1921 by Grasset.

42 Nicole Deschamps, "Avant-propos," *Maria Chapdelaine*, x.

43 Ibid.

44 Ibid., xi

45 Kathy Mezei, "Speaking White: Literary Translation as a Vehicle of Assimilation in Quebec," 20.

46 Ibid., 20–1.

47 Ibid., 21.

48 For an excellent overview of literary translation in Quebec in the 1990s see Simon, *Le Trafic des langues*.

49 Sherry Simon, "The True Quebec as Revealed to English Canada: Translated Novels 1864–1950," 41. W.H. Blake was the translator of *Maria*

Chapdelaine, also featured in Schogt's article, while Marquis was the translator of one of two other versions of *Les anciens Canadiens*.

50 Simon cites the case of the 1964 New Canadian Library edition of Roberts's translation of *Les anciens Canadiens* which gives Roberts's name on the cover page and not that of its author, Aubert de Gaspé.

51 Lorna Hutchinson and Nathalie Cooke, "How do you translate 'regard'? Rewriting Gabrielle Roy," in Jane Everett and François Ricard, eds., *Gabrielle Roy réécrite*, 108. On rewriting see Lefevere, *Translation, Rewriting, and the Manipulation of Literary Fame*.

52 Vanamal Viswanatha and Sherry Simon, "Srikantaiah and Kannada Translation," in Susan Bassnett and Harish Trivedi, eds., *Post-colonial Translation: Theory and Practice*, 176.

53 Ibid.

54 Ibid., 175.

55 Letter to William Arthur Deacon, 11 March 1946, in Lennox and Lacombe, eds., *Dear Bill*, 209.

56 These two publications were "The Jarvis Murder Case. By Gabrielle Roy, St. Boniface, Man. A Prize-Winning Short, Short Story," *The Free Press*, Winnipeg (12 January 1934), and "Jean-Baptiste takes a wife," *Toronto Star Weekly*, Toronto (19 December 1936).

57 In the case of short stories published in the periodical press, the translator's name is often not recorded. When, for example, the short story "Feuilles mortes" was published in *Maclean's* in June 1947, an anonymous English translation was published in parallel (see Everett and Ricard, eds., *Gabrielle Roy réécrite*, 162).

58 An index of Roy's correspondence that indicates which letters were written in English can be consulted on the website of the Groupe de Recherche sur Gabrielle Roy at http://www.gabrielle-roy.mcgill.ca.

59 Letter to William Arthur Deacon, 11 March 1946, in Lennox and Lacombe, eds., *Dear Bill*, 209.

60 Letter to Joyce Marshall, 25 April 1973, in Jane Everett, ed., *In Translation*, 93. All future references to the Roy–Marshall correspondence will be to Jane Everett's edition, *In Translation: The Gabrielle Roy–Joyce Marshall Correspondence*. Everett was kind enough to let me work on the unpublished proofs of her edition and the photocopied originals of the correspondence in Montreal in June 2005.

61 Letter to Gabrielle Roy, 3 June 1973, Ibid., 94.

62 Letter to Margaret Laurence, 6 March 1978, in Paul Socken, ed., *Intimate Strangers. The Letters of Margaret Laurence and Gabrielle Roy*, 52. This reference to the language barrier echoes the first exchange of letters

with Deacon when he explains in his letter of 16 February 1946: "It is unusual for a person speaking only English to take an interest in novelists, who write in French. But I believe it is time we tried to know each other across the language barrier." Roy takes up his point in her reply of 27 February 1946: "'To know each other across the language barrier,' as you put it, has always been my aim and I am truly delighted to see more and more signs of better understanding between Canadians of French and of English expression." See Lennox and Lacombe, eds., *Dear Bill*, 203.

63 Joan Hind-Smith, *Three Voices: The Lives of Margaret Laurence, Gabrielle Roy, Frederick Philip Grove*, 115.

64 Marshall, "Gabrielle Roy, 1909–1983," 44. See Bibliography for Joyce Marshall's other accounts of their working relationship.

65 See Jane Everett, "Introduction," *In Translation*, xx.

66 Marshall, "Gabrielle Roy, 1909–1983," 44.

67 Letter to Margaret Laurence, 11 March 1980, in Socken, ed., *Intimate Strangers*, 83.

68 For a discussion of the different models of the relationship between source text and target text, see Blodgett, "Towards a Model of Literary Translation in Canada," 189–206.

69 See Everett, "Introduction," *In Translation*, xx.

70 Schogt, *Linguistics, Literary Analysis, and Literary* Translation, 119.

71 *The Tin Flute*. Toronto: McClelland & Stewart, 1947.

72 Harry Binsse translated *La Petite Poule d'Eau: Where Nests the Water Hen*, Toronto: McClelland & Stewart 1951; *Alexandre Chenevert: The Cashier*, Toronto: McClelland & Stewart, 1955; *Rue Deschambault: Street of Riches*, Toronto: McClelland & Stewart, 1957, and *La Montagne secrète: The Hidden Mountain*, Toronto: McClelland & Stewart, 1962.

73 Letter to William Arthur Deacon, 16 March 1954, in Lennox and Lacombe, eds., *Dear Bill*, 305.

74 Letter to Joyce Marshall, 13 October 1968, *In Translation*, 87–8.

75 Ricard refers to this stage of Roy's relationship with her publishers as the "Canadianization" of her English-language translations. See Ricard, *Gabrielle Roy*, 379.

76 "Grand-mère et la poupée" was published in *Châtelaine* in October 1960, and Joyce Marshall's translation, "Grandmother and the Doll," appeared in the English language edition in the same month.

77 For bio-bibliographical material on Marshall's work as writer and translator, see Jane Everett's Introduction to *In Translation*, and Jane Everett, "Joyce Marshall, the Accidental Translator," in Agnès Whitfield, ed.,

Writing Between the Lines: Portraits of Anglophone Literary Translators.
Marshall translated *La Route d'Altamont: The Road Past Altamont*,
Toronto: McClelland & Stewart, 1966; *La Rivière sans repos:*
Windflower, Toronto: McClelland & Stewart, 1970, and *Cet été qui*
chantait: Enchanted Summer, Toronto: McClelland & Stewart, 1976.

78 Alan Brown translated *Un jardin au bout du monde: Garden in the*
Wind, Toronto: McClelland & Stewart 1977; *Ma vache Bossie: My Cow*
Bossie, Toronto: McClelland & Stewart, 1988; *Ces enfants de ma vie:*
Children of My Heart, Toronto: McClelland & Stewart, 1979; *Fragiles*
Lumières de la terre: The Fragile Lights of Earth, Toronto: McClelland
& Stewart, 1982, and *Courte-Queue: Cliptail*, Toronto: McClelland &
Stewart, 1980.

79 Letter to Gabrielle Roy, 2 May 1976, *In Translation*, 172.

80 Letter to Joyce Marshall, 24 March 1977, *In Translation*, 190.

81 Patricia Claxton translated *La Détresse et l'enchantement: Enchantment*
and Sorrow, Toronto: Lester and Orpen Dennys, 1987; *L'Espagnole et la*
Pékinoise: The Tortoise-shell and the Pekinese, Toronto: Doubleday Canada, 1989; and *Ma chère petite sœur: lettres à Bernadette, 1943–1970:*
Letters to Bernadette, Toronto: Lester and Orpen Dennys, 1990. She was
also the translator of François Ricard's biography of Roy, *Gabrielle Roy.*
Une vie: Gabrielle Roy: A Life, Toronto: McClelland & Stewart, 1996.

82 In addition to works already cited, see Jane Everett, "Le devenir-anglais
du texte et le rapport à l'écriture: Roy et Ferron," in Brigitte Faivre-
Duboz and Patrick Poirier, eds., *Jacques Ferron: le palimpseste infini*,
277–94; Everett, "Réécrire," in Everett and Ricard, eds., *Gabrielle Roy*
réécrite, 11–34.

83 Everett, "Introduction," *In Translation*, xxi–xxii.

84 Sophie Montreuil, "Re(re)dire: *The Hidden Mountain* revu par Gabrielle
Roy et Joyce Marshall," in Everett and Ricard, eds., *Gabrielle Roy*
réécrite, 91–105 [92].

85 Letter to Gabrielle Roy, 18 April 1967, *In Translation*, 16. Everett notes
that this is a reference to Colette, *La Maison de Claudine* (1922).

86 This particular name is interesting as it is a juxtaposition of two names
that occur separately in *La Rivière sans repos*, a text the two had worked
closely on from 1968 to 1970.

87 Letter to Joyce Marshall, 1 May 1970, *In Translation*, 61. The correspondence devotes a considerable amount of space to discussions
between the two women on Quebec separatism, the place of Quebec in
Canada, and their respective views of René Lévesque.

88 Letter to Joyce Marshall, 21 October 1970, *In Translation*, 69.

89 Letter to Gabrielle Roy, 3 June 1973, *In Translation*, 94.

90 Letter to Gabrielle Roy, 8 August 1976, *In Translation*, 179; letter to Joyce Marshall, 15 August 1976, *In Translation*, 179.

91 Roy wrote to Margaret Laurence, a great admirer of Marshall's work: "By the way, isn't [it] wonderful that Joyce Marshall won the great prize for translation this year!" Letter to Margaret Laurence, 4 June 1977, in Socken, ed., *Intimate Strangers*, 40.

92 Letter to Gabrielle Roy, 25 April 1977, *In Translation*, 191.

93 Letter to Gabrielle Roy, 27 October 1978, *In Translation*, 216.

94 See Fonds Gabrielle Roy, B58 Ch 2.

95 See Fonds Gabrielle Roy, B52 Ch 1–5.

96 Letter to Joyce Marshall, 13 October 1968, *In Translation*, 27.

97 Letter to Joyce Marshall, 2 October 1969, *In Translation*, 48.

98 Letter to Joyce Marshall, 14 January 1970, *In Translation*, 51–2.

99 Letter to Joyce Marshall, 29 January 1970, *In Translation*, 53. The slightly awkward English of some of the titles probably suggests that these are indications of ideas, not serious options.

100 Letter to Gabrielle Roy, 17 February 1970, *In Translation*, 54.

101 Letter to Joyce Marshall, 20 February 1970, *In Translation*, 56. Interestingly, the title used for the screenplay written by Paule Mason and Lee Reynolds was *River without Rest*. See Fonds Gabrielle Roy, B52, ch 15.

102 Letter to Gabrielle Roy, 25 March 1970, *In Translation*, 58.

103 Letter to Gabrielle Roy, 27 August 1974, *In Translation*, 138. The translator was Sheila Fischman.

104 Letter to Joyce Marshall, 13 April 1978, *In Translation*, 213.

105 Letter to Joyce Marshall, 11 March 1969, in *In Translation*, 37.

106 Letter to Joyce Marshall, late October–early November 1969, *In Translation*, 50–1. On this visit to Toronto in October 1969, for two weeks of intensive work with Joyce Marshall, see Ricard, *Gabrielle Roy*, 446–7.

107 Letter to Gabrielle Roy, 17 February 1970, *In Translation*, Appendix C, 244.

108 Letter to Joyce Marshall, 19 February 1970, *In Translation*, 55.

109 Montreuil, "Re(re)dire: *The Hidden Mountain* revu par Gabrielle Roy et Joyce Marshall," 103.

110 See Appendix D of Everett's edition of the Roy-Marshall correspondence for details of the changes as they appeared in the published versions.

111 Letter to Gabrielle Roy, 10 August 1973, *In Translation*, 100. One could, of course, argue that such instances of "unEnglishness" might have the effect of reminding the reader that they are reading a text

translated from French, but neither Marshall nor Roy appreciated such strategies or felt the need to correct any such lapse.

112 Letter to Gabrielle Roy, 13 August 1973, *In Translation*, 104.

113 Letter to Joyce Marshall, 11 March 1969, *In Translation*, 37.

114 Letter to Joyce Marshall, 4 September 1969, *In Translation*, 45.

115 See letter to Roy, 25 June 1974, *In Translation*, 135, in which Marshall refers to attending a conference of literary translators organized by the Canada Council in New Richmond, Gaspé, which was to lead to the setting up of this association.

116 The Canada Council first introduced grants for translation work in 1972–73.

117 Letter to Joyce Marshall, 28 September 1976, *In Translation*, 186.

118 Ricard gives the date of this decision as 1973, "after she had finished the translation *Enchanted Summer*" (see Ricard, *Gabrielle Roy*, 469), but this must be a confusion as Marshall was still working on the translation in the summer of 1975. See Marshall, "The Writer as Translator: A Personal View," 26. Roy reports in her letter of 5 February 1976 that Jack McClelland was already looking for a new translator for Roy and that Sheila Fischman had been suggested.

119 Letter to Joyce Marshall, 26 March 1976, *In Translation*, 168.

120 Ricard, *Gabrielle Roy*, 431.

121 Letter to Gabrielle Roy, 27 March 1974, *In Translation*, 130.

122 See Appendix E, *In Translation*.

123 See letter to Gabrielle Roy, 10 October 1975, *In Translation*, 165.

124 Letter to Joyce Marshall, 13 May 1976, *In Translation*, 175. In fact these French words are included in the published volume without italicization.

125 Letter to Gabrielle Roy, 8 August 1976, *In Translation*, 178. Roy does agree with Marshall's decision (see letter of 15 August 1976, *In Translation*, 180).

126 Letter to Gabrielle Roy, 19 September 1976, *In Translation*, 183. The review appeared in the *Globe and Mail* (18 September 1976), 39. The references for the words in French are as follows: *gatte, chaloupe, carillonneur* in *Enchanted Summer*, Toronto: McClelland & Stewart, 1976, 17–20; 120; 48.

127 The proofs I have consulted are held in the Fonds Gabrielle Roy at Library and Archives Canada, Ottawa. I am grateful to François Ricard for giving me permission to consult the archives and to Monique Ostiguy, Literary Archivist at Library and Archives Canada, who kindly prepared the material for me to consult in July 2005.

128 Schogt, *Linguistics, Literary Analysis, and Literary Translation*, 115–16.

129 It was Roy's practice to make a number of revisions to new editions of her works, with the result that, by the time Josephson's translation was published in 1947, her source text (the 1945 first edition) had already been revised by Roy for the Flammarion edition.

130 Page references after quotations refer to the following editions: *Alexandre Chenevert*, Montreal: Stanké, 1979 (AC) and *The Cashier*, New Canadian Library, Toronto: McClelland & Stewart, 1990 (C).

131 Vincent L. Schonberger, "The Problem of Language and the Difficulty of Writing in the Literary Works of Gabrielle Roy," *Studies in Canadian Literature* 14, no. 1 (1989), 136.

132 The incomplete name of the bank sounds rather awkward in English. In translation this is changed to "The Savings Bank" (C 35).

133 Frantz Fanon, *Peau noire, masques blancs*, 30.

134 The English translation refers here to *How to Win Friends and Influence People* (Dale Carnegie, 1936). The French title given by Roy certainly suggests this is the book she was thinking of, although the title of the current French translation is *Comment se faire des amis et influencer les autres*. However, a catalogue search of Library and Archives Canada reveals that an earlier (undated) translation was published by Hachette entitled *Comment se faire des amis pour réussir dans la vie*, translated and adapted by Denise Geneix.

135 The un-English transposition of *Home Ideal* for *Ideal Home* is probably an error, and indeed the English translation gives *Ideal Home*.

136 Lawrence Venuti, *The Translator's Invisibility: A History of Translation*, 15.

137 Godard, "Translations."

138 An interesting echo of these bilingual announcements appears at the end of *La Détresse et l'enchantement* as Roy describes her lodgings near the bus station on rue Dorchester: "'Départ pour Rawdon ... traque numéro sept ... track number seven ... départ pour Terrebonne ... traque numéro onze ... track number eleven ... ' Il m'arrivait en rêve de répéter: 'Traque numéro douze ... track number twelve ... ' ['Leaving for Rawdon, *traque numéro sept*, track number seven ... leaving for Terrebonne, *traque numéro onze*, track number eleven ... ' Sometimes I used to repeat in my sleep, '*Traque numéro douze*, track number twelve ... ']" (DE 500; 406).

139 Roy's representation of this character has been variously interpreted as either an example of Alexandre's fascination with the Other (and openness to ethnic, linguistic, and cultural diversity) or as illustrating his hostility to the Jewish Other. See Ben Shek, "'La généreuse disparité

humaine' dans l'œuvre de Gabrielle Roy, de *Bonheur d'occasion* à *La Détresse et l'enchantement*," *Etudes Canadiennes/Canadian Studies* 21, no. 1 (1986), 235–44, and Józef Kwaterko, "La problématique interculturelle dans *Alexandre Chenevert* de Gabrielle Roy," *University of Toronto Quarterly* 63, no. 4 (1994), 566–74. I see this not as an either/or but rather as an encounter that reveals Alexandre's own ambivalence and position, caught as he is in the contradiction between his humanist/internationalist concerns and his deep-seated distrust of the Other, reflecting the position of the petit-bourgeois francophone in Montreal.

140 On the reification of the Jew, Kwaterko comments: "He remains a cultural 'unknown,' perfectly accepted as 'other,' but indifferent, unable to provoke any intercultural encounter." See "La problématique interculturelle dans *Alexandre Chenevert* de Gabrielle Roy," 569.

141 Roy, *Bonheur d'occasion*, 153.

142 Gabrielle Roy, *The Tin Flute*, translated by Hannah Josephson, New Canadian Library No. 5. Toronto: McClelland & Stewart 1969, 98.

143 The corrected manuscript of Josephson's translation can be consulted in the Library and Archives Canada, Fonds Gabrielle Roy, boîte 29, chemises 4–12. There are up to eight minor corrections per page, often matters of punctuation, correction of typos, but also some changes of wording, discussed below.

144 Hugh MacLennan lived in Montreal and published his own bestseller, *Two Solitudes*, in 1945. It was MacLennan who had first brought Roy's novel to Deacon's attention.

145 W.H. New, *Encyclopaedia of Literature in Canada*, 1125.

146 See Roy's letter to Deacon, 30 May 1946, in Lennox and Lacombe, eds., *Dear Bill*, 223.

147 Ricard, *Gabrielle Roy*, 316.

148 Letter to William Arthur Deacon, 29 May 1947, in Lennox and Lacombe, eds., *Dear Bill*, 251.

149 Ricard, *Gabrielle Roy*, 262.

150 Simon, "The Language of Cultural Difference," 159.

151 Letter to Joyce Marshall, 4 April 1972, *In Translation*, 75.

152 Letter to Gabrielle Roy, 21 May 1972, *In Translation*, 75.

153 The editions used are the following: *Bonheur d'occasion*, Montreal: Boréal, 1993; *The Tin Flute*, translated by Hannah Josephson, Toronto: McLelland & Stewart, 1972; *The Tin Flute*, translated by Alan Brown, Toronto: McClelland & Stewart, 1989.

154 Fonds Gabrielle Roy, boîte 29, chemise 4, 3.

155 In the proofs, a marginal comment states: "St James for St Jacques etc but nobody knows Convent Street and 'Convent Street' sounds bastardized" (boîte 30, chemise 10, 229).

156 An example of this phenomenon is Hémon's descriptions of the Chapdelaine family home in *Maria Chapdelaine*.

157 In the United States such stores have been known by a range of price references over the years, "five and dime" also being used.

158 Mezei, "Speaking White," 20.

159 Ibid., 20–1.

160 Schogt, *Linguistics, Literary Analysis, and Literary Translation*, 118.

161 Jacques de Grandpré, "La traduction de 'Bonheur d'occasion,'" *Le Devoir*, 8 February 1947.

162 Lawrence Venuti, *The Translator's Invisibility*, 15.

163 Schogt, "'Pas *lonely* pantoute'," 347.

164 In Roy's corrections of the proofs for Brown's retranslation, there is a query from Brown about the register used by Jean to Florentine, which is slightly higher than in previous dialogue. Roy replies, in the margin: "In French his speech depends on who he's talking to. He might be more correct with her. At least he has education to speak properly. He relaxes more with his male acquaintances." See Fonds Gabrielle Roy, boîte 30, chemise 8, 79.

165 See Fonds Gabrielle Roy, boîte 30, chemise 11, 326.

166 For a fuller discussion of the representation of space in this novel see "Urban Quebec – Images of Montreal in Roy and Tremblay" in Rosemary Chapman, *Siting the Quebec Novel*, chapter 2, 83–149.

167 Schogt, "'Pas *lonely* pantoute'," 345.

168 Fonds Gabrielle Roy, boîte 30, chemise 7, 44, footnote.

169 Fonds Gabrielle Roy, boîte 30, chemise 12, 364.

170 Venuti, *The Scandals of Translation*, 12.

171 Sherry Simon, "Traduction et représentation identitaire," in Claude Duchet and Stéphane Vachon, eds., *La Recherche littéraire: objets et méthodes*, 313.

CHAPTER FIVE

1 Eva Mackey, *The House of Difference: Cultural Politics and National Identity in Canada*, 13.

2 For full details of Roy's journalistic work see the bibliography in François Ricard, *Gabrielle Roy*. I conducted my research using the copies of the original publications in Ottawa. The collection *Heureux les*

nomades et autres reportages 1940–1945, edited by Antoine Boisclair and François Ricard in the series Cahiers Gabrielle Roy, was published in 2007. The only existing translations into English of Roy's articles for the *Bulletin des Agriculteurs* being those for the selected articles published in *Fragiles Lumières de la terre*, I therefore refer to this edition for all cited translations. All other translations are my own.

3 The *Bulletin* also published "Bonheur d'occasion aujourd'hui" (*Bulletin des Agriculteurs*, January 1948) the text of Roy's acceptance speech to Royal Society of Canada, 1948, subsequently published with the title "Retour à Saint-Henri" in *Fragiles Lumières de la terre*. Subsequent references to articles from the *Bulletin des Agriculteurs* will be given in the text above, with the following format: title, BA, date, page number.

4 Ricard, *Gabrielle Roy,* 196.

5 Ricard reports that the circulation of the *Bulletin des Agriculteurs* rose from 63,000 in 1939 to 145,000 in 1948 (*Gabrielle Roy,* 196).

6 As Ricard points out, this represented three times the salary she had been earning as a teacher in Saint-Boniface (*Gabrielle Roy,* 224). The comparison with Quebec is even more striking; some rural schoolmistresses there were paid as little as $30 a month, with no pay for the vacation period (see Roy's reportage "Pitié pour les institutrices," BA, March 1942, 7).

7 On this point Ricard writes: "The only woman whose name figured in this section of the magazine and who occasionally figured on the cover, the only woman whose articles were considered on a par with those of masculine contributors, was Gabrielle Roy." (*Gabrielle Roy,* 209).

8 Ricard, *Gabrielle Roy,* 195.

9 René Labonté, "Gabrielle Roy, journaliste, au fil de ses reportages 1939–1945," *Studies in Canadian Literature* 7, no. 1 (1982), 107.

10 The following list gives the title of each article as it appears under the heading "Peuples du Canada" in *Fragiles lumières de la terre*, followed by the original title and date of publication in the *Bulletin des Agriculteurs*: "Les Huttérites," "Le plus étonnant: les Huttérites," November 1942; "De turbulents chercheurs de paix," "Turbulents chercheurs de paix," December 1942; "Les Mennonites," "Femmes de dur labeur," January 1943; "L'Avenue Palestine," "L'Avenue Palestine," January 1943; "Les Sudètes de Good Soil," "De Prague à Good Soil," March 1943; "Petite Ukraine," "Ukraine," April 1943; "Les pêcheurs de Gaspésie. 'Une voile dans la nuit'," "Une voile dans la nuit," May 1944.

11 Labonté, "Gabrielle Roy, journaliste," 101.

12 Ibid.

13 Cynthia Hahn, "Gabrielle Roy: portraits d'une voix en formation," in André Fauchon, ed., *Colloque international "Gabrielle Roy,"* 29.

14 See also Linda Clemente, "Gabrielle Roy: l'évolution d'un style narratif."

15 Two examples of this line of criticism will demonstrate its interest. Estelle Dansereau's article, "Des écrits journalistiques d'imagination aux nouvelles littéraires de Gabrielle Roy," compares "La vallée Houdou," published in *Amérique française*, Februrary 1945, and "Un vagabond frappe à notre porte," *Amérique française*, January 1946, with their later versions in *Un jardin au bout du monde* (1975). She concentrates on the lexical, stylistic, syntactic, and aesthetic choices made in the rewriting process. In "Petite histoire de la nouvelle 'Un jardin au bout du monde' de Gabrielle Roy," 360–81, Sophie Montreuil follows the transformations of the story of Martha Yaramko, from the glimpse of the character Masha in the reportage "De turbulents chercheurs de paix," *Bulletin des Agriculteurs*, December 1942, through the various unpublished *avanttextes* to the final text of 1975.

16 The interview is quoted in Carol J. Harvey, "Gabrielle Roy: reporter et romancière," in André Fauchon, ed., *Colloque international "Gabrielle Roy,"* 41.

17 See "Gabrielle Roy, la grande romancière canadienne. Une entrevue exclusive de Alice Parizeau," 118.

18 Jean-Paul Sartre, *Situations II*, 30.

19 Marc Gagné refers to an interview with Roy in which she declared that her journalistic writings "were based as much in fiction as in fact," *Visages de Gabrielle Roy, l'œuvre et l'écrivain*, 19.

20 See Ricard's finely argued discussion of Roy's decision to leave Manitoba, and the effect of this decision on her relationship with her mother (Ricard, *Gabrielle Roy*, 150–60, 218–22).

21 "Le Pays de *Bonheur d'occasion*," in François Ricard, Sophie Marcotte, and Jane Everett, eds., *Le Pays de* Bonheur d'occasion *et autres récits autobiographiques épars et inédits*, 89. The original text was published in the literary supplement of *Le Devoir* (18 May 1974): viii–ix.

22 In *La Route d'Altamont* and *Rue Deschambault* the narrator/protagonist, Christine, identifies herself with figures of both British and French colonial expansion and exploration – La Vérendrye, Sir Francis Drake, and Sir Walter Raleigh.

23 "Le Pays de *Bonheur d'occasion*," 88.

24 Stuart Hall, "Cultural Identity and Diaspora," in Patrick Williams and Laura Chrisman, eds., *Colonial Discourse and Postcolonial Theory: A Reader*, 392–403 [394].

25 Salman Rushdie, "The location of Brazil," in *Imaginary Homelands: Essays and Criticism 1981–1991*, 125.

26 *Heureux les nomades et autres reportages 1940–1945* includes twenty-eight of these reportages, "chosen for their literary qualities, for their historical interest and for the light that they throw on the art and the thinking of Gabrielle Roy at the time when she was working on *Bonheur d'occasion*" (HN 10).

27 Ricard's involvement in the preparation of this volume was considerable, but according to his account (*Gabrielle Roy*, 452–4), Roy had been encouraged by others, including Victor Barbeau and Gilles Marcotte, to publish a selection of her journalism. When Ricard met her in winter 1974, she had already prepared a selection for possible publication. Ricard's contribution was to advise particularly on the title and organization of the volume, but he also recommended omitting the two fictional pieces, to ensure greater cohesion.

28 This particular fact-finding trip was partly funded by the Montreal paper *Le Canada*, which had commissioned five reportages, one on the American construction of a road to Alaska for which she travelled on to Dawson Creek in British Columbia, and a series of four on farming in the prairies, "Regards sur l'Ouest." Roy also benefited from a free rail pass from Canadian National (Ricard, *Gabrielle Roy*, 212).

29 Gayatri Spivak, "Can the Subaltern Speak? Speculations on Widow-Sacrifice" (1985), quoted in Bill Ashcroft, *Post-Colonial Transformation*, 51.

30 Ashcroft, *Post-Colonial Transformation*, 51.

31 Incidentally, Roy's fluency in English was crucial to her ability to communicate directly in most of these immigrant communities.

32 Laurie Kruk, "Teaching/Reading Native Writing," in Cynthia Sugars, ed., *Home-Work: Postcolonialism, Pedagogy and Canadian Literature*, 308.

33 Of course, this fascination with the periphery recurs throughout Roy's work. To cite two examples: Martha Yaramko is described as living "en bordure du pays [on the edge of the country]" in "Un jardin au bout du monde" (JbdM 132; 140), and in *La Petite Poule d'Eau* Luzina comments explicitly on geography favouring the south as she consults a map of Canada to track the dispersal of her children across Canada (PPE 128–9; 120).

34 Linda Clemente makes a similar point about the way Roy uses antitheses throughout her work: "Nor does constructing a reportage, a novel or a character according to a binary paradigm mean proposing absolute opposites between which one has to choose. Such an interpretation fails to engage with Roy's creative process and reduces the complexity of the

narrative scheme." (Clemente, "Gabrielle Roy: l'évolution d'un style narratif," 231)

35 In the preceding chapters, I suggested that Roy's assumed reader would have some knowledge of English. It is interesting to note that her comments on linguistic hybridity require a similar familiarity with English and its abuses.

36 At the time Roy herself lived in the house of a Miss McLean on rue Dorchester on the fringes of Westmount. It is an interesting paradox that between 1937, when she left Saint-Boniface, and 1947, when she married Marcel Carbotte, Roy lived mostly in the homes of English speakers, in London, Upshire, Montreal, Rawdon, and Port Daniel, in all of which she felt loved and cared for.

37 In addition to some discussion of Léon Roy's work in *La Détresse et l'enchantement*, the settlement of Doukhobor immigrants in the Prairie provinces is represented in "La vallée Houdou" (*Un jardin au bout du monde*), that of Ruthenian immigrants in "Le puits de Dunrea," and the general concerns of immigrant settlement are the backdrop to "Le jour et la nuit" (both in *Rue Deschambault*).

38 The 1930s and 1940s saw a series of government-funded initiatives for the colonization of Abitibi-Témiscamingue, including the Gordon Plan (1932–34), the Vautrin Plan (1934–37), the Rogers-Auger Plan (1937–39) and the Plan Bégin in the 1940s. For details see Simon Tremblay, "La colonisation agricole et le développement du capitalisme en Abitibi de 1912 à 1950," *Anthropologie et Société* 6, no. 1 (1982).

39 In a later article Roy also wrote glowingly of the contribution of Canadian National, the railroad company that played a crucial role in the process of colonization. The fact that they partly sponsored her fact-finding tour may be relevant to her decision to praise the company in print.

40 A copy of the letter, dated 6 February 1942, is filed with the copies of Roy's articles for the *Bulletin des Agriculteurs* in the Fonds Gabrielle Roy (boîte 78a, chemise 6). This is my own translation from the French.

41 Ricard, *Gabrielle Roy*, 211.

42 Ibid., 214.

43 See Carol J. Harvey, "Gabrielle Roy, institutrice: reportage et texte narratif" for a comparison of this reportage with *Ces enfants de ma vie*.

44 Whereas the "institutrice" of the article receives a monthly salary of $30 for ten months of the year, Roy's salary in 1937 was $922 a year, which she could augment by teaching summer school.

45 See Roy, "*Mon cher grand fou …* ": *Lettres à Marcel Carbotte 1947–1979.*

46 Lori Saint-Martin, *La Voyageuse et la Prisonnière: Gabrielle Roy et la question des femmes*, 10.

47 Stuart Hall, "Cultural Identity and Diaspora," *Cultural Studies* 7, no. 3 (1993), 394.

48 James Clifford, *Routes: Travel and Translation in the Late Twentieth Century*, 2.

49 In *Rue Deschambault* the father's bond with the immigrants he settled is represented as paternalistic: "Qui saura jamais ce que, parmi ses Petits-Ruthènes, papa ressentait d'aise, de certitude! Isolés, loin de tout autre village, ne parlant pas encore la langue de leurs voisins, ils devaient s'en remettre à papa totalement, et la confiance était entière [Who can ever know what peace of mind, what certitude Papa felt among his Little Ruthenians? Isolated, far from any other village, not yet even speaking their neighbors' language, they must have relied wholly upon Papa, and the trust between them was total]" (RD 128; 75). But in stressing the strong sense of identification between colonizer and immigrant, the narrator suggests that the gulf between the two is in some way bridged: "Il disait: 'Mes gens, mes colons.' Et aussi: 'Mes immigrants', en accentuant le possessif, en sorte que ce mot: immigrant, plutôt que de signifier des étrangers, prenait une curieuse valeur de parenté [He spoke of 'my people, my settlers,' and likewise, 'my immigrants,' stressing the possessive pronoun so that this word 'immigrant,' rather than signifying a stranger, took on the curious value of blood relationship]" (RD 239; 145). A similar sense of "blood relationship" is evident in the title of Roy's auto-fictional account of teaching immigrant children, *Ces enfants de ma vie*.

50 For reasons of accessibility all references to articles from the "Peuples du Canada" series that were reprinted in *Fragiles Lumières de la terre* will be to the following edition: *Fragiles Lumières de la terre. Ecrits divers 1942–1970*. Montreal: Boréal 1996, indicated as (FL) in the references.

51 Roy had a number of Ukrainian friends in Winnipeg. One of them, Bohdan Hubicki, who had moved to London to study the violin, helped her settle in England. Stephen, with whom Roy had a brief love affair in England in spring-summer 1938, was also Ukrainian-Canadian, and worked as a secret agent for a Ukrainian nationalist organization. This throws light on the following line in the article: "Il en est d'attachés à leur rêve d'une libre Ukraine, plus qu'à la vie, plus qu'à la vérité [Some are attached to their dream of a free Ukraine, and to these it means more than life or truth]" (FL 82 ; 81).

52 The village that Roy names at this point is that of Tangent, in northern Alberta, the village where her sister Adèle was teaching at the time and

where Roy spent two months from 22 August to 14 October 1942 during her fact-finding trip across western Canada. Ricard's account describes this period as "this interlude of peace and friendship in her tumultuous life" (Ricard, *Gabrielle Roy*, 221).

53 Rushdie, "The location of Brazil," 124.

54 Bill Marshall, *Quebec National Cinema*, 7.

55 The additional article, "Les pêcheurs de Gaspésie. 'Une voile dans la nuit'" was first published as "Une voile dans la nuit," (BA, May 1944). Ricard states that while Roy felt that the other articles in the series "Peuples du Canada" were still relevant to the readers of 1978, "Les Gens de Chez-Nous" "contained opinions that could be misinterpreted," Ricard, *Gabrielle Roy*, 453.

56 In *Bonheur d'occasion* Florentine's rejection of Emmanuel's suggestion that they go to visit Caughnawaga acts as an indication of the gulf between his knowledge of, and openness to, the world and her ignorance and closed mentality (BO 345).

57 Arun Mukherjee, "Ironies of Colour in The Great White North: The Discursive Strategies of Some Hyphenated Canadians," *Oppositional Aesthetics: Readings from a Hyphenated Space*, 79.

58 Mary Louise Pratt, *Imperial Eyes: Travel Writing and Transculturation*, 4.

59 See Roy, "Le Pays de *Bonheur d'occasion*," 153, and 156–7, note 13.

60 See "Avertissement," in *Le Pays de* Bonheur d'occasion, 7. Excerpts from "Voyage en Ungava" had, however, been published in Roy's lifetime in Gagné, "*La Rivière sans repos* de Gabrielle Roy: étude mythocritique."

61 Roy, "Voyage en Ungava," *Le Pays de* Bonheur d'occasion, 101–28 [108]. Future references will be to this edition and will be indicated as follows (VU 108).

62 Fort Chimo, nowadays Kuujjuuaq, is in fact situated just about at the northern extent of the tree line and is part of the sub-Arctic, not the Arctic zone.

63 W.H. New, *Land Sliding: Imaginary Space, Presence and Power in Canadian Writing*, 12.

64 See Bill Ashcroft, Gareth Griffiths, and Helen Tiffin, *Post-Colonial Studies: The Key Concepts* (London: Routledge, 2000), 176, on the use of the term "*terra nullius*" and its role in imperial doctrine.

65 I am using the term here to refer to a person of mixed Inuit and White origin.

66 Ellen Babby, "*La Rivière sans repos*: Gabrielle Roy's 'Spectacular' Text," *Québec Studies* 2 (1984), 110.

67 See Estelle Dansereau, "Formations discursives pour l'hétérogène dans *La Rivière sans repos* et *Un jardin au bout du monde*," in Claude Romney and Estelle Dansereau, eds., *Portes de communications: études discursives et stylistiques de l'œuvre de Gabrielle Roy*, 119–36, and Dansereau, "Narrer l'autre: la représentation des marginaux dans *La Rivière sans repos* et *Un jardin au bout du monde*," in André Fauchon, ed., *Colloque international "Gabrielle Roy,"* 459–74.

68 See Gayatri Chakravorty Spivak, "Can the Subaltern Speak?" in Patrick Williams and Laura Chrisman, eds., *Colonial Discourse and Postcolonial Theory*, 66–111; Diana Brydon, "The White Inuit Speaks: Contamination as Literary Strategy," in Helen Tiffin and Ian Adam, eds., *Past the Last Post: Theorizing Post-Colonialism and Post-Modernism*; and Margery Fee, "Who Can Write as Other?" in Bill Ashcroft, Gareth Griffiths, and Helen Tiffin, eds., *The Post-Colonial Studies Reader*, 242–5.

69 Roy, *La Rivière sans repos* (Montreal: Boréal, 1995), 122. Subsequent references will be to this edition and indicated as follows (RSR 122).

70 Phyllis Webb, "Afterword" to Gabrielle Roy, *Windflower*, translated by Joyce Marshall (Toronto: McClelland & Stewart, 1989), 154.

71 Abdul R. JanMohamed, "The Economy of Manichean Allegory: the Function of Racial Difference in Colonialist Literature" (1985) in Diana Brydon, ed., *Postcolonialism: Critical Concepts in Literary and Cultural Studies*, 1055–84.

72 See Albert Memmi, *Portrait du colonisé, précédé du portrait du colonisateur*, 106.

73 On acculturation, see Robert Young, *Postcolonialism: An Historical Introduction*, 202.

74 Here the emphasis of my interpretation of the novel differs from that of Etienne Vaucheret, who judges Roy's representation of the Métis, Jimmy, in more sociological terms. See Etienne Vaucheret, "L'image des Inuit dans *La Rivière sans repos* de Gabrielle Roy," *Cahiers franco-canadiens de l'Ouest* 3, no. 1 (spring, 1991).

75 Frantz Fanon, *Les Damnés de la terre*.

76 Ashcroft, Griffiths and Tiffin, *The Post-Colonial Studies Reader*, 391.

77 Michael de Certeau, *L'Invention du quotidien. I. Arts de faire*, 60–1.

78 Roy, "Mon héritage du Manitoba," *Mosaic* 3, nos 3–4 (1970): 69–79 [69].

79 Ibid., 77 (FL, 164).

80 Rushdie, "The location of Brazil," 125.

81 See "Petite Ukraine" (FL 83). The figure of the Chinese restaurant owner will be developed as the central protagonist of the "Où iras-tu, Sam Lee Wong?" in *Un jardin au bout du monde* (1975).

82 Mukherjee cites here Atwood's "Introduction" to *The New Oxford Book of Canadian Verse in English*. Toronto: Oxford University Press 1982, xxxi.

83 Rushdie, "The location of Brazil," 124–5.

84 Ashcroft, *Post-Colonial Transformation*, 53.

Bibliography

WORKS BY GABRIELLE ROY

This is not an exhaustive bibliography of Roy's works. For a full bibliography see François Ricard, *Gabrielle Roy: une vie* (Montreal: Boréal, 1996), or consult the website of Le Groupe de Recherche sur Gabrielle Roy, http://www.gabrielle-roy.mcgill.ca. For all the texts that are discussed in this book, I have included: a) details of the first publication; b) the edition currently available; c) the abbreviated form of the title used in the body of the text for page references to works cited frequently (unless otherwise indicated in footnotes, all page references refer to the edition currently available); d) details of the English translation with date of the edition used where a subsequent edition is for page references).

Gabrielle Roy. *Bonheur d'occasion*. Montreal: Société des Editions Pascal, 1945 [2 vols.]. Montreal: Boréal, 1993 (BO)
The Tin Flute, Hannah Josephson, trans. Toronto: McClelland & Stewart, 1947 (1969).
The Tin Flute, Alan Brown, trans. Toronto: McClelland & Stewart, Ltd., 1980 (1989).
– *La Petite Poule d'Eau*. Montreal: Beauchemin, 1950; Montreal: Boréal, 1993 (PPE)
Where Nests the Water Hen. Harry L. Binsse, trans. Toronto: McClelland & Stewart, 1951 (1952).
– *Alexandre Chenevert*. Montreal: Beauchemin, 1954; Montreal: Boréal, 1995 (AC)
The Cashier. Harry L. Binsse, trans. Toronto: McClelland & Stewart, 1955 (1990).

– *Rue Deschambault*. Montreal: Beauchemin, 1955; Montreal: Boréal, 1993 (RD)
  Street of Riches. Harry L. Binsse, trans. Toronto: McClelland & Stewart, 1957 (1967).
– *La Montagne secrète*. Montreal: Beauchemin, 1961; Montreal: Boréal, 1994 (MS)
  The Hidden Mountain. Harry L. Binsse, trans. Toronto: McClelland & Stewart, 1962.
– *La Route d'Altamont*. Montreal: Éditions HMH, 1966; Montreal: Boréal, 1993 (RA)
  The Road Past Altamont. Joyce Marshall, trans. Toronto: McClelland & Stewart, 1966 (1989).
– *La Rivière sans repos*. Montreal: Beauchemin, 1970; Montreal: Boréal, 1995 (RSR)
  Windflower. Joyce Marshall, trans. Toronto: McClelland & Stewart, 1970 (1975).
  The 1970 translation does not include translations of the "Trois nouvelles esquimaudes." These have each been published separately in translation as follows: "The Satellites." Joyce Marshall, trans. *The Tamarack Review*, 74 (spring 1978):5–28; "The Telephone." Joyce Lubert, trans. *Matrix: New Canadian Writing*, 26 (spring 1988): 59–70; "The Wheelchair." Sherri Walsh, trans. *Breaking Free: A Cross-Cultural Anthology*. John Borovilos, ed. Scarborough, Ontario: Prentice-Hall Canada 1995, 124–32. Page references cited in the text refer to these translations.
– *Cet été qui chantait*. Quebec: Editions françaises, 1972; Montreal: Boréal, 1993 (CE).
  Enchanted Summer. Joyce Marshall, trans. Toronto: McClelland & Stewart, 1976.
– *Un jardin au bout du monde*. Montreal: Beauchemin, 1975; Montreal: Boréal, 1994 (JM).
  Garden in the Wind. Alan Brown, trans. Toronto, McClelland & Stewart, 1977.
– *Ces enfants de ma vie*. Montreal: Stanké, 1977; Montreal: Boréal, 1993 (CEV).
  Children of My Heart. Alan Brown, trans. Toronto: McClelland & Stewart, 1979 (2000).
– *Fragiles Lumières de la terre*. Montreal: Quinze, 1978; Montreal: Boréal, 1996 (FL).

The Fragile Lights of Earth. Alan Brown, trans. Toronto: McClelland & Stewart, 1982.

– *De quoi t'ennuies-tu, Éveline?* and *Ely! Ely! Ely!* Montreal: Boréal, 1988 (DQ).

– *La Détresse et l'enchantement*. Montreal: Boréal, 1984; Montreal: Boréal, 1996 (DE).
Enchantment and Sorrow. Patricia Claxton, trans. Toronto: Lester and Orpen Dennys, 1987.

– *Ma chère petite sœur: lettres à Bernadette, 1943–1970*: Toronto: Lester and Orpen Dennys, 1990.
Letters to Bernadette. Patricia Claxton, trans. Toronto, Lester and Orpen Dennys, 1990.

– *Le Temps qui m'a manqué*. Montreal: Boréal, 1997.

– *La Saga d'Eveline*, édition critique établie par Christine Robinson. Microfiche, LAC, 1998 (SE).

– *Le Pays de Bonheur d'occasion et autres récits autobiographiques épars et inédits*, edited by François Ricard, Sophie Marcotte, and Jane Everett. Montreal: Boréal, 2000.

– *"Mon cher grand fou ...": Lettres à Marcel Carbotte 1947–1979*, edited by Sophie Marcotte, with François Ricard and Jane Everett. Montreal: Boréal, Cahiers Gabrielle Roy, 2001.

– *Femmes de lettres. Lettres à ses amies 1945–78*, edited by Ariane Léger and François Ricard, with Sophie Montreuil and Jane Everett. Montreal: Boréal, Cahiers Gabrielle Roy, 2005.

– *Heureux les nomades et autres reportages 1940–1945*, edited by Antoine Boisclair and François Ricard. Montreal: Boréal, Cahiers Gabrielle Roy, 2007.

ARCHIVAL SOURCES

Fonds de l'Association d'éducation des Canadiens français du Manitoba, consulted at the Centre du patrimoine franco-manitobain, Saint-Boniface, Manitoba.

Department of Education archives, consulted at the Department of Education Library (IRU), Winnipeg, and the Provincial Archives of Manitoba, Winnipeg.

Fonds Gabrielle Roy (MSS 1982–11/1986–11), Library and Archives Canada, Ottawa.

PUBLISHED SOURCES.

Allard, Jacques. "Le chemin qui mène à La Petite Poule d'Eau." *Les Cahiers de Sainte Marie* 1 (May 1966), 55–67.

Anderson, Benedict. *Imagined Communities: Reflections on the Origin and Spread of Nationalism.* London: Verso, 1983.

Appel, René and Pieter Muysken. *Language Contact and Bilingualism.* London: Edward Arnold, 1987.

Ashcroft, Bill. *Post-Colonial Transformation.* London: Routledge, 2001.

Ashcroft, Bill, Gareth Griffiths, and Helen Tiffin, eds. *The Empire Writes Back: Theory and Practice in Post-Colonial Literatures.* London: Routledge, 1989.

–, eds. *The Post-Colonial Studies Reader.* London: Routledge, 1995.

–, eds. *Post-Colonial Studies: The Key Concepts.* London: Routledge, 2000.

Atlas historique du Canada, Volume II, La transformation du territoire 1800–1891. Montreal: Presses de l'Université de Montréal, 1993.

Aunger, E.A. "Dispersed Minorities and Segmental Autonomy: French Language School Boards in Canada." *Nationalism and Ethnic Politics* 2, no. 2 (1996): 191–215.

Babby, Ellen Reisman. "*La Rivière sans repos*: Gabrielle Roy's 'Spectacular' Text." *Québec Studies* 2 (1984), 105–17.

Baril, Paul. "Trémulations d'un cadavre encore chaud: l'enseignement des valeurs culturelles en milieu minoritaire." *Cahiers franco-canadiens de l'Ouest* 4, no. 1 (printemps 1992): 7–28.

Bassnett, Susan and André Lefevere. *Constructing Cultures: Essays on Literary Translation.* Clevedon: Multilingual Matters, 1998.

Bassnett, Susan and Harish Trivedi, eds. *Post-colonial Translation: Theory and Practice.* London: Routledge, 1999.

Berlant, Lauren. *The Queen of America Goes to Washington City.* Durham: Duke University Press, 1997.

Berman, Antoine. *Les Tours de Babel: Essais sur la traduction.* Mauzevin: Trans-Europ-Repress, 1985.

– "Translation and the Trials of the Foreign," translated by Lawrence Venuti, in Lawrence Venuti, ed. *The Translation Studies Reader.* London: Routledge, 2000, 284–97.

Bhabha, Homi K. "Signs Taken for Wonders" (1985), in Bill Ashcroft, Gareth Griffiths, and Helen Tiffin, eds. *The Post-Colonial Studies Reader.* London: Routledge, 1995, 29–35.

– *The Location of Culture.* London: Routledge, 1994.

Blaut, J.M. "History Inside Out: the Argument" (1993), in Diana
   Brydon, ed. *Postcolonialism: Critical Concepts in Literary and
   Cultural Studies*. London: Routledge, 2000, 1692–1738.

Blay, J. *L'Article 23: les péripéties législatives et juridiques du fait français
   au Manitoba 1870–1986*. Saint-Boniface: Editions du Blé, 1987.

Blodgett, E.D. "How do you say 'Gabrielle Roy'?," in Camille La
   Bossière, ed. *Translations in Canadian Literature, Reappraisals:
   Canadian Writers*. Ottawa: University of Ottawa Press, 1983, 13–34.

– "Towards a Model of Literary Translation in Canada." *TTR:
   Traduction, Terminologie, Rédaction* 4, no. 2 (1991): 189–206.

Brault, Jacques. *Poèmes des quatre côtés*. Chambly: Editions du Noroît,
   1975.

Britton, Celia. *Edouard Glissant and Postcolonial Theory: Strategies of
   Language and Resistance*. Charlottesville and London: University Press
   of Virginia, 1999.

Britzman, Deborah P. "Cultural Myths in the Making of a Teacher:
   Biography and Social Structure in Teacher Education." *Harvard
   Educational Review* 56, no. 4 (November 1986): 442–55.

Brown, Craig, ed. *Histoire générale du Canada*. Montreal: Boréal, 1990.

Brydon, Diana. "The White Inuit Speaks," in Helen Tiffin and Ian Adam,
   eds. *Past the Last Post: Theorizing Post-Colonialism and
   Post-Modernism*. Calgary, Alberta: University of Calgary Press, 1990.

– "Introduction: Reading Postcoloniality, Reading Canada." *Essays on
   Canadian Literature* 56 (fall 1995): 1–19.

– "Postcolonial Pedagogy and Curricular Reform." Keynote Address at
   Red Deer College, Alberta, 1997. <http://publish.uwo.ca/-dbrydon/
   red_deer.html>.

–, ed. *Postcolonialism: Critical Concepts in Literary and Cultural Studies*,
   5 vols. London: Routledge, 2000.

Certeau, Michel de. *L'Invention du quotidien. I. Arts de faire*. Paris:
   Gallimard, 1990.

Chafer, Tony. *The End of Empire in French West Africa*. Oxford: Berg,
   2002.

Chapman, Rosemary. *Siting the Quebec Novel*. Bern: Peter Lang, 2000.

– "A (Post)colonial Perspective on the Examination System," in Anthony
   Bushell and Hinrich Siefken, eds. *Experiencing Tradition: Festschrift
   for Keith Spalding*. York: Ebor Press, 2003, 250–8.

– "Resisting Colonialism in Manitoba: The Case of Gabrielle Roy," in
   Charles Forsdick and David Murphy, eds., *Francophone Studies:
   Postcolonial Issues*. London: Arnold, 2003, 242–52.

– "Writing of/from the Fourth World: Gabrielle Roy and Ungava."
  Québec Studies 35 (spring/summer 2003): 45–62.
– "L'Espace francophone dans l'œuvre manitobaine de Gabrielle Roy."
  Globe 6, no. 1 (2003): 85–105.
– "French and English in Gabrielle Roy's Autobiographical Work." *The
  French Review*, special issue, "Le Québec et le Canada francophone"
  78, no. 6 (May 2005): 1127–37.
Chaudenson, Robert. "Diglossie créole, diglossie coloniale." *Cahiers de
  l'Institut de linguistique de Louvain* 2 (1984): 20–9.
Clemente, Linda. "Gabrielle Roy: l'évolution d'un style narratif." *Cahiers
  franco-canadiens de l'Ouest* 8, no. 2 (1996): 219–37.
Clifford, James. *Routes: Travel and Translation in the Late Twentieth
  Century*. Cambridge, Massachusetts: Harvard University Press, 1997.
Cloutier-Wojechewska, Cécile and Réjean Robidoux, eds., *Solitude
  rompue*. Ottawa: University of Ottawa Press, 1986.
Cobb, David. "Seasons in the Life of a Novelist: Gabrielle Roy." *The
  Canadian* (1 May 1976): 10–13.
Cormier, Marianne. "Finalités justes ou attentes démesurées? Le débat
  autour de l'école en milieu minoritaire." *Francophonies d'Amérique* 17
  (spring 2004): 55–63.
Courchesne, Georges. *Nos Humanités*. Nicolet: Procure de l'Ecole
  Normale, 1927.
Craig, G.M., ed. *Lord Durham's Report*. Toronto: McClelland &
  Stewart, 1963.
Cronin, Michael. *Across the Lines: Travel, Language, Translation*. Cork:
  Cork University Press, 2000.
Cudjoe, Selwyn. *Eric Williams Speaks: Essays on Colonialism and
  Independence*. Wellesley, Massachusetts: Calaloux, 1993.
Dansereau, Estelle. "Des écrits journalistiques d'imagination aux
  nouvelles littéraires de Gabrielle Roy." *Francophonies d'Amérique* 2
  (1992): 115–27.
– "Formations discursives pour l'hétérogène dans *La Rivière sans repos*
  et *Un jardin au bout du monde*," in Claude Romney and Estelle
  Dansereau, eds. *Portes de communications: études discursives et
  stylistiques de l'œuvre de Gabrielle Roy*. Sainte-Foy, Quebec: Presses
  de l'Université Laval, 1995, 119–36.
– "Narrer l'autre: la représentation des marginaux dans *La Rivière sans
  repos* et *Un jardin au bout du monde*," in André Fauchon, ed.
  Colloque international "Gabrielle Roy." Saint-Boniface: Presses
  universitaires de Saint-Boniface, 1996, 459–74.

Deleuze, Gilles and Félix Guattari. *Kafka. Pour une littérature mineure.* Paris: Minuit, 1975.

Delson-Karan, Myrna. "The Last Interview: Gabrielle Roy." *Québec Studies* 4 (1986).

Derrida, Jacques. *Le Monolinguisme de l'autre.* Paris: Galilée, 1996.

Desruisseaux-Talbot, Amélie, Nadine Bismuth, and François Ricard, eds., with Jane Everett and Sophie Marcotte. *Rencontres et entretiens avec Gabrielle Roy 1947–1979.* Montreal: Boréal, 2005, collection "Cahiers Gabrielle Roy."

Dion, Robert, Hans-Jürgen Lüsebrink, and János Riesz, eds. *Ecrire en langue étrangère. Interférences de langues et de cultures dans le monde francophone.* Quebec: Editions Nota Bene, 2002.

Docker, J. "The Neo-colonialist Assumption in University Teaching of English," (1978) in Bill Ashcroft, Gareth Griffiths, and Helen Tiffin, eds. *The Post-Colonial Studies Reader.* London: Routledge, 1995, 443–6.

Dubé, J-P. *Le Cercle Molière: 75ᵉ anniversaire.* Winnipeg: Le Cercle Molière, 2001.

Duchet, Claude and Stéphane Vachon, eds. *La Recherche littéraire: objets et méthodes.* Montreal: XYZ, éditeur 1993.

Durham, John George Lambton, Charles Buller, and Edward Gibbon Wakefield. *The Report and Despatches of the Earl of Durham, His Majesty's High Commissioner and Governor-General of British North America.* London: Ridgways, 1839.

Everett, Jane. "Le devenir-anglais du texte et le rapport à l'écriture: Roy et Ferron" in Brigitte Faivre-Duboz and Patrick Poirier, eds. *Jacques Ferron: le palimpseste infini.* Montreal: Lanctôt, 2002, 277–94.

– *In Translation: The Gabrielle Roy–Joyce Marshall Correspondence.* Toronto: University of Toronto Press, 2005.

– and François Ricard, eds. *Gabrielle Roy réécrite.* Quebec: Editions Nota Bene, 2003.

Fahmy-Eid, Nadia and Micheline Dumont, eds. *Maîtresses de maison, maîtresses d'école: femmes, famille et éducation dans l'histoire du Québec.* Montreal: Boréal, 1983.

Faivre-Duboz, Brigitte and Patrick Poirier, eds. *Jacques Ferron: le palimpseste infini.* Montreal: Lanctôt, 2002.

Fanon, Frantz. *Peau noire, masques blancs.* Paris: Seuil, 1952.

– *Les Damnés de la terre.* Paris: Maspéro, 1961.

Fauchon, André, ed. *Colloque international "Gabrielle Roy."* Saint-Boniface: Presses universitaires de Saint-Boniface, 1996.

Fee, Margery. "Who Can Write as Other," in Bill Ashcroft, Gareth
    Griffiths, and Helen Tiffen, eds. *The Post-Colonial Studies Reader.*
    London: Routledge, 1995.

Filteau, Gérard. *Organisation scolaire de la province de Québec:
    historique, législation et règlements.* Montreal: Centre de Psychologie
    et de Pédagogie, 1954.

Finkel, Alvin and Margaret Conrad with Veronica Strong-Boag. *History
    of the Canadian Peoples*, vol. II, 1867 to the Present. Toronto: Copp
    Clark Pitman, 1993.

Friedmann, Susan Stanford. *Mappings: Feminism and the Cultural
    Geographies of Encounter.* Princeton: Princeton University Press,
    1998.

Gaffield, Chad. *Language, Schooling, and Cultural Conflict.* Montreal:
    McGill-Queen's University Press, 1987.

Gagné, Marc. *Visages de Gabrielle Roy.* Montreal: Librairie Beauchemin,
    1973.

– "*La Rivière sans repos* de Gabrielle Roy: étude mythocritique." *Revue
    de l'Université d'Ottawa* (July–September 1976): 364–90.

Gagnon, Nicole. "L'idéologie humaniste dans la revue *L'Enseignement
    secondaire*." *Recherches sociographiques* 4, no. 2 (1963): 167–200.

Gandhi, Leela. *Postcolonial Theory: A Critical Introduction.* Edinburgh:
    Edinburgh University Press, 1998.

Gauvin, Lise. *Langagement. L'écrivain et la langue au Québec.* Montreal:
    Boréal, 2000.

– "Passages de langues," in Robert Dion, Hans-Jürgen Lüsenbrink, and
    János Riesz. *Ecrire en langue étrangère: interférences de langues et de
    cultures dans le monde francophone.* Quebec: Editions Nota Bene,
    2002, 23–42.

– *La fabrique de la langue: de François Rabelais à Réjean Ducharme.*
    Paris: Editions du Seuil, 2004.

–, ed. *L'Ecrivain francophone à la croisée des langues. Entretiens.* Paris:
    Karthala, 1997.

– and Jean-Pierre Bertrand, eds. *Littératures mineures en langue majeure:
    Québec, Wallonie-Bruxelles.* Brussels: Peter Lang; Montreal: Presses de
    l'université de Montréal, 2003.

Glissant, Edouard. *Introduction à une poétique du divers.* Paris:
    Gallimard, 1996.

Gobard, Henri. *L'Aliénation linguistique. Analyse tétraglossique.* Paris:
    Flammarion, 1976.

Godard, Barbara. "Translations." *University of Toronto Quarterly* 58, no. 1 (fall 1988), online version.

- "Between Performative and Performance: Translation and Theatre in the Canadian/Quebec Context." *Modern Drama* 43, no. 3 (fall 2000): 327–58.
- "L'Éthique de traduire: Antoine Berman et le 'virage éthique' en traduction." *TTR: Traduction, Terminologie, Rédaction* 14, no. 2 (2001): 49–82.
- "La traduction comme réception: les écrivaines québécoises au Canada anglais." *TTR: Traduction, Terminologie, Rédaction* 15, no. 1 (2002): 65–101.

Goldie, Terry. *Fear and Temptation: The Image of the Indigene in Canadian, Australian, and New Zealand Literatures*. Montreal and Kingston: McGill-Queen's University Press, 1989.

Goodson, Ivor and Peter Medway, eds. *Bringing English to Order: The History and Politics of a School Subject*, Studies in Curriculum History Series 14. London: Falmer, 1990.

Grandpré, Jacques de, "La traduction de 'Bonheur d'occasion,'" *Le Devoir*, 8 February 1947.

Groulx, Lionel. *Mes Mémoires*. Montreal: Fides, 1972.

- *L'Enseignement français au Canada. Volume II. Les écoles des minorités*. Montreal/Paris: Editions Leméac/Editions d'aujourd'hui, 1979.

Grutman, Rainier. *Des langues qui résonnent*. Montreal: Fides, 1997.

Hahn, Cynthia. "Gabrielle Roy: portraits d'une voix en formation," in André Fauchon, ed. *Colloque international "Gabrielle Roy."* Saint-Boniface: Presses universitaires de Saint-Boniface, 1996, 29–39.

Hall, Stuart. "Culture, Community, Nation." *Cultural Studies* 7, no. 3 (1993): 349–63.

- "Cultural Identity and Diaspora," in Patrick Williams and Laura Chrisman, eds. *Colonial Discourse and Post-Colonial Theory: A Reader*. New York: Harvester Wheatsheaf, 1994, 392–403.

Handbook to the Canadian Readers, Books II-III-IV-V. Toronto: Gage & Nelson, 1928.

Harasym, Sarah, ed. *The Post-colonial Critic: Interviews, Strategies, Dialogues: Gayatri Chakravorty Spivak*. New York: Routledge, 1990.

Harel, Simon. *Le Voleur de parcours. Identité et cosmopolitisme dans la littérature québécoise contemporaine*. Longueil: Préambule, 1989.

- *L'Etranger dans tous ses états*. Montreal: XYZ, 1992.

Harvey, Carol J. "Gabrielle Roy, institutrice: reportage et texte narratif." *Cahiers franco-canadiens de l'Ouest* 3, no. 1 (spring 1991) 31–42.

– *Le Cycle manitobain de Gabrielle Roy*. Saint-Boniface: des Plaines, 1993.

– "Gabrielle Roy: reporter et romancière," in André Fauchon, ed. *Colloque international "Gabrielle Roy,"*, Saint-Boniface: Presses universitaires de Saint-Boniface, 1996, 41–52.

Healy, J.J. "The Melting of the Mosaic: Landscape, Power and Ethnicity in Post-Confederation Canada," in Jean Burnet, Danielle Juteau, Enoch Padolsky, Anthony Raspovich, and Antoine Sirois, eds. *Migration and the Transformation of Cultures*. Toronto: Multicultural History Society of Ontario, 1992, 55–89.

Heble, Ajay, Donna Palmateer Pennee, and J.R. (Tim) Struthers, eds. *New Contexts of Canadian Criticism*. Peterborough, Ontario: Broadview Press, 1997.

Hémon, Louis. *Maria Chapdelaine*. Montreal: Boréal, Express, 1980.

Herriot, A.A. "School Inspectors of the Early Days in Manitoba," *MHS Transactions*, Series 3 (1947–48) (online version).

Hicks, D. Emily. *Border Writing: The Multidimensional Text*. Minneapolis: University of Minnesota Press, 1991.

Hind-Smith, Joan. *Three Voices: The Lives of Margaret Laurence, Gabrielle Roy, Frederick Philip Grove*. Toronto: Clarke, Irwin & Co., 1975.

Jaenen, C.J. "Le français au Manitoba: fruit de l'histoire ou d'une contrainte extérieure?" *Langue et société* 13 (spring 1984): 3–16.

JanMohamed, Abdul R. "The Economy of Manichean Allegory: the Function of Racial Difference in Colonialist Literature" (1985), in Diana Brydon, ed. *Postcolonialism: Critical Concepts in Literary and Cultural Studies*. London: Routledge, 2000, 1055–84.

Johnson, F. Henry. *A Brief History of Canadian Education*. Toronto: McGraw-Hill, 1968.

Johnston, Anna and Alan Lawson. "Settler Colonies," in Henry Schwarz and Sangeeta Ray, eds. *A Companion to Postcolonial Studies*. Oxford: Blackwell, 2000, 360–76.

Jones, David C., Nancy M. Sheehan and Robert M. Stamp, eds. *Shaping the Schools of the Canadian West*. Calgary, Alberta: Detselig Enterprises, 1979.

Kohlmeister, Benjamin, and George Kmoch. *Journal of a Voyage from Okkak, on the Coast of Labrador, to Ungava Bay, Westward of Cape Chudleigh; Undertaken to explore the Coast, and visit the Esquimaux in that unknown Region.* London: 1811. The text is currently available as an e-text at www.mun.ca/rels/hrollmann/morav/texts/ungava.html.

Kroetsch, Robert. "Unhiding the Hidden," in Bill Ashcroft, Gareth Griffiths, and Helen Tiffin, eds. *The Post-Colonial Studies Reader.* London: Routledge, 1995, 394–6.

Kwaterko, Józef. "La problématique interculturelle dans *Alexandre Chenevert* de Gabrielle Roy." *University of Toronto Quarterly* 63, no. 4 (1994): 566–74.

Labonté, René. "Gabrielle Roy, journaliste, au fil de ses reportages 1939–1945." *Studies in Canadian Literature* 7, no. 1 (1982): 90–108.

Lawson, Alan. "Postcolonial Theory and the 'Settler' Subject." *Essays on Canadian Writing* 56 (fall 1995): 20–36.

Lefevere, André. *Translation. Rewriting and the Manipulation of Literary Fame.* London: Routledge, 1992.

Lemelin, André and Claude Marcil. *Le Purgatoire de l'ignorance: l'éducation au Québec jusqu'à la Grande réforme.* Montreal: MNH, 1999.

Lennox, John and Michèle Lacombe, eds. *Dear Bill: The Correspondence of William Arthur Deacon.* Toronto: University of Toronto Press, 1988.

Létourneau, Jocelyn. "Langue et identité au Québec aujourd'hui. Enjeux, défis, possibilités." *Globe. Revue internationale d'études québécoises* 5, no.2 (2002): 79–110.

Lintvelt, Jaap and François Paré, eds. *Frontières flottantes. Shifting Boundaries.* Amsterdam, New York: Rodopi, 2001.

Loomba, Ania. "Overworlding the 'Third World,'" (1991) in Patrick Williams and Laura Chrisman, eds. *Colonial Discourse and Post-Colonial Theory: A Reader.* New York: Harvester Wheatsheaf, 1994, 305–23.

Macaulay, Thomas. "Minute on Indian Education," in Bill Ashcroft, Gareth Griffiths, and Helen Tiffin, eds. *The Post-Colonial Studies Reader.* New York: Routledge, 1995, 428–30.

Mackey, Eva. *The House of Difference: Cultural Politics and National Identity in Canada.* London: Routledge, 1999.

Maclaren, I.S. "The Aesthetic Map of the North, 1845–1859," in Kenneth S. Coates and William R. Morrison, eds. *Interpreting Canada's North: Selected Readings.* Mississauga: Copp Clark Pitman, 1989, 18–51.

McLaren, Peter. *Schooling as a Ritual Performance: Towards a Political Economy of Educational Symbols and Gestures.* London: Routledge, and Kegan Paul, 1986.

Marchand, Anne-Sophie. "La Francophonie plurielle au Manitoba."
  Francophonies d'Amérique 17 (spring 2004): 147–159.

Marcotte, Sophie. "Réécritures de l'enfance dans 'Mes études à
  Saint-Boniface' et *La Détresse et l'enchantement* de Gabrielle Roy."
  Voix et images 86 (winter 2004): 99–113.

Marshall, Bill. *Quebec National Cinema.* Montreal and Kingston:
  McGill-Queen's University Press, 2001.

Marshall, Joyce. "Gabrielle Roy 1909–1983." *Antigonish Review* 55
  (autumn 1983): 35–46.

– "Gabrielle Roy, 1909–1983: Some Reminiscences." *Canadian
  Literature* 101 (summer 1984): 183–4.

– "The Writer as Translator: A Personal View." *Canadian Literature*
  117 (summer 1988): 25–9.

– "Remembering Gabrielle Roy." *Brick* 39 (summer 1990): 58–62.

– "Introduction to 'Between Writers: From a Correspondence,' by Joyce
  Marshall and Gabrielle Roy." *Brick* 73 (summer 2004): 81–98.

Maufort, Marc and Franca Bellarsi, eds. *Reconfigurations: Canadian
  Literatures and Postcolonial Identities/Littératures canadiennes et
  identités postcoloniales.* Brussels: Peter Lang, 2002.

Memmi, Albert. *Portrait du colonisé, précédé du portrait du colonisateur.*
  Corrêa: Edns Buchet/Chastel, 1957.

Meschonnic, Henri. *Poétique du traduire.* Paris: Verdier, 1999.

Mezei, Kathy. "Speaking White: Literary Translation as a Vehicle of
  Assimilation in Quebec." *Canadian Literature* 117 (summer 1988):
  11–23.

Milot, Louise and Jaap Lintvelt, eds. *Le Roman québécois depuis 1960.*
  Quebec: Presses de l'Université Laval/CRELIQ, 1992.

Mohanty, S.P. " 'Us and Them': On the Philosophical Bases of Political
  Criticism." *New Formations* 8 (summer 1989): 55–80.

Montreuil, Sophie. "Petite histoire de la nouvelle 'Un jardin au bout du
  monde' de Gabrielle Roy." *Voix et images* XXIII, 2, 68 (winter 1998):
  360–81.

– "Re(re)dire: *The Hidden Mountain* revu par Gabrielle Roy et Joyce
  Marshall," in Jane Everett and François Ricard, eds., *Gabrielle Roy
  réécrite.* Quebec: Editions Nota Bene, 2003, 91–105.

Morgan, Janice and Colette T. Hall, eds. *Redefining Autobiography in
  Twentieth-Century Women's Fiction.* New York: Garland, 1991.

Morgan, Robert. "The 'Englishness' of English Teaching," in Ivor
  Goodson and Peter Medway, eds. *Bringing English to Order.* Lewes:
  Falmer Press, 1990, 197–241.

Morton, W.L. "Manitoba schools and Canadian nationality, 1890–1923," in David C. Jones, Nancy M. Sheehan, and Robert M. Stamp, eds. *Shaping the Schools of the Canadian West*. Calgary, Alberta: Detselig Enterprises, 1979, 3–13.

Moss, Laura, ed. *Is Canada Postcolonial? Unsettling Canadian Literature*. Waterloo, Ontario: Wilfrid Laurier University Press, 2003.

Moura, Jean-Marc. *Littératures francophones et théorie postcoloniale*. Paris: Presses universitaires de France, 1999.

Mukherjee, Arun. P. "Ideology in the Classroom: A Case Study in the Teaching of English Literature in Canadian Universities." *Dalhousie Review* 66, 1, no. 2 (1986): 22–30.

– *Towards an Aesthetics of Opposition: Essays on Literature, Criticism, and Cultural Imperialism*. Stratford, Ontario: Williams, 1988.

– "Ironies of Colour in The Great White North: The Discursive Strategies of Some Hyphenated Canadians," *Oppositional Aesthetics: Readings from a Hyphenated Space*. Toronto: TSAR Publications, 1994.

Murray, Heather. "English Studies in Canada and the Case of Postcolonial Culture." *Essays on Canadian Writing* 56 (fall 1995): 51–77.

New, W.H. *Land Sliding: Imaginary Space, Presence and Power in Canadian Writing*. Toronto: University of Toronto Press, 1997.

– *Encyclopaedia of Literature in Canada*. Toronto: University of Toronto Press, 2002.

Ngugi Wa Thiong'o. *Moving the Centre: the Struggle for Cultural Freedoms*. London: James Currey, 1993.

– "The Language of African Literature," in Patrick Williams and Laura Chrisman, eds. *Colonial Discourse and Post-Colonial Theory: A Reader*. New York: Harvester Wheatsheaf, 1994, 435–55.

O'Neil, John D. "The Politics of Health in the Fourth World: a Northern Canadian Example," in Kenneth S. Coates and William R. Morrison, eds. *Interpreting Canada's North: Selected Readings*. Toronto: Copp Clark Pitman, 1989, 279–97.

O'Neill-Karch, Mariel. "Gabrielle Roy et William Arthur Deacon: une amitié littéraire." *Cultures du Canada français* 9 (1992): 75–97.

Parizeau, Alice. "Gabrielle Roy, la grande romancière canadienne." *Châtelaine* (avril 1966).

Phillipson, R. *Linguistic Imperialism*. London: Oxford University Press, 1991.

Pratt, Mary Louise. *Imperial Eyes: Travel Writing and Transculturation*. London: Routledge, 1992.

Procès Edmond. *Modèles français: extraits des meilleurs écrivains, avec notices*, II. Brussels: A. Lesigne, 1935.

- *Modèles français: extraits des meilleurs écrivains, avec notices*, III. Brussels: A. Lesigne, 1928.

- *Modèles français*, IV. Brussels: A. Lesigne, 1936.

Renaud, Norbert. "Le collège classique: la maison d'enseignement, le milieu d'études, les fins et les moyens." *Etudes Littéraires* (December 1981): 415–38.

Ricard, François. "La métamorphose d'un écrivain: essai biographique." *Etudes littéraires* 17, no. 3 (hiver 1984): 441–55.

- *Gabrielle Roy: une vie*. Montreal: Boréal, 1996.

- *Gabrielle Roy: A Life*. Patricia Claxton, trans. Toronto: McClelland & Stewart, 1999.

- and Ariane Leger, eds., with Sophie Montreuil and Jane Everett. *Femmes de lettres. Lettres de Gabrielle Roy à ses amies 1945–1978*. Montreal: Boréal, 2005, collection "Cahiers Gabrielle Roy.".

Robinson, Christine. "Etude génétique du 'Printemps revint à Volhyn,'" in Jane Everett and François Ricard, eds. *Gabrielle Roy réécrite*. Quebec: Editions Nota Bene, 2003, 55–74.

Rocheron, Yvette and Christopher Rolfe, eds. *Shifting Frontiers of France and Francophonie*. Bern: Peter Lang, 2004.

Ross, Mgr François-Xavier. *Pédagogie théorique et pratique*, 3e édition. Quebec: Imp. Charrier et Dugal, 1924.

Ross, Vincent. "La structure idéologique des manuels de pédagogie québécois." *Recherches sociographiques* 10, nos. 2/3 (1969): 171–96.

Rushdie, Salman. *Imaginary Homelands: Essays and Criticism 1981–1991*. London: Granta Books, 1992.

Said, Edward W. *Culture and Imperialism*. London: Vintage, 1994.

Saint-Martin, Lori. *Lectures contemporaines de Gabrielle Roy. Bibliographie analytique des études critiques (1978–1997)*. Montreal: Boréal, Les Cahiers Gabrielle Roy, 1998.

- *La Voyageuse et la prisonnière. Gabrielle Roy et la question des femmes*. Montreal: Boréal, Les Cahiers Gabrielle Roy, 2002.

Sartre, Jean-Paul. *Situations II*. Paris: Gallimard, 1948.

Schogt, Henry. "'Pas *lonely* pantoute?'" in Cécile Cloutier-Wojechewska and Réjean Robidoux, eds. *Solitude rompue*. Ottawa: University of Ottawa Press, 1986, 340–50.

- *Linguistics, Literary Analysis, and Literary Translation*. Toronto: University of Toronto Press, 1988.

Schonberger, Vincent L. "The Problem of Language and the Difficulty of
   Writing in the Literary Works of Gabrielle Roy." *Studies in Canadian
   Literature* 14, no. 1 (1989): 127–38.
Schwarz, Henry and Sangeeta Ray, eds. *A Companion to Postcolonial
   Studies.* Oxford: Blackwell, 2000.
Sheehan, Nancy, "Indoctrination: Moral Education in the Early Prairie
   Schoolhouse," in David Jones, Nancy Sheehan, and Robert Stamp, eds.
   Shaping the Schools of the Canadian West. Calgary: Detselig
   Enterprises, 1979, 222–35.
Shek, Ben. "Quelques réflections sur la traduction dans le contexte
   socio-culturel canado-québécois." *Ellipse* 21 (1977): 111–17.
 – "'La généreuse disparité humaine' dans l'œuvre de Gabrielle Roy, de
   Bonheur d'occasion à *La Détresse et l'enchantement.*" *Etudes
   Canadiennes/Canadian Studies* 21, no. 1 (1986): 235–44.
Simon, Sherry. "The True Quebec as Revealed to English Canada:
   Translated Novels 1864–1950." *Canadian Literature* 117 (summer
   1988): 31–43.
 – "The Language of Cultural Difference: Figures of Alterity in Canadian
   Translation," in Lawrence Venuti. *Rethinking Translation: Discourse,
   Subjectivity, Ideology.* London: Routledge, 1992, 159–76.
 – "La traduction inachevée," in Simon Harel, ed. *L'Etranger dans tous
   ses états: enjeux culturels et littéraires.* Montreal: XYZ 1992, 27–38.
 – "Traduction et représentation identitaire," in Claude Duchet and
   Stéphane Vachon, eds. *La Recherche littéraire: objets et méthodes.*
   Montreal: XYZ, 1993, 311–20.
 – *Le Trafic des langues: traduction et culture dans la littérature
   québécoise.* Montreal: Boréal, 1994.
 – "Translating and Interlingual Creation in the Contact Zone. Border
   Writing in Quebec," in Susan Bassnett and Harish Trivedi, eds.
   Post-colonial Translation: Theory and Practice. London and New
   York: Routledge, 1999, 58–74.
Sirois, Antoine. "Gabrielle Roy et le Canada anglais." *Etudes littéraires*
   17, no. 3 (winter 1984): 469–79.
Skiba, Richard. *Internet TESL Journal,* III, 10 (October 1997).
Slemon, Stephen. "Unsettling the Empire: Resistance Theory for the
   Second World." *World Literature Written in English* 30, no. 2 (1990):
   30–41.
 – "The English Side of the Lawn." *Essays on Canadian Writing* 56
   (1995): 274–86.

- "The Scramble for Postcolonialism," in Bill Ashcroft, Gareth Griffiths, and Helen Tiffin, eds. *The Post-Colonial Studies Reader*. London: Routledge, 1995, 45–52.

Smith, Rowland, ed. *Postcolonizing the Commonwealth: Studies in Literature and Culture*. Waterloo, Ontario: Wilfrid Laurier University Press, 2000.

Socken, Paul G., "Gabrielle Roy as Journalist." *Canadian Modern Languages Review* 30, no. 2 (1974): 96–100.

–, ed. *Intimate Strangers. The Letters of Margaret Laurence and Gabrielle Roy*. Winnipeg: University of Manitoba Press, 2004.

Söderlind, Sylvia. *Margin/Alias: Language and Colonization in Canadian and Québécois Fiction*. Toronto: University of Toronto Press, 1991.

Spivak, Gayatri Chakravorty. *The Post-Colonial Critic*. New York: Routledge, 1990.

- "The Politics of Translation," *Outside in the Teaching Machine*. New York: Routledge, 1993, 179–200.

- "Can the Subaltern Speak? Speculations on Widow-Sacrifice," in Patrick Williams and Laura Chrisman, eds. *Colonial Discourse and Post-Colonial Theory*. London: Harvester 1994, 66–111.

Sugars, Cynthia, ed. *Home-Work: Postcolonialism, Pedagogy and Canadian Literature*. Ottawa: University of Ottawa Press, 2004.

- *Unhomely States: Theorizing English-Canadian Postcolonialism*. Peterborough, Ontario: Broadview Press, 2004.

Taillefer, Jean-Marie. "Les Franco-manitobains et l'éducation 1870–1970: une étude quantitative." Unpublished PhD dissertation, Department of History, University of Manitoba, 1988.

Thomas, Clara and John Lennox. *William Arthur Deacon: A Canadian Literary Life*. Toronto: University of Toronto Press, 1982.

Tiffin, Helen and Ian Adam, eds. *Past the Last Post: Theorizing Post-Colonialism and Post-Modernism*. Calgary: University of Calgary Press, 1990.

Tougas, Gérard. *La Littérature canadienne-française*. Paris: PUF, 1974.

Tremblay, Simon. "La colonisation agricole et le développement du capitalisme en Abitibi de 1912 à 1950." *Anthropologie et Sociétés* 6, no. 1 (1982): 229–53.

Trevelyan, C.E. *On the Education of the People of India*. London: Longman, Orme, Brown, Green, and Longmans, 1838.

Trudgill, Peter. *Sociolinguistics: An Introduction to Language and Society*. London: Penguin, 2000.

Turcotte, Pierre-André. "Sécularisation et modernité: les frères éducateurs et l'enseignement secondaire public, 1920–1970." *Recherches sociographiques*, 30, no. 2 (1989): 229–48.

Tymoczko, Maria. "Post-colonial Writing and Literary Translation," in Susan Bassnett and Harish Trivedi, eds. *Post-colonial Translation: Theory and Practice*. London and New York: Routledge, 1999, 19–40.

Vaucheret, Etienne. "L'image des Inuit dans *La Rivière sans repos* de Gabrielle Roy." *Cahiers franco-canadiens de l'Ouest* 3, no. 1 (spring 1991): 81–96.

Venuti, Lawrence. *The Translator's Invisibility: A History of Translation*. London: Routledge, 1995.

– *The Scandals of Translation: Towards an Ethics of Difference*. New York: Routledge, 1998.

– ed. *Rethinking Translation: Discourse, Subjectivity, Ideology*. London: Routledge, 1992.

Viswanatha, Vanamal and Sherry Simon. "Srikantaiah and Kannada Translation," in Susan Bassnett and Harish Trivedi, eds. *Post-colonial Translation: Theory and Practice*. London and New York: Routledge, 1999, 58–74.

Viswanathan, Gauri. "The Beginnings of English Literary Study in British India," in Bill Ashcroft, Gareth Griffiths and Helen Tiffin, eds., *The Post-Colonial Studies Reader*. London: Routledge, 1995, 431–7.

Whitfield, Agnès. "Gabrielle Roy's *Children of My Heart* or Portrait of the Artist as a Young Woman," in Janice Morgan and Colette T. Hall, eds. *Redefining Autobiography in Twentieth-Century Women's Fiction*. New York: Garland, 1991, 209–25.

– "Altérité et identité: tensions narratives dans *Ces Enfants de ma vie* de Gabrielle Roy," in Louise Milot and Jaap Lintvelt, eds. *Le Roman québécois depuis 1960*. Quebec: Presses de l'Université Laval/CRELIQ, 1992, 167–80.

– *Writing Between the Lines: Portraits of Anglophone Literary Translators*. Waterloo, Ontario: Wilfrid Laurier University Press, 2006.

Whitlock, Gillian. "Outlaws of the Text" (1992), in Bill Ashcroft, Gareth Griffiths, and Helen Tiffin, eds. *The Post-Colonial Studies Reader*. London: Routledge, 1995, 349–52.

Williams, Patrick and Laura Chrisman, eds. *Colonial Discourse and Post-Colonial Theory: A Reader*. New York: Harvester Wheatsheaf, 1994.

Willinsky, John. *Learning to Divide the World: Education at Empire's End*. Minneapolis: University of Minnesota Press, 1998.
Young, Robert. *Colonial Desire*. London: Routledge, 1995.
– *Postcolonialism: An Historical Introduction*. Oxford: Blackwell, 2001.

Index

DATE DUE